Outdoor Furniture

Outdoor Furniture

30 Great Projects for the Deck, Lawn and Garden

Bill Hylton

with Fred Matlack & Phil Gehret

Illustrations by Frank Rohrbach

Photographs by Mitch Mandel

Rodale Press, Emmaus, Pennsylvania

The authors and editors who compiled this book have tried to make all of the contents as accurate and as correct as possible. Plans, illustrations, photographs, and text have all been carefully checked and cross-checked. However, due to the variability of local conditions, construction materials, personal skill, and so on, neither the author nor Rodale Press assumes any responsibility for any injuries suffered or for damages and other losses incurred that result from the material presented herein. All instructions and plans should be carefully studied and clearly understood before beginning construction.

Senior Woodworking Editor: Jeff Day
Copy Editor: Sarah Dunn
Editorial assistance: Stacy Brobst and Karen Earl-Braymer

Cover design by Darlene Schneck
Interior design by Jerry O'Brien
Cover photography by Mitch Mandel

If you have any questions or comments concerning this book, please write:
      Rodale Press
      Book Reader Service
      33 East Minor Street
      Emmaus, PA 18098

Library of Congress Cataloging-in-Publication Data

Hylton, Bill.
      Outdoor furniture : 30 great projects for the deck, lawn, and garden / Bill
Hylton, Fred Matlack, & Phil Gehret ; illustrations by Frank Rohrbach ;
photographs by Mitch Mandel.
            p.   cm.
      ISBN   0-87596-105-3   hardcover
      1. Outdoor furniture.   I. Matlack, Fred.   II. Gehret, Phil.   III. Title.
IV. Title: Outdoor furniture : thirty great projects for the deck, lawn, and
garden.
TT197.5.09H96   1992
684.1'8—dc20   91-32271
                                                                              CIP

Distributed in the book trade by St. Martin's Press

      4   6   8   10   9   7   5   3   hardcover

CONTENTS

The Designer Collection

The Traditional Collection

INTRODUCTION

A hammock's easy to make. The hard part is waiting for the trees to grow big enough to support the hammock *and* you.

Wait no more! *Outdoor Furniture* has an easy-to-make hammock, as well as a laminated oak stand to support it *and* you. We call it the "Sun Lounger."

That's just one of the projects to be found in *Outdoor Furniture*. Tables, chairs, swings, chaise lounges, and even a traditional porch rocker are included. Go ahead. Flip through the pages. You'll see that the designs are varied. You'll find something that really appeals to you, and I hope you see a project or two that surprises you.

In creating the book, our two goals were (a) to provide an interesting, exciting mix of furniture projects—something for every taste, budget, and skill level—and (b) to present each project in thorough, lucid detail. Assuming that you already have a book or two on woodworking, we included nothing in *Outdoor Furniture* but projects. There's no chapter on techniques, no appendix with a rundown on tools or joints or glues.

It's just projects.

And what a showcase of outdoor furniture.

You want a porch swing? We've got two different styles to choose from. Plus a glider and a porch rocker!

A picnic table? We've got an all-in-one unit, a round table with stools, a rectangular table with a diagonal-striped top. There's even one you can fold up for storage.

How about a chaise lounge? There's a redwood 2 × 4 version, a mahogany designer number with a cushy pad, a fixed-back oak style, even a webbed-seat trundle chaise.

For every piece of furniture, there's a style to suit every taste, and there's a variety of constructions to accommodate—or challenge—any skill level and tool inventory. The All-America Picnic Table requires only a drill-driver and a circular saw to complete, but the Vineyard Ensemble can't be built outside of a well-equipped shop.

The project presentations are also shaped to serve a diversity of needs. Skim through the pages again: High-lighted tips and how-to photos present time-saving shortcuts and proven techniques you can use in *any project*. Page more slowly: Photos show what the finished projects look like in typical backyard settings. "Builder's Notes" discuss the salient aspects of every project. Where a specific tool or glue or finish is pertinent to the project, detailed information about it is presented in the notes. Tool and Shopping lists let you know what tools are necessary and how much wood is required so you won't get started on a project you can't complete.

Once you do start, the information you need is all there. Dimensioned drawings, gridded patterns, isolated details—we've got hundreds of revealing and helpful two-color drawings. Scores of how-to photos clarify important woodworking operations and assembly procedures. Step-by-step directions list the work sequence and articulate *how* to do the tasks necessary to build each project. All of these features support you novices or weekend woodworkers as you build a project.

As for those of you who are veteran woodworkers, who don't need—or want—all the guidance, you can simply peruse the Cutting List and dimensioned illustrations and set to work. If a technique is unfamiliar, the explanation is there.

And don't assume, you veterans, that there are no challenges for you in *Outdoor Furniture*. The Terrace Ensemble—table and four chairs, 10-foot-diameter canvas-covered umbrella, and tea trolley—is handsome and expensive-looking with its mortise-and-tenon construction in solid oak. Too, there's the Vineyard Ensemble, a deep-cushioned chair with an ottoman and a flagstone-topped side table: It's a deceptively challenging project that demands you know how to use your band saw. And don't overlook the Wheelwright Serving Cart: You have to make the spoked wheels and wooden casters that give it mobility.

As you've doubtless noted, these projects aren't all in redwood. Some are made of oak, a few of cedar, one ensemble is mahogany. You can use pine.

All of the projects were constructed in Rodale's Design Center workshop.

The Authorial Team

Bill Hylton has been writing and editing Rodale Press books for 20 years. He created Rodale's first woodworking title, *Build It Better Yourself* (more than 650,000 copies sold), as well as its most recent backyard building title, *Projects for Outdoor Living* (more than 125,000 copies sold since 1990). Bill was the editor of *Outdoor Furniture* and, with assistance from freelancers Roger Yepsen and Jim Barrett, wrote its text.

Fred Matlack and **Phil Gehret** have been building projects for Rodale's magazines and books for 12 years. They've designed and constructed hundreds of projects, ranging from solar food dryers to toys to antique repro-

ductions. All but one of the projects in *Outdoor Furniture* were designed and constructed by Fred 'n' Phil.

Frank Rohrbach created *Outdoor Furniture*'s countless illustrations. A longtime draftsman, Frank illustrated *The Backyard Builder* and other books. He is a regular contributor to *American Woodworker* magazine.

Mitch Mandel took all the photos in *Outdoor Furniture*. A Rodale photographer for more than 12 years, Mitch is an avid and accomplished woodworker. He is a contributing writer and photographer for *American Woodworker* magazine.

THE
QUICK-AND-EASY
COLLECTION

CALIFORNIA REDWOOD ENSEMBLE

A Super Set from a Weekend's Work

Easy as this set is to build, it offers a lot of action: The lounger's a mobile recliner, the table folds for storage, and even the chair and settee can be hung in a glider stand for some easy swingin'.

CALIFORNIA REDWOOD ENSEMBLE CHAIR AND SETTEE

The motivating concept behind these outdoor seats, and behind the lounger and table that complement them, is "Quick and Easy." What could be more contemporary!

Eschewing their stationary power tools, Rodale woodworkers Fred Matlack and Phil Gehret created a collection of pieces that are made with a standard lumberyard stock, using home-handyman power tools. The pieces are easy to build in almost no time at all. Perfect backyard projects for the weekend woodworker.

The chair is the foundation of the ensemble, and it displays the aesthetic and engineering motifs characteristic of the whole ensemble: redwood 2 × 4 lumber, simply tapered legs supporting a slatted seat and backrest, and basic butt-joint construction fastened with the increasingly popular galvanized drywall-type screw.

The settee is simply a wider version of the chair—the back slats, seat slats, and apron are longer on the settee than on the chair, but the side assemblies are identical. The building procedures are the same for both pieces. And either can be accommodated in the optional glider stand.

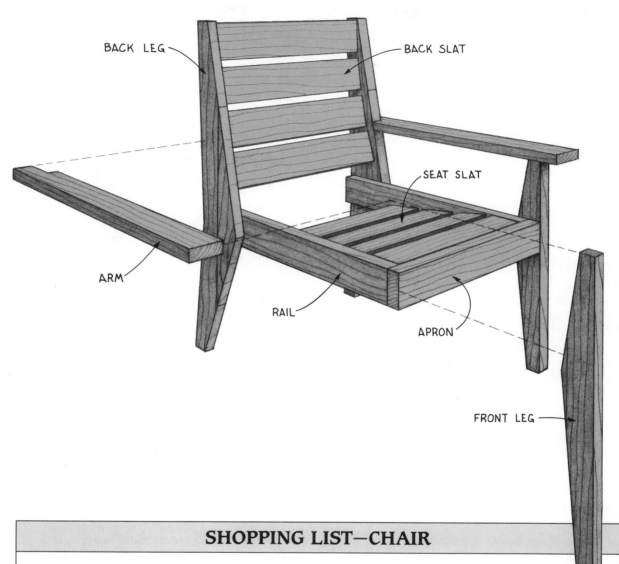

BACK LEG

BACK SLAT

SEAT SLAT

ARM

RAIL

APRON

FRONT LEG

SHOPPING LIST—CHAIR

LUMBER
5 pcs. 2 × 4 × 8' construction heart redwood

HARDWARE AND SUPPLIES
42 pcs. #6 × 3" galvanized drywall-type screws
10 pcs. #6 × 2" galvanized drywall-type screws

FINISH
Clear water repellent or clear exterior finish

SHOPPING LIST—SETTEE

LUMBER
8 pcs. 2 × 4 × 8' construction heart redwood

HARDWARE AND SUPPLIES
42 pcs. #6 × 3" galvanized drywall-type screws
10 pcs. #6 × 2" galvanized drywall-type screws

FINISH
Clear water repellent or clear exterior finish

CUTTING LIST—CHAIR

PIECE	NUMBER	THICKNESS	WIDTH	LENGTH	MATERIAL
Back legs*	2	1½"	3½"	36"	Redwood
Back leg tapers*	2	1½"	3½"	24"	Redwood
Front legs	2	1½"	3½"	22½"	Redwood
Rails	2	1½"	3½"	23"	Redwood
Seat slats	4	1½"	3½"	19"	Redwood
Apron	1	1½"	3½"	22"	Redwood
Back slats	4	1½"	3½"	22"	Redwood
Arms	2	1½"	3½"	27"	Redwood

*Cut the back legs and back leg tapers from 2 × 8 stock to avoid edge-joining 2 × 4s.

CUTTING LIST—SETTEE

PIECE	NUMBER	THICKNESS	WIDTH	LENGTH	MATERIAL
Back legs*	2	1½"	3½"	36"	Redwood
Back leg tapers*	2	1½"	3½"	24"	Redwood
Front legs	2	1½"	3½"	22½"	Redwood
Rails	2	1½"	3½"	23"	Redwood
Seat slats	4	1½"	3½"	41"	Redwood
Apron	1	1½"	3½"	44"	Redwood
Back slats	4	1½"	3½"	44"	Redwood
Arms	2	1½"	3½"	27"	Redwood

*Cut the back legs and back leg tapers from 2 × 8 stock to avoid edge-joining 2 × 4s.

Builder's Notes

Three characteristics dominate this project from the builder's perspective. First, it is made of redwood, long the traditional wood for outdoor projects. Second, it is joined in simple butt joints secured with screws. (No, glue isn't necessary.) Third, it is a hand and portable power tool project.

Materials. Redwood is the traditional choice for outdoor projects because of its natural beauty and weatherability. In fact, commercial outdoor furniture made of other woods is often stained to give it a "redwood look." This rugged ensemble is made from the real thing, and it would be the ideal group to furnish a redwood deck.

Though redwood is naturally resistant to weather's punishment, only the darker-colored heartwood (cut from the center portion of the tree) resists decay; the lighter, cream-colored sapwood does not. When selecting lumber, avoid pieces that contain sapwood.

For this project, we used construction heart redwood. This grade contains a few knots and other slight defects but is much less expensive than clear all-heart redwood.

Unless you live on the West Coast, your local lumberyard may not stock redwood in sizes other than standard 2 × 4s. The ensemble was designed with this limitation in mind—note that we edge-joined two pieces of 2 × 4 stock to achieve the required 7-inch width for the back legs of the chair and settee. To avoid making this splice, cut the back legs from 2 × 8 stock if it's available in your area.

(There *are* alternatives, of course. You can use cedar, which is a good "outdoor" lumber, though it is soft and easily dented. And think seriously about plain old Douglas fir. It is considerably less expensive than redwood. Given a sound outdoor finish—one that you maintain year after year—the entire ensemble will last for decades.)

The screws used to fasten the parts of the chair and

CUTTING DIAGRAM—CHAIR

2 x 4 x 8'

BACK LEG	BACK LEG	FRONT LEG

2 x 4 x 8'

BACK LEG TAPER	BACK LEG TAPER	FRONT LEG	RAIL

2 x 4 x 8'

RAIL	APRON	BACK SLAT	BACK SLAT

2 x 4 x 8'

ARM	ARM	BACK SLAT	SEAT SLAT

2 x 4 x 8'

BACK SLAT	SEAT SLAT	SEAT SLAT	SEAT SLAT	

CUTTING DIAGRAM—SETTEE

2 x 4 x 8'

BACK LEG	BACK LEG	FRONT LEG

2 x 4 x 8'

BACK LEG TAPER	BACK LEG TAPER	FRONT LEG	RAIL

2 x 4 x 8'

RAIL	ARM	ARM	

2 x 4 x 8'

APRON	SEAT SLAT	

2 x 4 x 8'

SEAT SLAT	SEAT SLAT	

2 x 4 x 8'

SEAT SLAT	BACK SLAT	

2 x 4 x 8'

BACK SLAT	BACK SLAT	

2 x 4 x 8'

BACK SLAT	

settee are the drywall type. Designed to be driven with a power screwdriver, they have a profile and thread pitch calculated to expedite power driving. Its bugle-shaped head is billed as being self-countersinking, and to a large extent it is. The particular screws we used are galvanized; they are often packaged as "decking screws" or "all-purpose screws." Although they are more expensive than nails, they hold better than nails.

Be sure you purchase galvanized screws intended for exterior use. And always drill pilot holes for the screws, so the wood doesn't split.

Tools and techniques. This is very much a circular-saw project. The primary guideline was to design an ensemble that could be constructed using typical hand and portable power tools. No table saws, no band saws, no drill presses. Just something to build on a spring weekend.

A nearly essential tool is a drill-driver. You'll need forearms like Popeye if you expect to drive all the screws in the chair and settee by hand. Best bet: a drill fitted with a pilot hole bit in one hand, a drill-driver with a Phillips bit in the other. Where the directions call for a very deep countersink, remember that redwood is relatively soft and that, with the torque of a drill-driver forcing it, the screw itself can create a countersink. In other words, countersink the pilot hole as deep as you can, then drive the screw as deep as you can.

Finish. When your chair and settee are completed, they'll look great. But a finish can prolong their attractiveness and their structural integrity by mollifying the effects of sunlight and moisture on the wood.

Curiously, the finish we ultimately applied enhances the strength of redwood—its resistance to the effects of moisture—but does relatively little to bolster its resistance to the effects of sunlight. The heart of redwood is naturally rot-resistant. Moreover, because it is a very light (not dense) wood, it is relatively resistant to cupping and splitting. But sunlight will turn the wood gray.

The challenge here is to find a finish that protects your redwood furniture without concealing its inherent beauty. Presuming you want to keep it looking natural, you can eliminate paint and stains from consideration,

TOOL LIST

Backsaw	Ruler
Bar clamps	Saber saw
Circular saw	Sander(s)
Drill	Sandpaper
Pilot hole bit	Sawhorses
Framing square	Screwdriver
Level	Tack cloth
Paintbrush	Tape measure
Router	Try square
¼" rounding-over bit	Yardstick

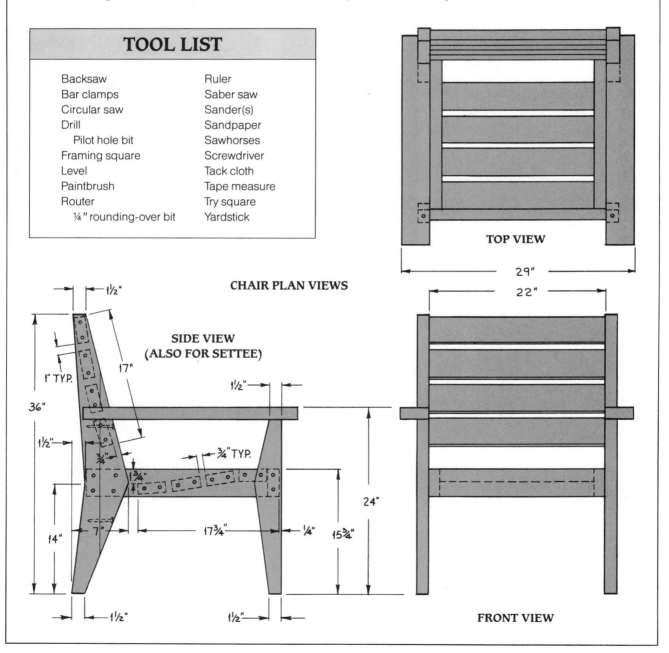

TOP VIEW

29"

CHAIR PLAN VIEWS

SIDE VIEW
(ALSO FOR SETTEE)

1½"

17"

1" TYP.

36"

1½"

¾"

¾" TYP.

1¾"

7"

17¾"

¼"

14"

1½"

1½"

1½"

22"

24"

15¾"

FRONT VIEW

even though these are the finishes that protect most effectively against photodegradation (the degrading effects of the sun).

So what did we use? A plain water repellent.

Water repellents are popular for applications where you want to retain the natural appearance of wood while protecting it from cracking and warping. They contain no pigment and darken the wood only slightly. The first application to smooth surfaces is usually short-lived. When a blotchy discoloration starts to show, the wood should be cleaned with a liquid household bleach and detergent solution, then re-treated. During the first few years, retreatment will be an annual affair. But after the wood has weathered to a uniform color, it will need refinishing only when it becomes discolored by fungi.

To prevent mildew and fungi that can discolor the surface, use a water-repellent preservative, which is a water repellent that contains a fungicide. Because this is only a surface treatment, the fungicide will not prevent rot.

Alternative finishes include exterior-grade penetrating oils and exterior-grade varnishes.

SETTEE PLAN VIEWS

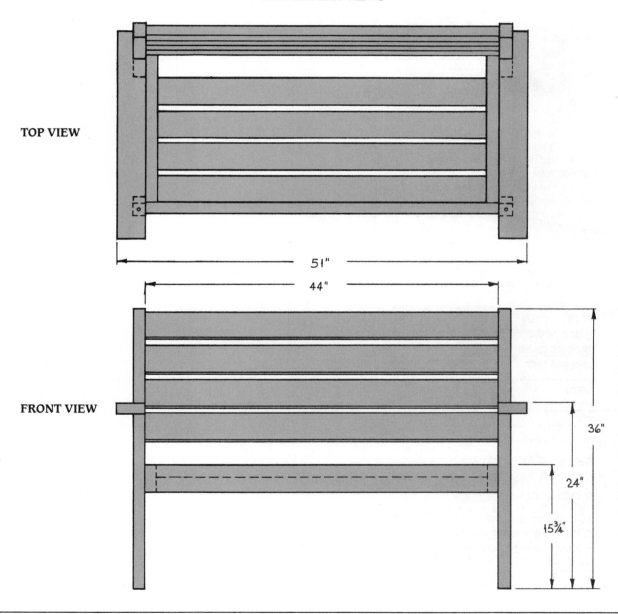

TOP VIEW

FRONT VIEW

1. Make the back and front legs. Cut stock to length for the front and back legs, then lay out and cut the tapers on each, as shown in the *Leg Layout*.

The back legs are assembled by edge-joining the two pieces with 3-inch-long screws. Drill pilot holes for the fasteners, countersinking them deeply, as shown in the *Side View*. Using a router and a ¼-inch rounding-over bit, radius all legs.

Outside tapers for the front and back legs can be cut with a circular saw. To do this safely, clamp the workpiece to a long 2 × 4 supported on sawhorses. Set your saw to *just* break through the workpiece, so you don't unduly weaken the support board. You'll have to reposition the clamp after the initial cut.

Support the pieces for the back legs on sawhorses, and cut the inside tapers with a saber saw. Equip the saw with the widest blade you have to ensure the cut is straight and true.

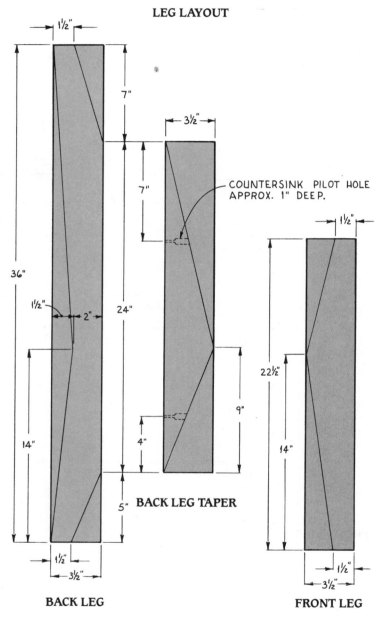

LEG LAYOUT

COUNTERSINK PILOT HOLE APPROX. 1" DEEP.

BACK LEG

BACK LEG TAPER

FRONT LEG

2. Make the seat. Cut the rails, seat slats, and apron to length. Radius all exposed edges.

The seat slats form a slight curve, as shown in the *Side View.* Using the drawing as a guide, mark the positions of the front and rear seat slats on the inside faces of the rails. Flex a thin strip of scrap—¼-inch plywood, plastic laminate, even a thin yardstick—to form a curve connecting the positions of the front and rear slats, and scribe the curve on the rail. (An extra pair of hands makes this as easy to do as it is to say.) When both rails are marked, lay out the positions of the middle two seat slats, spacing them approximately ¾ inch apart.

Drill pilot holes, then drive 3-inch screws through the rails into the ends of the seat slats. Fasten the apron to the front ends of the rails in the same manner.

---

3. Fasten the legs to the seat assembly. Start by marking the rail location on the inside of the legs; refer to the *Side View* for this information. Lay a front leg and a back leg on the benchtop. Stand the seat assembly on edge, positioning the rail on top of the legs.

Fasten the back leg first. Drill a pilot hole, then drive a single 2-inch screw through the rail and into the leg. Then use a framing square and long straightedge to square up the leg to the rail, and drive three more screws into the joint. The front leg is "tacked" in place with a single screw.

Repeat the process to install the second back leg and to tack the second front leg in place. Set the chair (or settee) on its feet now, square up the front legs with a framing square, and drive additional screws through the legs into the rails.

Above: A framing square and straightedge, used as shown, help you "square up" the back legs to the seat. A single screw holds the parts in position, yet enables you to pivot the leg to square it up.

Right: To square up the front legs, hang the framing square from the rail. This enables you to square up the front leg with one hand and drive screws with the other.

4. **Fasten the back slats to the back legs.** You need to position the slats on the legs so the backrest is slightly curved. On the inside of the back legs, mark the locations of the top and bottom back slats, as shown in the *Side View*. As with the seat, use a flexible strip to establish the arc between the top and bottom slats, and scribe it on the legs.

Install the top slat first. Drill pilot holes and drive two 3-inch screws through the legs into each end of the slat. Repeat the process to install the other three slats.

TIP

Use a tourniquet-type clamp—sometimes called a Spanish windlass—to hold the back slats in position while you drill pilot holes and drive screws. The tourniquet pulls the legs together, pinching the slat and holding it in place. To make the tourniquet, simply loop a piece of sturdy twine around the legs, then use a short stick to twist the twine, as shown. This arrangement has two advantages: It's far cheaper than a long bar clamp or pipe clamp, and it won't leave jaw marks on the wood.

---

5. **Fasten the arms to the legs.** Cut the arms to length, and radius all the exposed edges. The arms must be scribed and notched to fit around the back legs, as shown in the *Top View*. To scribe an arm for cutting, rest it on the front leg, butt it against the side of the leg, and mark the angle of the back leg on it. Make sure the arm is level from front to back. Cut the notch with a backsaw or hand saw.

Fasten each arm to the legs by driving 3-inch screws through the arm into the front leg and 2-inch screws through the back leg into the arm.

To mark the notch where the arm fits around the back leg, rest the arm on the front leg, line it up against the back leg, and run a pencil along the edge of the leg, marking the arm. You can level the arm visually, as done here, or with more exactitude by resting a level on the arm.

---

6. **Apply a finish.** Sand the entire piece with fine-grit sandpaper, smoothing any sharp or splintery edges. Apply the clear finish of your choice and let it dry. Now, sit down and relax—it's done!

CALIFORNIA REDWOOD GLIDER STAND

What is it about gliders that evokes nostalgic feelings? It's a wistful image. The spacious porch with gaudy striped awnings. A cooling breeze coming just at dusk. Murmuring voices, comforting voices. The creak of the glider.

Is it the gentle rocking? Is it the creaking of the wood and the pivots? Even people who never had a porch feel it.

Well, whatever it is, with this glider stand, you can have it, too. Embue your California redwood settee with that nostalgic—and very pleasant—quality. If you've successfully completed the settee, you'll find the stand easy to build.

The glider stand doesn't have to be restricted to the settee, of course. By shortening the cross members, you can make it accommodate the chair.

SHOPPING LIST

LUMBER
2 pcs. 2 × 4 × 8' construction heart redwood
1 pc. 2 × 4 × 10' construction heart redwood

HARDWARE AND SUPPLIES
28 pcs. #6 × 3" galvanized drywall-type screws
1 pc. ⅛" × ¾" × 72" steel strap
1 pc. ½" × ½" × 60" aluminum channel

HARDWARE AND SUPPLIES—CONTINUED
8 pcs. ¼" × 2" hex-head bolts, washers, and locknuts
8 pcs. #6 × ½" roundhead wood screws

FINISH
Clear water repellent or clear exterior finish

CUTTING LIST

PIECE	NUMBER	THICKNESS	WIDTH	LENGTH	MATERIAL
Legs	4	1½"	3½"	23"	Redwood
Bottom rails	2	1½"	3½"	25"	Redwood
Top rails	2	1½"	3½"	27"	Redwood
Cross members	2	1½"	3½"	49"	Redwood

CUTTING DIAGRAM

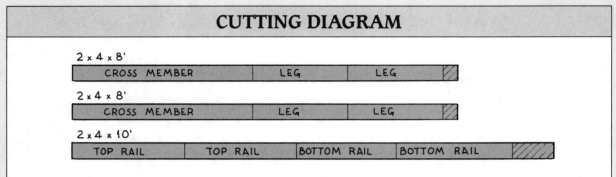

2 x 4 x 8'

| CROSS MEMBER | LEG | LEG | |

2 x 4 x 8'

| CROSS MEMBER | LEG | LEG | |

2 x 4 x 10'

| TOP RAIL | TOP RAIL | BOTTOM RAIL | BOTTOM RAIL | |

GLIDER STAND PLAN VIEWS

SIDE VIEW

FRONT VIEW

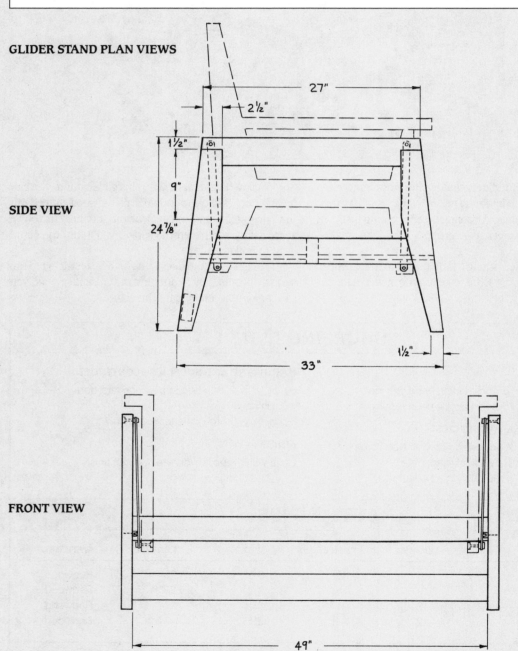

Builder's Notes

The glider stand consists of two identical side frames, joined by two cross members. You hang the settee in the stand by means of four metal supports, which allow the swinging action. Use the same materials for the stand that you used for the chair and settee. The tool requirements and the techniques you use are essentially the same, too.

To complete the glider, build the settee on page 4, but cut 4 inches off the bottom of each leg. This maintains the settee's height, yet allows attachment to the stand, as shown in the *Side View*. Most important, it provides the ground clearance necessary for swinging.

TOOL LIST

Bar clamps	Router
Centerpunch	¼" rounding-over bit
Circular saw	Ruler
Drill	Saber saw
¼" dia. bit (for metal)	Sander(s)
¾" dia. spade bit	Sandpaper
Countersink bit	Sawhorses
Pilot hole bit	Screwdriver
File	Tack cloth
Hacksaw	Tape measure
Hammer	Try square
Paintbrush	Wrench

1. Cut and assemble the legs and rails. Lay out and cut the four legs, as shown in the *Leg Layout*. You can lay out each leg individually, or just lay out one and, after cutting the tapers and mitering the ends, use it as a template to lay out the others. In any case, cut the tapers with a circular saw; clamp the leg to a 2 × 4 supported on sawhorses to safely manage this operation.

Cut the lower rails to size, mitering the ends at a 75 degree angle, as shown in the *Side View*. Lay out the top rails, as shown in the *Top Rail Layout,* and cut them out. Use a saber saw to cut the notches.

The legs and rails are fastened together with deeply countersunk 3-inch screws. To ensure that the completed assemblies are flat and true (as opposed to wracked or twisted), set them in position on a workbench, then clamp them to the benchtop (but not to each other). With the pieces clamped down, drill pilot holes through the edges of the legs into the ends of the rails (see the *Side View*), countersinking the holes as much as 1¾ inches. Drive the screws.

Complete the work on these assemblies by radiusing all exposed edges.

LEG AND TOP RAIL LAYOUTS

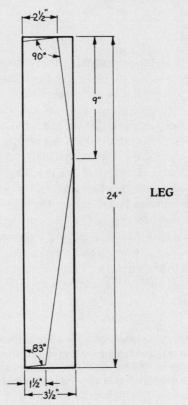

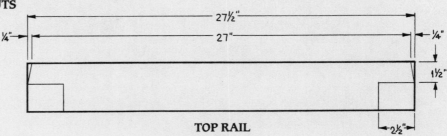

2. **Join the two leg-and-rail assemblies.** Cut the cross members and radius all four sides. To join the two leg-and-rail assemblies, position the cross members, as shown in the *Side View* and *Front View*. After drilling pilot holes, drive 3-inch screws through the back legs and the bottom rails into the ends of the cross members.

3. **Make the metal supports and rub rails.** From the ⅛-inch by ¾-inch steel strap, cut four 17-inch pieces. Radius the ends with a file or grinder, and drill ¼-inch-diameter holes at each end, as indicated in the *Side View*. From the ½-inch by ½-inch aluminum channel, cut four rub rails 14½ inches long. There are two rub rails attached to each bottom rail, one on each side of the center cross member. Spray paint both sides of these metal pieces (rub rails *and* supports) with a rust-preventive paint before assembly.

TIP

Mark the center of each hole you drill in metal with a centerpunch and hammer. The centerpunch will dimple the metal, and this tiny depression will prevent the drill bit from wandering across the metal surface as you start the drill.

---

4. **Hang the seat (settee) in the glider stand.** In the top rails of the glider stand and bottom ends of the seat (settee), drill ¼-inch holes with ¾-inch-diameter by ¼-inch-deep counterbores, as indicated in the *Front View*. Before screwing on the rub rails and hanging the seat, sand the seat and stand and apply a finish to both.

After the finish is dry, install the rub rails along the bottom rails of the stand (see the *Side View*). Use four equally spaced screws in each. Drill holes in the rub rails for the roundhead wood screws, then screw them in place.

Fasten the top end of each support to the glider stand with bolts, washers, and locknuts. Then, using scrap blocks of wood to raise the seat to the correct height inside the stand, fasten the bottom ends of the metal supports to the seat legs with bolts, washers, and locknuts.

The rub rails extend from the edge of the legs (front and back) in along the bottom rails to the center crosspiece. They prevent the seat from swaying side to side in the stand; that way the protruding pivot bolts can't gouge the stand or the seat.

CALIFORNIA REDWOOD ENSEMBLE CHAISE LOUNGE

This reclining chaise is a natural complement to the California Redwood Ensemble, but it doesn't always have to stick to the group. Unlike the chairs and table, it has wheels, so it can easily be moved to the sunny spot. With its reclining back, it was designed for sunbathing.

The special hardware that supports the backrest is nifty. Because of its similarity to the principle of the cog railway, we're calling the hardware pieces cog-latch braces. Just as the railway's cog system prevents the train from slipping back as it advances up a steep grade, so do these braces prevent the backrest from dropping back. As you raise the backrest, a latch engages a cog, maintaining the backrest's position. To drop it into the fully reclining position, you must raise it up as far as it will go, *then* lower it.

Just as it is easy to build, the lounger is easy to use. Roll it to the sunny spot, lift the back a click or two, stretch out, and just broil.

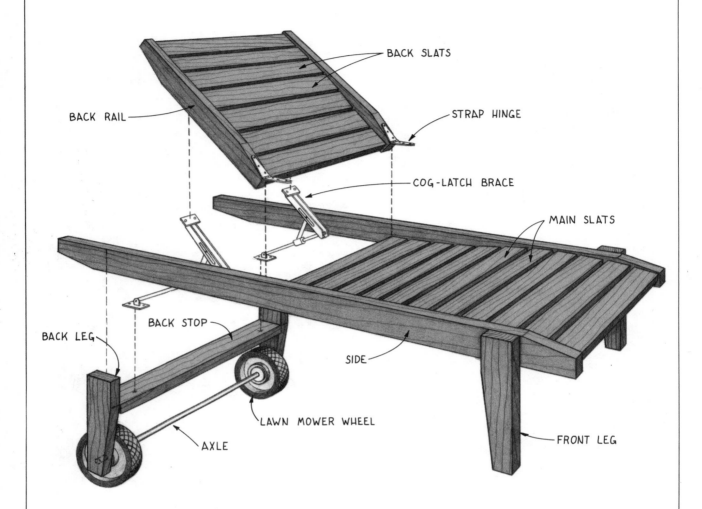

BACK SLATS

BACK RAIL

STRAP HINGE

COG-LATCH BRACE

MAIN SLATS

BACK LEG

BACK STOP

SIDE

LAWN MOWER WHEEL

AXLE

FRONT LEG

SHOPPING LIST

LUMBER

5 pcs. 2 × 4 × 10' construction heart redwood
1 pc. 2 × 4 × 8' construction heart redwood

HARDWARE AND SUPPLIES

80 pcs. #6 × 3" galvanized drywall-type screws
12 pcs. #6 × 1½" galvanized drywall-type screws
8 pcs. #8 × 2½" galvanized drywall-type screws
2 pcs. 7" dia. wheels with rubber tires
1 pc. ½" dia. × 26" steel rod
4 pcs. ½" dia. flat washers
2 pcs. ⅛" dia. cotter pins
2 pcs. 6" strap hinges
1 pr. cog-latch braces*

FINISH

Clear water repellent or clear exterior finish

*Sold by Constantine's, 2050 Eastchester Road, Bronx, NY 10461 (1-800-223-8087 or 212-792-1600) as slant/tilt table hardware (part number FH702). And by The Woodworker's Store, 21801 Industrial Blvd., Rogers, MN 55374 (612-428-2199) as drafting table hardware (part number D5660).

CUTTING LIST

PIECE	NUMBER	THICKNESS	WIDTH	LENGTH	MATERIAL
Sides	2	1½"	3½"	72"	Redwood
Main slats	11	1½"	3½"	21"	Redwood
Back rails	2	1½"	3½"	28"	Redwood
Back slats	7	1½"	3½"	17¾"	Redwood
Back stop	1	1½"	3½"	24"	Redwood
Back legs	2	1½"	3½"	12½"	Redwood
Front legs	2	1½"	3½"	14"	Redwood

CUTTING DIAGRAM

2 × 4 × 10'
| SIDE | BACK RAIL | BACK SLAT |

2 × 4 × 10'
| SIDE | BACK RAIL | BACK SLAT |

2 × 4 × 10'
| MAIN SLAT | MAIN SLAT | MAIN SLAT | MAIN SLAT | MAIN SLAT | BACK LEG |

2 × 4 × 10'
| MAIN SLAT | MAIN SLAT | MAIN SLAT | MAIN SLAT | MAIN SLAT | BACK LEG |

2 × 4 × 10'
| BACK SLAT | BACK SLAT | BACK SLAT | BACK SLAT | BACK SLAT | FRONT LEG | FRONT LEG |

2 × 4 × 8'
| MAIN SLAT | BACK STOP |

Builder's Notes

A companion project to the chair and settee that opened this chapter, the lounger is constructed with the same materials and uses the same tools and techniques as those earlier projects. If you are building only this project from the ensemble, then by all means read the "Builder's Notes" accompanying the California Redwood Chair and Settee project on page 6.

A few hardware items are unique to the lounger, but you can get most of them at your local hardware store or home center. The wheels, for example, are intended for lawn mowers. The cog-latch braces that support the backrest may be harder to come by, though. There doesn't seem to be a common name used by all retailers. Having obtained our set through the mail, we list two sources (see the "Shopping List").

TOOL LIST

Bar clamps	Ruler
Centerpunch	Sander(s)
Circular saw	Sandpaper
Drill	Sawhorses
⅛" dia. bit (for metal)	Screwdriver
½" dia. bit	Spring clamps
Countersink bit	Tack cloth
Pilot hole bit	Tape measure
Hacksaw	Try square
Hammer	
Paintbrush	
Router	
¼" rounding-over bit	
⅜" V-groove bit	

PLAN VIEWS

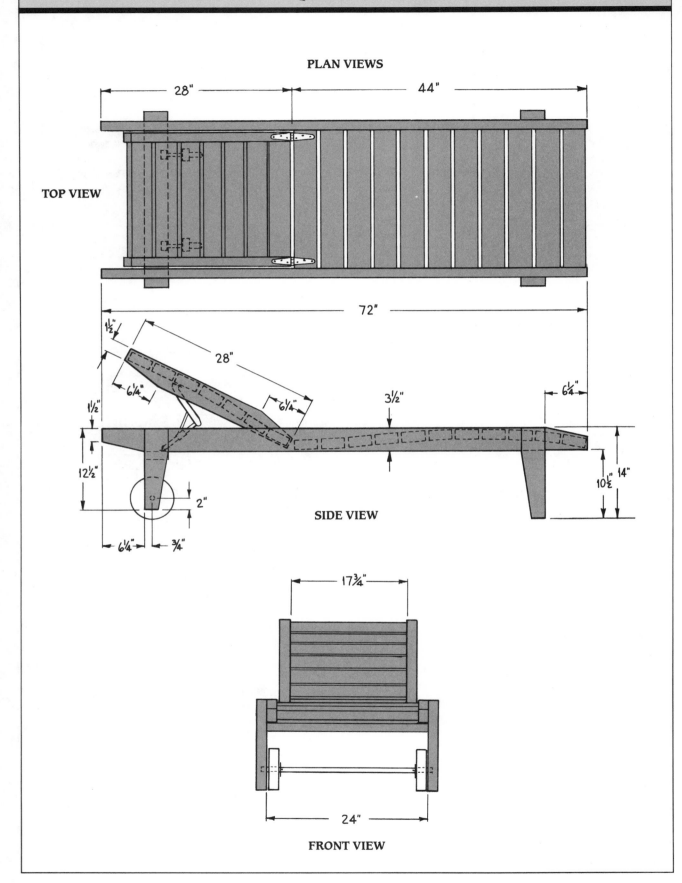

TOP VIEW

28"   44"

72"

1½"

28"

6¼"   6¼"   3½"   6¼"

1½"

12½"   14"   10½"

2"

6¼"   ¾"

SIDE VIEW

17¾"

24"

FRONT VIEW

1. Cut and assemble the parts for the lounge frame. Cut the sides and main slats for the lounge frame to the lengths specified by the "Cutting List." Lay out and cut the tapers at each end of the side pieces, as shown in the *Side View.* Use a router with a ¼-inch

rounding-over bit to radius all sharp edges.

Assemble the frame by joining the two sides with the end slat and hinge slat.

Establish the contour of the lounge seat next. Stand the partially assembled frame on one side. Hold a strip of plastic laminate or thin plywood on edge against the side. Flex the strip to the desired curve, then, to hold the curve, clamp the strip to the front and hinge slats (use spring clamps). Trace the curve on the side piece. To duplicate the line on the second side, take measurements at several points along the line, then transfer them to the second side. Flex the strip to connect the marks, clamp it, then trace the curve.

That done, fasten the remaining nine slats to the sides with 3-inch screws, following the curve.

To establish the seat contour, flex a strip of plastic laminate or thin plywood until it takes on a curve you like. Use spring clamps to secure the strip to the front and hinge slats, holding the curve so you can trace it with a pencil, marking the side.

2. Make the legs. Cut the front and back legs to length, then taper the sides, as shown in the *Side View.* You can cut the tapers with a portable circular saw if you clamp the leg blanks to a larger piece of scrap. Drill ½-inch-diameter by 1-inch-deep stopped holes into the inside faces of the back legs for the wheel axle, as shown

in the *Side View.* Radius all exposed edges of the legs.

Attach the front legs to the lounge frame with 2½-inch screws. When marking the leg positions on the sides, use a try square and pencil to make sure the legs are exactly perpendicular to the sides.

3. Install the wheel assembly. Cut the back stop to fit between the back legs and, with 3-inch screws, fasten it to the bottom edge of the lounge sides.

Cut the 26-inch axle for the wheel assembly from ½-inch-diameter steel rod. As shown, the axle is "captured" by the legs. Likewise, each wheel is captured between a leg and a cotter pin. Drill two ⅛-inch holes in the axle for these cotter pins. The exact positions of the holes are best determined by dry assembling the axle, wheels, and legs. Allow about ¼ inch of side-to-side play for each wheel.

Attach one of the back legs to the lounge side and back stop. Next, insert the axle in the leg hole. Slide on a washer, a wheel, two more washers, the second wheel, and yet another washer. Then, temporarily attach (or clamp) the second leg, capturing the axle and wheels between the legs. Slide the wheels against their respective legs, and mark the axle for the cotter-pin holes.

Remove the axle from the assembly, drill the holes, then reassemble the components. Install the cotter pins in the axle.

To install the axle, fasten one of the back legs to the lounge side and back stop, insert the wheel/axle assembly, then add the other back leg to capture the axle between the two legs.

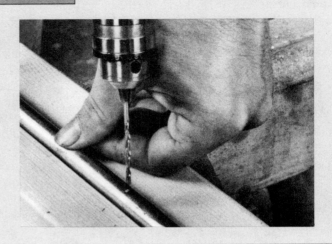

Drilling the cotter-pin holes in the steel axle can be done with a hand-held drill just as well as with a drill press. But here are two tips to make the job easier, regardless of the tool you use.

First, make a V-block to cradle the axle. Plow a groove in a scrap of 2 × 4 with a router and a V-groove bit. As shown, the V-block will keep the axle from rolling as you try to drill.

Then use a hammer and centerpunch to dimple the axle where the hole should be. This little depression will be enough to constrain the bit as you start to drill, preventing it from skittering off mark.

4. Cut and assemble the backrest. Cut the backrest rails and slats to the lengths specified by the "Cutting List," then taper the ends of the back rails, as shown in the _Side View._ With the router and ¼-inch rounding-over bit, radius all the edges that will be exposed.

Using the drawing as a guide, establish the contour formed by the slats on the rails, as you did for the lounge sides. Fasten the back slats to the back rails with 3-inch screws.

5. Install the backrest. Center the backrest between the lounge sides, and install the hinges.

The cog-latch braces must now be installed, and

positioning them is a trial-and-error proposition. They must be aligned so that they'll work together without binding _and_ allow the back to hinge down perfectly flat.

Begin by propping the back in an upright position. Use 1½-inch screws to attach the top end of each brace to the third back slat from the top (one at each end of the slat, flush against the side rails). Use a C-clamp or short bar clamp to secure the bottom end of each brace to the back stop, as shown. Test the action of the backrest. As necessary, loosen one or both clamps, shift the brace(s), and retighten the clamp(s). When you are satisfied with the action of the braces, fasten the bottom ends with the 1½-inch screws and remove the clamps.

A short bar clamp holds the lower end of the cog-latch brace in place while you test the action. Both braces must work in concert without binding, and to do that, they must be perfectly aligned.

6. Apply a finish. Sand the entire piece with fine-grit sandpaper, smoothing any sharp or splintery edges. Apply the clear finish of your choice and let it dry.

That's it—the chaise is ready to be wheeled out to a spot in the sun.

CALIFORNIA REDWOOD ENSEMBLE FOLDING TABLE

This sturdy, 6-foot-long table will hold a smorgasbord of snacks, making your redwood ensemble the focal point of backyard gatherings. If you think it's a bit too big for everyday use on your deck or patio, no problem— just fold up the legs and store it neatly out of the way.

The table complements the ensemble visually. The taper of the leg echoes that of the other pieces of the ensemble. And the joinery of the leg assembly echoes that used for the glider stand.

A bit of ingenuity went into the construction of the table. After testing it, we discarded hardware we had bought that supposedly was designed especially for folding tables; the play in the mechanisms made the table far too wobbly. A pensive stroll through the aisles of the local hardware store led to a different solution: stepladder braces. Like your picnic table, a stepladder in use is laden with precious cargo and must be rock-steady. The braces work perfectly.

SHOPPING LIST

LUMBER

4 pcs. 2 × 4 × 12′ construction heart redwood
2 pcs. 2 × 4 × 10′ construction heart redwood
1 pc. 2 × 4 × 8′ construction heart redwood

HARDWARE AND SUPPLIES

80 pcs. #6 × 2½″ galvanized drywall-type screws
24 pcs. #6 × 1¼″ galvanized drywall-type screws

HARDWARE AND SUPPLIES—CONTINUED

4 pcs. 6″ light-duty T-strap hinges
4 pcs. stepladder braces

FINISH

Clear water repellent or clear exterior finish, if
desired

CUTTING LIST

PIECE	NUMBER	THICKNESS	WIDTH	LENGTH	MATERIAL
Tabletop slats	8	1½″	3½″	72″	Redwood
Tabletop cleats	3	1½″	3½″	29¼″	Redwood
Brace blocks	4	1½″	3½″	16″	Redwood
Legs	4	1½″	3½″	27″	Redwood
Leg crosspieces	2	1½″	3½″	17¼″	Redwood

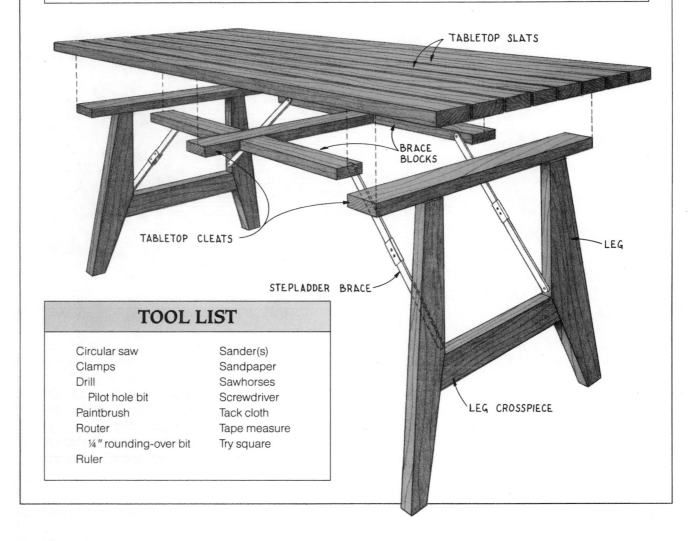

TABLETOP SLATS

BRACE BLOCKS

TABLETOP CLEATS

STEPLADDER BRACE

LEG

LEG CROSSPIECE

TOOL LIST

Circular saw
Clamps
Drill
  Pilot hole bit
Paintbrush
Router
  ¼″ rounding-over bit
Ruler

Sander(s)
Sandpaper
Sawhorses
Screwdriver
Tack cloth
Tape measure
Try square

PLAN VIEWS

TOP VIEW

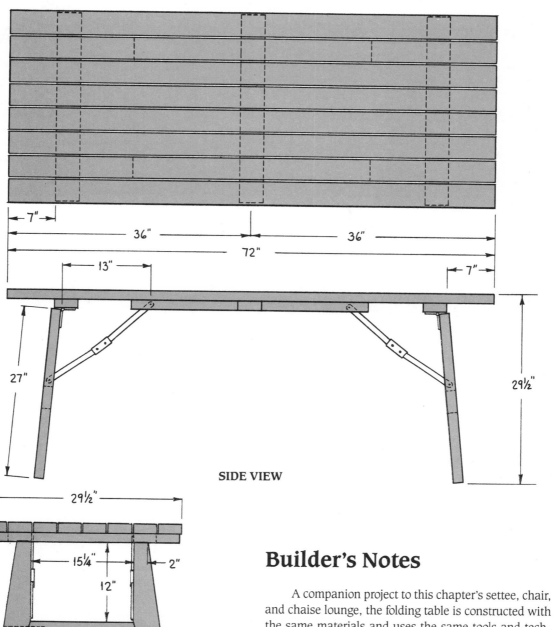

SIDE VIEW

END VIEW

Builder's Notes

A companion project to this chapter's settee, chair, and chaise lounge, the folding table is constructed with the same materials and uses the same tools and techniques as those earlier projects. If you are building only this project from the ensemble, then by all means read the "Builder's Notes" accompanying the California Redwood Chair and Settee project on page 6.

One hardware item, the stepladder brace, is unique to the folding table, but you should be able to get it at a well-stocked hardware store or home center.

CUTTING DIAGRAM

2 x 4 x 12'
| TABLETOP SLAT | TABLETOP SLAT |

2 x 4 x 12'
| TABLETOP SLAT | TABLETOP SLAT |

2 x 4 x 12'
| TABLETOP SLAT | TABLETOP SLAT |

2 x 4 x 12'
| TABLETOP SLAT | TABLETOP SLAT |

2 x 4 x 10'
| TABLETOP CLEAT | TABLETOP CLEAT | TABLETOP CLEAT | LEG |

2 x 4 x 10'
| LEG | LEG | LEG | LEG CROSSPIECE | LEG CROSSPIECE |

2 x 4 x 8'
| BRACE BLOCK | BRACE BLOCK | BRACE BLOCK | BRACE BLOCK |

1. Cut and assemble the pieces for the top.
Cut the tabletop slats, tabletop cleats, and brace blocks to the lengths specified by the "Cutting List." Using a router and a ¼-inch rounding-over bit, radius all edges of the tabletop slats and the exposed edges of the cleats and brace blocks.

On a workbench or other flat surface, arrange the slats, spacing them evenly to form a top 29½ inches wide. Making sure that the slat ends are perfectly aligned and the tabletop is square, position the cleats across the tabletop, as shown in the *Top View,* and fasten them in place with 2½-inch screws. Use the same size screws to attach the brace blocks to the underside of the tabletop.

2. Lay out and cut the legs. Cut four blanks for the tapered legs to the length specified by the "Cutting List." Lay out the tapered sides and angled ends on one leg, cut the leg out, then use it as a template to lay out the other three. Here's how to lay out that first leg:

• Use a straightedge to extend the line of the inside edge of a brace block across the hinge cleat, as shown in the *Leg Layout.*

• Mark the hinge alignment line on the end tabletop cleat, as shown. The intersection of this line with the

After marking the location of the leg and hinge on a cleat, align the leg blank to the marks and lay out the taper angle. Visually align the straightedge with the inside edge of the brace block beneath.

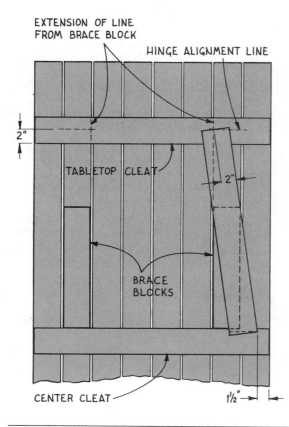

EXTENSION OF LINE FROM BRACE BLOCK

HINGE ALIGNMENT LINE

2"

TABLETOP CLEAT

2"

BRACE BLOCKS

CENTER CLEAT

1½"

first line is the key alignment point on the end tabletop cleat.

● Measure and mark a line across the center tabletop cleat 1½ inches from the end, as shown.

● At the end of a leg blank, measure and mark 2 inches from the outer edge, as shown.

● Position the leg across the cleats, as shown, with its mark lined up with the alignment point on the end tabletop cleat and its foot flush with the line on the center tabletop cleat.

● Place a straightedge on top of the leg, visually align it with the inside edge of the brace block, and scribe the taper line on the leg. Use the straightedge to mark the top and foot of the leg for cutting; align it visually with the cleats to do this.

● Finally, follow the *End View* to mark the line of the second taper.

Use a circular saw to cut the shape of the leg. For safety's sake, clamp the leg blank to a scrap 2 × 4 supported on sawhorses when you make these cuts. After the other three legs are laid out, cut them in the same way.

3. **Build the leg assemblies.** Cut the leg crosspieces to length, mitering the ends as shown in the *End View.* Assemble both leg sets by drilling pilot holes through the sides of the legs into the ends of the crosspieces, as indicated in the *End View,* then driving 2½-inch screws.

With a router and a rounding-over bit, radius the edges of the two assemblies.

TIP

Here's how to ensure that both leg assemblies will be perfectly flat and will match each other. First, lay out the pieces for the first assembly on a flat bench, and clamp them, not to each other but to the benchtop, as shown. Drill pilot holes and drive the screws. Remove the clamps, lay the pieces for the second assembly on top of the first, and clamp both to the benchtop. You'll see immediately whether or not the assemblies are matched. If they are, install the screws in the second assembly.

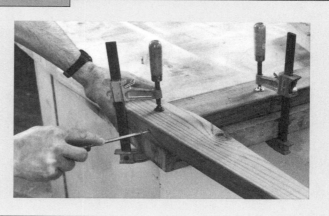

4. **Attach the leg assemblies to the tabletop.** Center the strap leaf of the hinges on the ends of the table legs, and fasten the hinges with 1¼-inch screws. Then rest each assembly on the underside of the table-top in its folded position. Clamp the assembly to the tabletop, and drive 1¼-inch screws in the exposed screw holes of the hinge's butt leaf. Now, open up the assembly and drive screws into the remaining holes in the hinge leaf.

To locate the screw holes for the stepladder braces on the brace blocks and legs, use the braces themselves. With both the legs and braces folded, set the braces next to the leg and brace block. Fasten one end to the leg, the other to the brace block. Use 2½-inch screws. Check the action of the leg; it should open easily and completely, as should the braces. If the setup works to your satisfaction, duplicate the procedure to install the other leg assembly.

After attaching the leg assembly to the tabletop, align the folded stepladder brace against the brace block and the leg, and drive the screws to secure it. The position of the second brace must parallel the position of the first for the setup to work smoothly.

5. **Apply a finish.** Lightly sand all surfaces with fine-grit sandpaper and apply the same clear finish you used for the other pieces in the ensemble. If the deeply counterbored screw holes in the legs bother you, you can fill these with a plastic wood dough or putty before sanding and finishing the project.

Now, let's eat outdoors!

ALL-AMERICA PICNIC TABLE

The Backyard's Rugged Standby

This project is called the All-America Picnic Table simply because it's the rugged standby seen all over America—in campgrounds, parks, roadside rests, and at least a few million backyards. The time-honored design has survived for several reasons: It's easy to build with a few basic tools and standard lumber available at any lumberyard, it will seat a family of six comfortably, and it's durable enough to outlast a lifetime of picnics.

Of course, no outdoor furniture book would be complete without one!

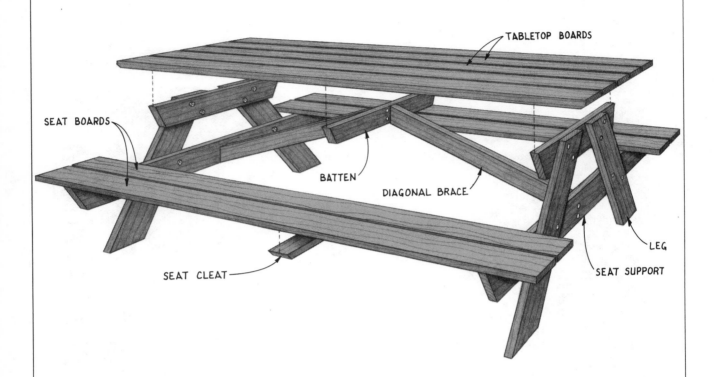

TABLETOP BOARDS

SEAT BOARDS

BATTEN

DIAGONAL BRACE

LEG

SEAT SUPPORT

SEAT CLEAT

SHOPPING LIST

LUMBER

12 pcs. 2 × 6 × 8' clear all heart redwood
2 pcs. 2 × 4 × 8' clear all heart redwood

HARDWARE AND SUPPLIES

16 pcs. ¼" × 3½" galvanized carriage bolts,
  washers, and nuts
1 box #6 × 2½" galvanized drywall-type screws
1 box #6 × 3" galvanized drywall-type screws

FINISH

Clear water repellent or clear exterior finish

CUTTING LIST

PIECE	NUMBER	THICKNESS	WIDTH	LENGTH	MATERIAL
Legs	4	1½"	5½"	33"	2 × 6 redwood
Seat supports	2	1½"	5½"	55½"	2 × 6 redwood
Battens	3	1½"	3½"	28½"	2 × 4 redwood
Diagonal braces	2	1½"	3½"	42"	2 × 4 redwood
Tabletop boards	5	1½"	5½"	96"	2 × 6 redwood
Seat boards	4	1½"	5½"	96"	2 × 6 redwood
Seat cleats	2	1½"	5½"	11½"	2 × 6 redwood

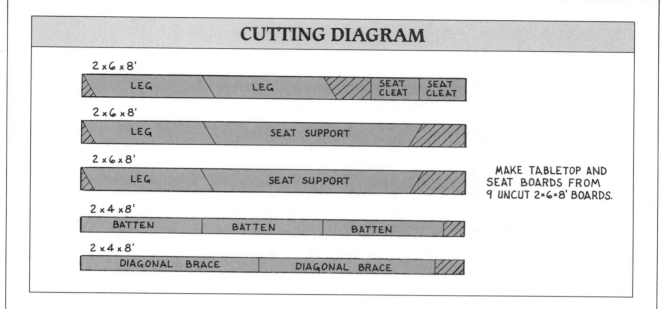

Builder's Notes

The All-America Picnic Table is an *ideal* project for the complete novice. It is, first of all, imminently practical—you get a piece of furniture you and your family will use for years to come. The materials, though not cheap, are readily available throughout North America. The necessary tools are few and commonplace. (If you really reduce the project to its simplest form, you can get by with a handsaw and a hammer.) And finally, the woodworking processes are basic ones that you'll use again and again as you learn, gain experience, and tackle more demanding projects.

From the drawings and the text, you'll learn how to build a nice, basic picnic table with top-quality lumber and heavy-duty hardware, simple solid joinery, and a few craftsman-like touches, among them the chamfered ends on the tabletop and seat boards, and the hidden fasteners. Following these directions explicitly will require you to purchase premium materials and to have a selection of power tools (and accessories). In the following notes, you'll find specific tips on saving money and time, and simplifying the work.

The table shown is one of dozens crafted by Rodale Press's John Keck for the fair-weather use of the company's employees. Though Keck's picnic tables get fair-weather use, they also get—and withstand—year-round abuse. Because each table is one bulky piece, it's a tough item to store out of the weather. Attesting to the durability of the design and materials is the fact that these tables are left outdoors year-round, in all kinds of weather—spring rains, summer sun, fall frosts, winter snow and ice. Many are five or more years old, and still supporting the heartiest of picnics. And picnickers!

Materials. Perhaps the most obvious thing about the materials is that fully half the boards you buy never get cut. They're used at full length and width in the project.

The next most obvious thing is that we—or at least John Keck—used the premium grade of redwood. Is this *necessary?* Of course not. Buy down a grade. Or select a different wood. But do try to avoid knots and other defects that may undermine the strength of the project. You don't want a seat board to break at a knot and dump Aunt Martha on the ground. (She just might have a litigious reaction.) And select a species that will weather well; your picnic table (like ours) will surely have to withstand the worst that your local climate has to offer.

TOOL LIST

Circular saw	Sander(s)
Clamps	Sandpaper
Drill	Sawhorses
¼" dia. bit	Screwdriver
⅜" dia. bit	Sliding T-bevel
Long-shank Phillips bit	Tack cloth
Pilot hole bit	Tape measure
Hammer	Try square
Paintbrush	Wrench
Protractor	Yardstick

PLAN VIEWS

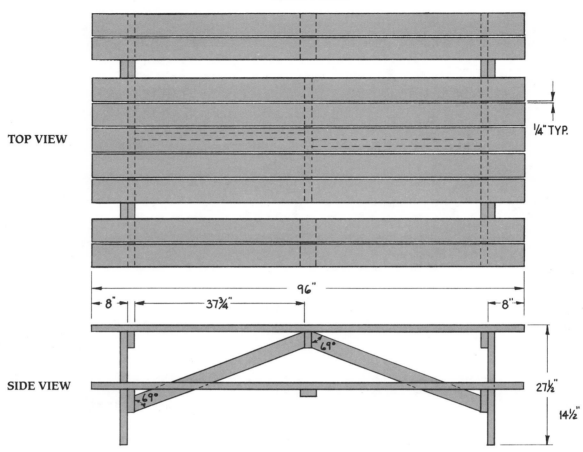

TOP VIEW

¼" TYP.

SIDE VIEW

96"

8" 37¾" 8"

69°

69°

27½"

14½"

END VIEW

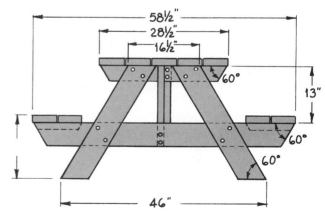

58½"

28½"

16½"

60°

13"

60°

60°

46"

Think more than once before substituting pressure-treated wood for the redwood in this project, however. Your first thought, of course, will be that this lumber is a lot less expensive. But your second thought ought to be a question: Do I want to eat from a table made of a material that's thoroughly impregnated with an arsenic compound? One that will kill any insects that try to eat it?

If you are willing to paint or varnish your table (and recoat it, say, every other year), you could use construction-grade material—pine, spruce, fir, hemlock, or whatever is commonly used in your area.

Less obvious, perhaps, are the hardware options. The "Shopping List" specifies carriage bolts and drywall-type screws as the fasteners to use. In the original table, almost four dozen lag screws were used to attach the tabletop and seat boards. The drywall-type screws are a less costly choice that is completely satisfactory. Moreover, you can use the screws throughout the project.

Or you can use nails. Not just any nails, of course, but galvanized nails with threaded or ringed shanks. They often are sold under the name "decking nails" or "pressure-treated wood nails."

Tools and techniques. The woodworking tools you have and the techniques you use are always entwined. The picnic table shown was built using shop tools: a radial arm saw to chamfer the seat and tabletop boards, and a drill press to make the pilot holes and counterbores in the battens and seat supports. The directions below outline how to build the table using portable tools exclusively—a circular saw and a ⅜-inch power drill. But the cutting necessary is so minimal that you can use a handsaw to do it.

Laying out the miters for the legs, braces, and seat supports can be done in a variety of ways. Use a protractor to set a sliding T-bevel, then scribe along the bevel's blade to mark the wood. With a chop saw or radial arm saw at your disposal, you don't have to mark the lumber at all; just set the saw and cut. To aid the woodworker using a circular saw, several companies make relatively inexpensive guides—saw protractors and so-called speed squares. You clench the guide to the wood with one hand, and slide the saw along it with the other. You'll find the guides at most home centers and hardware stores.

Making all the pilot holes and counterbores is one of the biggest parts of this project. As noted, this work was originally done on a drill press. There's no reason, though, why it can't be done with a hand-held power drill. The point of the approach is to conceal the fasteners, both for the aesthetic benefit and to avoid providing water with spots to accumulate and penetrate, leading to rot.

But if *really* quick-and-easy is what you want, you can skip the counterboring and simply drive screws or nails through the tabletop boards into the battens. The heads will be visible, but the work will be expedited and the tool requirements minimized.

Finish. The picnic table shown doesn't have a finish. Redwood is as resistant to the effects of moisture as a wood can be. The heart of redwood is naturally resistant to the growth of rot-producing fungi. Moreover, redwood is very light (not dense). Thus, the table won't rot, and it is relatively resistant to cupping and splitting.

After a year or two in the sun, the redwood's natural color slowly shifts to a silvery-gray. You can try to fight this color shift with finishes containing ultraviolet absorbers (UVAs). How successful you will be depends upon how diligent you are at keeping the table's finish fresh.

1. Cut the legs, seat supports, and battens.

Cut these pieces to the lengths specified by the "Cutting List." Then miter the ends of each piece at the angles indicated in the *End View.*

Drill and counterbore pilot holes in each batten. Since you eventually will drive two 3-inch screws through each batten into each tabletop board, a total of ten are needed. Lay out the holes, as shown in the *Batten Layout.*

Drill the counterbores first, making each ⅜ inch in diameter by 1¾ inches deep. Don't bore them too deep, or you'll risk having screws emerge through the tabletop during assembly. Next, drill pilot holes for the screws; if your bit isn't long enough to completely penetrate the batten—and it probably won't be—make them as deep as you can.

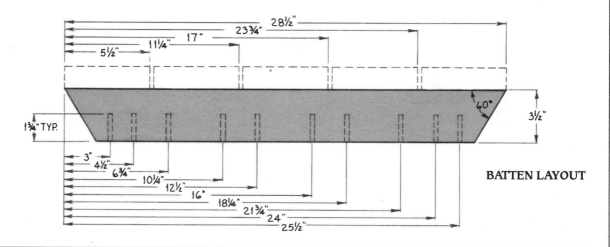

BATTEN LAYOUT

You can mark the miters with a sliding T-bevel and protractor. Or, you can use a saw protractor. This simple device can guide any miter up to 60 degrees. With it, you simply mark the length of your piece with a tape measure, then hold the protractor or square tightly to the stock at the appropriate angle. With the base shoe of your saw against the guide, align the blade with the mark and make the cut.

To simplify drilling the counterbores, mark the proper depth on the drill bit by wrapping tape around it, leaving a little flag. When the flag brushes the batten's surface, the counterbore is just deep enough.

2. **Assemble the leg units.** Begin the assembly process by laying a batten and a seat support on a flat surface and arranging the legs on top of them, as shown in the *End View.* Clamp the legs in place and drill ¼-inch-diameter holes for the carriage bolts that will hold the parts together. Two bolts in each joint should be sufficient. Insert the bolts into the legs and through the batten or support, then add a washer and nut. Tighten it down.

TIP

You can save a little hardware money by fastening the leg assemblies with 2½-inch galvanized drywall-type screws, rather than carriage bolts. Drive four screws into each joint.

---

3. **Assemble the tabletop.** When you buy them, the five tabletop boards should be the correct length. Select the best side of each, and arrange them on your sawhorses or a flat surface with the good side down.

Rest the center batten (the one not used when you assembled the legs) on the tabletop boards, centering it as shown in the *Top View.* Space the top boards evenly, so the two outside top boards are flush with the end of the batten. An easy way to do this is to use scraps of

¼-inch plywood as spacers between the boards.

Drive 3-inch screws through the batten into the tabletop boards. If you use a drill-driver, you'll need a long-shanked Phillips bit (Black & Decker sells bits in lengths up to 6 inches). Don't be too aggressive when driving the screws; redwood is pretty soft, and the torque of a drill-driver can bury the screws to the degree that their points will emerge through the tabletop boards. (If your counterbores prove to be too deep, simply substitute shorter screws.)

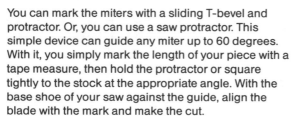

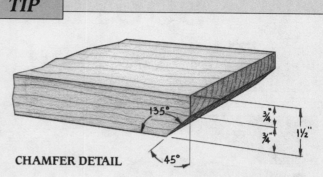
4. **Attach the leg assemblies to the tabletop.** Mark the positions of the leg assemblies across the tabletop boards. Support one assembly in an upright position (have a helper do this, or clamp the assembly to the tabletop), then drive 3-inch screws through the battens into the tabletop boards. Attach the second leg assembly in the same manner.

5. **Cut and install the diagonal braces.** Cut the diagonal braces to length, and miter the ends, as shown in the *Side View.* With the table still upside down, attach the diagonal braces to the seat supports and center batten with 3-inch screws, driving two screws at each joint.

6. **Install the seat boards.** With the table still upside down, drill pilot holes and 3¾-inch-deep counterbores through the bottom edges of the seat supports for the 2½-inch screws that attach the seat boards. Position the holes, as shown in the *Seat Support Detail.*

Get some help to turn the table onto its feet; if you can stand it on sawhorses, it will make the seat installation a little easier. Position the seat boards on the supports and clamp them. Then drive 3-inch screws through the supports into the seat boards.

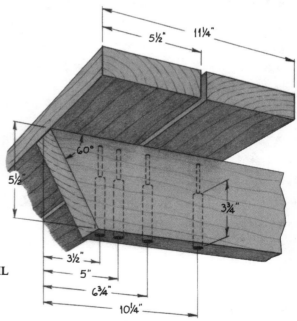

SEAT SUPPORT DETAIL

7. **Apply a finish.** After a once-over with a finish sander, apply a clear exterior finish such as CWF, or a water repellent such as Thompson's Water Seal.

SOUTHERN PINE TABLE AND BENCHES

Simply Elegant for Deck or Patio

This smart pine table and bench set, with its sleek tapered legs, mitered corners, and diagonal board top, is a fine example of such simple elegance. The clean lines and finished appearance will add just the right touch of class to your deck or patio. But don't let the light, somewhat delicate look of the table and benches fool you—they're plenty sturdy. The set will seat six adults comfortably with plenty of elbow room.

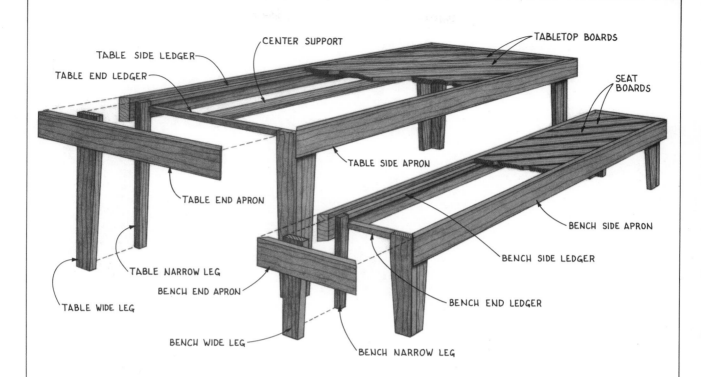

Labels in the illustration:

CENTER SUPPORT
TABLETOP BOARDS
TABLE SIDE LEDGER
TABLE END LEDGER
SEAT BOARDS
TABLE SIDE APRON
TABLE END APRON
BENCH SIDE APRON
TABLE NARROW LEG
BENCH SIDE LEDGER
BENCH END APRON
TABLE WIDE LEG
BENCH END LEDGER
BENCH WIDE LEG
BENCH NARROW LEG

SHOPPING LIST

LUMBER

2 pcs. 5/4 × 4 × 10' #2 pine
2 pcs. 5/4 × 3 × 10' #2 pine
4 pcs. 5/4 × 6 × 12' #2 pine
12 pcs. 1 × 4 × 8' #2 pine

HARDWARE AND SUPPLIES

1 box #6 × 2" galvanized drywall-type screws
3 boxes #6 × 1½" galvanized drywall-type screws
2 tubes construction adhesive, 10-oz. size

FINISH

Semitransparent preservative stain

Builder's Notes

This is an excellent project for the beginning woodworker. It's built with lumber that's basic stock at any good lumberyard, and the essential tools will be in a basic tool kit. The required cutting and the joinery techniques specified are basic and easily mastered. A shop isn't necessary; you can cut the parts and assemble them in your yard.

Materials. On the "Shopping List," we've included enough lumber and hardware to build the table and two benches.

TOOL LIST

Bar clamps
Caulking gun
Circular saw
Drill
  Phillips bit
  Pilot hole bit
Hammer
Paintbrush
Router
  ¼" rounding-over bit
Sander(s)
Sandpaper
Saw for ripping
Sawhorses
Screwdriver
Tack cloth
Tape measure
Yardstick

CUTTING LIST

PIECE	NUMBER	THICKNESS	WIDTH	LENGTH	MATERIAL
Table					
Wide legs*	4	1⅛"	3½"	28¼"	5/4 × 4
Narrow legs*	4	1⅛"	2½"	28¼"	5/4 × 3
End aprons	2	1⅛"	4½"	36"	5/4 × 6
Side aprons	2	1⅛"	4½"	72"	5/4 × 6
End ledgers	2	¾"	1⅛"	26¾"	5/4[†]
Side ledgers	2	¾"	1⅛"	62½"	5/4[†]
Center support	1	¾"	3½"	67½"	1 × 4
Tabletop boards	19	¾"	3½"	various[‡]	1 × 4
Benches					
Wide legs*	8	1⅛"	3½"	14¾"	5/4 × 4
Narrow legs*	8	1⅛"	2½"	14¾"	5/4 × 3
End aprons	4	1⅛"	4½"	16"	5/4 × 6
Side aprons	4	1⅛"	4½"	72"	5/4 × 6
End ledgers	4	¾"	1⅛"	6½"	5/4[†]
Side ledgers	4	¾"	1⅛"	62½"	5/4[†]
Seat boards	16	¾"	3½"	various[§]	1 × 4

*Dimensions of piece before tapers are cut
[†]Use scrap ripped from apron piece.
[‡]Approx. 60 lineal feet; cut to fit.
[§]Approx. 50 lineal feet; cut to fit.

CUTTING DIAGRAM

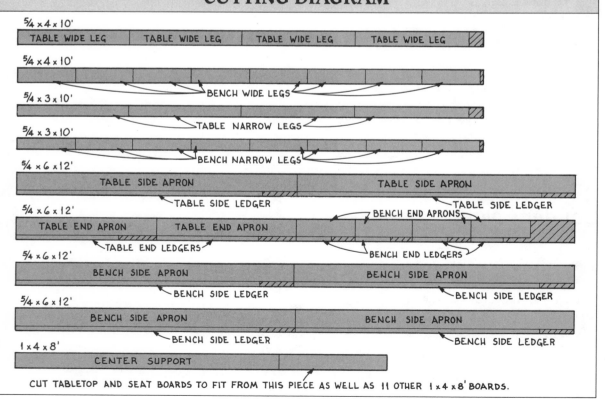

CUT TABLETOP AND SEAT BOARDS TO FIT FROM THIS PIECE AS WELL AS 11 OTHER 1 x 4 x 8' BOARDS.

TABLE PLAN VIEWS

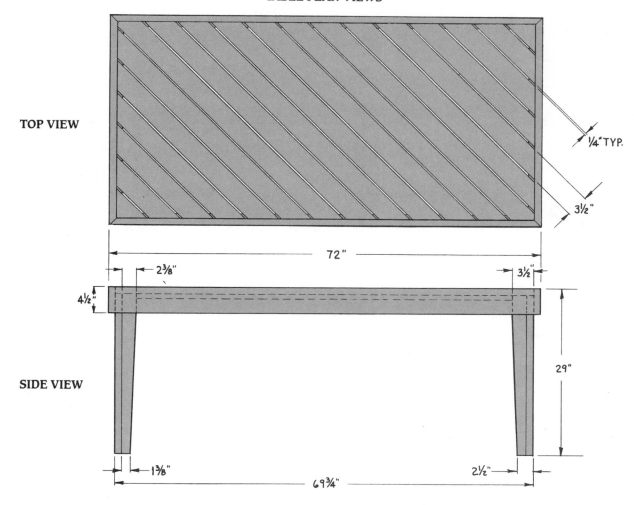

TOP VIEW

¼" TYP.

3½"

SIDE VIEW

72"

2⅜"

3½"

4½"

29"

1⅜"

2½"

69¾"

Five-quarter (5/4) stock measures approximately 1⅛ inches. The pine we used is generally available in the same widths and lengths as the more familiar 1-by material. Number 2 grade is perfectly suitable for this project. (A price check at your local lumberyard probably will reveal that a clear grade costs double—or even more—what the number 2 grade does.)

We used screws—the galvanized drywall-type—and construction adhesive to assemble both the table and the benches. Screws cost more than nails, and considering the number used in this project, you almost *need* a drill-driver to install them. (In fact, the drywall-type screws are designed to be power-driven.) But screws hold better: They can be tightened if time, wood movement, and hard use loosens them, and the process of installing them isn't likely to whack the parts you are joining out of alignment.

END VIEW

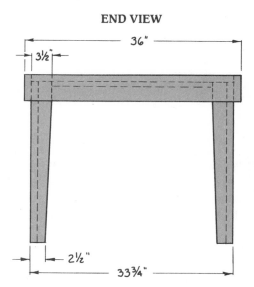

36"

3½"

2½"

33¾"

BENCH PLAN VIEWS

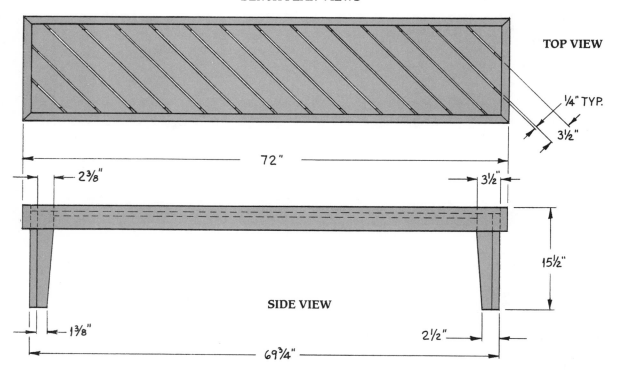

TOP VIEW

¼" TYP.

3½"

72"

2⅜"

3½"

3½"

15½"

SIDE VIEW

1⅜"

2½"

69¾"

END VIEW

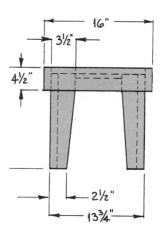

16"

3½"

4½"

2½"

13¾"

Construction adhesive is packaged in tubes like caulk. You need a caulking gun to apply it. Buy a waterproof adhesive that's suitable for bonding wood to wood. When applying it, run a *narrow* bead along *one* of the pieces to be joined; otherwise, any excess glue may show on the finished piece.

Tools and techniques. The construction of this set is easily accomplished with hand tools and two portable power tools—a drill and a circular saw. While you do have to make a lot of miter cuts and some taper cuts, you can make all of them with a circular saw. You do have to rip the aprons to width, which is most easily done on a table saw. But even the rip can safely and effectively be done with a circular saw. Equipping the saw with a combination blade will permit you to make all the rips, miter cuts, taper cuts, and crosscuts without swapping blades.

Finish. To finish the set, we chose a gray semitransparent preservative stain to give a weathered appearance. Semitransparent stains are only moderately pigmented and thus do not totally hide the wood grain. They penetrate the wood surface, are porous, but do not form a surface film like paints. As a result, they will not blister or peel, even if moisture moves through the wood. Penetrating stains are oil-based or alkydbased (synthetic oil), and some may contain a fungicide. Semitransparent stains are not inherently resistant to moisture, but some have a water repellent such as paraffin. Moderately pigmented latex stains also are available, but they do not penetrate the wood surfaces as do the oil-based stains.

Stains come in an ever-increasing variety of colors, but not as many as paint or solid-color stains. White is not available. We used a light gray color.

1. Cut and assemble the table legs. Cut and taper the eight pieces necessary to form the legs; follow the dimensions in the *Table Plan Views*. With a router and a ¼″ rounding-over bit, radius each tapered side.

To form the legs, join a narrow leg piece to a wide leg piece using construction adhesive and 2-inch screws. Note in the *Table Side View* and *Table End View* that the wide leg piece is always oriented to adjoin the table's end apron. To achieve this, you must assemble the legs in mirror-image pairs. Don't make all four legs the same. After assembling the legs, radius the outside corner formed by the two leg pieces.

To assemble a leg, glue and screw a narrow leg to a wide one. Run a bead of construction adhesive on the wide leg, then press the narrow leg in place. Drill pilot holes, then drive the screws. Three screws per leg are sufficient.

TIP

To make the tapered leg pieces safely with a circular saw, try cutting the tapers *before* sawing the piece to length.

You'll be cutting four legs from a 10-foot length of 5/4 stock. Rest the board across two sawhorses. Mark the crosscut for the first leg, then lay out the taper with the narrowest part at the butt end of the board. Lay out a second leg piece at the opposite end of the same board. With the circular saw, cut the tapers for both pieces, then crosscut them from the board. Lay out two more legs on the remaining stock, then cut them out.

2. Cut and assemble the aprons. From the 5/4 × 6 stock, rip the side and end aprons to the width specified by the "Cutting List." Save the waste from the rips to make the side and end ledgers.

The four apron pieces are joined to each other with end miter joints. To prepare the aprons, set your portable circular saw to cut a 45-degree bevel, then use it to crosscut the aprons to length. Be sure to orient the bevel cuts as shown in the *Table Top View.*

Radius the edges (but not the ends) of the apron pieces with the router and a ¼-inch rounding-over bit. Arrange the apron pieces on your bench, and assemble them into a frame with construction adhesive and 2-inch screws. At each joint, you should drive two screws through the side apron into the end apron, as well as two through the end apron into the side apron. To anchor the aprons during assembly, use bar clamps, applying one jaw to the top edge of the apron and the other to the underside of the work surface. A scrap of wood between the jaw and the apron will protect the workpiece.

3. **Attach the legs to the aprons.** First, lay out and cut the two triangular corner pieces for the tabletop. With the apron assembly upside down on your bench, slip this piece under each leg at each corner to position the legs while you attach them to the apron assembly. Attach the legs to the aprons with construction adhesive and 1½-inch screws.

With the apron assembly clamped to the workbench and the triangular corner piece used as a spacer, apply construction adhesive and fit the leg in place. Drive a couple of screws through each leg piece into the apron assembly.

4. **Cut and attach the ledgers.** Use the scrap ripped from the aprons to make the ledgers. Cut two end ledgers and two side ledgers to the dimensions specified by the "Cutting List."

Apply a bead of construction adhesive to each ledger, press the ledger in place, and drive several 1¼-inch screws through the ledger into the apron. Align the top surface of each ledger flush with the top of the legs, as shown in the *Table Side View* and *Table End View,* so the tabletop boards will be flush with the top edge of the aprons.

5. **Cut and attach the tabletop boards and center support.** Measure, mark, and cut the diagonal top boards to fit inside the frame formed by the aprons. The best way to do this is to start at diagonally opposite corners with the triangular pieces, setting them loosely in place. Then measure, cut, and loose-fit successive boards, leaving a ¼-inch space between each. The process will ensure you get a uniform layout. The last board to be cut will be the middle one; if it needs to be wider or narrower than the others to close the last gap it won't throw off the symmetry of the top.

When all the boards are cut and fitted, number them with a pencil and remove them from the frame. With a router and a ¼-inch rounding-over bit, radius the top edges of the boards, including the mitered ends.

To install the tabletop boards, start at the corners and work toward the middle. After you have four boards installed at each corner, attach the center support to the boards with screws and adhesive. The center support is attached only to the boards, not to the ledgers; it serves merely to tie the boards together. Install the remaining boards, gluing and screwing them to the ledgers and center support from underneath.

Install the tabletop boards with the table standing on its legs. Apply a short bead of adhesive to a board, press the board in place, then drill pilot holes and drive two galvanized 1¼-inch screws through the ledger into the board. The center support can be installed as soon as you get four boards installed at each end.

6. **Cut and assemble the bench frames.** The benches are made exactly the way the table is made. The dimensions are different, of course, and they have no center supports. Otherwise, they are the same.

Cut the bench legs to the dimensions specified by the "Cutting List." Repeat the process described in step 1 of cutting the tapers, then crosscutting the legs to length. Rip the aprons to width, saving the waste for the ledgers.

As you crosscut the aprons to length, bevel the ends for end miter joints.

Assemble the legs and the apron framework with construction adhesive and 2-inch screws. Cut the triangular corner pieces for the bench seats, and use them as spacers in positioning the legs for attachment to the apron frames. Use the adhesive and 1¼-inch screws to attach the legs.

7. **Cut and install the seat boards.** This operation is also a repeat of the corresponding table-construction step. Start at diagonally opposite corners, setting the triangular pieces loosely in place. Measure, cut, and loose-fit successive seat boards, leaving a ¼-inch space between each. After all the boards are cut, radius the top edges of the boards, including the mitered ends, with a router and a ¼-inch rounding-over bit.

Start installing the seat boards at the corners of the benches and work toward the middle. Apply a short bead of adhesive to a seat board, press it in place, then drill pilot holes and drive two 1¼-inch screws through the ledger into the seat board.

8. **Apply a finish.** Sand the table and benches, then apply a semitransparent preservative stain. For a more finished look, you can cover the exposed screw heads with wood putty prior to staining.

PICNIC TABLE AND BENCHES IN THE ROUND

A Round Table to Serve Summer's Conversations

The prototypical picnic table—the granddaddy of them all—is the familiar redwood-colored one with "sawbuck" 2 × 4 legs and 2 × 6 plank top. It has a couple of matching benches with the same redwood color, sawbuck legs, and plank seats. And why shouldn't it be the prototype? Easy to make, it is nevertheless sturdy and durable. Inexpensive, it looks "right" in a wooded glade, on a grassy terrace, or on a sunny deck.

Because an outdoor furniture book would be incomplete without one, here it is. Don't recognize it? That's because it's round. Making it round doesn't make it any more difficult to build, but roundness enhances its role

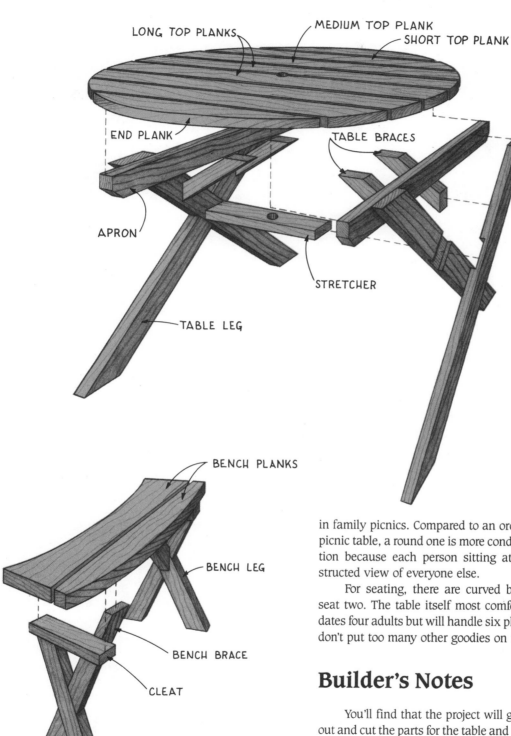

LONG TOP PLANKS
MEDIUM TOP PLANK
SHORT TOP PLANK
END PLANK
TABLE BRACES
APRON
STRETCHER
TABLE LEG

BENCH PLANKS
BENCH LEG
BENCH BRACE
CLEAT

in family picnics. Compared to an ordinary rectangular picnic table, a round one is more conducive to conversation because each person sitting at it has an unobstructed view of everyone else.

For seating, there are curved benches that each seat two. The table itself most comfortably accommodates four adults but will handle six place settings if you don't put too many other goodies on it.

Builder's Notes

You'll find that the project will go faster if you lay out and cut the parts for the table and the benches at the same time, then assemble each separately. The shopping and cutting lists assume you'll be making the table and three curved benches.

Materials. Any number of woods can be used to construct this table and benches. Woods that are either

SHOPPING LIST

LUMBER

1 pc. 2 × 6 × 8' construction-grade lumber
2 pcs. 2 × 6 × 10' construction-grade lumber
1 pc. 2 × 4 × 8' construction-grade lumber
1 pc. 2 × 4 × 10' construction-grade lumber
1 pc. 2 × 3 × 12' construction-grade lumber
1 pc. 5/4 × 6 × 10' #2 pine
2 pcs. 5/4 × 6 × 12' #2 pine

HARDWARE AND SUPPLIES

8 pcs. ⅜" × 3½" galvanized carriage bolts,
  washers, and nuts
4 pcs. ⅜" × 4" lag screws and washers
16 pcs. #12 × 2½" flathead wood screws
1 lb. 10d spiral decking nails
1 box #6 × 2" galvanized drywall-type screws
1 box #6 × 2½" galvanized drywall-type screws

FINISH

Exterior paint or clear exterior finish of your choice
  for all pieces

CUTTING LIST

PIECE	NUMBER	THICKNESS	WIDTH	LENGTH	MATERIAL
Long top planks	2	1½"	5½"	45¾"	2 × 6
Medium top planks	2	1½"	5½"	44¾"	2 × 6
Short top planks	2	1½"	5½"	40"	2 × 6
End planks	2	1½"	5½"	30½"	2 × 6
Aprons	2	1½"	2½"	41¾"	2 × 3
Table legs	4	1½"	3½"	44¼"	2 × 4
Stretcher	1	1½"	3½"	18⅛"	2 × 4
Table braces	4	1½"	2⅜"	12½"	2 × 3
Bench planks	6	1¹⁄₁₆"	5½"	36"	5/4 × 6 pine
Bench legs	12	1¹⁄₁₆"	2½"	16¼"	5/4 × 6 pine
Bench braces	6	1¹⁄₁₆"	2½"	11"	5/4 × 6 pine
Cleats	6	1¹⁄₁₆"	2½"	9"	5/4 × 6 pine

naturally or artificially rot resistant are the obvious choices.

Redwood is traditional for picnic tables, and it has several advantages. It looks attractive, and it is naturally rot resistant. Equally important, it is not as dense as other woods (like hardwood or pressure-treated wood). A table or bench made of it won't be too heavy. The top and bench planks will resist cupping and cracking. Moreover, redwood is readily available in both the 2-by and 5/4 (five-quarter) stock specified for this project.

Pressure-treated wood is (mostly) southern yellow pine. It is fairly dense, and as such is prone to cupping and cracking. It will also yield a heavy piece of furniture. And it has the disadvantage of being laden with chromated copper arsenate, which poisons any fungi or insects that try to consume the wood. Is this a good choice for a picnic table?

We chose common construction-grade lumber for the table, pine for the benches. The exact wood you get

TOOL LIST

Bar clamps
Clamps
Drill
  ⅜" bit
  Countersink bit
  Pilot hole bit
Hammer
Hole saw, 1¾" dia.
Paintbrush
Power miter saw
Radial arm saw
  Dado set
Rasp
Router
  ¼" rounding-over bit

Saber saw
Sander(s)
Sandpaper
Saw for crosscutting
Saw for ripping
Sawhorses
Screwdriver
Tack cloth
Tape measure
Trammel
Try square
Wrench
Yardstick

CUTTING DIAGRAM

2 × 6 × 8'

| LONG TOP PLANK | LONG TOP PLANK | |

2 × 6 × 10'

| MEDIUM TOP PLANK | SHORT TOP PLANK | END PLANK |

2 × 6 × 10'

| MEDIUM TOP PLANK | SHORT TOP PLANK | END PLANK |

2 × 4 × 10'

| TABLE LEG | TABLE LEG | STRETCHER |

2 × 4 × 8'

| TABLE LEG | TABLE LEG | |

2 × 3 × 12'

| APRON | APRON | TABLE BRACE | TABLE BRACE | TABLE BRACE | TABLE BRACE |

5/4 × 6 × 10'

| BENCH PLANK | BENCH PLANK | BENCH PLANK | CLEAT / CLEAT |

5/4 × 6 × 12'

| BENCH PLANK | BENCH PLANK | BENCH PLANK | CLEAT CLEAT BENCH BRACE / CLEAT CLEAT BENCH BRACE |

5/4 × 6 × 12'

| BENCH LEG | BENCH LEG | BENCH LEG | BENCH LEG | BENCH LEG | BENCH LEG | BENCH LEG | BENCH LEG |
| BENCH LEG | BENCH LEG | BENCH LEG | BENCH LEG | BENCH BRACE | BENCH BRACE | BENCH BRACE | BENCH BRACE |

when you order 2-by lumber may vary—it will probably be hemlock, fir, or spruce. Any of these will be satisfactory. A thorough finishing job is essential, of course.

The leg assembly for the table is made from 2 × 4s; the top, 2 × 6s. Because 2-by lumber (1½ inches thick) would have made the benches too bulky, we built them from 5/4 stock, which measures 1 1/16 inches thick. Be picky when you select the wood—you're going to sit and eat on those boards. You want them to be fairly clear and free of defects.

All fasteners should be galvanized or otherwise weather-resistant. For the benches, we used galvanized drywall-type screws because they drive easier than flathead wood screws when using a power screwdriver or drill-driver. Drill pilot holes for all screws.

Tools and techniques. The essential tools for this project are on the "Tool List." The ideal crosscutting tool for this project is the power miter saw, which makes fast, accurate miters; there are a lot of them to cut. You'll also need a saber saw to make curved cuts.

The umbrella hole in the table was made on a drill press fitted with a 1¾-inch-diameter hole saw. But the hole saw can be chucked in a ½-inch portable drill for the operation (and some hole saws will fit a ⅜-inch chuck), so the drill press is not essential.

To draw the arcs for the tabletop and benchtops, you *can* make a simple string compass, using a non-stretching mason's twine. Attach one end of the twine to a nail for a pivot point, the other end to a pencil. We used a trammel, however. We made it up using commercial trammel points and a 5-foot-long strip of wood about the width and thickness of a yardstick. The trammel is a little bit easier for a lone woodworker to manipulate.

Finish. As noted above, a durable outdoor finish is essential to the longevity of your picnic table and benches (or stools), especially if you follow our lead and build it of pine or fir. What you need in a finish is something that tempers the effects of sunlight and moisture on the wood.

Moisture affects wood several ways. It is a critical requirement for the growth of the fungi that rot wood. When it soaks into wood, it causes it to swell. As it migrates out of the wood, it causes the wood to shrink.

This cyclical expansion and contraction produces tensions within the wood that are released when the wood cups, cracks, splits, and checks. In general, the denser the wood, the more prone it is to cracking and cupping.

Sunlight damages wood in a process called photodegradation. The ultraviolet rays of the sun turn the wood gray and cause its exposed surfaces to disintegrate. In most applications, this surface erosion is too slow to worry about—about ¼ inch per century for softwoods, even less for dense hardwoods.

Paint does the best overall job of protecting wood

outdoors. It is best for preventing erosion. Paint has more pigment than solid-color and semitransparent stains, and pigment is what blocks out the sun's degrading effects. Also, paint forms a film on the wood (instead of soaking in, as stain does), which further retards erosion.

In general, oil-based paints are more resistant to moisture than latex paints. The advantage of latex paints is that they are easier to apply, dry quicker, and clean up with water. Cleanup for oil paints requires mineral spirits.

Before brushing on our paint, we applied a coat of water-repellent preservative. Applied before priming, the water-repellent preservative greatly prolongs the life of the paint. Water-repellent preservatives are mixtures of petroleum solvents, paraffin, resins, or drying oils that seal the wood against surface water (but not water vapor), and preservatives like copper naphthenate and pentaclorophenol that prevent the growth of mildew and fungi.

TABLE PLAN VIEWS

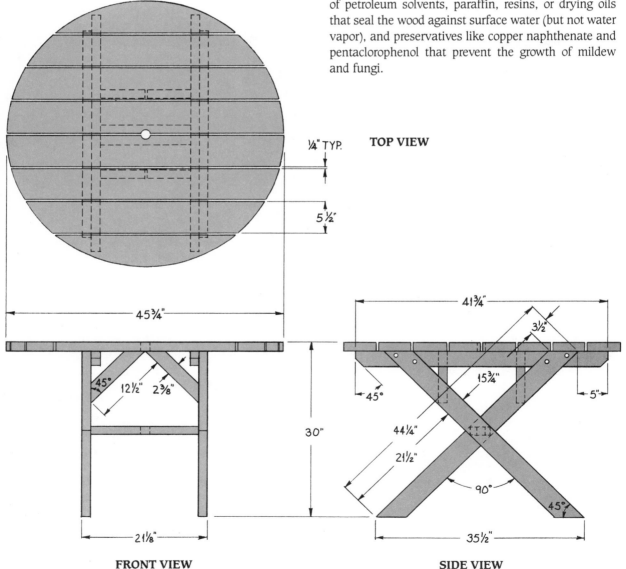

TOP VIEW

FRONT VIEW

SIDE VIEW

1. Cut the parts to size. Rip and crosscut all the parts for the table and benches to the sizes specified by the "Cutting List."

Miter the ends of the table legs and braces at 45 degrees, as shown in the *Table Front View* and the *Table Side View.* Miter the ends of the bench legs at 65 degrees, the bench braces at 45 degrees.

Chamfer the ends of the table aprons to remove sharp corners on which you could bump your legs.

TIP

To avoid mixing up the table parts and bench parts, make neat stacks of cut stock, so you know which parts belong to which piece of furniture. It also helps to label each part or stack of identical parts; if you don't want to spend extra time sanding off pencil marks, though, write the name of each part on a Post-it note and attach it to the part.

The power miter saw is the optimal tool for mitering the table and bench legs. The workpiece remains stationary, while the motor and blade arc in a chopping motion— hence the popular name, chop saw—to make the cut. A stop block—we used a small hand screw clamped on the fence—allows you to cut lengths of stock into parts of uniform length and with the proper miters, quickly and without repetitive layout work.

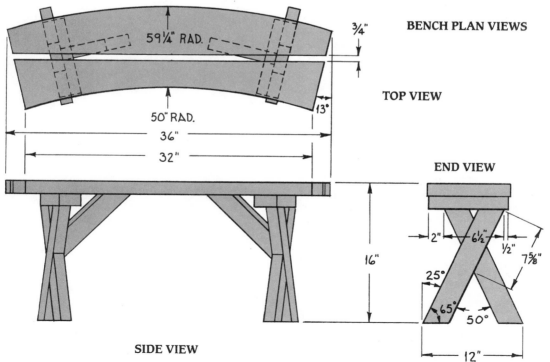

BENCH PLAN VIEWS

TOP VIEW

END VIEW

SIDE VIEW

2. Lay out and cut the lap joints in the legs. The table legs intersect at 90 degrees; the bench legs intersect at 50 degrees. Working with the dimensions shown in the *Table Side View* and *Bench End View,* mark the positions of the lap joints on each set of legs for the table and benches.

To cut the lap joints, you can fit a radial arm saw or table saw with a dado set and make several passes to remove the material between the marked lines. If you don't have a dado set, you can make a series of parallel cuts (about ¼ inch apart) with your saw, then chisel out the waste. Set the depth of the blade to make cuts exactly half the thickness of the stock.

Note: From this point on, steps for assembling the table and benches will be listed separately. You'll probably find it easier to work on the benches until you get them completely assembled, then do the table. After assembly, you can sand and finish all the pieces at one time.

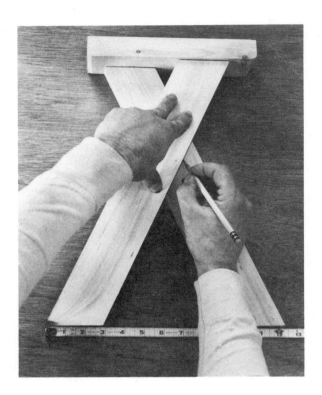

To lay out the lap joints on the legs, lay one leg atop the other, with the top ends flush against a straightedge (for the bench legs, you can use one of the cleats as a straightedge, as shown here). Use a tape measure to set the distance between the bottom ends of the legs to determine the layout position.

3. Make the bench leg subassemblies. Put the bench legs together to form an X, and radius the edges of the leg assembly with a router and a ¼-inch rounding-over bit. To attach the cleats to the tops of the legs, drill countersunk pilot holes, then drive 2-inch galvanized drywall-type screws through the cleats into the legs. Attach the braces to the legs, centering one end of the brace over the lap joint where the legs cross.

Radius the leg edges after the laps are cut but before the bench is assembled. Test fit two legs together, clamp them to the workbench, and run a router along the edges to be radiused. The rounded edges will flow from part to part, and you won't accidentally radius an edge that you shouldn't.

TIP

The easiest way to mount the braces on the leg subassemblies is to screw one end of the brace to a scrap of plywood, as shown. Then butt the upside-down leg subassembly against the other end of the brace. Drill pilot holes, then drive flathead wood screws through the leg's lap joint into the brace. Back out the screw that attaches the brace to the scrap plywood, and the subassembly is ready for the next step.

---

4. Lay out and cut the bench planks. Clear a space on the shop floor and lay out two of the bench planks. Use a trammel or string compass to scribe the curved edges of the benchtop. The pivot point for the outer edge should be 59¼ inches from that edge. After scribing that arc, shorten the radius of your trammel or string compass by 9¼ inches and, without moving the planks or changing the pivot point, draw the inside arc.

After drawing the arcs, mark across the ends of both boards at a 13-degree angle, as indicated in the *Bench Top View.*

Lay out the rest of the bench planks in the same manner, then cut them out with a saber saw. (Or cut out the first pair of planks and use them as templates to lay out the other planks.) Clean up the saw marks with a rasp or belt sander, then radius the edges of each plank with a router and a ¼-inch rounding-over bit.

---

5. Attach the leg assemblies to the bench planks. Position a pair of bench planks on your workbench with a ½-inch gap between them. Align the ends. Position the leg assemblies on the planks, 4 inches from each end, with the cleats running roughly parallel to the plank ends. Drill countersunk pilot holes, then drive a couple of 2-inch screws through each cleat into each plank and one through each brace into the plank.

With all three benches assembled, you are ready to complete the table.

Final assembly of the benches is straightforward. Position the bench planks, set the leg assemblies in place, drill pilot holes, then drive the screws. Your ⅜-inch electric drill can do more than bore holes; it can also drive screws into them.

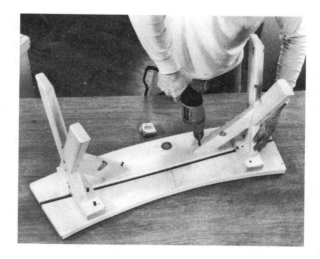

Laying out the bench planks is easier than it might seem. The ideal situation is one that allows you to sketch some layout lines on the floor or a benchtop.

- Place the two planks on the work surface, about ½ inch apart, and set the trammel to the proper radius.
- Set the point on the midpoint of the outer plank's edge and scribe an arc on the work surface. The pivot point will be somewhere along this arc.
- Set the point on one corner of the inner plank and scribe an arc on the work

surface. Then set the point on the opposite corner of the inner plank and scribe a second arc, intersecting the first.

- Sight (or scribe a line) from the midpoint of the outer plank to the crossing arcs. The pivot point is where this line intersects the first arc.
- Once the pivot point is located, scribe the cutting line on the outer plank, as shown in the photo. To scribe the cutting line on the inner plank, reset the trammel to the proper radius and, using the same pivot point, mark the plank.

LOCATING THE PIVOT POINT

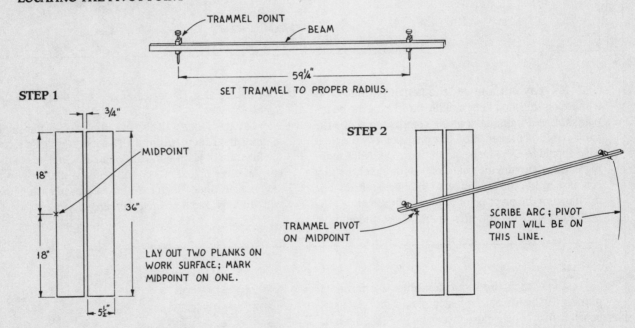

STEP 1

STEP 2

6. **Cut the umbrella hole in the tabletop planks and the stretcher (optional).** If you want to be able to mount a large umbrella in the table, you'll need to drill holes in the tabletop and table stretcher for the umbrella pole. Clamp the two long top planks together with a ¼-inch spacer in between. Mark the center point on the inside edge of both planks. With a hole saw of the

appropriate diameter (the same as that of the pole, usually 1¾ inch), drill a hole centered between them. Depending upon the hole saw you use, you may need to bore from one side until the pilot bit emerges through the other, then flip the work over and complete the hole from the second side.

Drill a matching hole in the center of the stretcher.

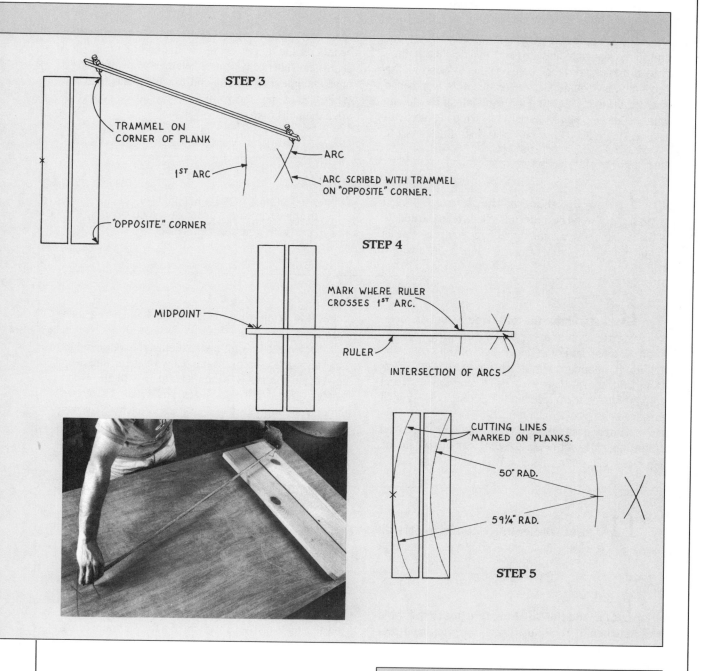

STEP 3

TRAMMEL ON CORNER OF PLANK

ARC

1ST ARC

ARC SCRIBED WITH TRAMMEL ON "OPPOSITE" CORNER.

"OPPOSITE" CORNER

STEP 4

MARK WHERE RULER CROSSES 1ST ARC.

MIDPOINT

RULER

INTERSECTION OF ARCS

CUTTING LINES MARKED ON PLANKS.

50" RAD.

59¼" RAD.

STEP 5

7. Sand the table parts. With a router and a ¼-inch rounding-over bit, radius the exposed edges of all the table parts. Dry assemble the legs to radius their edges as you did with the bench legs. Then sand all the parts of the table to remove any rough spots on the wood.

Now would be a good time to stain the parts and apply the first coat of clear finish, or, if you're painting the table, apply the first coat of paint.

TIP

If you're painting the table, apply a liberal coat of paint to parts that will be joined, and assemble them while the paint is still wet. When the paint dries, it will help seal the joints against moisture, preventing decay.

8. Assemble the tabletop. Measure the aprons and all the planks to find the exact middle of each, then draw a mark across the boards at this location with a pencil and try square. Set the aprons on a workbench 15⅛ inches apart. Starting at the middle of the aprons with the long top planks, tack the tabletop in place with 10d decking nails. Use scraps of ¼-inch-thick stock to space the planks evenly. Make sure you center the boards on the aprons so all the marks line up. (If the boards aren't perfectly centered on the aprons, you won't have enough stock at one end to cut a perfect circle.) When you're sure the planks are positioned correctly, drive the nails home.

9. Saw the shape of the tabletop. Tack a small scrap of wood over the umbrella hole in the middle of the tabletop. Drive a nail through the scrap to serve as the pivot for your string compass. Mark a circle with a radius of 22⅞ inches on the top planks.

Cut the circle with a saber saw, then clean up the saw marks with a rasp or belt sander.

10. Assemble the table frame. Turn the tabletop over, so the aprons are up. Put the table legs together in an X, then clamp the upper ends of the legs to the aprons, positioning them as shown in the *Table Side View*. Drill ⅜-inch-diameter holes through the legs and aprons and bolt them together with ⅜-inch by 3½-inch carriage bolts, washers, and nuts.

Carefully position the stretcher so that it's centered on the lap joints of the leg-apron assemblies where the legs cross. Clamp the stretcher between the legs with a bar or pipe clamp while you install the ⅜-inch by 4-inch lag screws.

For a neat-looking installation, drill counterbores large enough to accept the lag screw washers, and deep enough so the screw heads are flush with the wood surface. Then, drill pilot holes and drive the screws through the lap joints and into the stretcher. The lag screws not only attach the legs to the stretcher, but secure the legs to each other.

11. Install the leg braces. With the table still upside down, set the table braces in place, as shown in the *Table Front View* and the *Table Side View*. Fasten them in position with 2½-inch screws.

12. Add the finishing touches to the table and benches. If necessary, use a router to round-over any remaining sharp edges. Sand all surfaces smooth, and apply the paint or finish of your choice.

We painted our table and benches, but the job wasn't as straightforward as it might seem. To extend the life of the paint, we applied a coat of a water-repellent preservative first. This we applied following the directions on the can, giving it a full 72 hours to dry. After the required time had passed, we primed the table and benches with a pigmented shellac. This both primed the surface and sealed the knots to prevent them from "bleeding" through the paint. Finally, we applied two coats of a semi-gloss latex exterior paint.

CONTOURED ENSEMBLE

Smoothly Curved for Comfort with Style

Take one look at these pieces and you can see what sets them apart from the other projects in this section. The slats are attached to curved frame members and accommodate the body a little more graciously than standard outdoor furniture. A less obvious difference is the joinery. The plans call for half-lap joints, a way of bringing two boards together that is stronger than butt joints but not very difficult to make.

CONTOURED ENSEMBLE CHAIR, BENCH, AND SWING

Although these projects may not be quite as quick and easy as the others offered in this section, their sturdy construction is worth a little extra effort.

Consider the half-lap joint that is the heart of this furniture. To make the joint, both pieces of wood give up half their thickness. The boards have a good deal of gluing surface, which helps to make a stronger union. And the steps or "shoulders" of the laps meet to further reinforce the joint.

Rodale woodworker Phil Gehret made this furni-ture out of oak, a dense and attractive hardwood that makes its weight known the first time you pick up an assembled piece and try to move it. Lighter woods will serve well enough, among them several weather-resistant species that won't demand anything in the way of maintenance.

Laying out the curves you see here shouldn't cause you any problem, even if you can't draw a straight line. You'll read how to enlarge the scaled-down patterns using either the grid method or a pantograph. Note that

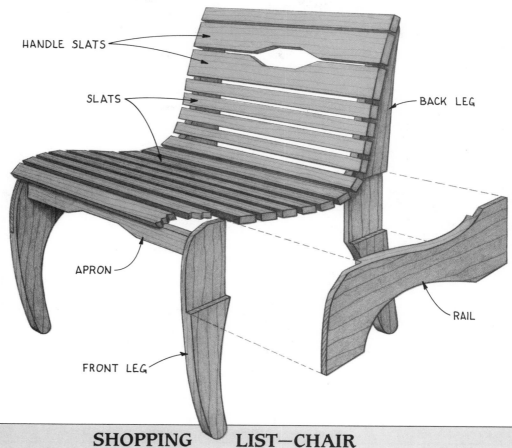

HANDLE SLATS

SLATS

BACK LEG

APRON

FRONT LEG

RAIL

SHOPPING LIST—CHAIR

LUMBER
6¼ bd. ft. 5/4 white oak
5 bd. ft. 4/4 white oak

HARDWARE AND SUPPLIES
4 pcs. #6 × 2½" galvanized drywall-type screws
32 pcs. #6 × 1¼" galvanized drywall-type screws
Resorcinol glue

FINISH
Clear water repellent or clear exterior finish

SHOPPING LIST—BENCH

LUMBER
8½ bd. ft. 5/4 white oak
10 bd. ft. 4/4 white oak

HARDWARE AND SUPPLIES
6 pcs. #6 × 2½" galvanized drywall-type screws
48 pcs. #6 × 1¼" galvanized drywall-type screws
Resorcinol glue

FINISH
Clear water repellent or clear exterior finish

SHOPPING LIST—SWING

LUMBER
7¼ bd. ft. 5/4 white oak
10 bd. ft. 4/4 white oak

HARDWARE AND SUPPLIES
4 pcs. #6 × 2½" galvanized drywall-type screws
32 pcs. #6 × 1¼" galvanized drywall-type screws
Resorcinol glue

FINISH
Clear water repellent or clear exterior finish

CUTTING LIST—CHAIR

PIECE	NUMBER	THICKNESS	WIDTH	LENGTH	MATERIAL
Back legs	2	1⅟₁₆″	5½″	29″	5/4 oak
Front legs	2	1⅟₁₆″	3½″	15″	5/4 oak
Rails	2	1⅟₁₆″	5½″	27½″	5/4 oak
Apron	1	¾″	2¼″	17⅞″	4/4 oak
Handle slats	2	¾″	2¼″	22″	4/4 oak
Slats	14	¾″	1½″	22″	4/4 oak

CUTTING LIST—BENCH

PIECE	NUMBER	THICKNESS	WIDTH	LENGTH	MATERIAL
Back legs	2	1⅟₁₆″	5½″	29″	5/4 oak
Front legs	2	1⅟₁₆″	3½″	15″	5/4 oak
Rails	2	1⅟₁₆″	5½″	21½″	5/4 oak
Center back	1	1⅟₁₆″	5½″	19″	5/4 oak
Center rail	1	1⅟₁₆″	5½″	20″	5/4 oak
Apron	1	¾″	2¼″	41⅞″	4/4 oak
Handle slats	2	¾″	2¼″	46″	4/4 oak
Slats	14	¾″	1½″	46″	4/4 oak

CUTTING LIST—SWING

PIECE	NUMBER	THICKNESS	WIDTH	LENGTH	MATERIAL
Backs	3	1⅟₁₆″	5½″	19″	5/4 oak
Rails	2	1⅟₁₆″	5½″	21½″	5/4 oak
Center rail	1	1⅟₁₆″	5½″	20″	5/4 oak
Apron	1	¾″	2¼″	41⅞″	4/4 oak
Handle slats	2	¾″	2¼″	46″	4/4 oak
Slats	14	¾″	1½″	46″	4/4 oak

all or part of the curved frame pattern is used in each piece of the ensemble. The full frame occurs in the chair and bench; it loses its legs for the swing and the middle frame of the bench. In the following project, a table borrows only the front leg and its mirror image. Note that in both the bench and swing, the middle frame is cut short at the front edge to accommodate the apron.

Builder's Notes

The lap joint used in this project is a step up from the butt joint, but it remains a simpler affair than a mortise-and-tenon or dovetail joint. Although you can use a router, circular saw, or table saw to cut the laps, the work will go faster with a radial arm saw equipped with a dado cutter.

Materials. The furniture shown is made of oak. The decay resistance of oak depends on the particular species; white oak is one of the better woods in this respect, while red oak is among the less resistant. Unless protected with a clear finish, oak will be darkened by precipitation. Woods that weather without such dramatic discoloration include redwood, cedar, mahogany, and cypress. Pine is both affordable and readily available, but it needs to be varnished or painted to extend its useful life.

As is the case with all hardwoods, oak is not a dimension lumber, which means it isn't stocked at every lumberyard and it isn't available in predictable sizes.

PATTERNS

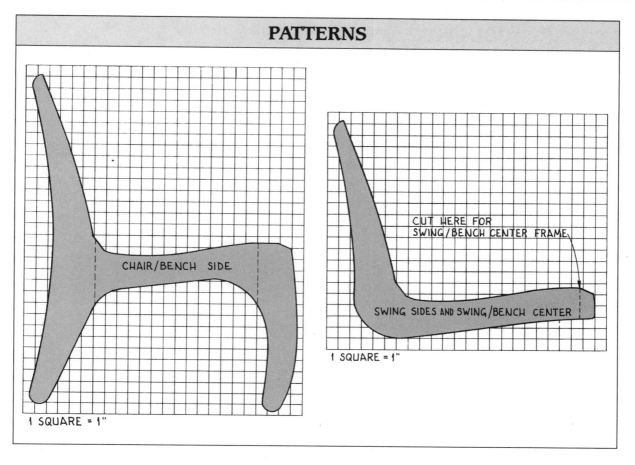

CHAIR/BENCH SIDE

1 SQUARE = 1"

CUT HERE FOR
SWING/BENCH CENTER FRAME

SWING SIDES AND SWING/BENCH CENTER

1 SQUARE = 1"

Thicknesses are standardized, but not widths and lengths.

The thicknesses are couched in terms of quarters of an inch. A four-quarter (4/4) board is actually ¾ inch thick; the missing ¼ inch is lost to the shrinkage that accompanies drying and to the planing that smooths the board. Similarly, a 5/4 (five-quarter) board is 1 1/16 inches thick, an 8/4 board 1¾ inches thick.

The "Shopping List" for the bench specifies the purchase of 8½ board feet of 5/4 oak. With hardwoods, you must keep the dimensions of the necessary parts in mind when you shop. A board might contain the requisite number of board feet without having the correct dimensions to give you the parts you need. Remember that you may have to work around knots and other defects, so be prepared to buy more wood than you strictly need.

Although the plans call for the frames to be made out of 5/4 stock, you can adapt these projects to use standard 2 × 4s and 2 × 6s.

Tools and techniques. The core procedure in building these pieces is making rectilinear frames. The horizontal member is joined to the two verticals with lap joints. The laps are best cut with a dado blade on a radial

arm saw. You can do the job with a dado blade on a table saw, but you won't be able to see the blade in the act of cutting. A circular saw or router will also handle half-laps.

The joints are glued together; screws aren't necessary. Finally, the full-size pattern is traced on these rough frames and then cut out with a saber saw.

As with other projects in this book, these pieces will come together more quickly if you use an electric drill or drill-driver to sink the drywall-type screws. Driving more than a few screws by hand gets to be a chore. If you will be using drywall screws in oak, plan on drilling pilot holes; this step is a help but not a requirement with softer woods.

Finish. Three prime considerations in choosing an exterior wood finish (in no particular order) are: what the finish looks like, the conditions under which the wood will be used, and the kind of wood you are finishing.

The last consideration may be the first you look at. If you, like us, build your contoured furniture pieces of oak (or another hardwood), you will undoubtedly avoid any finish that will obscure the wood's figure and color. You'll use a clear (or natural) finish such as an exterior-

TOOL LIST

Belt sander	Router
Circular saw	¼" rounding-over bit
Clamps	Ruler
Drill	Saber saw
Pilot hole bit	Sandpaper
Finishing sander	Sawhorses
Paintbrush	Screwdriver
Plug cutter	Tack cloth
Radial arm saw	Tape measure
Dado set	Try square

Like every other outdoor finish, you must renew penetrating oil every couple of years.

Neither of these finishes does the best job of protecting wood outdoors. That job is done by paint. If you build of pine, you ought to give prime consideration to paint. Paint has more pigment than other finishes, and pigment is what blocks out the sun's degrading effects. Also, paint forms a film on the wood (instead of soaking in, as stain does), which further retards erosion. In general, oil-based paints are more resistant to moisture than latex paints.

grade varnish or an exterior-grade penetrating oil.

Varnishes, including urethane, provide a beautiful natural finish, but unfortunately, they don't hold up outdoors unless protected from direct exposure to sunlight. Varnish forms a film, which can peel. To develop the most durable film, varnish manufacturers recommend applying three to six thin coats.

Penetrating oil, in contrast, is easy to apply. You brush on a generous application and let it penetrate the wood. Before it has time to completely dry, you apply a second coat. Then you are done. It takes the oil 48 to 72 hours to completely dry and for the odor to disappear.

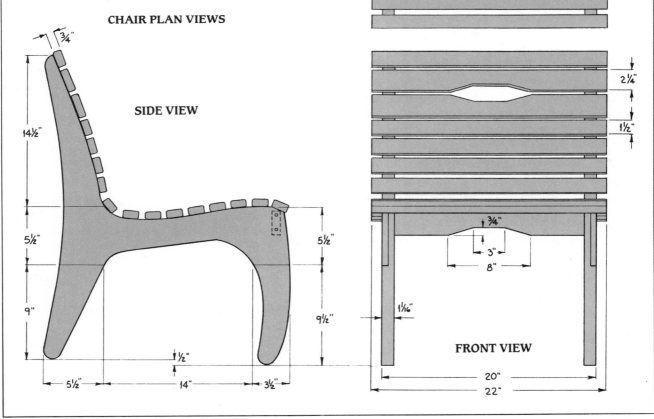

TOP VIEW

FRONT VIEW

CHAIR PLAN VIEWS

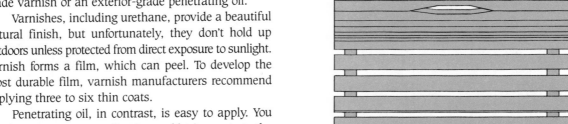

SIDE VIEW

BENCH PLAN VIEWS

TOP VIEW

FRONT VIEW

SIDE VIEW

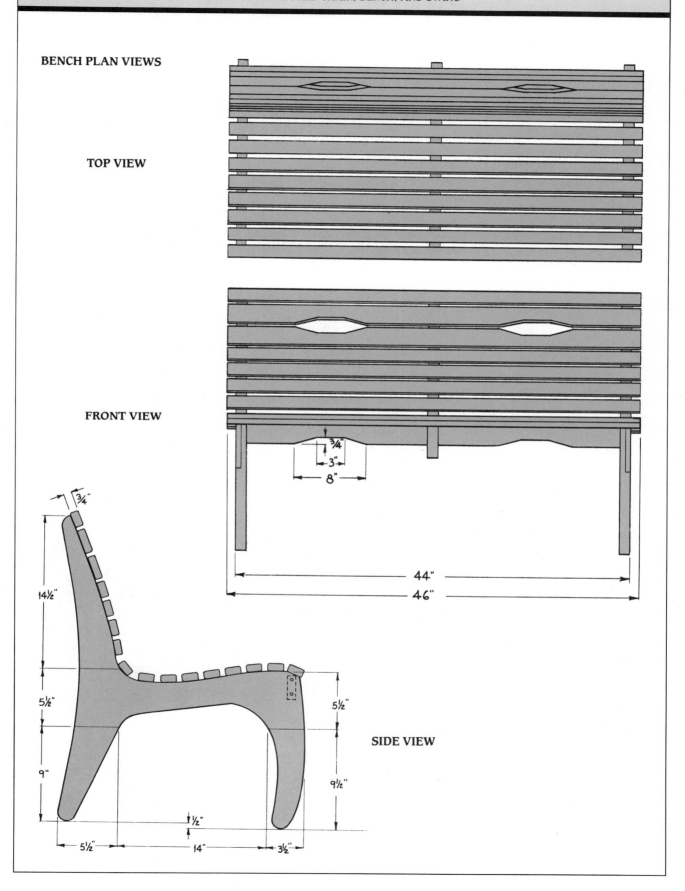

1. **Rough-cut the back legs, front legs, and rails.** The basic frames are the side and center rails. (The chairs require only side rails; the bench and the swing are wide enough that the slats need extra support in the middle, which the center rail provides.) Although these rails have a curved contour in the finished furniture pieces, they are assembled of rectilinear boards.

The side frames for the chair and bench are identical, each being formed of a front and a back leg connected by a rail. The swing's side frames obviously don't have legs, and neither do the center frames required for the bench and swing.

Begin making the seating project you have chosen by cutting the legs and rails to the lengths specified by the "Cutting List."

---

2. **Cut the lap joints.** Lay out the half-lap joints on the boards, as shown in the *Rough Frame Assemblies* drawing.

Although you can use any number of tools to cut laps—beginning with a backsaw and ranging through router, circular saw, and table saw—we found the *best*

SWING PLAN VIEWS

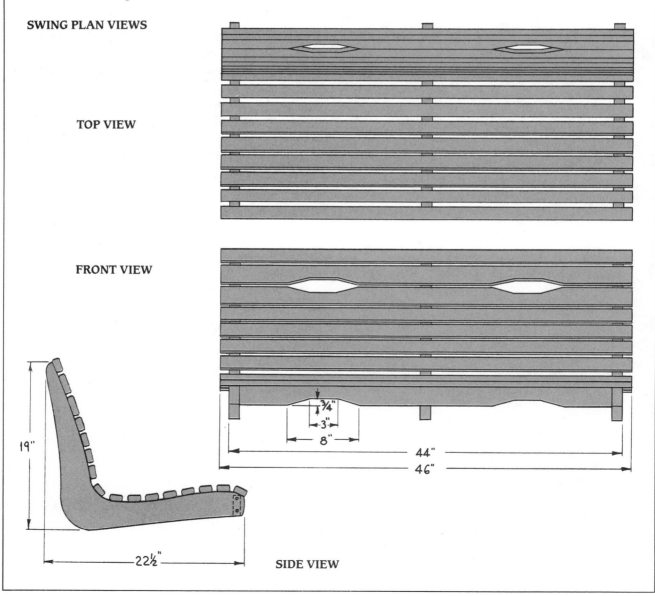

TOP VIEW

FRONT VIEW

19"

3⁄4"
3"
8"
44"
46"

22½"

SIDE VIEW

tool to cut these particular laps was the radial arm saw.

To make fast work of this operation, fit the saw with a dado cutter to remove as much waste as possible with each pass, and clamp a stop block to the saw fence to accurately control the length of each lap. Adjust the blade height to cut halfway through the 5/4 stock. Although the depth of the cut is crucial, the exact placement of the laps is not. That's because you will be cutting out the curved frame from this rough assembly. If one board sticks a bit beyond another, the error will be

cut away and consigned to the scrap pile.

Work methodically to avoid getting the joints mixed up. All are cut to the same depth, but there are two different lengths, and the laps on the back legs are T-laps rather than end laps. So set your stop block for the front legs first, and cut the laps on those. Use the same setting to lap the back ends of the rails. Reset the stop block and lap the front ends of the rails. Finally, set two stop blocks to lap the back legs.

ROUGH FRAME ASSEMBLIES

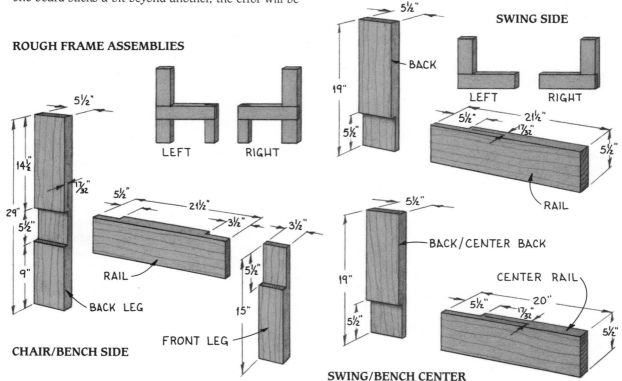

CHAIR/BENCH SIDE

BACK LEG

RAIL

FRONT LEG

SWING SIDE

LEFT   RIGHT

BACK

RAIL

BACK/CENTER BACK

CENTER RAIL

SWING/BENCH CENTER

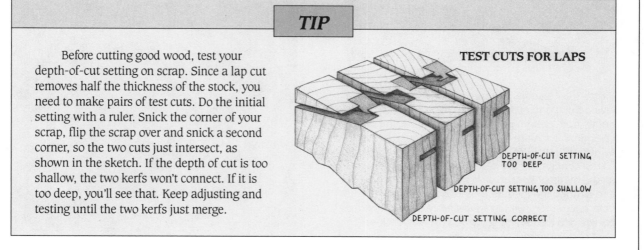

TIP

Before cutting good wood, test your depth-of-cut setting on scrap. Since a lap cut removes half the thickness of the stock, you need to make pairs of test cuts. Do the initial setting with a ruler. Snick the corner of your scrap, flip the scrap over and snick a second corner, so the two cuts just intersect, as shown in the sketch. If the depth of cut is too shallow, the two kerfs won't connect. If it is too deep, you'll see that. Keep adjusting and testing until the two kerfs just merge.

TEST CUTS FOR LAPS

DEPTH-OF-CUT SETTING TOO DEEP

DEPTH-OF-CUT SETTING TOO SHALLOW

DEPTH-OF-CUT SETTING CORRECT

3. Glue up the frames. Once you're certain that the surfaces of the lap joints are smooth and consistent, assemble the frames using resorcinol glue.

Note that you have to make a left side frame and a right side frame; the two are not identical, they are mirror images. Ideally, when you look at the assembled chair (or bench or swing), the horizontal line of the rail is unbroken. To avoid mix-ups, assemble the left and right frames side by side, as shown in the *Rough Frame Assemblies* drawing.

---

4. Enlarge the frame pattern and transfer it to the rough frames. Enlarge the patterns as accurately as possible. An indifferent job of laying out these curved lines can spoil the project.

The grid method of enlarging a pattern is simple and traditional. Note the grid superimposed on the frame patterns. To make a full-size pattern, lay out a 1-inch grid on a sheet of paper measuring at least 23 by 29 inches for the chair or bench, and at least 19 by 23 inches for the swing. (If you are making only the swing, you needn't bother drawing the legs.) Next, transfer reference points from the grid in the book to the one you've drawn: These are the points at which the outline of the frame pattern crosses a grid line. Finally, play "connect the dots" with the points you've plotted on the large grid. Don't just draw lines; try to fair them into graceful curves that come close to those in the book's pattern.

If you don't trust yourself with even this level of freehand drawing, you can use a pantograph, a drafting device that consists of two inverted, interlocking Vs. As you trace the original drawing with a stylus, a pencil point on another arm of the pantograph draws a larger (or smaller) version with good accuracy. Pantographs are available at art supply and drafting stores.

Left: A pantograph looks ungainly, and, frankly, it is. But it can help you make pattern enlargements fairly quickly. The device is mounted on a drawing board or on a piece of smooth plywood and adjusted to the scale of enlargement necessary. With the stylus, trace around the pattern in the book, and the pantograph's pencil will produce a rough enlargement. "Rough" means the lines will waver and wander; you will need to use a straightedge and flexible curve to align the straights and contour the curves, as shown here. Though it seems double work, it still is faster than drawing a grid and plotting points.

Right: You can enlarge any pattern in this book by laying out a grid at the scale specified, then plotting points from pattern to grid. If, for example, the pattern specifies "1 square = 1"," you must draw a grid with 1-inch squares. (You don't, however, have to grid the "dead spaces" on the pattern; only grid the general shape of the pattern outline.) After plotting the points and connecting them freehand, go back over the enlarged pattern with a straightedge and French curves or a flexible curve, giving it a well-defined, continuous contour.

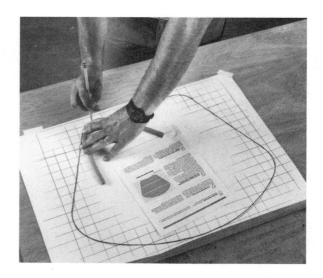

There are a couple of ways to transfer the outline of the frame from the full-size pattern to the rough frame assemblies. You can place sheets of carbon paper between the pattern and the wood, then tape the pattern in place and trace along the outline. Or, turn the pattern over and draw a wide, heavy line where you see the outline through the paper, using a soft (number one) pencil. Then flip the pattern right-side up, tape it in place, and use a harder pencil to trace with enough pressure to leave a line of graphite on the wood.

If you plan on making a number of pieces—the complete ensemble, perhaps, or a few chairs—you may want to make a durable template. This cut-out pattern is used to trace the outline on frames.

If you are making the bench or swing, note that the pattern shows that the front edge of the center frame must be cut short in order to accommodate the apron that will run across the piece.

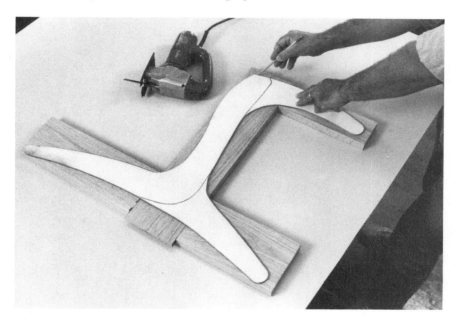

To make a template, enlarge the pattern onto something more durable than a sheet of paper (we used lauan plywood) and cut it out. You also can use cardboard, posterboard, or Masonite (hardboard). Place the template on each side assembly and trace around it. Note that the template shown is marked with lines that show where to eliminate the legs for the swing frames and the middle bench frame; you can use the entire template for chair and bench end frames, then saw off the template's legs and use it to lay out these smaller frames.

5. Cut out the frames. Use a saber saw to cut out the frames, taking care not to stray inside the line. If necessary, use a belt sander, hand plane, or file to remove excess wood down to the line. Use a router and a ¼-inch rounding-over bit to radius all edges.

Even though this frame is made of 5/4 oak, a saber saw can manage the job. Clamp the workpiece to a bench or sawhorse, making sure that the area to be sawed is cantilevered out over the edge of the support.

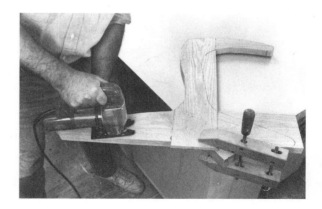

6. Cut the apron and slats. Cut the apron, 14 narrow (1½ inch) slats, and two wide (2¼ inch) handle slats. Lay out the cutouts in one edge of the apron and in both handle slats, as shown in the *Plan Views*. Make the cutouts with a saber saw. Again, use a router and a ¼-inch rounding-over bit to radius all edges.

7. **Assemble the chair.** With a helper, attach the slats and apron to the frames. Use screws, driven into counterbored pilot holes, then cover the screws with wood plugs glued into the counterbores. Sink one 1¼-inch screw in either end of each slat, and two 2½-inch screws through either side of the frame and into the apron. On the bench and swing, drive two additional 2½-inch screws through the apron and into the front edge of the center frame.

Make the plugs from scraps of the working stock, using a plug cutter. Apply resorcinol glue to the counterbores with a cotton swab. To make the plugs as inconspicuous as possible, try to pick plugs that match the wood's color, and align the plug's grain with the surrounding grain.

8. **Apply a finish.** Sand the piece with fine-grit sandpaper. If the wood needs to be protected from the elements, apply a clear finish or exterior paint.

CONTOURED ENSEMBLE TABLE

An ensemble is a group working together to achieve a single effect. In outdoor furniture terms, you have an ensemble when the different furniture pieces have the same aesthetic appearance. Though the pieces function differently, they work together visually.

This table, though it serves a different function from the contoured chair and bench, clearly springs from the same aesthetic. If you've built the contoured bench or chair, or the lounger that follows, and you want to add a table, then you'll surely choose a complementary design. And this table not only uses the same materials and joinery, it borrows part of the chair's side pattern for its legs. (If a contoured chair were to mutate into an end table, this is what you'd get.)

The construction process is a virtual repeat of the chair's: Make up the leg frames using lap joints, cut the curvilinear shape, and screw the slats and aprons to the leg assemblies to complete the construction.

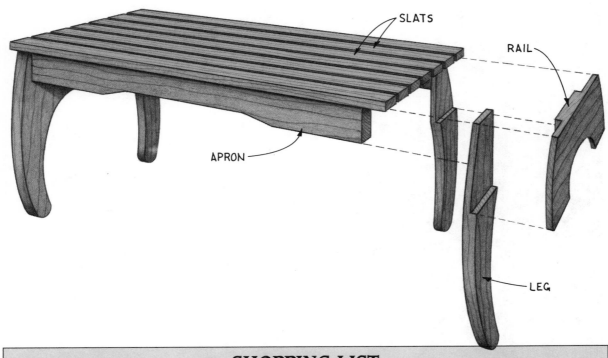

SHOPPING LIST

LUMBER

3½ bd. ft. 5/4 white oak
4 bd. ft. 4/4 white oak

HARDWARE AND SUPPLIES

8 pcs. #6 × 2½" galvanized drywall-type screws
14 pcs. #6 × 1¼" galvanized drywall-type screws
Resorcinol glue

FINISH

Clear water repellent or clear exterior finish

CUTTING LIST

PIECE	NUMBER	THICKNESS	WIDTH	LENGTH	MATERIAL
Legs	4	1⅟₁₆"	3½"	15"	5/4 oak
Rails	2	1⅟₁₆"	5½"	14"	5/4 oak
Aprons	3	¾"	2¼"	27⅞"	4/4 oak
Slats	7	¾"	1½"	32"	4/4 oak

Builder's Notes

The construction of the contoured table closely mimics that of the chair (or bench or swing). If you are building only the table, by all means read over the "Builder's Notes" for the chair on page 58 before you begin cutting wood. In addition, skim through the step-by-step section as well; it details the best way to cut the laps and assemble the side frames, how to enlarge the patterns, and so forth. The building tips there may prove useful in constructing the table.

PATTERN

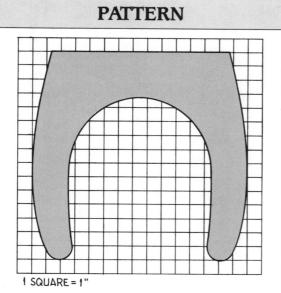

1 SQUARE = 1"

TOOL LIST

Belt sander
Drill
  Countersink bit
  Pilot hole bit
  Plug cutter
Finishing sander
Hand screws
Paintbrush
Radial arm saw
  Dado set

Router
  ¼" rounding-over bit
Ruler
Saber saw
Sandpaper
Sawhorses
Screwdriver
Tack cloth
Tape measure
Try square

PLAN VIEWS

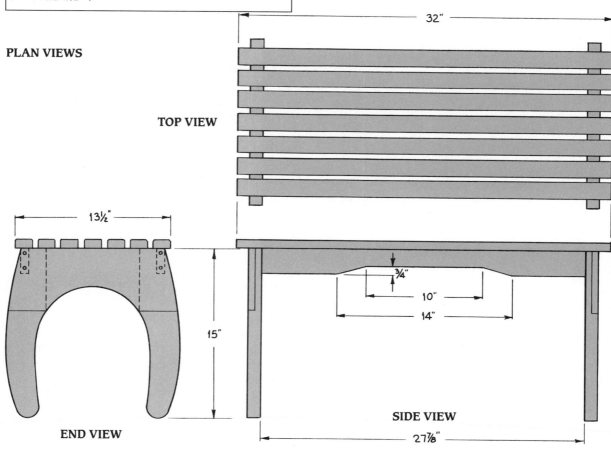

TOP VIEW

END VIEW

SIDE VIEW

1. Cut the legs and rails. Cut the parts needed to make a pair of rough frames to the sizes specified by the "Cutting List." Each frame consists of two legs bridged at the top by a rail.

2. **Cut the laps and glue up the frames.** Lay out the laps on the legs and rails. Cut them on a radial arm saw equipped with a dado cutter.

Once you're certain that the surfaces of the lap joints are smooth and consistent, assemble the frames using resorcinol glue. Clamp the assemblies with hand screws. Note that both frames are identical.

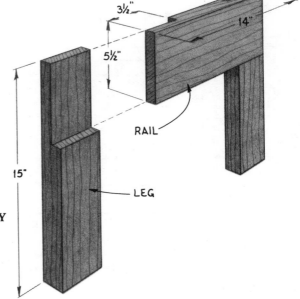

ROUGH END FRAME ASSEMBLY

---

3. **Cut the frames to their final contour.** Enlarge the frame pattern and transfer it to the rough frames. The table derives its charm from the legs, so take care when laying them out.

For cutting the contours, use a saber saw. If you stray from the line, it should be to the outside of the pattern, into waste wood. Use a belt sander to remove any excess wood down to that line.

Using a router and a ¼-inch rounding-over bit, radius all but the top edges.

---

4. **Cut the aprons and slats.** Note the cutouts in the aprons; lay them out, as shown in the *Side View*, and cut them with a saber saw or band saw. Again, use a router and a ¼-inch rounding-over bit to radius all edges of the slats and the lower edges of the aprons.

---

5. **Assemble the table.** Attach the slats and aprons to the frames. Note that the frames are juxtaposed so that, when the assembled table is viewed from each end, the rails will be seen to overlap the legs. To assemble the parts, use screws, driving them into counterbored pilot holes. Cover the screws with wood plugs glued into the counterbores. Sink one 1¼-inch screw through each end of each slat, and two 2½-inch screws through each frame and into the aprons.

Make the plugs from scraps of the working stock, using a plug cutter. Apply resorcinol glue to the counterbores with a cotton swab. To make the plugs as inconspicuous as possible, try to pick plugs that match the wood's color, and align the plug's grain with the surrounding grain.

---

6. **Apply a finish.** Sand the table with fine-grit sandpaper. If you've chosen a wood that needs to be protected from the weather, apply a clear finish or exterior paint.

CONTOURED ENSEMBLE CHAISE LOUNGE

Here is a rakish chaise lounge to complete the Contoured Ensemble. The back is fixed, sparing you the trouble of dealing with any hardware. The lines are graceful, and seem to advertise that this is a comfortable place to relax.

This project has something in common with its ensemble kin. Take a look at the front legs, and you'll see that they are the same as those on the chair, bench, and table. The back legs, though different from the others in the set, are true to the ensemble's style. The side rails and backs add their own sinuous curves.

Structurally, the two side frames, which look like elongated versions of those on the other furniture, are the core. The rails meet the legs in half-lap joints, forming the side frames. The slats tie the two frames together.

SHOPPING LIST

LUMBER

10¼ bd. ft. 5/4 white oak
9¼ bd. ft. 4/4 white oak

HARDWARE AND SUPPLIES

8 pcs. #6 × 2½" galvanized drywall-type screws
62 pcs. #6 × 1¼" galvanized drywall-type screws
Resorcinol glue

FINISH

Clear water repellent or clear exterior finish

CUTTING LIST

PIECE	NUMBER	THICKNESS	WIDTH	LENGTH	MATERIAL
Front legs	2	1⅟₁₆"	3½"	15"	5/4 × 4 oak
Back legs	2	1⅟₁₆"	3½"	16"	5/4 × 4 oak
Rails	2	1⅟₁₆"	5½"	59"	5/4 × 6 oak
Backs	2	1⅟₁₆"	3½"	28"	5/4 × 4 oak
Apron	1	¾"	2¼"	19⅞"	5/4 × 3 oak
Brace	1	¾"	3"	19⅞"	4/4 × 4 oak
Handle slats	2	¾"	2¼"	24"	4/4 × 3 oak
Slats	29	¾"	1½"	24"	4/4 × 2 oak

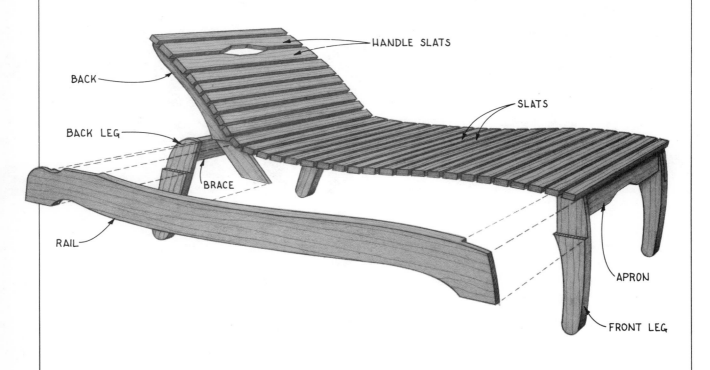

PLAN VIEWS

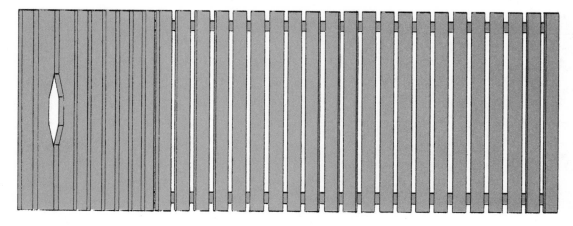

TOP VIEW

SIDE VIEW

½" TYP.

15"

9½"

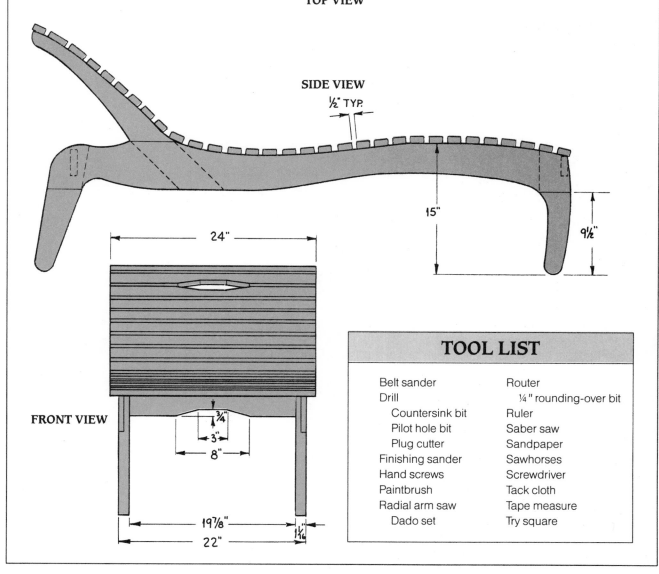

24"

FRONT VIEW

¾"

3"

8"

19⅞"

1½"

22"

TOOL LIST

Belt sander	Router
Drill	¼" rounding-over bit
Countersink bit	Ruler
Pilot hole bit	Saber saw
Plug cutter	Sandpaper
Finishing sander	Sawhorses
Hand screws	Screwdriver
Paintbrush	Tack cloth
Radial arm saw	Tape measure
Dado set	Try square

PATTERN

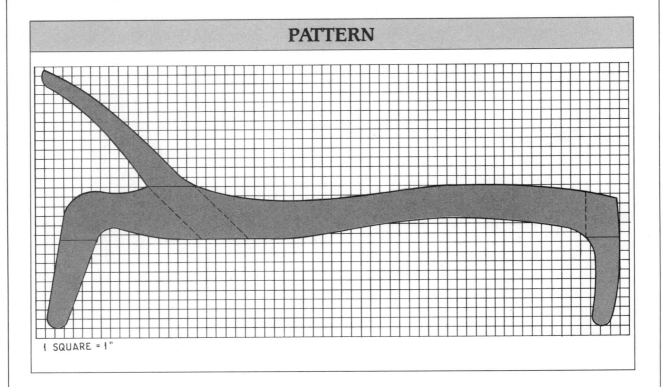

1 SQUARE = 1"

Builder's Notes

The construction of the contoured chaise lounge closely mimics that of the chair (or bench or swing). If you are building only the lounger, by all means read over the "Builder's Notes" for the chair on page 58 before you begin cutting wood. In addition, skim through the step-by-step section as well; it details the best way to cut the laps and assemble the side frames, how to enlarge the patterns, and so forth. The building tips there may prove useful in constructing this project.

---

1. **Cut the legs, rails, and backs.** Cut the parts of the two frames, each consisting of two legs, a back, and a rail. The chaise has an additional pair of half-laps, where the backs meet the rails. Otherwise, the procedure for making the two frames is similar to that given for the other projects this chapter.

---

2. **Make the lap joints.** Lay out the lap joints on the boards, making sure that you will be able to cut out the finished shapes of the legs and backs at the correct angles. The back leg is canted 10 degrees from the rail, and the back is canted 45 degrees. The front leg is at a standard 90 degree angle. Note also that you have to make a left frame and a right frame; the two are not identical. The laps will be cut in the *insides* of the rails. So, when you look at the assembled lounge from either side, the legs and the back will be seen to pass behind the rail. We found that the best tool for cutting the laps is a radial arm saw equipped with a dado blade, though you could use a router or circular saw.

Check that the surfaces of the lap joints are smooth and consistent. Then glue up the frames using resorcinol glue.

ROUGH SIDE FRAME ASSEMBLY

BACK

3½"

28"   135°

59"

5½"   15"

3½"

FRONT LEG

RAIL

80°

16"

BACK LEG

3½"

Left: Cutting the half-laps with the radial arm saw, a good tool to use for this task. Since you move the cutter over the workpiece, you can see the cut you are making as you make it. Also, the workpiece is stationary while the cut is being made. Since the chaise sides are large (and heavy, if you are using oak), this is a distinct safety advantage. After each pass, you shift the position of the workpiece.

Below: Gluing up a rough frame for the chaise. Mix resorcinol glue in a paper cup, and use a cheap brush to apply it. The hand screws shown distribute their clamping pressure over a broad area, but you can also use bar clamps or C-clamps.

3. **Cut the frame contours.** Draw a full-size copy of the pattern given here. Make sure your drawing captures the grace of the plan's curves. Then transfer the full-size pattern onto the rough frames.

Use a saber saw to cut out the frames; they will be too unwieldy to cut on the band saw. Take care not to stray inside the line. If necessary, use a belt sander to remove excess wood down to the line. Finally, use a router with a ¼-inch rounding-over bit to radius all the edges that will be exposed on the completed project.

4. **Cut the apron, brace, and slats.** Cut the apron, brace, narrow (1½ inch) slats, and the wide (2¼ inch) handle slats, as specified by the "Cutting List." Lay out the cutouts in one edge of the apron and the handle slats, and in both edges of the brace, as shown in the *Typical Cutout* drawing. Make the cutouts with a saber saw. Again, use a router with a ¼-inch rounding-over bit to radius the exposed edges of each slat and the apron.

TYPICAL CUTOUT

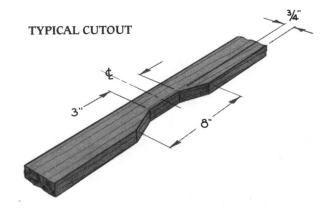

5. **Assemble the chaise.** With a helper, attach the slats, apron, and brace to the frames. Use screws, driven into counterbored pilot holes, then cover the screws with wood plugs glued into the counterbores. Sink one 1¼-inch screw in each end of every slat. Use two 2½-inch screws through either side of the frame and into the apron and brace.

Make the plugs from scraps of the working stock, using a plug cutter. Apply resorcinol glue to the counterbores with a cotton swab. To make the plugs as inconspicuous as possible, try to pick plugs that match the wood's color, and align the plug's grain with the surrounding grain.

Cutting plugs is done with a plug cutter, which can be chucked in a drill press or a hand-held power drill. To get loose plugs—like dowels—simply bore completely through the stock; each new plug you cut will eject the previous one from the cutter. But you can also stop the boring and leave the plugs attached to the stock. When you need one, break it out with a screwdriver or chisel.

6. **Apply a finish.** Go over the chaise with fine-grit sandpaper. If the wood needs to be protected from the elements, apply a clear finish or exterior paint.

THE
GARDEN
COLLECTION

TRUNDLE CHAISE

A Web-Seated Armchair with Pull-Out Footrest

This nifty chair and footrest was inspired by a wicker chaise I saw in a catalog of high-tone garden furniture. We liked the form of the piece, but making a *wicker* project . . .? Fred Matlack, who runs Rodale's woodworking shop, worked the form in his mind and came up with this version.

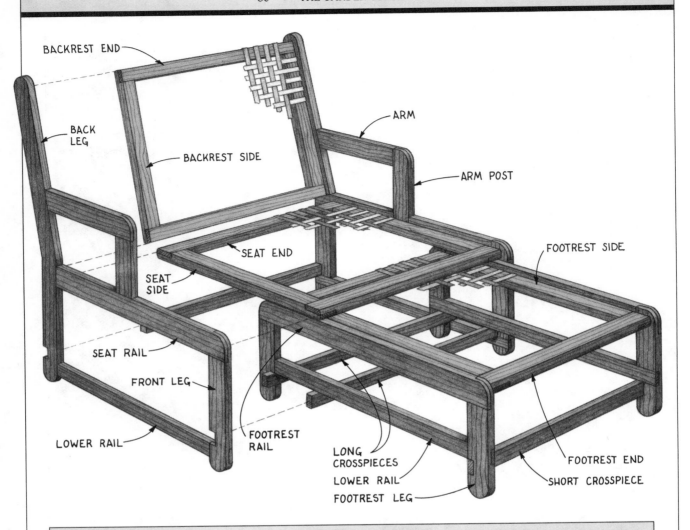

BACKREST END

BACK
LEG

BACKREST SIDE

ARM

ARM POST

SEAT END

SEAT
SIDE

FOOTREST SIDE

SEAT RAIL

FRONT LEG

LOWER RAIL

FOOTREST
RAIL

LONG
CROSSPIECES

LOWER RAIL

FOOTREST LEG

FOOTREST END

SHORT CROSSPIECE

SHOPPING LIST

LUMBER
4½ bd. ft. 5/4 white oak
10½ bd. ft. 4/4 white oak

HARDWARE AND SUPPLIES
100 yd. (approx.) 1" wide cotton webbing
12 pcs. 16 ga. × ½" nails
44 pcs. #8 × 2" brass flathead screws

HARDWARE AND SUPPLIES—CONTINUED
16 pcs. #8 brass finish washers
Resorcinol glue

FINISH
Exterior-grade penetrating oil

The piece is a collection of half-lap frames. Three rectangular ones are for the woven seat and back and footrest. Four others are the side frames (two for the chair, two for the footrest). The seat and back are joined to the side frames with screws. We selected brass flathead screws with brass finish washers; these say, "Yeah, we're screws holding this together, but we're wearing our good duds."

Fred used oak for the frames, after trying pine. The pine simply didn't seem substantial enough to "take" the weaving. The weaving is inch-wide cotton webbing purchased at a local tent, canopy, and awning company. It really is black and white.

I like this chair a lot. It is surprisingly comfortable. The weaving is firm, and the back is fairly erect. With a couple of scatter pillows under the small of your back,

CUTTING LIST

PIECE	NUMBER	THICKNESS	WIDTH	LENGTH	MATERIAL
Web frames					
Seat/footrest sides	4	1⅛"	1½"	30"	5/4 oak
Backrest sides	2	1⅛"	1½"	22"	5/4 oak
Seat/backrest ends	4	1⅛"	1½"	24"	5/4 oak
Footrest ends	2	1⅛"	1½"	22"	5/4 oak
Side frames					
Back legs	2	¾"	5"	36"	4/4 oak
Seat rails	2	¾"	2½"	33½"	4/4 oak
Front legs	2	¾"	2½"	14"	4/4 oak
Arms	2	¾"	2½"	19½"	4/4 oak
Arm posts	2	¾"	2½"	11½"	4/4 oak
Lower rails	4	¾"	1½"	33"	4/4 oak
Footrest rails	2	¾"	2½"	33"	4/4 oak
Footrest legs	4	¾"	2½"	12"	4/4 oak
Long crosspieces	3	¾"	1½"	25⅝"	4/4 oak
Short crosspiece	1	¾"	1½"	23⅝"	4/4 oak

it's a great chair for reading, where you want to be sort of erect but not bolt upright. And the weaving does have give without being saggy and hammocky. Moreover, the proportions and dimensions of the chair are tailored to someone my size (a bulky 6 footer).

A feature of the piece that I like, and that prompted the name, is that the footrest is interconnected with the chair. You can slide it in under the chair to get it out of the way. But because they're interlinked, you can't pick up the chair without also picking up the footrest.

Builder's Notes

You face mostly modest challenges with this project. The frame is put together with half-laps, a relatively simple joint. The weaving requires little skill but a generous measure of patience. Expect to spend two or three hours weaving each of the three panels.

Materials. A prototype web frame made of pine didn't hold up quite as well to the stresses of all those taut webs as Fred Matlack had hoped. He switched to a strong, easily available (in our area, anyway) hardwood, white oak. In addition to greater strength than pine, the oak has greater decay resistance. But oak's sturdiness comes at the price of weight—and keep in mind that the footrest doesn't detach.

You could switch to some other hardwoods—the decay resistance of cherry, locust, and walnut compares favorably with that of the white oak. But these three woods are premium materials. Hardwoods like poplar and maple, plentiful in many parts of the country, are poor choices for outdoor projects because of the low decay resistance. (I suggest hardwoods because it doesn't seem that the traditional outdoor woods—redwood and cedar—would be any better under stress than pine.) A compromise would be to make the web frames from oak, and the side frames from another stock.

If you've never tackled a hardwood project, this is actually a good one to start with. The required pieces are relatively uniform in width; the joinery is basic. And the finished project is very practical.

As I've noted with other projects, hardwoods aren't stocked by every lumberyard or building center. Where they are, you'll find them in rough-sawn form. The thicknesses are standardized, but the widths and lengths of individual boards are random. You have to keep the "Cutting List" handy so you select boards that will economically yield all the parts you need. And unless you have a jointer and a thickness planer, you'll need to have the dealer dress the boards you buy.

It should take only a phone call or two to track down a source for the 1-inch-wide cotton webbing (sometimes called tape). In our area, it's available both from a canopy and awning business, and from fabric stores. If you want or need to order it through the mail, try Shaker Workshops, P.O. Box 1028, Concord, MA 01742, or Connecticut Cane and Reed Company, P.O. Box 1276, Manchester, CT 06040. We used white and black web-

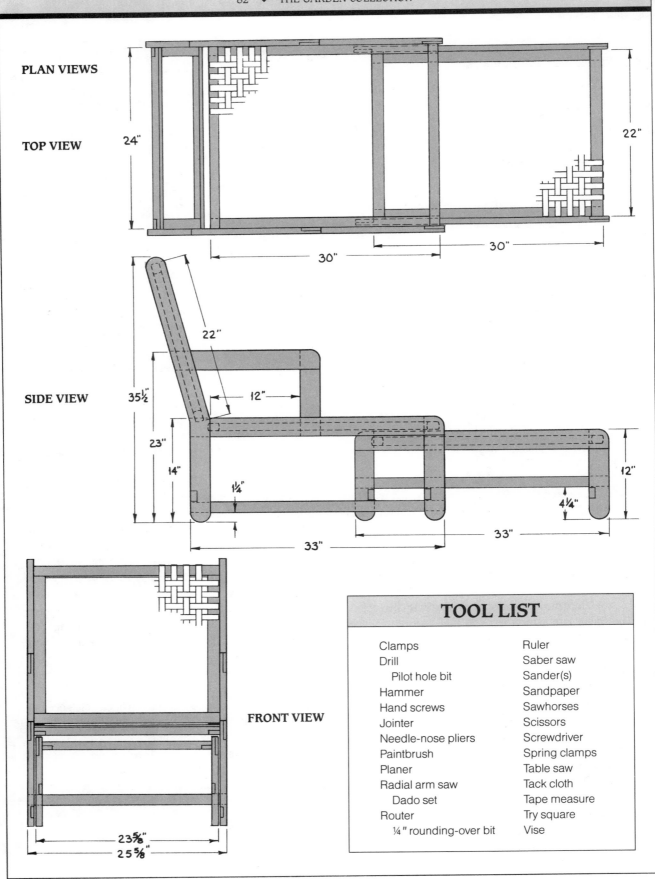

PLAN VIEWS

TOP VIEW

24"

22"

30"

30"

SIDE VIEW

22"

12"

35½"

23"

14"

1¼"

12"

4¼"

33"

33"

FRONT VIEW

23⅝"

25⅝"

TOOL LIST

Clamps
Drill
  Pilot hole bit
Hammer
Hand screws
Jointer
Needle-nose pliers
Paintbrush
Planer
Radial arm saw
  Dado set
Router
  ¼" rounding-over bit

Ruler
Saber saw
Sander(s)
Sandpaper
Sawhorses
Scissors
Screwdriver
Spring clamps
Table saw
Tack cloth
Tape measure
Try square
Vise

bing for a starkly geometric effect, but many colors are available. Use your imagination.

Tools and techniques. The joinery is fairly simple, and thus the required tools are typical of the hobby woodworker's shop. To dress the wood, you should have a jointer and a table saw, at a minimum. But since you can have the wood planed when you buy it—for an additional charge, of course—you don't absolutely need the jointer.

Half-lap joints are little trouble if made with a radial arm saw and a dado blade. The blade does the work with repeated passes over the lap, in full view. A router will serve well enough; so will a table saw and a dado blade, although you won't be able to monitor the blade's progress.

What shaping of parts is necessary can be accomplished satisfactorily with a saber saw, though a band saw would make quicker work of it.

No special tools are needed to do the webbing.

Two slightly different routes present themselves to the builder of this project. To build the chaise along the first route, you would cut the parts, build the frames, apply a finish to the entire project, do the weaving, and finally, assemble the piece. By the other, you would build and finish the web frames, then start the weaving. While the weaving is progressing, you take woodworking breaks and build and finish the side frames. At about the time the weaving is completed, the side frames are too, and the piece can be assembled.

In the following step-by-step directions, we take the latter approach. At about three hours per panel, the weaving is time-consuming. And unless you have an unusually large collection of clamps, you will need to glue up the frames one or two at a time.

Finish. The finish used on this chaise is CWF, a favorite of the Rodale woodworkers. A penetrating oil, it goes on quickly in two coats applied about a half-hour apart. You don't have to sand the project between coats. Since both coats go on in the same work session, you only have to clean up once. So using CWF—or any other penetrating oil graded for outdoor use—minimizes a task that, to a lot of us woodworkers, is really a chore.

Lest you forget, you do have to apply the finish to the web frames before you weave them. If penetrating oil is what you use, allow them to dry thoroughly before beginning the weaving.

---

1. Prepare the stock. Hardwood, as you know, generally is stocked in a rough-sawn state. To prepare it for use, you need to joint and plane it to reduce it to working thicknesses and to smooth the faces and edges.

Generally, this routine is followed:

• Crosscut the boards to rough working lengths first. That is, assuming the stock is close to the desired width, you measure off each part, allowing an extra inch or so, and crosscut it.

• Smooth one face on the jointer, making as many passes as necessary to really smooth it and remove all the saw marks.

• Joint one edge. Hold the jointed face against the jointer fence as you joint the edge; this will ensure that the edge is square to that face.

• Turn to the planer. Run the board through the planer as many times as is required to reduce the board to the desired thickness, resetting the cutters after each pass. (When planing a lot of parts, the usual practice is to set the planer, run all of them through, reset the planer and run them all through again, and so forth. That way, all the boards will end up at the same thickness.)

• Rip the boards to within 1/16 inch of the final width, then trim away that last 1/16 inch—and at the same time smooth away the saw marks—on the jointer.

The result is a board whose surfaces are flat and at right angles to their neighbors, and whose faces are parallel to each other.

There are some alternatives, although the results won't always be ideal.

If you lack a planer, you can often get away with jointing a face and an edge, then resawing the rough face on the table saw and cleaning up the cut on the jointer. The faces will be flat, but they may not be perfectly parallel.

If you lack a jointer, you can smooth both faces in a planer, and hand plane the edges. Here, one potential shortcoming is that the edges will be out of square with the faces. Another is that the faces won't be absolutely flat (the feed rollers of a big planer can exert enough pressure on a cupped board to flatten it; when the pressure is off the board, it recups.)

The obvious solution—and it can be a time-saver as well, if you are pressed for shop time—is to buy from a lumberyard or dealer that can surface the boards to your specifications.

2. Cut and assemble the parts for the web frames. Each web frame is simple: four lengths of wood joined together into a rectangle with half-lap joints. Each frame is a different size, but the frame members are all the same girth, so the laps to be cut are all the same. For each frame, cut two sides and two ends to the sizes specified by the "Cutting List." Mark an identification on each piece, so you know which frame it is for.

Cut the laps next. Possibly the best tool for cutting laps is the radial arm saw equipped with a dado cutter. Clamp a block to the backstop to govern the length of the lap. When the workpiece is butted to the block, the cutter will make the shoulder cut. Pull the workpiece back from the block and make another pass or two with the cutter to complete the lap. The workpiece is always sta-tionary when it's being cut, the cut is not concealed from your view (as it is on the table saw), and the dado cutter hogs away a major amount of the waste with each pass.

With the laps completed, glue the frames together. Use resorcinol glue and pinch each joint with a hand screw, speed clamp, spring clamp, or the like until the glue sets. As you apply the clamps, be sure the frame is square and flat.

After the glue has set and the clamps are off, sand the frames carefully. Radius the edges, inside and out, top and bottom, with a router and a ¼-inch rounding-over bit. Dust the frames with a tack cloth, then apply two coats of an exterior-grade penetrating oil, with the second coat going on within a half hour of the first, when it is still wet.

WEB FRAME JOINERY

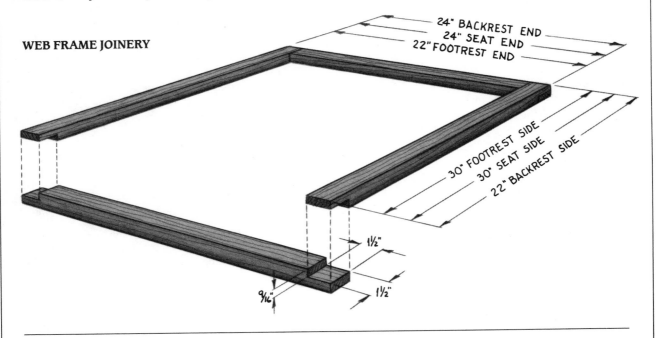

24" BACKREST END
24" SEAT END
22" FOOTREST END
30" FOOTREST SIDE
30" SEAT SIDE
22" BACKREST SIDE
1½"
1½"
9/16"

3. String the warp on a web frame. You'll weave the three web frames one at a time. And while work on the weaving is progressing, you can move ahead on building and finishing the side frames. The weaving is done in two steps: stringing the warp, and weaving. Stringing the warp is easy. The actual weaving takes far more time.

The warp is the aggregation of webs through which the weaver is interlaced. String the warp webbing on the frame from end to end. Nail the starting end to the frame near a corner. You could simply loop it around the outside of the frame, but there's a good possibility it will simply slip off if the frame should get tipped the wrong way. Moreover, weaving on such a warp is somewhat more difficult. It's better to loop the webbing under and over the end frame members, as shown in *Stringing the Warp,* in a figure-eight course.

STRINGING THE WARP

Top: The starting end of the webbing is attached to the frame with a ½-inch nail. These nails are pretty small, so save your fingers and use needle-nose pliers to hold it for the first couple of hammer blows. Then wrap the webbing around itself and the frame member, covering the nail, before stretching it to the opposite end of the frame. Note that the attachment point is about ½ inch from the inside corner.

Center: String the warp in a figure-eight course; that is, over one frame member and under the opposite one. Leave the warp somewhat slack, and keep the loops a little more than the width of the tape apart. All of these things will help ease the job of weaving. Incidentally, note the size of the webbing roll.

Bottom: To tack down the end of the tape, crowd the second-to-last loop with the last. Wind the tape around the frame member and tack it down, just as you did the starting end. Then pull the last loop into its proper position, as shown, covering the nail and the end.

Before cutting the web and tacking the end, secure it with a spring clamp and adjust the spacing and tension of the webbing. Fred Matlack, who built and wove the chaise, provides two "don'ts."

• *Don't* make the warp too tight. As you weave, it tightens dramatically, and if you start with it too tight, you'll never be able to complete the weaving. Try to duplicate the tension shown in the photograph; the strands don't sag noticeably.

• *Don't* get the warp strands too close together. Weaving becomes extremely difficult. Each strand should be slightly more than the tape's width away from its neighbors.

When you are satisfied with your warp, cut off the webbing with enough margin to allow you to wrap it around the frame and nail it. Note that the last strand is pushed aside temporarily so that the nail can be driven. After the warp is secured, work the strand back in place to conceal the nailed end.

TIP

Since you don't want to be passing the entire roll of webbing through the warp, you need to cut a weaver. But you can't splice the webbing if you run short, so you need to estimate pretty accurately how long the weaver must be.

Do this: Nail the starting end in place and then simply wrap the correct number of courses around the frame, as shown. Don't bother interweaving the weave with the warp—this is just a trial run. When you've finished, add an extra margin for error, and cut. If you *do* end up short, there's a way to avoid having to cut another length of webbing and starting over. Back out the last course of weave, and reposition each previous course so that you can get by with one fewer.

4. Weave the panel. The weaver is very well named—it requires you to snake a strand into the warp. To make it easier to fish the weave through those tight places, use only as much webbing as you think the job will take, cutting that amount off the roll. Another way to speed the job along is to anchor the frame in a vise, so it is held upright at a comfortable working height, leaving both hands free.

Attach the weaver (which is often called the woof or the weft) as you did the warp. Nail the starting end of

Because the weaver is so long at the outset of the project, you can't work with the free end. Rather, grasp the weaver fairly close to the secured end and lace it through the warp, creating the first row, and simultaneously trailing the excess through the warp. Here Fred is about to pull the excess through.

the web to the frame, about ½ inch from the corner (closer will give the woven panel a "pulled" corner). Wrap the webbing around the frame to conceal the cut end and the nail.

Weaving is a simple matter of snaking the strand of webbing over and under and over and under the warp strands. The weaver is—at first anyway—a very long piece, so work close to its secured end. Fold it back on itself and snake a double strand through the warp. Then pull through the excess, which is everything up to the free end. The free end is always the last through (not the first). After you have the excess through, go back and tidy up the webbing, flattening each strand in the warp, pulling the weaver up. This done, loop the weaver around the outside of the frame, and head back. On the return course, you will pass over the warp strands you passed under on the previous pass, and vice versa.

On the first weave, you want to tighten the warp, so go over the high side of each warp strand. With each subsequent pass, the tension of the woven surface will increase. When you are finished, the woven surface will be recessed between the frame members, as shown in the *Weaving Section View.* Anchor the last course as you did the end of the warp; that is, work the last strand temporarily aside, loop the free end around the frame and tack it, then move the weaver back to cover and conceal the end and nail.

WEAVING SECTION VIEW

In weaving the panels in the chaise shown, Fred worked—with the frame in the vise—from the top down to about the middle of the frame. Then he turned the frame and worked up to complete the panel. This kept

A needle-nose pliers makes a good tool for aligning and straightening the webs. It has a pointed tip to worm into the weave without damaging the material, as well as a handle to provide leverage for moving the web. As you can see, the webbing bunches and folds when you push it with the pliers, but you can easily spread it flat again by "spearing" the far edge and pulling it.

the work area of the frame at a comfortable height for him. You can work from the bottom up or the top down, whichever is better for you.

---

5. **Cut the parts for the side frames.** From the 4/4 (four-quarter) stock, cut the legs, rails, arms, arm posts, and crosspieces. For everything but the back legs, this is pretty much a rip and crosscut operation. The back legs, however, need to be carefully laid out on a 5-inch-wide board, as shown in the *Back Leg Layout.* Orienting the leg properly on the board is important so that the leg has the maximum strength the wood's grain structure can offer. The back legs can be cut out with a saber saw, though a band saw will do a better job in less time.

With the parts cut, lay out and cut the various laps. See the *Chair Side Frame Joinery* and *Footrest Side Frame Joinery* drawings. Keep in mind that the chair's two side frames are mirror images of each other, not duplicates. Pay attention, too, to which face each lap is cut into. The arm, for example, has the lap for the back leg cut into the outer face, while the lap for the arm post is cut into the inside face. As you did the web frame laps, cut these on the radial arm saw equipped with a dado cutter. The end laps can be cut assembly-line fashion, using stop blocks to help control the size of the cuts.

Even the laps for the lower rails can be positioned with stop blocks.

Lay out and cut the notches in the legs for the cross-pieces next. And while you are at it, round off the foot ends of the two front legs and the four footrest legs. All these cuts can be handled with a saber saw or, better, on the band saw.

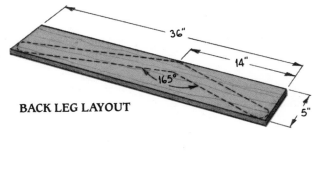

BACK LEG LAYOUT

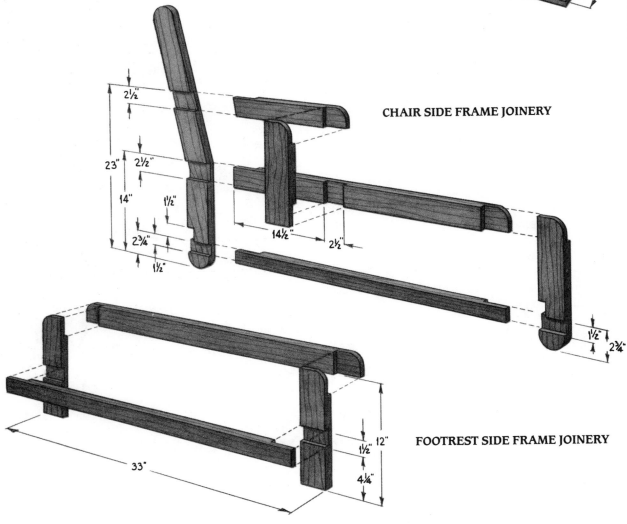

CHAIR SIDE FRAME JOINERY

FOOTREST SIDE FRAME JOINERY

6. Assemble the side frames. Glue up the side frames of the chair and footrest, pretty much the way you did the web frames. If you cut the laps correctly, the frames should square, but check with a try square and do whatever you can during clamping to keep the frames square. Make sure they are flat, too.

After the clamps are off, cut the corners that must be rounded off—the junction of arm and arm post, of seat rail and front leg, of footrest rail and leg. Use a saber saw. At the same time, trim off any excess at the laps, such as where the arm joins the back leg.

You can ensure good fitting end laps if you cut some of the parts a bit long. The rail joins the back leg, for example, just where it bends. Leaving the rail end square and trimming it flush to the leg's edge after glue-up guarantees a good appearance. Similarly, by cutting a T-lap (such as the arm-to-back-leg joint) as a cross-lap, you can be sure the joint won't slip open during glue-up because it is locked in place mechanically. After the clamps are off, trim off the excess with a saber saw.

7. **Apply a finish.** Sand all the assemblies thoroughly. Using a router and a ¼-inch rounding-over bit, radius the edges of the side frames, inside and out. Dust the frames with a tack cloth to remove all the dust.

Apply two coats of an exterior-grade penetrating oil. The second coat should go on while the first coat is still wet. Give the first coat 15 to 30 minutes to penetrate the wood surface before applying the second.

8. **Assemble the chaise.** We chose to attach the panels to the side frames with showy brass screws, five on each side of the footrest and seat web frames, and three on each side of the back web frame. The screws in the chair sides are fitted with brass finish washers, which make them stand proud of the wood's surface. But with the footrest, such an arrangement would interfere with the sliding action; here the screws are countersunk just enough to make them flush. In each case, drill pilot holes through the side frames and into the web frames.

After the web frames and side frames are assembled, add the crosspieces. These side-to-side members fit into the notches in the lower legs, and they are secured with brass screws driven through the crosspiece into the leg. Install a long crosspiece at the back of the chair and the short crosspiece at the front of the footrest. Slide the foot-

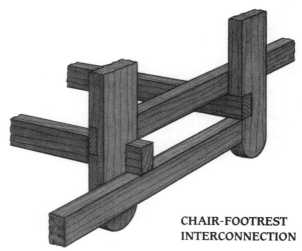

CHAIR-FOOTREST INTERCONNECTION

rest under the chair and install the two remaining long crosspieces. These serve to trap the footrest between the side frames of the chair.

TIP

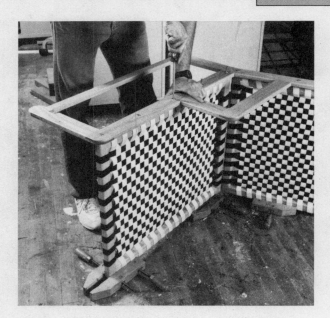

Hand screws can serve as extra hands to help you assemble the web frames between the side frames. Apply two of the wooden-jawed clamps to one side of the backrest frame and two to the side of the seat frame. Stand the frames on the hand screws, as shown. Place the first side frame on them, get the three assemblies properly lined up, then drill pilot holes and drive the screws. With the first side attached, you can turn the assembly over, remove the hand screws, and attach the second side frame.

TERRACE ENSEMBLE

Old-World Charm for Your Terrace

With its classic table and chairs, canvas umbrella, and tea trolley, this ensemble would be at home in a formal English garden or outside an Italian villa. The reward of having the ensemble to adorn your terrace equals the challenge of building it.

TERRACE ENSEMBLE TABLE AND CHAIRS

The inspirations for this table and chair set were the various classy and expensive teak outdoor furniture sets that are widely advertised, particularly in mail-order landscaping catalogs. You can't help but admire these handsomely designed, well-crafted pieces.

Because this table and chair set is much more elegant than your run-of-the-mill patio furniture, it deserves special care. Until you're done, you'll have a substantial amount of money and time invested, too much to just plop it on the deck or patio and leave it there through the seasons. Although oak is a durable hardwood and the design is a sturdy one, an outdoor environment takes its toll on any wood furniture, and you'll want to keep this set looking its best. So pick a protected spot for it—under a patio awning or a sundeck trellis, for example—and definitely do not leave it outside all year round.

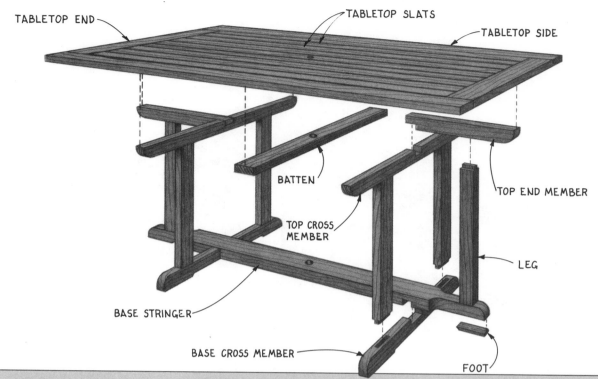

SHOPPING LIST—TABLE

LUMBER
50 bd. ft. 8/4 white oak
42 bd. ft. 5/4 white oak
4½ bd. ft. 4/4 white oak

HARDWARE AND SUPPLIES
1 box #6 × 1⅝" galvanized drywall-type screws
1 box #6 × 2¾" galvanized drywall-type screws
Resorcinol glue

FINISH
Exterior-grade penetrating oil, such as CWF

CUTTING LIST—TABLE

PIECE	NUMBER	THICKNESS	WIDTH	LENGTH	MATERIAL
Top cross members	2	1¾"	2"	34"	8/4 oak
Top end members	2	1¾"	2"	17¾"	8/4 oak
Base stringer	1	1¾"	4"	62"	8/4 oak
Base cross members	2	1¾"	2½"	26"	8/4 oak
Feet	2	¾"	1¾"	5¾"	scrap
Legs	6	1¾"	2½"	24"	8/4 oak
Tabletop ends	2	1"	4"	30"	5/4 oak
Tabletop sides	2	1"	4"	73"*	5/4 oak
Tabletop slats	9	1"	3"	66"	5/4 oak
Batten	1	1"	4"	34"	5/4 oak

*Trim to a finished length of 72" *after* assembly.

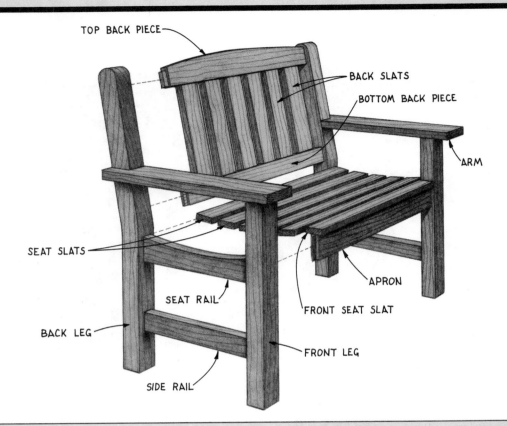

TOP BACK PIECE
BACK SLATS
BOTTOM BACK PIECE
ARM
SEAT SLATS
SEAT RAIL
BACK LEG
SIDE RAIL
FRONT SEAT SLAT
APRON
FRONT LEG

SHOPPING LIST—ARMCHAIR

LUMBER
9¼ bd. ft. 8/4 white oak
6¾ bd. ft. 5/4 white oak
1½ bd. ft. 4/4 white oak

FINISH
Exterior-grade penetrating oil, such as CWF

HARDWARE AND SUPPLIES
1 box #6 × 1⅝" galvanized drywall-type screws
Resorcinol glue

CUTTING LIST—ARMCHAIR

PIECE	NUMBER	THICKNESS	WIDTH	LENGTH	MATERIAL
Front legs	2	1⅞"	2"	23¾"	8/4 oak
Back legs	2	1⅞"	5"	35½"	8/4 oak
Side rails	2	1⅞"	2"	15"	8/4 oak
Seat rails	2	1⅞"	2¾"	15"	8/4 oak
Top back piece	1	1"	3½"	22"	5/4 oak
Bottom back piece	1	1"	2½"	22"	5/4 oak
Back slats	6	¾"	1¾"	14½"	4/4 oak
Apron	1	1"	2½"	22½"	5/4 oak
Seat slats	5	1"	2"	23¾"	5/4 oak
Front seat slat	1	1"	2"	20"	5/4 oak
Arms	2	1"	2¾"	19"	5/4 oak

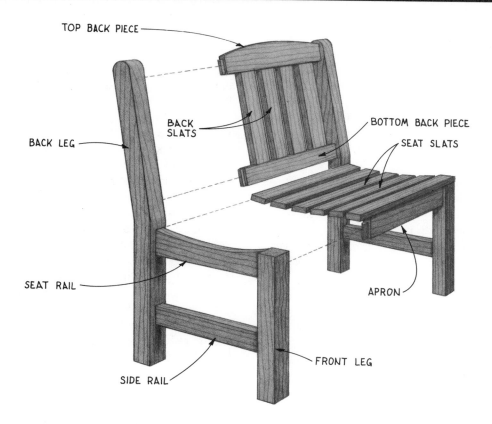

SHOPPING LIST—CHAIR

LUMBER

8½ bd. ft. 8/4 white oak
3½ bd. ft. 5/4 white oak
1 bd. ft. 4/4 white oak

HARDWARE AND SUPPLIES

1 box #6 × 1⅝" galvanized drywall-type screws
Resorcinol glue

FINISH

Exterior-grade penetrating oil, such as CWF

CUTTING LIST—CHAIR

PIECE	NUMBER	THICKNESS	WIDTH	LENGTH	MATERIAL
Front legs	2	1⅞"	2"	15¾"	8/4 oak
Back legs	2	1⅞"	5"	35½"	8/4 oak
Side rails	2	1⅞"	2"	15"	8/4 oak
Seat rails	2	1⅞"	2¾"	15"	8/4 oak
Top back piece	1	1"	3½"	16¼"	5/4 oak
Bottom back piece	1	1"	2½"	16¼"	5/4 oak
Back slats	4	¾"	1¾"	14½"	4/4 oak
Apron	1	1"	2½"	16¾"	5/4 oak
Seat slats	6	1"	2"	18"	5/4 oak

Builder's Notes

This project is one of our more demanding ones. For the woodworker looking for a challenge, here it is. The basic material is oak, a wood that demands attention from you *before* it's ready to be worked. The principle joint is the mortise and tenon, one that takes practice to master and time to cut and fit, one that many experienced woodworkers avoid. And the work is extensive, with a table and two kinds of chairs listed on the work order. But the result is a gratifyingly handsome set of furniture for the terrace or patio.

The table is rectangular for a reason. Were it square, its leg assembly would be less able to resist wracking. The tabletop would tend to rotate, twisting the legs, spilling the iced tea, disrupting the conversation. So we made the table rectangular.

You can make the chairs with or without arms—both types are covered on the drawings and instructions. Make sure you use the appropriate cutting list for the type you're making because the length of some parts are different. Rather than simply extend the front leg to support the arm, you need to widen the seat also. If you don't, the chair turns out to be too narrow—particularly between the arms—for all but the most slender fannies.

Materials. While teak is the material that comes to mind as the natural choice for this sort of outdoor furniture, we all have (or should have) reservations about using teak. Oak is readily available here in the eastern United States, it looks very good, and white oak is a species that has better than average decay resistance (its relative, red oak, is considerably less decay resistant). So oak is a good choice for this upscale outdoor furniture ensemble, and it is the choice we made.

If you haven't already worked with a hardwood, you'll find that buying the lumber can be a challenge in itself. Hardwoods aren't stocked at every lumberyard. When they are, they are usually stocked in pretty unpredictable dimensions. While thicknesses are standardized, lengths and widths are not. The length is whatever length the log was—nothing is trimmed off to square the board's ends. The width is the maximum the sawyer could eke out of the log. The standard unit—particularly for pricing purposes—is the board foot, a volumetric measure calculated by multiplying the thickness in inches by the width in inches by the length in feet, then dividing the result by 12.

The upshot of all this is that you may have to shop around just to find the species you want. (Phil Gehret, who built the table and chairs, purchased the material, kiln dried, from a local sawmill.) Then, too, you must keep the dimensions of the necessary parts in mind when you shop. Our "Shopping List," specifying so many board feet of such-and-such a thickness, isn't quite good enough. Rather than predetermining that you need so many boards of a particular size, you have to look at what's available and judge which ones will give you the parts you need. It's tricky, because it's easy to misjudge, to forget a couple of key parts, or to overlook a major defect you can't work around. So give yourself some leeway and buy a little extra.

As you close the deal for the wood, consider its state. It is probably rough-sawn. Before you can start cutting parts and joints, the wood has to be reduced to working thicknesses and surfaced to make it smooth and flat. If you have—or have access to—a thickness planer and a jointer, you can do this work yourself. If you don't have these tools, be prepared to pay the lumber dealer to do it for you.

Tools and techniques. As does much fine furniture, this set employs a lot of mortise-and-tenon joinery. Tenons are pretty easy to make; you can cut them with a router, on a table saw, with a radial arm saw, or on a band saw. But mortises are more of a challenge for the hobby woodworker. The standard procedure is to drill a series of holes inside the mortise layout lines to rough it

TOOL LIST

Band saw	Paintbrush
Bar or pipe clamps	Planer
Belt sander	Router
Chisels	¼" rounding-over bit
Clamps	¾" straight bit
Drill	Rubber mallet
Pilot hole bit	Ruler
Drill press	Saber saw
⅜" Forstner bit	Sandpaper
¾" Forstner bit	Saw for crosscutting
⅜" plug cutter	Sawhorses
Countersink bit	Screwdriver
Hollow-chisel mortising	Table saw
attachment	Dado cutter
Finishing sander	Miter gauge
Hand plane	Tack cloth
Hand screws	Tape measure
Hole saw, 1¾"	Try square
Jointer	Yardsticks

out. To do this, you use a bit that's the width of the desired mortise, perhaps $\frac{1}{16}$ inch smaller. Then you clean up and square the mortise walls with a chisel.

The holes you bore should be perfectly straight and aligned, and all bored to the same depth. You *can* do the job with a portable electric drill fitted with a 90-degree drill guide, but such contrivances are often clumsy and awkward to use. A drill press will do the job much more quickly and accurately. The holes will be plumb, and you can adjust the machine so the holes will be of a consistent depth. You can mount a fence on the table to help position the mortises. Fitted with a hollow-chisel mortising attachment (that bores square holes), the drill press becomes even more efficient.

When making mortise-and-tenon joints, it's best to cut all the mortises first, then cut the corresponding tenons for an exact fit. Number each joint so you know which tenon fits into which mortise and how they should be oriented.

Making the chairs amounts to a small production run. You need four chairs at minimum, so you are making duplicates of every part. Minimize layout work by using setups effectively, and you'll save time and work. Keep the parts organized and clearly labeled, and you'll save time.

A detailing procedure that crops up again and again in these projects is rounding-over the exposed edges of the parts. It seems to be a signature touch on the part of Fred Matlack and Phil Gehret, Rodale's woodworking project mavens. They radius the edges of everything they build.

It isn't *always* as easy as running the part by the rounding-over bit on the router table, though. In this project, you can deal with the legs and the tabletop slats, among other parts, that way. But you need to be careful where two parts join; here you want the radius on one edge to blend into the radius on the other. The easiest way to achieve this effect, of course, is to machine the edges after assembly. But "easiest" isn't always possible. Sometimes you have to dry assemble joints, mark edges, then disassemble and machine.

It seems like a lot of trouble, but the details often do. Until they pay off in the finished project.

Finish. Unless protected with a finish, oak will weather poorly. It darkens rather dramatically, for example. A clear finish, given the attractiveness—not to say the expensiveness—of the wood, is in order.

For this ensemble, we used CWF, a penetrating oil especially formulated for outdoor use. (CWF, the brand name, stands for Clear Wood Finish.) The theory of the penetrating oil finish is that it, as the name indicates, penetrates the wood's surface and seals it. By keeping standing water—from rain, dew, the lawn sprinkler—from soaking in, the finish minimizes the expansion and contraction that lead to warping, checking, splitting, and joint failure. The finish helps prevent molds and mildew from getting established, and helps keep the wood's natural resins from baking out under the hot sun.

Generally, manufacturers instruct you to brush on the oil liberally, letting it penetrate. And, in fact, when you brush it on you can see it soak into the wood. After 15 minutes to a half-hour, apply more. While these finishes generally are supposed to dry in 24 to 48 hours, in my experience, it often takes three to five days for the solvent smells to dissipate. CWF actually seems to form a surface film as it dries to a matte sheen.

Initially, the finish will darken the wood somewhat. And as the piece weathers, the finish *will* break down and allow the wood to darken and turn silvery-gray. The solution, of course, is to renew the finish every couple of years.

Table

1. **Cut and shape the base parts.** Cut the two base cross members and the base stringer to the sizes specified by the "Cutting List." Following the *Base Stringer Layout* and the *Base Cross Member Layout,* mark the sizes and locations of the mortises for the legs and the laps that join the three pieces, as well as the final contours.

Cut the laps first, using a router and a straight bit. Though the cross members are thicker than the stringer at this point, bear in mind that after the cross member contours are cut, they'll be the same thickness as the stringer at the laps. Plan to cut the laps a hair undersize, then to refine the fit by paring with a chisel. To prevent tearout that could mar the project, clamp scraps to each

---

TIP

A Forstner bit bores a clean, flat-bottomed hole, which makes it an excellent bit to use in roughing out mortises. Investing in a couple of sizes—say ⅜ inch and ¾ inch—would enable you to tackle mortise-and-tenon joinery effectively, without incurring the expense of a hollow-chisel mortising attachment.

---

side of the workpiece. Then clamp parallel straightedges across the workpiece, positioned to control the width of the lap. Cut each in several passes; oak is pretty hard, and the router is primarily a trimming tool, so don't try to cut more than an additional ⅛ inch with each pass. You can save some time by clamping the two cross members together and lapping both at the same time. After rough-cutting the laps with the router, fit the parts together and refine the width and depth of the laps using a chisel.

Next, cut the mortises. If you have a hollow-chisel mortising attachment, use it. If you don't, select a bit that is the same diameter as the width of the mortises, and chuck it in your drill press. Clamp a fence to the drill press table, positioning it so the center point of the bit will enter the centerline of the workpiece. Drill a series of slightly overlapping holes the length of the mortise. Cut the two mortises in the stringer, then reset the fence and rough out the mortises in the cross members. (If possible, maintain the drill press setup for roughing out the top cross member mortises.) With a chisel, pare the sides and ends of the mortises to square them and bring them to their final dimensions.

If you are planning to use an umbrella with the table, cut the hole for its post in the stringer. Use a 1¾-inch hole saw, boring as deep as possible from one side. Then withdraw the cutter, turn the stringer over, and complete the operation from the other side.

The final operation in this step is to cut the contours. Do this on a band saw. After cutting, sand the surfaces to remove saw marks.

BASE STRINGER LAYOUT

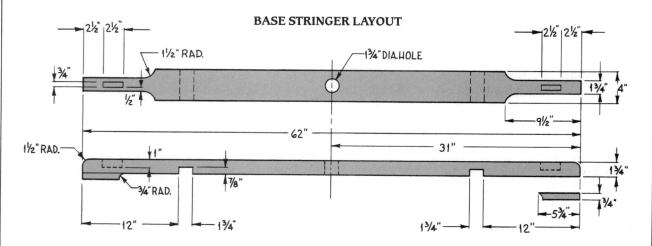

BASE CROSS MEMBER LAYOUT

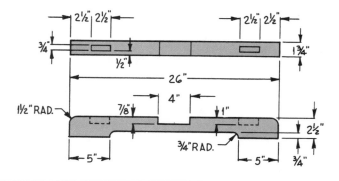

TABLE PLAN VIEWS

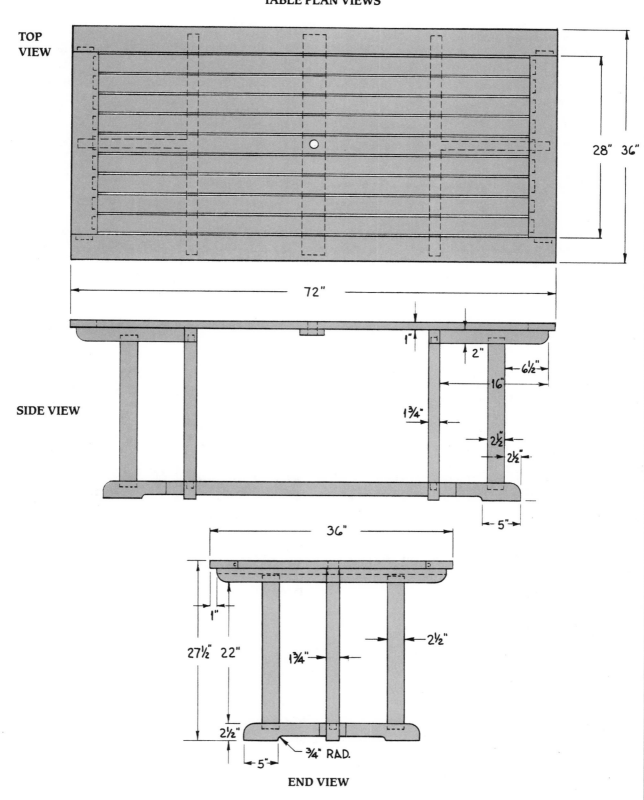

TOP VIEW

28" 36"

72"

SIDE VIEW

1"

2"

6½"

16"

1¾"

2½"

2½"

5"

36"

1"

2½"

27½" 22"

1¾"

2½"

5"

¾" RAD.

END VIEW

2. **Cut and shape the top members.** This step is pretty much a repeat of the previous step, but with different parts. Rough-cut the four top members to the sizes specified by the "Cutting List." Following the *Top Cross Member Layout* and the *Top End Member Layout,* mark the sizes and locations of the laps, mortises, and contours that must be cut.

Cut the laps first, again using a router and straight bit. Remember to clamp scraps on each side of the workpieces to prevent tearout. Remember, too, that you can clamp like parts together and lap both at the same time. And to get the proper fit, rough-cut the laps just a tad undersize, and in a process of alternately test fitting and paring with a chisel, bring them to their final fit.

Cut the mortises next. Since these mortises match those in the base cross members, you can use the same drill press setup to rough them out. Pare them to their final dimensions with a chisel.

Finally, cut the contours of the parts on the band saw, then sand away the tool marks with a belt sander.

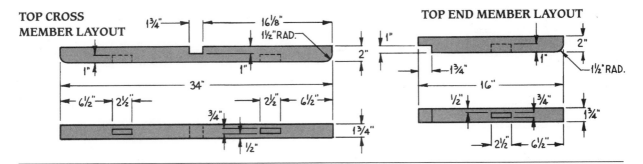

3. **Assemble the base and top frames.** Dry assemble the top frame and the base frame one last time. If the lap joints fit to your satisfaction, glue and screw the parts together. Use resorcinol glue. With the base, drive a couple of 1⅝-inch screws through the bottoms of the cross members into the stringer. With the top frame, drive the same number of screws through the tops of the cross members into the end members.

Cut and glue the feet to the stringer. Cut two scraps to the size specified by the "Cutting List." Set the base assembly on a flat surface, and measure from the bottom of the stringer to the surface. If necessary, plane the feet to that thickness, then glue them to the underside of the stringer at each end. After the glue sets, sand the three frames.

Although the feet are integral to the base cross members, they have to be glued to the base stringer. Because of the size of the stringer, this is an easier and less wasteful approach. After the stringer is joined to the cross members, cantilever an end off the workbench and glue and clamp a foot in place.

4. **Cut and tenon the legs.** Cut the six legs to the size specified by the "Cutting List."

Each leg is tenoned on both ends, as shown in the *Leg Tenon Detail.* While you can cut the tenons with a router and a straight bit, it probably is easiest to cut them on a table saw with a dado cutter. Set up the dado cutter, and position the rip fence so it is the length of the tenon away from the *outside* of the blade. When the end of the leg is butted against the fence, the blade will cut the tenon's shoulder. Set the depth of cut to give you a tenon that's just a tad fat. Make test cuts on a scrap of the leg stock to confirm the accuracy of your settings. When cutting the tenons, guide the leg with the miter gauge. Make a series of passes; on the last, the butt end of the leg should be against the rip fence. With the saw set up, you can quickly cut tenons on both ends of each leg.

After all the tenons are cut, carefully fit them to particular mortises. On each leg, one tenon has to fit a mortise in a base member, while the other tenon has to fit a mortise in the corresponding top member. Assuming you did cut the tenons a bit thick, use a chisel to pare the tenon's cheeks until an appropriate, snug fit is obtained.

Finally, using a router and a ¼-inch rounding-over bit, radius the edges of the legs.

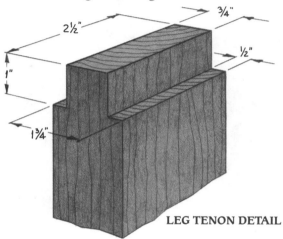

LEG TENON DETAIL

TIP

After paring a tenon to fit a particular mortise, mark both so you don't get them mixed up later. To avoid accidental erasures, chisel Roman numerals (what else?), locating the marks where they'll be concealed after assembly. If you mark surfaces that adjoin when properly assembled, you can indicate the correct orientation of tenon in mortise.

5. Assemble the table base.

The radiused edge is a characteristic of virtually all the pieces in this book, and the Terrace Ensemble is no exception. To work all the exposed edges sometimes takes some doing, and with the table, some edges have to be worked before assembly and some after. Before actually gluing the legs to the base and top frames, use the router and a ¼-inch rounding-over bit to radius all the appropriate edges.

Assembly of the table base is a two-person operation. You need to apply glue to both mating surfaces; in this case, the mortise as well as the tenon. Resorcinol glue is runny, and it stains. If you hold the mortises upside down, glue can run out, drip on other parts of the project, and stain them.

Turn the two top frames so the mortises face up. Apply glue to them and to the tenons on the legs. Fit the legs into the top frames. Then apply glue to the lower tenons and the base mortises. With a helper, lift one leg-and-top-frame unit, turn it right-side up, and fit the tenons into the base mortises. Repeat with the second unit.

Dry assemble the table's base to determine which edges—or sections of edges—can be radiused before assembly, and which must wait until after assembly. Make a practice run around the assembly with the router—Be sure it's turned off!—marking starting and stopping points, as above, and determining on which surfaces you'll have to rest the router to get all the spots. While it's easiest to machine individual pieces, you want to blend one part into another where they join, so some edges have to be machined in an assembled state.

(continued)

Above: The legs can be radiused before assembly. The stringer and cross members are best worked in an assembled state, with the router riding on their top surfaces. *Right:* Where their edges fair into the legs, they have to be worked with the router bearing on their side surfaces.

The most important thing shown in the photos is the sequence necessary to fair the leg and stringer together. The stringer's shape and the router base's diameter dictate that you do part of the stringer with the leg removed, and part with the leg in place. Note also at right that you must block up the assembly to gain clearance when working from the side.

Apply bar or pipe clamps to hold the parts firmly together. Remember that with resorcinol glue, great pressure is not necessary. Rather, you need to hold the parts together and leave them undisturbed until the glue cures.

6. Cut the joinery on the tabletop parts. Constructed of 5/4 (five-quarter) stock, the tabletop consists of nine 3-inch-wide slats, surrounded by a frame of 4-inch-wide boards. Mortises and tenons are used to join all the pieces together.

Start by cutting all the tabletop parts to the sizes specified by the "Cutting List."

The slats and ends are tenoned on both ends, and the tenons are shouldered on all four sides. Set up the table saw for tenoning by installing the dado cutter; the width

of cut isn't important except to minimize the number of passes required to complete a tenon. Set the depth of cut to $5/16$ inch, or just a hair less. Position the rip fence 1 inch from the *outside* of the cutter. When cutting the tenons, guide the workpieces with the miter gauge.

After all the tenons are cut, lay out the mortises on the ends and the sides, following the *Tabletop Joinery* drawing. If cut properly, the sides will be 1 inch longer than their finished length. Lay out the mortises so the extra length is divided, with half at each end.

TABLETOP JOINERY

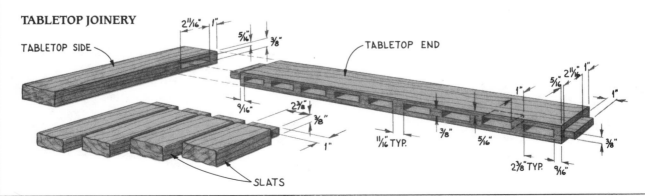

(The extra length serves two purposes here. By making the sides overlong, then trimming them flush with the ends after assembly, you ensure that one won't come up a tad short. Perhaps more important, there's only 5/16 inch of end-grain stock between the mortise and the butt end in the finished piece. Oak splits relatively easily, so having an extra ½ inch of stock there during assembly helps ensure that it doesn't break as you force the tenon in the mortise.)

Now cut the mortises. Since all are centered on the edge of 5/4 stock and all are ⅜ inch wide, set up the drill press with a fence to position the mortises uniformly. Set the depth stop so the mortises will be just over 1 inch deep. Drill out the waste with a ⅜-inch bit, perferably a Forstner bit. Lay out all the parts and mark the joints—which tenon goes into which mortise—then, using a chisel, pare the mortises to accommodate their tenons.

---

7. Assemble the tabletop.

Start by dry assembling the tabletop parts. Better to find out now about any problems with fit than after you've mixed and spread the glue. With the parts together, mark on the tabletop sides where the ends meet them.

Knock the assembly apart. With a router and a ¼-inch rounding-over bit, radius the edges of the slats. Radius the inner edges of the sides, too, beginning where one end meets the side and terminating where the other end meets it.

Repeat the assembly process, this time using glue. Capture the slats between the ends, then the ends between the sides. Apply pipe or bar clamps across the top and bottom of the tabletop. Use scrap as cauls between the clamp jaws and the wood to prevent damage.

After the glue sets and the clamps are off, cut and

Although many parts are coming together in precision-fitted joints, assembly of the tabletop is easily a one-person operation. A dry run is advisable; although you may have fit the joints individually, you need to make sure they fit in concert. A dry run is shown here.

Top: Lay out the parts on a benchtop. Align the slats carefully, then position the ends and sides. Note that all the joints are clearly and legibly marked, so each tenon goes into the mortise to which it was fitted. The letters on the tenons should be visible even after a coat of maroon resorcinol is applied, and the markings on the end will be erased by the finish sanding. Cock the tabletop end slightly, so you can progressively align each slat tenon, getting a corner of it into the appropriate mortise. As you move to the next slat and the next, previously started joints will be gradually closed up. Use a rubber mallet, which won't deface the wood. After all the tenons have been started into their mortises, drive the end home.

Repeat the process to install the other tabletop end. Then fit the tabletop sides to the assembly. The sides lock the assembly together, serving to clamp the slats between the ends. In the final gluing-up process, apply bar or pipe clamps across each end of the tabletop.

Bottom: Note the pencil mark on the side piece where the edge radiusing ends; the mark was made in a previous dry fitting, before the edge was routed. Note also that the extra length of the sides—though it is for other purposes—provides a means of dismantling the tabletop after a dry assembly; a mallet blow on the projecting corner will drive the side off its tenons.

attach the batten to the underside of the tabletop, centered across the slats. Drill and countersink pilot holes, then drill a screw through the batten into each side and slat. If you plan to use an umbrella with the table, use a hole saw to cut a pole hole through the center of the top and batten. Work from the top of the table until the hole saw's pilot bit penetrates the batten, then turn the assembly over and complete the hole from the bottom.

Finally, trim the "wild" ends of the sides with a saber saw or circular saw, then radius the outside edges of the tabletop with a router and a ¼-inch rounding-over bit.

8. Attach the tabletop to the base assembly.

Center the tabletop on the base. With hand screws, clamp the tabletop to the top cross members. Working underneath the table, drill and countersink pilot holes, then drive screws up through the top cross members into each of the slats. Also drive several screws through each of the top end members into the center slat.

9. Finish the table.

Sand the entire table. As noted in the "Builder's Notes," we used CWF, an exterior-grade penetrating oil. Following the manufacturer's instructions, we brushed on a liberal application, let it soak into the wood for about 20 minutes, then brushed on another coat. We let the finish dry for two or three days before putting the table to use.

Chairs

1. Make templates for laying out the legs, top back piece, and seat rail.

Several of the chair parts are involved or judgmental to lay out. To expedite the work, and to keep the parts as uniform as possible (since you'll be making four or more chairs), it's a good idea to make templates for these parts. Use thin plywood, posterboard, or heavy cardboard for the templates.

Prepare a template for the back leg first. On a piece of ¼-inch plywood the size of the leg blank (as specified by the "Cutting List"), mark the outline of the leg, as shown in the *Leg Layouts*. Include the mortises needed for the back assembly. With a saber saw, cut out the template, including the mortises. You will lay this template on the leg blank and trace around it with a pencil, and you need to be able to mark the mortises at the same time.

Do the back top piece and the seat rail templates next. Remember there are two sizes of back top pieces: one for the armchair, and a shortened one for the regular chair. Start with a piece of ¼-inch plywood that is the size of the tenoned blank for the particular part, *excluding* the tenons. Both these parts have a curved edge, and the contour of the curve is up to you (you could even decide you want no curve at all). Assuming you do want a

Make a template for the back legs from plywood or hardboard. Since there are eight back legs to lay out—if you build a set of four chairs—it saves time to lay the leg out once on "template stock," then use the template to lay out the eight legs. Mark the mortise size and locations on the template, then cut "windows" in the template so you can mark the mortises on the stock. The template can then be cut out with a saber saw.

LEG LAYOUTS

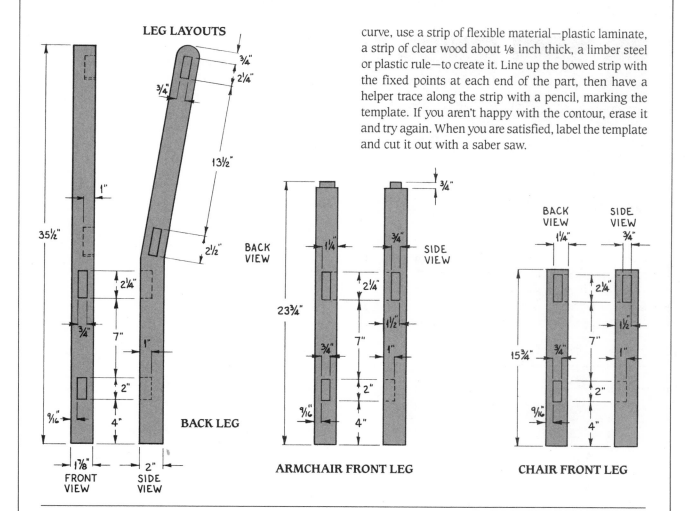

BACK LEG

ARMCHAIR FRONT LEG

CHAIR FRONT LEG

curve, use a strip of flexible material—plastic laminate, a strip of clear wood about ⅛ inch thick, a limber steel or plastic rule—to create it. Line up the bowed strip with the fixed points at each end of the part, then have a helper trace along the strip with a pencil, marking the template. If you aren't happy with the contour, erase it and try again. When you are satisfied, label the template and cut it out with a saber saw.

2. Make the front and back legs. Cut the front and back legs to the sizes specified by the "Cutting List." If you are duplicating our set, you need eight back leg blanks, two front legs for the armchair, and six front legs for the regular chairs.

Lay out the back legs using the template. Orient the template on the leg blank so both the top and bottom ends align with one edge of the blank and the kink aligns with the opposite edge; this should get the grain direction oriented in the leg for maximum strength (or

Using the template allows you to orient the leg layout quickly. You can try several different orientations, minimizing the impact of defects as much as possible, economizing on materials. Trace around the template and inside the mortise "windows." Keep close stock of the legs you lay out, to ensure that you produce a left and a right for each chair you make.

minimum weakness). Trace around the template, then cut the legs on the band saw. Sand the cut edges smooth.

Do the mortises next. The mortises to be cut into the front and back edges of the legs are all ¾ inch wide and 1+ inches deep, and centered across the stock. Consult the *Leg Layouts* for the length and positioning of the mortises. Remember that you need mirror-image pairs of legs. Laying them out in pairs will help ensure you get the required lefts and rights.

Chuck a ¾-inch bit in the drill press—a Forstner bit is particularly good for this sort of work, since it cuts a clean-sided, flat-bottomed hole. Clamp a fence to the

ARMCHAIR PLAN VIEWS

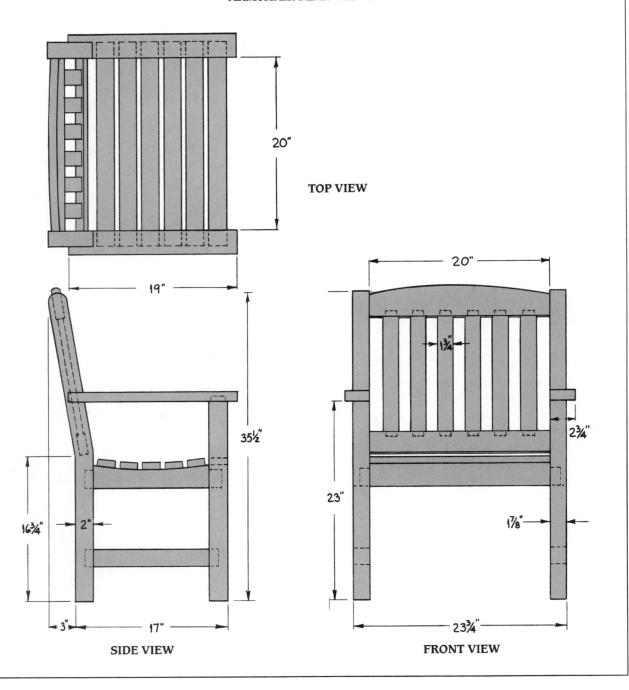

20"

TOP VIEW

19"

35½"

16¾"   2"

3"   17"

SIDE VIEW

20"

1¾"

2¾"

23"

1⅞"

23¾"

FRONT VIEW

drill press table, positioned to center the rough mortise across the width of the leg as much as possible. (You can then perfect the centering by drilling out each mortise, then turning the workpiece around and drilling it again with the opposite side against the fence.)

With the drill press set up in this way, you can

CHAIR PLAN VIEWS

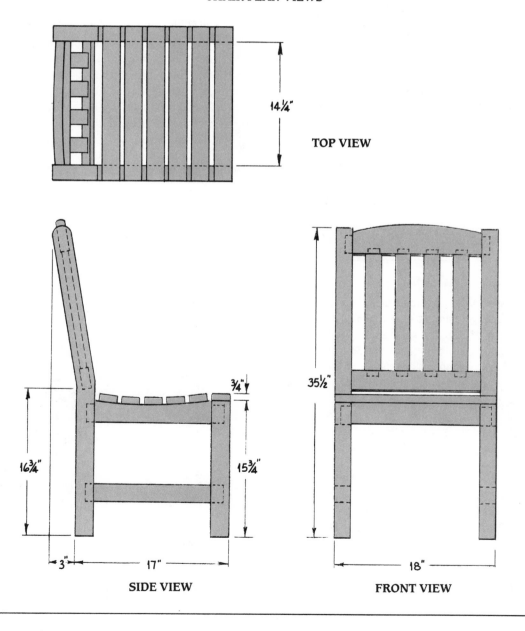

14¼"

TOP VIEW

¾"

16¾"   15¾"

3"   17"

35½"

18"

SIDE VIEW   **FRONT VIEW**

simplify mortise layout: Just mark the ends of the mortises, and the setup will establish the sides. Line up the leg blanks side by side. Mark the ends of the mortises on one leg, then use a square to extend them across the lot.

Rough out the seat and side rail mortises in the back legs first. If need be, cut a block from scrap to support the leg on the drill press table while you rough out the mortise closest to the kink. Then, rough out the same mortises in the front legs, and the back mortises in the back legs. After adjusting the fence position, rough out the apron mortises in the front legs. (You need to adjust the fence position because the legs are wider than they are thick.) As you cut these mortises, you'll notice that they break through into the mortises for the seat rails. Square up the mortises with a chisel, removing the ridges left by the round drill bit.

3. Cut and tenon the rails, aprons, and back parts.

The most efficient way to produce these parts is to cut them all to size, then to rough out all the tenons. Refining the tenons and cutting the arcs in the seat rails and the top back pieces will be done later. For now, just cut the parts to the sizes specified by the "Cutting List." Since four chairs will require stacks of parts—as many as 18 back slats, for example—be sure to label each piece as it leaves the saw, and make room for tidy stacks, one for each kind of part.

Next, cut tenons on both ends of each of these pieces. All of the tenons are cut using a table saw equipped with a dado cutter; it makes sense to maximize your use of the setup. As you did in other tenoning operations on this project, use the rip fence as a stop to set the tenon length. Set the depth of cut carefully, and test your setting on scraps of the working stock before cutting good parts. And always guide the workpiece over the dado cutter using the miter gauge.

- On the seat and side rails, cut tenons ¾ inch thick and 1 inch long, shouldered on two sides.
- On the aprons, top back pieces, and bottom back pieces, cut tenons ¾ inch thick and 1 inch long, also shouldered on two sides. NOTE that this stock is thinner than the rails, so reduce the depth of cut to get the desired tenon thickness.
- On the back slats, cut tenons ⅜ inch thick and ½ inch long. Shoulder them on all four sides.

The final operation is to cut the tenon on each front leg of the armchair that joins the leg to the arm.

4. Assemble the side frames.

Begin this process by matching sets of parts—a front and a back leg with a side and a seat rail. Then pair these sets of parts to make up chairs, adding to each chair an apron and all the parts for a back assembly. Mark each part, so you know which side frame and which chair it is for. Check carefully to ensure each chair will have a left and a right side frame.

Fit the rail tenons to their mortises next. Fit the side rails first. Pare the tenons with a chisel until a snug fit is attained.

Do the seat rails next. Each seat rail tenon must be shortened by cutting away ½ inch of it, forming a shoulder across the top. The front tenon must be mitered, as shown in the *Rail- and Apron-to-Leg Detail,* so it doesn't prevent the apron tenon from seating in its mortise. Both of these refinements can be made on the band saw. At the same time, you can also cut the concave arc for the seat. Use the template you made to

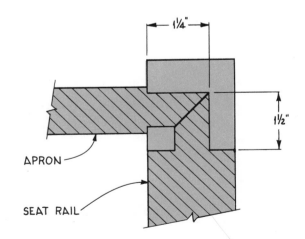

RAIL- AND APRON-TO-LEG DETAIL

lay this out. After cutting the rail, pare the tenons until they fit their respective mortises.

After dry assembling a frame to check how all the joints fit, apply resorcinol glue to mortises and tenons, assemble the frame, and apply clamps. Use scrap cauls between the clamp jaws and the wood to prevent damage. Be sure the frame is flat, not wracked or twisted. Continue this process until all the frames are assembled.

After the glue has set and the clamps are removed, radius all exposed edges with a router and a ¼-inch rounding-over bit.

5. Assemble the backs. Although the back slats have been tenoned, there are no mortises in the tops and bottoms for them to fit into. Lay out the mortises, as shown in the *Back Assembly Joinery* drawing. Rough out the mortises on the drill press, then square them with a chisel. While you are working with the chisel, fit the slat tenons to their mortises.

Now, before going any further, use the template for the top back pieces and lay out the convex arc on each top. Cut them on the band saw, then sand the edges smooth. With a router and a ¼-inch rounding-over bit, radius the top (curved) edges of the tops and the bottom edges of the bottoms. Radius all the edges of the slats.

Fit the tenons on the tops and bottoms to their mortises in the back legs. Then, to be sure the tenons will fit their mortises when the slats are in place, assemble each back unit without glue, both to finalize the fit of all the joints together, and to test the fit to the legs. When you are satisfied with the way everything fits, glue up each back assembly. Again, protect the wood from clamp damage with cauls. And be sure each back is flat and square.

One operation—squaring the roughed-out mortises—performed two ways: cutting with a chisel and shop-made mallet, and paring. In either case, the mortise has been roughed out with a drill bit in a drill press. The pencil marks across the workpiece indicate the "ends" of the mortise. The sides are established by the drill press setup, while the bit diameter matches the mortise width. The ridges between the holes need to be removed, the sides pared flat, and the corners squared.

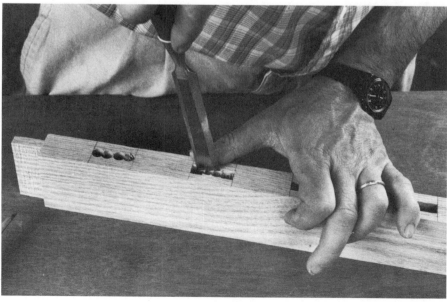

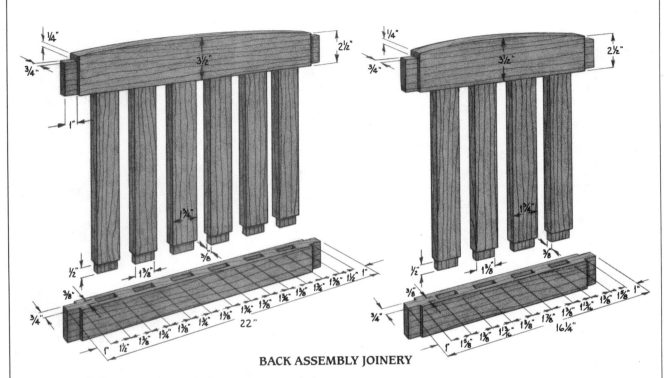

BACK ASSEMBLY JOINERY

If you are making several chairs—and you are—it is worthwhile to make a template of the back's curve and trace it onto the workpieces. Note that the mortises and the tenons have already been cut—done while the piece is square.

6. Assemble the chairs. Connect the two side frames at the back with the back assembly and at the front with the apron to form the chair frame. You should already have assured yourself that the back assemblies fit their respective side frames. You still have to fit the apron, however.

On the band saw, miter the end of the apron tenons, as you did the tenons on the seat rails. Also cut away ½ inch of the tenon height, forming a shoulder across the top of the tenon. If necessary, pare each tenon with a chisel to fit it to its mortise. Finally, radius the bottom edges with a router and a ¼-inch rounding-over bit.

After dry assembly has assured you the parts fit satisfactorily, glue them together. Apply clamps overnight; you can use bar or pipe clamps, or you can wrap a band clamp around the assembly. In any case, remember that great pressure is not going to improve the set of the resorcinol glue, so don't invest more effort here than is necessary.

7. **Cut and install the seat slats.** Cut the seat slats to the sizes specified by the "Cutting List." The slats for the regular chair are uniformly sized, but the armchair requires two different lengths. Radius the two exposed edges of each.

Attach five slats to the seat rail, spacing the slats equally. Attach the sixth slat to the front legs and apron. On the armchair, the front slat is shorter than the others and fits between the front legs; it is attached to the apron. Use glue and 1⅝-inch galvanized screws, driving the screws into counterbored pilot holes.

For a finished appearance, conceal the screw heads with wooden plugs, which you glue into the counterbores. Use a plug cutter—match it to the diameter of the counterbores—to cut the plugs from scrap stock.

8. **Cut and attach the arms to the armchair.** Cut the arms to the size specified by the "Cutting List." Radius the edges with a router and a ¼-inch rounding-over bit. Notch the back end of the arm to fit around the back leg. Lay out and cut the mortise for the front leg tenon.

Attach the arm by fitting the mortise onto the tenon, aligning the back end so the arm is level, and driving a screw through the edge of the arm into the back leg. Lock the arm on the leg tenon with a screw driven through the edge of the arm into the tenon. Counterbore both pilot holes, and cover the screws with wooden plugs.

9. **Finish the chairs.** Sand the chairs carefully. Apply two coats of an exterior-grade penetrating oil. Apply the second coat while the first coat is still wet, about 15 to 30 minutes after the initial application.

TERRACE ENSEMBLE UMBRELLA

This umbrella has been a big hit with everyone who has seen it. Though it looks devilishly complicated, it is quite simple to build, because it is cleverly done. It just takes time. Sewing the cover may be the most difficult part of the project.

The inspiration for the Terrace Umbrella was the Italian market umbrellas, which sell for about $500 to $700 a pop. A base costs extra, of course. Fred Matlack,

who designed and built our Terrace Umbrella, estimates that his version has less than $100 in materials in it, including the fabric for the cover and the oak for the base.

The umbrella uses a relatively small amount of oak, ripped into a pole and many slender arms and struts. But it requires (what seems like) a couple of pounds of hardware—angle plates, *lots* of picture hangers, some S-hooks, screws, and machine screws with locknuts.

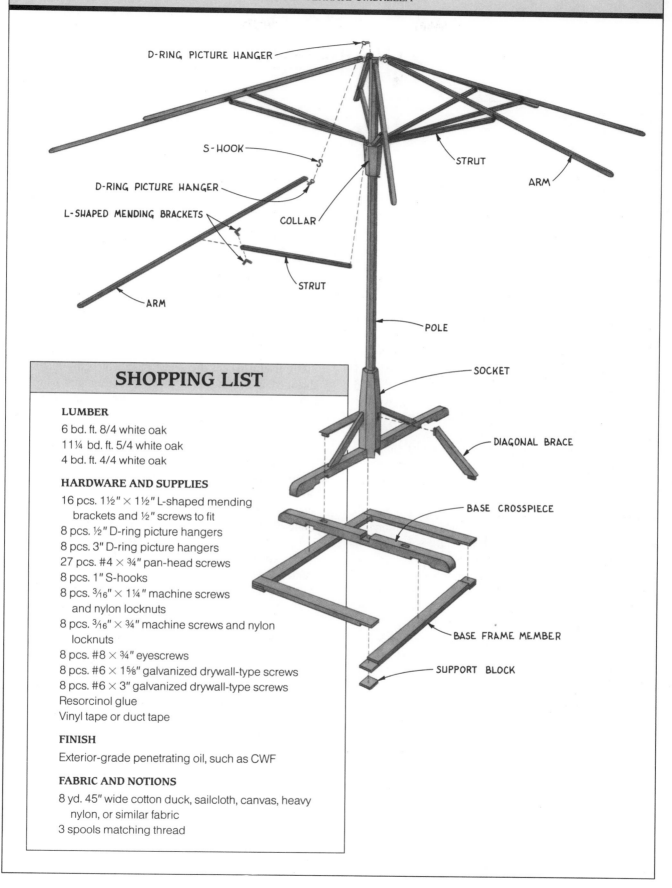

D-RING PICTURE HANGER

S-HOOK

STRUT

ARM

D-RING PICTURE HANGER

L-SHAPED MENDING BRACKETS

COLLAR

STRUT

ARM

POLE

SOCKET

DIAGONAL BRACE

BASE CROSSPIECE

BASE FRAME MEMBER

SUPPORT BLOCK

SHOPPING LIST

LUMBER

6 bd. ft. 8/4 white oak
11¼ bd. ft. 5/4 white oak
4 bd. ft. 4/4 white oak

HARDWARE AND SUPPLIES

16 pcs. 1½" × 1½" L-shaped mending
   brackets and ½" screws to fit
8 pcs. ½" D-ring picture hangers
8 pcs. 3" D-ring picture hangers
27 pcs. #4 × ¾" pan-head screws
8 pcs. 1" S-hooks
8 pcs. ³⁄₁₆" × 1¼" machine screws
   and nylon locknuts
8 pcs. ³⁄₁₆" × ¾" machine screws and nylon
   locknuts
8 pcs. #8 × ¾" eyescrews
8 pcs. #6 × 1⅝" galvanized drywall-type screws
8 pcs. #6 × 3" galvanized drywall-type screws
Resorcinol glue
Vinyl tape or duct tape

FINISH

Exterior-grade penetrating oil, such as CWF

FABRIC AND NOTIONS

8 yd. 45" wide cotton duck, sailcloth, canvas, heavy
   nylon, or similar fabric
3 spools matching thread

CUTTING LIST

PIECE	NUMBER	THICKNESS	WIDTH	LENGTH	MATERIAL
Umbrella					
Pole	1	1½"	1½"	96"	8/4 oak
Struts	8	½"	¾"	30"	4/4 oak
Arms	8	1"	1½"	56"	5/4 oak
Collar segments	8	1"	1½"	8"	5/4 oak
Umbrella Base (optional)					
Socket segments	8	1"	1½"	20"	5/4 oak
Base crosspieces	2	1⅞"	2⅜"	42"	8/4 oak
Diagonal braces	4	1"	1⅞"	16"	5/4 oak
Base frame members	4	¾"	1⅞"	30"	4/4 oak
Support blocks	4	½"	1⅞"	1⅞"	4/4 oak

Builder's Notes

Although it looks amazingly complex to build, you don't have to be a veteran woodworker to make the umbrella frame and optional umbrella base—the building techniques are pretty straightforward. But it will take more than a few hours to fashion all the parts and assemble them.

The umbrella consists of three elements: the frame, the base, and the fabric cover. The frame consists of a pole, eight arms that hang from the pole top, and eight struts that link the arms to a collar that slides up and down the pole. The engineering design requires the struts to ride against the pole, so when the umbrella is opened, the stress is on the strut and the pole. The cover consists of eight triangular panels that are stitched together. The cover has pockets that fit over the ends of the arms and secure it on the frame. You need the base if you plan to use the umbrella alone, rather than as a sunshade for the ensemble's table and chairs.

Materials. The frame and the base are made of white oak. If you are building just the umbrella, it may be worthwhile for you to skim through the "Builder's Notes" accompanying the Terrace Table and Chairs project on page 96. Information on buying oak is there.

Although the frame doesn't use much wood in its construction, it does use a lot of hardware, all of which should be available at a good hardware store. The photos and drawings that illustrate the construction of the umbrella show what the various hardware bits look like. And, of course, the "Shopping List" tells how many of each piece you should buy.

One interesting bit of hardware used in the frame is the stop nut. It has a nylon insert that keeps the nut in position, even when it isn't jammed tight. This is particularly useful where the screw onto which the nut is threaded is serving as a pivot. The elements being hinged can be given adequate operating clearance without the fear that the nut will work off the screw. In the case of the umbrella, the struts can be left loose enough to pivot easily.

Tools and techniques. The tools used to make the umbrella aren't unusual, and the techniques used add up to standard woodworking. The one stumper was the sliding collar. How to make it—gluing up beveled strips—came easily. How to shape it came hard. Throughout much of the construction, Fred worked with a short blocky collar, which is seen in a number of the procedural photos. The obvious solution to its ungainly appearance was to taper it, but how? Doing it on the jointer would be too hazardous, on the band saw, too complicated. The hand plane was the solution.

Sewing. Making the fabric umbrella cover requires only basic sewing skills. Fred Matlack stitched up the cover shown using a typical home sewing machine. A heavy-duty commercial model isn't required. The cover is, however, a daunting project if you've never used a sewing machine before.

The umbrella shown has a cover made of duck, a cotton fabric. It isn't too heavy, but it isn't waterproof either. For our purposes, that seems fine, since the umbrella is intended to shade you from the sun, rather than shield you from the rain. Sailcloth or a lightweight canvas would be a good choice. They are heavier than the duck; while that makes them more durable, it also makes them more demanding to sew.

TOOL LIST

Band saw
Belt sander
Chisel
Clamps
Drill
   ³⁄₁₆" dia. bit
   ½" dia. bit.
   Pilot hole bit
Finishing sander
Hand plane
Jack plane
Jointer
Paintbrush
Planer
Router
Router, table-mounted
   ¼" rounding-over bit
   ¾" straight bit
Rubber mallet
Ruler
Sandpaper
Saw for crosscutting
Sawhorses
Screwdriver
Sewing machine
Snug hand clamp
Steel square
Table saw
   Dado cutter
   Miter gauge
Tack cloth
Tape measure
Try square
Vise
Wrenches

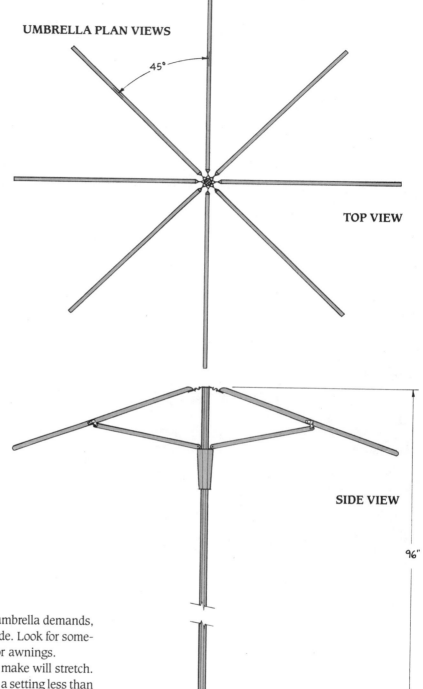

UMBRELLA PLAN VIEWS

45°

TOP VIEW

SIDE VIEW

96"

If canvas is what you feel your umbrella demands, consider seriously having a cover made. Look for someone who makes and sells draperies or awnings.

Bear in mind that the cover you make will stretch. Fred fitted the cover to the umbrella at a setting less than fully open, knowing that it would stretch. He didn't want it to end up too loose and billowy. The first few times the umbrella was opened fully, the fabric was taut, but, as you can see in the photo, it now has a loose, casual appearance.

Note: All the photos show the proper procedure, but some of them reflect the development process. For example, the sliding collar was originally short and straight. The photos depicting the gluing-up process, the installation of the struts, and the drilling of the support-pin holes in the pole all show the original collar. Afterwards, Fred made a second, longer, tapered collar, which is seen in the photo of the finished umbrella.

Umbrella Frame

1. Make the umbrella pole. Start by cutting the pole blank to the dimensions specified by the "Cutting List."

The pole must be cut to an octagonal shape, with each face ⅝ inch wide. You can use a band saw or jointer to accomplish this, but we did it on the table saw. Clamp an expendable board to the rip fence to protect it and the blade. Retract the blade, tilt it to 45 degrees, turn the saw on, and carefully raise the blade until it just cuts into the fence. On a scrap the same thickness as the workpiece, make a test cut and measure the width of the cut face. If it is less than ⅝ inch wide, the fence is too close to the blade. If it is more than ⅝ inch wide, the fence is too far away from the blade. Adjust the fence's position accordingly. When you've got the setup, cut the pole.

Note: This setup is something of a compromise. You do have to remove the saw guard, but the top of the blade is buried in the fence facing at all times, and the workpiece covers the blade through most of the cut, protecting the fingers. The compromise is kickback of the waste. The waste will be trapped between the blade and the fence, and will get hurled back. Be forewarned and stand well to the side, so you don't get speared.

An alternative setup would be to feed the work between the blade and the fence. That would eliminate the kickback, but would expose a sizable portion of the blade throughout the cut. Moreover, with this alternative setup, the workpiece would be ruined if it drifted from the fence.

When the pole is completed, sand it smooth and apply two coats of an exterior-grade penetrating oil.

Rip a ⅝-inch-wide chamfer along each edge of the pole blank to form an octagonal pole. Cut the chamfers by clamping an auxiliary wood fence to the fence of the table saw, setting the blade to 45 degrees, and raising it (with the saw running) just into the board, as shown. Cut test chamfers on a scrap of the correct thickness and adjust the fence (retracting the blade each time you move the fence, then resetting it) until the saw cuts a ⅝-inch-wide chamfer. Then cut the pole. **Caution:** When cutting chamfers with this setup, the waste pieces tend to kick back, so don't stand directly behind the blade.

2. Make the struts and arms. Cut the eight struts to the dimensions specified by the "Cutting List." Study the *Strut Layout.* Cut a 3/16-inch-wide by ¾-inch-deep slot in one end of each strut, then drill a 3/16-inch-diameter hole through both ends. Round off the ends last. You can do this with a saber saw or on a band saw, but it may be easiest to stack and clamp the struts in a vise, then freehand a rounded profile on the ends with a belt sander. By stacking the struts, you'll get a fairly uniform profile on all of them. The purpose here is not to duplicate a perfect radius, but to create a smooth curve that will index smoothly against the pole and arm as the umbrella is raised and lowered.

Next, cut the arms to the dimensions specified by the "Cutting List." Study the *Arm Layout.* Line up all eight arms on their sides and pencil an alignment mark across them, 28 inches from the "pole end." Roll them over and duplicate the mark on the opposite face. Round off the pole ends, as shown, and taper and round the outer ends. As you did with the struts, stack and clamp the arms in a vise, then work them with a belt sander. The idea is to soften the profiles, not duplicate a specific shape.

Do any necessary touch-up sanding on both the struts and the arms, then apply two coats of an exterior-grade penetrating oil.

When the finish is dry, mount two L-shaped mending brackets on each arm. The top holes in the brackets should be aligned to accept the bolt that will fasten the strut to the arm.

Finally, fasten the 3-inch D-ring picture hangers to the pole end of the arms using pan-head screws.

STRUT LAYOUT

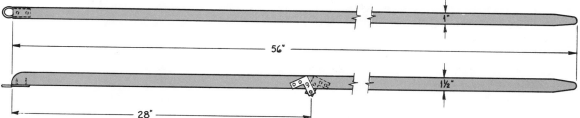

ARM LAYOUT

When attaching the mending brackets to the arms—one to each side—orient them so the holes for the strut-mounting bolt are aligned but the bracket-mounting screws are offset. Note that the bolt hole is aligned with the pencil mark on the arm, and that the outside corner of the bracket is flush with one edge of the arm and the inside end corner with the other edge. When the time comes, you'll be able to slip a machine screw through the brackets and struts.

TIP

Use a tenoning jig on your table saw to cut the slots in the struts. The blade will produce the required 3/16-inch slot in two passes, simultaneously centering the slot across the width of the strut.

The typical shop-made tenoning jig—see the plan—straddles the rip fence and has a fixed stop against which to clench (or, better, clamp) the workpiece. When positioning the fence, measure from the face of the jig to the blade. The depth of the slot is determined, of course, by the depth-of-cut setting on the table saw.

In this application, stand the strut on end, side against the jig, locked against the stop. Push the jig along the fence, passing the strut over the blade. Turn the strut 180 degrees and make a second pass. This will bring the slot to the full width desired, and ensure that you have the same thickness of stock on either side of the slot.

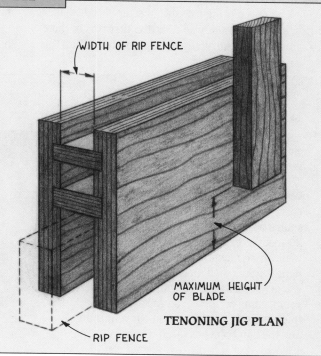

TENONING JIG PLAN

3. **Make the collar.** The collar is made up of eight segments that, when glued up, form an octagonal tube to fit over the pole. Sized properly, the collar should be just loose enough to move up and down the pole freely. As you can see from some of the how-to photos, the basic collar is pretty blocky. So once the collar is glued up, you'll want to plane it to a tapered shape.

Begin by studying the *Collar Detail.* It is easiest to cut uniform segments if you bevel one length of stock, then crosscut the eight segments from it. Rip the stock to the size specified by the "Cutting List," then bevel the edges, as indicated in the drawing, at 22½ degrees. You can rip the bevels on the table saw, using a setup similar to that used to chamfer the umbrella pole. Crosscut the segments to length.

To assemble the collar, lay the segments side by side on two strips of tape, as shown in the photo. Plastic tape is best, because it has some elasticity, but duct tape, masking tape, or any other tape will do. Before applying glue, roll up the segments and tape the bundle. Now you can test how it fits on the pole: It must be loose enough to slide easily, but without excessive play. You decide what "excessive" is; it's your umbrella. If the collar is too tight, cut new segments. Too loose, plane them a little. When the fit is satisfactory, open up the bundle, apply glue to each mating face, then reroll the bundle.

When the glue dries, use a hand plane to taper the collar to the final dimensions. Because the collar is fully tapered, you need to cut a couple of scrap-wood wedges to help secure it in the vise after the first two or three facets are tapered. An alternative approach is to butt the

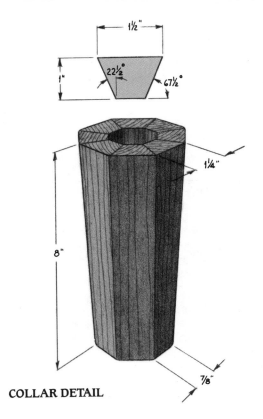

COLLAR DETAIL

collar's bottom end against a bench dog, then clamp it to the benchtop with a speed clamp or C-clamp, the clamp's jaw inside the collar. After the collar is suitably tapered, radius the top and bottom edges with a rounding-over bit in a table-mounted router.

Do any touch-up sanding that is necessary, then apply two coats of an exterior-grade penetrating oil.

TIP

To truss up the sliding collar while the glue set, we used a Snug band clamp. It is a ½-inch-wide strip of mildly elastic plastic. When you buy it (Woodcraft Supply, 210 Wood County Industrial Park, P.O. Box 1686, Parkersburg, WV 26102-1686 is the only source we know of, by the way), you get a 20-foot piece, but you can cut it into somewhat shorter lengths. Just wrap the band tightly around and around the collar. When you get to the last loop, wrap the band over your thumb, as shown, so you can tuck the free end under the band. Pull out your thumb, and the band pinches the end.

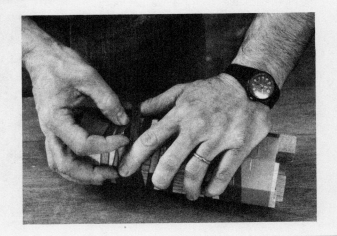

Assembling the sliding collar. Cut the eight pieces and lay them on two pieces of tape, as shown. With the tape linking them together, the segments roll right up in proper alignment. The excess tape wraps around, keeping them bundled. Thus dry assembled, you can test the collar's fit on the pole. If it is okay, peel back the tape, unroll the bundle, and spread glue on the mating surfaces.

4. Attach the struts to the collar.

Each strut is connected to the sliding collar by a ¾-inch machine screw run through an eyescrew. The idea is to have the strut actually ride against the pole, so the stresses are transferred directly from the strut to the pole, not to the collar. The eyescrews need to be positioned so that happens.

It works best to install one strut at a time. Drill a pilot hole, then turn an eyescrew into place. Slip the strut's slot over the eyescrew, insert the screw, and secure it with a stop nut. Remember that the stop nut will hold its position on the screw without being jammed tight, so the strut can be allowed to pivot freely. Repeat the process until all the struts are installed.

TIP

Working space is at a premium, and it is tough to get good leverage on the eyescrews. Use a 10d nail as a lever.

The last strut is tricky to install. To provide working room for your screwdriver, you need to align the last eyescrew almost parallel to one of its neighbors. After the screw is set, you simply twist the strut into proper position.

5. Attach the arms to the top of the pole.

Each arm is attached to the pole with two D-ring picture hangers and an S-hook. One hanger is attached to the arm (this you've already done), and the other to the top of the pole. Snag each ring in a loop of the S-hook, then crimp the loops closed.

The first step in doing this is to fasten the eight hangers to the top of the pole. It's really much easier than it looks. Drill a pilot hole in the very center of the top of the pole. Run one pan-head screw through the top holes of all eight hangers, driving it partway into the pilot hole. Because all eight arms will be attached to this one screw, the stresses on it will be equalized, thus minimizing the chance that the pole will split.

Spread the hangers out around the pole-top, arranging a D-ring picture hanger over each flat. Drive a pan-head screw through each hanger and tighten it. Drill a pilot hole for each screw, of course. Finally,

tighten the center screw.

Attach the arms next. Crimp an S-hook onto each arm's D-ring. Then hook an arm onto each D-ring on the pole, crimping it in place. It helps to clamp the pole in a vise while you do this.

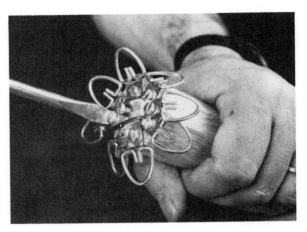

The top of the pole is congested with hardware. The center screw is the first one started, the last one tightened. It penetrates all eight picture hangers, so that the stresses are equalized around it, preventing the pole from splitting. Start that first screw, then arrange the connectors so one D-ring is aligned with each flat on the pole. Drive an additional screw through each connector, then tighten the center screw.

TIP

When crimping the S-hooks, use locking-grip pliers. The jaws of these pliers can be preset; they'll snap to that setting when the handles are squeezed. You can thus give each S-hook a uniform crimp (if such details are important to you).

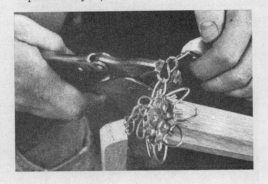

---

6. Complete the umbrella frame. Join the pole-arm assembly to the collar-strut assembly. To do this, secure the collar in a vise with the struts splayed out around it. Slide the pole into it. One by one, align the struts between the mounting brackets on the arms and bolt them in place. Again, use machine screws and stop nuts.

Finally, drill a series of holes through the pole for a support pin. You push the collar up the pole, insert a pin in a hole, then let the collar settle back onto the pin. While you could pick the setting you like and drill a hole at that setting only, you'll get a better umbrella if you have several stops leading up to the maximum opening.

Left: Link strut and arm with a machine screw and stop nut. The engineering of the umbrella is pretty clear here: The weight of the umbrella is transferred from the arms to the struts through direct contact. The assembly bolts serve merely as pivot points, not as weight bearers.

Right: To select positions for support-pin holes, you can work with a ruler and pencil, or you can be more direct. With the pole secured in a vise, slide the collar up the pole. When the setting "looks right," drill a hole. In any case, make a range of holes.

Umbrella Base

The design of the base puts eight feet on the ground to virtually eliminate tippiness. There are two main crosspieces cross-lapped together. These provide four of the feet. Next, a secondary framework is half-lapped together and fitted to the bottom of the first structure.

Now you have eight feet on the ground. A socket is added to accept the umbrella pole.

Build the eight-footed base first, then make the socket and fit it to the base. Finally, add the diagonal braces.

1. **Prepare the stock.** Unless you have purchased surfaced stock, prepare your lumber for use, jointing and planing it to reduce it to working thicknesses and to smooth the faces and edges. As you work, it is often productive to crosscut the various parts to a rough length, which is about an inch or two longer than the size specified by the "Cutting List." Be sure you label these pieces. Don't do too much to size the stock for the socket until you are ready to bevel-rip the segments.

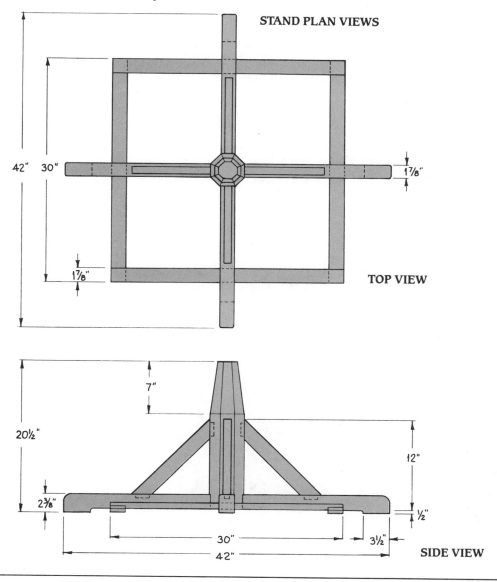

STAND PLAN VIEWS

TOP VIEW

SIDE VIEW

2. **Make the crosspieces.** Cut the crosspieces to the final dimensions specified by the "Cutting List." Lay out the recess in the bottom edge that forms the feet. (See the *Stand Side View.*) Cut the recesses on the band saw.

Cut the cross-lap joint that connects the two cross-pieces. Cutting the laps with a router and straight bit may be the least problematic approach. If you work on the table saw with a dado cutter, the two members are effectively different thicknesses because of the recesses that form the feet, so you need to lay out the laps fully and work carefully.

3. **Make the secondary frame.** Cut (or trim) the four secondary frame members to size, then cut half-lap joints at each end of each piece. Assemble the members to form a square frame, as shown in the *Stand Top View*. As you glue up this assembly, be sure the frame is square and flat.

Without glue, assemble the two crosspieces, and turn the assembly upside down on a flat surface. Position the secondary frame on it, also upside down. Mark where the frame members intersect the crosspieces, scribing along both sides of each frame member on the crosspieces. Notch the crosspieces to accept the frame; the scribed lines delineate the shoulders of the notches. You won't be able to cut these notches (or laps) with a router, because of their proximity to the feet, so cut them on the table saw with a dado cutter. All are cut at the same depth-of-cut setting.

Cut the support blocks and attach them to the secondary frame, one at each corner. You may want to cut the blocks a bit on the fat side, then plane or sand them to fit. You want all eight "feet" on the ground.

4. **Make the base socket.** First, cut the socket segments to the dimensions specified by the "Cutting List." As you do this, rip converging bevels on the edges, as shown in the *Base Socket Detail*. Cut these bevels at 22½ degrees. (These segments are the same as the sliding collar segments but for their length.)

As you did in making the sliding collar, lay out the segments on two pieces of duct or packing tape. Roll up the segments to check how tight the seams will be and to see if the pole will fit into it okay. Make any adjustments necessary, either by planing material from mating surfaces, or by cutting new segments. When the parts are right, apply glue to the mating surfaces, roll the segments into the socket, seal the tape, and apply a band clamp.

Lay out and cut the socket's fingers next. Start on the socket's bottom end, scribing lines as shown in the *Base Socket Detail*. First scribe "diameter" lines to divide the area into quarters. Measure $15/16$ inch to each side of these two lines and scribe four more lines. These four lines will outline four triangular areas at the edges of the

BASE SOCKET DETAIL

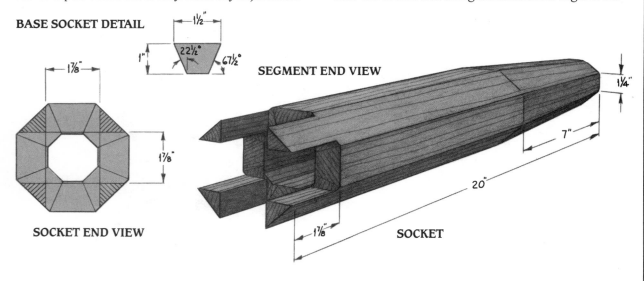

SEGMENT END VIEW

SOCKET END VIEW

SOCKET

Here's how to lay out the cuts that create the four fingers that "clutch" the base assembly.

Left: With the socket blank in a vise, twice scribe its diameter, dividing the end into quarters (in the photo, the ruler covers the second line). *Center:* Measure and scribe a second set of lines—four in all—which are $^{15}/_{16}$ inch to each side of the first two lines. *Right:* The photo shows—among other things—the areas delineated by the layout lines. The fingers are the triangular areas NOT X'ed. Every segment that has an X is to be cut away.

With the fingers delineated on the end of the socket, extend lines onto the socket sides. With the tongue of a small steel square butted against the end of the socket, scribe along the inner edge of the body (or blade). Measure and mark how deep to cut along the line.

socket. These are the fingers. To complete the layout, extend lines from the corners of these triangles 1⅞ inches up the sides of the socket, thus establishing the length of the fingers. Connect these lines around the perimeter of the socket. To avoid confusion as you cut at the band saw, outline the four triangular areas that are the ends of the fingers, and mark the waste—Fred used Xs.

Before actually cutting, double-check your layout against the actual dimensions of the crosspieces to assure a snug fit. Cut out the waste on the band saw. To ensure a snug fit, cut shy of your layout lines. Check the fit, and trim on the band saw or pare with a chisel, as appropriate.

Clamp the nearly completed socket in a vise and taper the top end with a hand plane. The taper should start just above the point where the diagonal braces will be mortised in. (See the *Stand Side View*.)

Hand plane the socket to get the taper. Clamp the socket in a vise and work with a jack plane. The degree of taper is an aesthetic judgment. The *Base Socket Detail* gives some indication of what we did, but you can alter the profile of the taper to suit yourself.

---

5. **Make the diagonal braces.** Cut the four diagonal braces to size, mitering the ends at 45 degrees in the process. The tenons are surprisingly easy to cut on the table saw. The miter gauge—set to the desired 45 degree angle—guides the workpiece and establishes the proper tenon angle. The distance from the (outside of the) blade to the fence is the length of the tenon. The first cut, made with the end of the workpiece butted against the fence, establishes the tenon shoulder. Repeated subsequent cuts remove the waste.

Set the depth of cut to properly establish the thickness of the tenon. After you've cut the tenon, redirect it by nipping off the corners, as shown in the *Brace Tenon Detail*.

BRACE TENON DETAIL

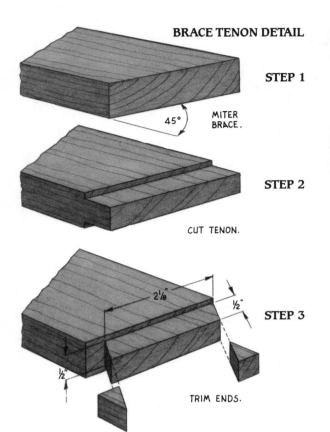

STEP 1

45°   MITER
        BRACE.

CUT TENON.

STEP 2

2⅛"   ½"

½"

STEP 3

TRIM ENDS.

Cut the brace tenons on the table saw, using the fence and miter gauge to guide the work and control the cut. Here, one side has been cut, and the second side is just being started. Angling the miter gauge as shown helps hold the workpiece to the fence; if the gauge were angled the opposite way, the work would tend to drift away from the fence as you cut. The wood backing on the miter gauge—a common enhancement—offers better support for the workpiece.

6. Cut the mortises for the diagonal braces.
Lay out the mortise locations on the crosspieces and the socket, as shown in the *Stand Side View*. To establish the starting point for measurements on the crosspieces, set the socket in place and scribe a line along the socket on each crosspiece. Measure from this line to the far end of the mortise, then measure back to establish the mortise length.

To cut the mortises, bore out most of the waste on the drill press (or with a portable drill and a 90-degree guide). Set the stop to make the mortise depth equal the tenon length plus about ¹⁄₁₆ inch (to provide a glue pocket). Drill a series of holes inside the mortise lines, using a bit equal to the mortise width. Then clean up the walls of the mortise with a chisel.

TIP

Getting the diagonal braces to fit their mortises precisely is pretty tricky because of the way the brace position shifts as the piece seats against the socket and crosspieces. You can circumvent fitting problems if you (a) wait to trim the tenons until after the mortises are cut, and (b) cut the mortises short. Fit the tenons to the socket mortises first. Then, with the braces fitted to the socket, lower it onto the crosspieces and mark the tenons for trimming.

7. Assemble the entire base. Dry assemble all the parts one last time to make sure everything fits. Radius the exposed edges of all parts with a router and a ¼-inch rounding-over bit. To ensure that the rounded edges blend into one another where parts connect, mark these spots while the unit is still dry assembled.

To assemble the base, first glue the crosspieces together, then add the secondary frame. Glue the diagonal braces to the socket, then lower the brace/socket assembly onto the crosspiece assembly.

After the glue has dried, touch-up sand the assembly and apply an exterior-grade penetrating oil.

Dry assemble the base to confirm how the parts fit. Work in this sequence: Join the crosspieces and fit the secondary frame in place. With the braces seated in the mortises cut into the socket, settle the brace-socket unit into place atop the base assembly. The fingers will settle into the crotches of the crosspieces, and the tenons on the braces will drop into their mortises. A rubber mallet is a good persuader.

Umbrella Covering

The fabric cover is a relatively simply sewing project. (Unless, of course, you've never sewn before.) The cover is made up of eight triangular panels, two octagonal patches, and eight small pockets that fit over the ends of the arms. You must hem all the pieces, then sew them together. If you *do* sew, the most difficult part of this project is dealing with all the layers of cloth, and manipulating the cover as it reaches completion—it is 10 feet in diameter, after all.

1. **Cut the parts from the fabric.** The cover is composed of eight wedge-shaped panels and an octagonal pole patch. Eight small pockets, each of which fits over the end of an arm, are sewn between panels. These pockets keep the cover on the umbrella. Study the *Cover Plan;* cut eight panels, eight pockets, and two caps to the sizes shown.

2. **Stitch up the arm pockets.** Each of the eight 6-inch-square pieces of fabric is hemmed, folded, and sewn into a pocket that fits onto an arm of the umbrella.

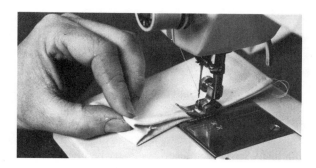

Start by sewing a flat, simple hem along one edge, as shown in the *Pocket Sewing Sequence.* Fold the piece across the hem and fold in the two adjoining edges. Starting at the hemmed end, sew the folded edges of the pocket together. As you reach the unhemmed end, fold in the ends of the fabric, then finish the seam, turning the pocket as you sew to continue the seam across the end, closing the end. The hemmed end remains open.

The pockets that fit over the arms and hold the cover onto the umbrella framework are made from a single square of fabric. The cloth is folded in half and sewed along two edges to form the pocket. As you sew, fold the cut edges of the cloth in so they won't unravel. Here the end edges and corners are folded in as the stitching progresses along the folded-in sides.

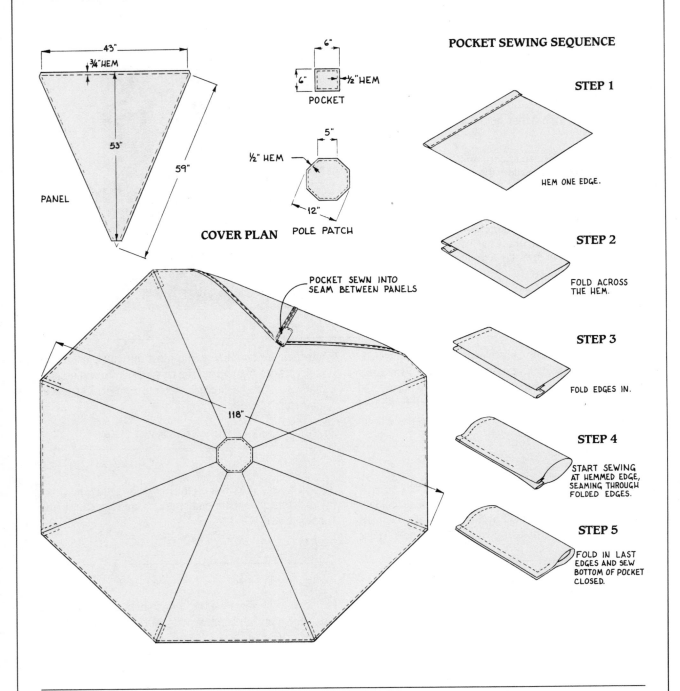

43"
¾" HEM
53"
59"
PANEL

6"
6"
½" HEM
POCKET

5"
½" HEM
12"
POLE PATCH

COVER PLAN

118"

POCKET SEWN INTO
SEAM BETWEEN PANELS

POCKET SEWING SEQUENCE

STEP 1
HEM ONE EDGE.

STEP 2
FOLD ACROSS
THE HEM.

STEP 3
FOLD EDGES IN.

STEP 4
START SEWING
AT HEMMED EDGE,
SEAMING THROUGH
FOLDED EDGES.

STEP 5
FOLD IN LAST
EDGES AND SEW
BOTTOM OF POCKET
CLOSED.

3. **Hem and sew together the panels.** Sew a double hem—the kind shown in the *Panel Hemming Sequence*—around the edges of each cover panel. As you do this, you'll discover the vexation of sewing "on the bias." Fabric has a grain, and it folds easily on the grain. But on the bias, which is crossing the grain, the cloth wants to unroll, making hemming pretty exasperating.

After the panels are hemmed, you must sew them together along their sides, sandwiching an arm pocket into each seam at the outer perimeter. To sew the panels, lay one on top of another, face to face. Line up the hemmed edges carefully, then stitch along the existing hem stitches, joining the two panels together. Start at the inside and sew toward the outer perimeter. When you get within 8 inches of the end, stop and tuck an arm pocket into the seam. The pocket's open end should face the cover's center, and the pocket itself should hang out of the seam like a tab. Line up the seam of the pocket with the panels' hems and sew. Work slowly because the needle must go through some 14 layers of fabric—eight layers in the hems of the pocket and six in the two panel hems. Finish the seam, sewing the pocket and two panels together.

Now unfold the panels and spread a third atop them, again face to face. Line up the hemmed edges and sew the third to the second. Again, as you near the outer perimeter, incorporate a pocket into the seam. In like manner, add the fourth panel and pocket, fifth, and so on, until the entire cover is sewn together.

Finally, bind the untidy ends of the panels along the pocket seam with a buttonhole or zig-zag stitch to reinforce and finish off the seam. Trim these ends with scissors.

PANEL HEMMING SEQUENCE

STEP 1 DOUBLE-HEM EDGES OF THE PANELS.

FOLD ONCE,

STEP 2 AND AGAIN,

STEP 3 THEN STITCH.

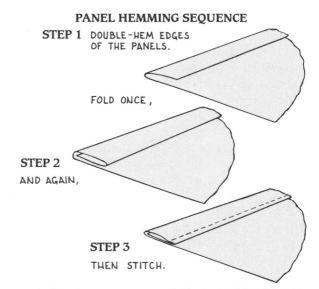

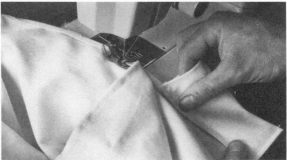

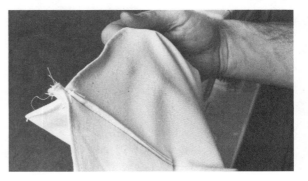

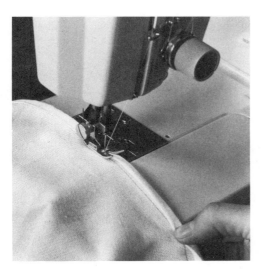

Above: Hemming the cover panels is as easy as this. With an ordinary #2 pencil, draw a line about ¾ inch from the cut edge. Fold the cloth once, then again, bringing the fold to the line. Sew along the centerline of the fold.

Top right: As you sew the panels together, tuck an arm pocket into the seam, just at the outer perimeter of the cover. The open end of the pocket faces the center of the umbrella, the hems all overlap, and the pocket is on the underside of the cover (with all the hems). *Center right:* When you are done, the seam will end in an untidy clump. *Bottom right:* Using a buttonhole stitch, reinforce the corner, then trim off the frayed edges and errant threads.

4. **Finish off the cover's center hole.** The center of the cover is an untidy opening—frayed seams and hems and stray threads. If you fit the cover on the umbrella frame now, the pole and the hardware connecting the arms to it will jut through the hole. A two-piece octagonal patch fits over (and under) this hole, providing a reinforced cover over the pole top and handsomely finishing off the cover.

Double-hem the two octagonal pieces of cloth already cut for the patch. Lay one patch atop the other, faces out, and carefully align the hems. Sew a circular seam, about 4 inches in diameter, in the center of the two patches, joining them together. Fit the patch into the hole, and arrange one layer of the patch overlapping the cover underneath and the other overlapping on top. Center and align the patch, and stitch around its edges, fastening it to the cover.

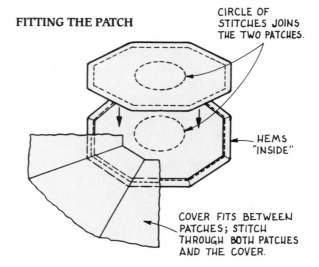

FITTING THE PATCH

CIRCLE OF STITCHES JOINS THE TWO PATCHES.

HEMS "INSIDE"

COVER FITS BETWEEN PATCHES; STITCH THROUGH BOTH PATCHES AND THE COVER.

This last operation is easier said than done. Starting at the outer perimeter of the nearly 10-foot-diameter cover, you have to carefully work it under the foot of the sewing machine until the central area is beneath the needle. As you pull the cover under the foot, roll it up to make it a bit easier to maneuver through the sewing machine.

When the cover is all done, the top looks like this. The loose ends of the panels are concealed by the octagonal center patch. The patch's corners are aligned with the seams between panels, and the whole is neatly stitched together.

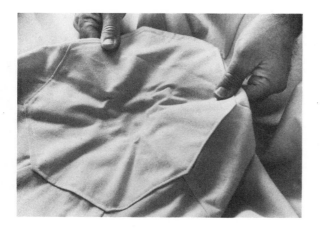

5. **Fit the covering onto the frame.** With the umbrella pole clamped upright either in a vise or in the base, open it about halfway. Drape the covering over the open frame, and slip the pockets over the ends of the arms, starting with one arm and working around the circumference of the frame.

After you've installed the cover, push up on the collar to open the umbrella more fully and to stretch the cover tight.

TERRACE ENSEMBLE TEA TROLLEY

The final piece in the Terrace Ensemble is this tea trolley. Whether you like tea or not, you'll find this little cart handy for keeping snacks, beverages, and table settings close at hand. This furniture set is definitely upper crust stuff, hence the British affectation on the name.

The design of the trolley echoes the slatted tabletop and the arched chairs. Like the rest of the pieces in the set, it's made of oak. The wheels and casters are part of a purchased set. While the white plastic casters seem a little retrograde for this project, the back wheels look great and save a lot of work.

The project includes a separate tea tray, an optional part of the trolley. Two of the trays will fit on the top of the trolley, so you might make two as part of the project. But then, you don't have to make any.

TOP SLATS

TOP END RAIL

HANDLE

TOP SIDE RAIL

SIDE APRON

END APRON

BACK LEG

BOTTOM SLATS

SIDE RAIL

END RAIL

FRONT LEG

SHOPPING LIST—TROLLEY

LUMBER
10 bd. ft. 5/4 white oak
7¾ bd. ft. 4/4 white oak
1 pc. 1⅜" dia. × 36" white oak dowel*

HARDWARE AND SUPPLIES
Tea cart wheel kit*
2 pcs. #6 × 1⅝" flathead wood screws
6 pcs. #6 × 2" flathead wood screws
8 pcs. #6 × 1⅝" galvanized drywall-type screws
Resorcinol glue

FINISH
Exterior-grade penetrating oil finish, such as CWF

*Available from Constantine's, 2050 Eastchester Road, Bronx, NY 10461 (1-800-223-8087).

CUTTING LIST—TROLLEY

PIECE	NUMBER	THICKNESS	WIDTH	LENGTH	MATERIAL
Front legs	2	1"	2"	22¼"	5/4 oak
Back legs	2	1"	2"	19¼"	5/4 oak
Side aprons	2	1"	4½"	29"	5/4 oak
Side rails	2	1"	2¼"	29"	5/4 oak
End aprons	2	1"	4½"	15⅜"	5/4 oak
End rails	2	1"	2¼"	15⅜"	5/4 oak
Bottom slats	5	¾"	2⅜"	30"	4/4 oak
Top side rails	2	1"	2"	37½"	5/4 oak
Top end rails	2	1"	2"	20¾"	5/4 oak
Top slats	7	¾"	2½"	33"	4/4 oak
Handle	1	1⅜" dia.		21"	oak dowel

TROLLEY PLAN VIEWS

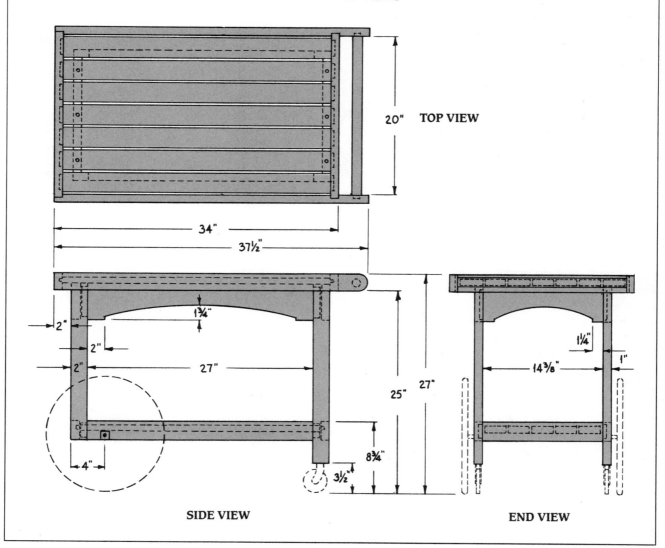

TOP VIEW

SIDE VIEW

END VIEW

Builder's Notes

A companion project to this chapter's table and chairs, the tea trolley is constructed with the same materials and uses the same tools and techniques as the earlier project. If you are building only this project from the ensemble, then by all means read the "Builder's Notes" accompanying the Terrace Table and Chairs project on page 96.

The elements unique to this piece of the ensemble are the wheels and casters. Don't worry—you won't have to make them. We purchased the elaborate rubber-tired spoke wheels as a part of a set that included the axle, hardware, and front casters as well. Because oak wheels weren't available—only cherry, maple, and walnut—we selected the wood (maple) that most closely matched the color of our white oak.

TOOL LIST

Chisels	Planer
Clamps	Router
Drill	¼" rounding-over bit
Pilot hole bit	Rubber mallet
Drill press	Ruler
⅜" bit	Saber saw
¾" bit	Sander(s)
⅜" plug cutter	Sandpaper
⅜" rabbeting bit	Saw for crosscutting
1" Forstner bit	Screwdriver
Countersink bit	Table saw
Hollow-chisel	Dado cutter
mortising	Miter gauge
attachment	Tack cloth
Jointer	Tape measure
Paintbrush	Try square
Pipe clamps	

Trolley

1. **Make the legs.** Cut the front and back legs to the sizes specified by the "Cutting List." Following the *Leg Layouts,* mark the sizes and locations of the mortises for the aprons and rails.

Next, cut the mortises. If you have a hollow-chisel mortising attachment, use it. If you don't, select a bit that is the same diameter as the width of the mortises, and chuck it in your drill press. Clamp a fence to the drill press table, positioning it so the center point of the bit will enter the center of the mortise. Rough out the mortise by drilling a series of slightly overlapping holes, starting at one end and working to the other. With a chisel, pare the sides and ends of the mortises to square them and bring them to their final dimensions.

Finally, drill holes for the casters in the front legs. You can drive the metal caster sockets into the holes now, or you can wait until after a finish has been applied.

LEG LAYOUTS

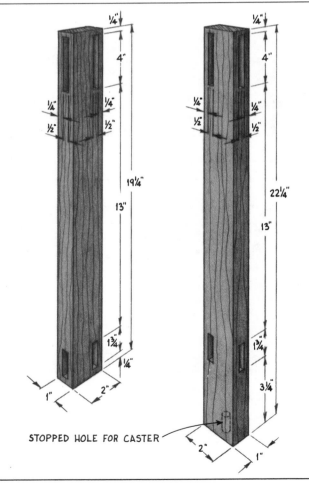

STOPPED HOLE FOR CASTER

2. **Make the side aprons and side rails.** Cut the side aprons and side rails to the sizes specified by the "Cutting List." Tenon both ends of each side rail and side apron to fit the corresponding mortises in the legs. Details of the apron are shown in the *Apron Layouts.*

While you can cut the tenons with a router and straight bit, it probably is easiest to cut them on a table saw with a dado cutter. Set up the dado cutter, and position the rip fence so it is the length of the tenon away from the *outside* of the blade, in this case 1 inch. When the end of the leg is butted against the fence, the blade will cut the tenon's shoulder. Set the depth of cut, in this case to 3/16 inch, and make test cuts on a scrap of the working stock to confirm the correctness of your settings. (Fit your test tenon to a mortise to be sure you don't cut too much.) To expedite things, all the tenons are designed to be formed by removing 3/16 inch of material from both faces and one or both edges. With the saw set up, you can quickly cut tenons on both ends of each apron and rail. When cutting the tenons, guide the workpiece with the miter gauge.

After all the tenons are cut, carefully fit them to particular mortises. Use a chisel to pare the tenon or the mortise until an appropriate, snug fit is obtained.

Lay out and cut the curve on the bottom edge of the side aprons next. Consult the *Apron Layouts.* Mark the high and low points, then flex a strip of thin plywood or plastic laminate to find a pleasing arc that connects the points. Have a helper trace the curve. Cut the arc on the band saw or with a saber saw. After cutting one side apron, use it as a template to lay out the second.

Finally, cut the notches in the side rails for the axle. In the wheel-and-caster set we purchased, the axle rod is housed in a 1-inch by 1-inch strip of oak. Measure the strip in your set, then cut a notch for the strip in the bottom edge of each side rail, as shown in the *Trolley Side View.* Use a band saw or saber saw.

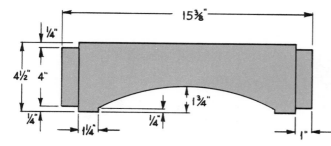

APRON LAYOUTS

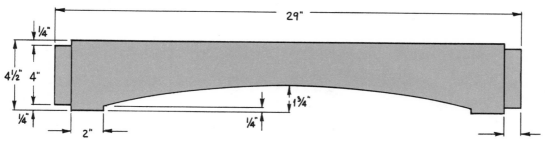

---

3. **Assemble the side frames.** Without glue, assemble the two side frames. When you are satisfied that all the joints fit properly, knock the frames apart, sand the parts, then reassemble them with resorcinol glue.

After the glue has set and the clamps are off, radius the inside edges of the side frames and outer edges of the legs and the side rails using a router and a ¼-inch rounding-over bit.

---

4. **Make the end aprons and remaining rails.** Cut the end aprons and all the remaining rails—two end rails, two top side rails, and two top end rails—to the sizes specified by the "Cutting List."

As you can see in the *Bottom-Rail-to-Slats Joinery* drawing, the (lower) end rails are mortised to accept the bottom slats and tenoned to join the side frames. The end aprons also are tenoned to join the side frames. Tenon both ends of each end rail and apron. Use the same setup you used to tenon the side rails and aprons.

Using the flexible strip method described in step 2 and the points indicated in the *Apron Layouts,* create and trace the arc on one end apron. Cut the arc on the band saw or with a saber saw, then use that piece as a template to lay out the second end apron. Cut it, too.

Cut the joinery in the top side rails next. Consult the *Top-Rail-to-Slats Joinery* drawing. In each side rail you must (in no particular order):

● Cut a 1-inch-wide, ⅜-inch-deep rabbet across one end.

● Cut a 1-inch-wide, ⅜-inch deep dado whose centerline is 4 inches from the other end.

● Bore a 1-inch-diameter, ½-inch-deep hole, located midway between the dado and the closest end.

● Round off the "handle end."

The rabbets and dadoes can be cut with a router and straight bit, or with a table saw and dado cutter. If you don't have a Forstner bit to bore the holes for the handle, be very careful that the center spur of whatever bit you *do* use doesn't penetrate the workpiece and spoil the appearance. Test your setup on a piece of scrap if you aren't sure.

Mortise the end rails and the top end rails next. Lay out the mortises, then set up the drill press to rough them out, fitting it with a ⅜-inch bit and clamping a fence to the table. Although the lower rails and the top rails are of different widths, the mortises in both are ⅜ inch wide and are 1 1/16 inch from the top edges. Thus, you should be able to cut all the mortises with the same setup.

BOTTOM-RAIL-TO-SLATS JOINERY

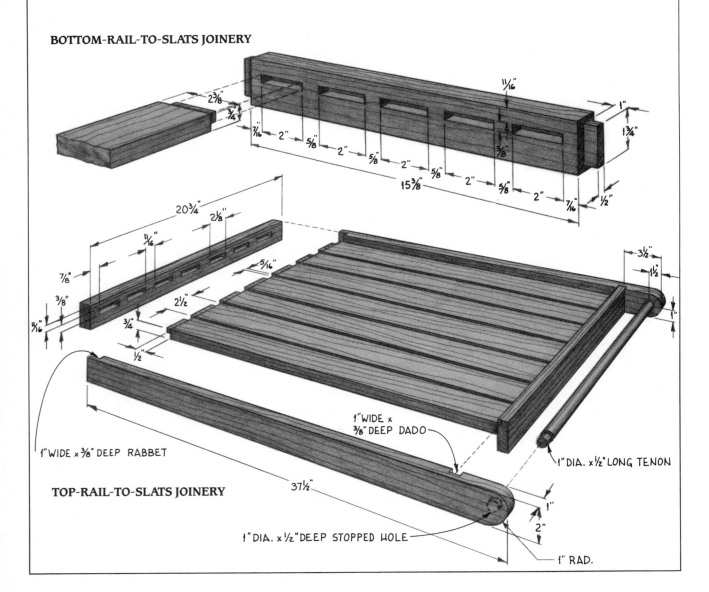

TOP-RAIL-TO-SLATS JOINERY

1"WIDE × ⅜" DEEP RABBET

1"WIDE × ⅜" DEEP DADO

1" DIA. × ½" LONG TENON

1" DIA. × ½" DEEP STOPPED HOLE

1" RAD.

5. **Cut and tenon the slats.** From the 4/4 (four-quarter) oak stock, cut the five bottom slats and seven top slats to the sizes specified by the "Cutting List." With a router and a ¼-inch rounding-over bit, radius the edges of all the slats.

Tenon both ends of all the slats, as indicated in the two joinery drawings. The tenons should be ½ inch long and shouldered on both sides and both edges. Cut the tenons with a dado cutter on the table saw. It's a good idea to cut a test tenon on scrap and fit it to an end-rail mortise before cutting the slats.

6. **Assemble the trolley frame.** Before gluing the frame together, assemble all the parts without glue to ensure that everything fits properly *and* to rehearse the assembly routine. While you have the frame together, use the router and the rounding-over bit to radius exposed edges, blending intersecting edges.

While it is strong and waterproof and gap-filling, resorcinol glue is also runny and guaranteed to stain. Mix up a small batch in a paper cup and brush it on with an acid brush or a cheap paintbrush. Apply glue both to the interior of the mortise and to the tenon. Be careful not to dribble it on exposed surfaces. And choreograph the assembly to avoid having it leak out of open mortises.

Here is the trolley frame assembly process. *Above:* Start with the bottom shelf. Apply glue to the mortises and the slat tenons. Fit the slats into the mortises and force them in place. To avoid having glue dribble out of the mortises onto the assembly, always lower the tenons into the mortises. So turn the assembly over, lowering the tenons into the mortises in the rail that's resting on the benchtop. Line up the tenons to get them started in the mortises. The rubber mallet is there to persuade the joints to close tightly.

Top right: The side frames are already glued up. Set one out, stand the bottom shelf assembly in place, and add the end aprons. Then, with a helper, lift that and flip it over, so you can set it onto the second side frame. Line up the tenons in the mortises and use the mallet to drive them home.

Bottom right: With the trolley upside down, apply pipe clamps. No clamps are needed parallel to the slats, since their joints have already been snugged with the persuader and are secured by the side assemblies. Besides, resorcinol is a filling glue, meaning that clamping doesn't affect its curing action.

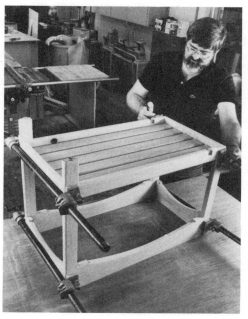

7. Assemble the trolley top. Before you can assemble the top, you have one last part to make, and that's the handle. Cut the oak dowel to the length specified by the "Cutting List." At the table saw, cut a 1-inch-diameter, ½-inch-long tenon on each end.

Now dry assemble the top to check how the joints fit. While the top is together, run over all the exposed edges with the router and the rounding-over bit. Then knock the works apart so you can glue it up.

As you assemble the top with glue, remember to keep the open mortises up, fitting the tenons down into them. When all the slats are fitted into one top end rail, upend this assembly, so you can lower the tenons into the mortises in the remaining top end rail. Lay out a side rail, stand the slat assembly in the rabbet and dado, fit the handle into its socket, then upend this assembly to fit it to the remaining side rail. Then apply clamps. You'll probably need a helper. Unless you have three hands.

Cut the handle tenons on the table saw. Set the miter gauge roughly parallel to the saw arbor and clamp the bar to the table saw so it can't move. Set the fence-to-blade distance to equal the length of the tenon (measure from the outside of the blade). Feed the workpiece into the blade and rotate it. The fence keeps the tenon from getting too long; the miter gauge holds the work perpendicular to the blade. This is not something you can do with the saw guard in place.

8. Attach the top to the frame. After you have the clamps removed from both the trolley frame and the trolley top, you can mount the top on the frame. Position the top as shown in the *Trolley Plan Views,* and drive galvanized drywall-type screws through the slats into the end aprons. You need use only six screws, one through each end of the second, fourth, and sixth slats. Conceal the screw heads beneath plugs cut from scraps of the oak used to make the trolley.

TIP

Drill a pilot hole for every screw you use. The screws will go in easier, they won't split the wood, and they'll actually hold better. The pilot hole bit setup we use bores a tapered, countersunk pilot hole in one operation. It consists of a tapered twist drill bit, a countersink, and a stop collar. Adjust the amount that the bit projects from the countersink so the depth of the hole matches the length of the screw. The optional, adjustable stop collar controls the depth of the countersinking action. The bits are matched to the screw gauges.

To conceal the screws that secure the top assembly to the frame, cut wood plugs from scraps of your working stock. Use a plug cutter, and try to match the color of the plug to the color of the slat. When you drill the pilot hole, adjust the depth stop to prevent the counterbore from getting too deep; you want the plug to stand a bit proud of the slat surface. *Left:* Apply glue to the counterbore with a cotton swab, then insert a plug. *Right:* Line up the grain in the plug with the grain in the slat. After the glue sets, you can pare the plug flush with the slat using a sharp chisel.

9. **Apply a finish, then install the wheels and casters.** Sand the entire assembly one last time, dust it well with a tack cloth, then apply two coats of an exterior-grade penetrating oil. We used a product called CWF (for Clear Wood Finish). With this product, you apply the second coat while the first is still wet, which is to say about 15 to 30 minutes after the initial application.

After the finish dries, install the axle, wheels, and casters.

The axle, as supplied, is housed in a strip of wood. Fit the axle into the notches cut for it. Drill a pilot hole in the seam between the oak axle strip and the edge of the notch. Drive in a galvanized drywall-type screw to hold it in place.

Tea Tray

1. **Prepare the stock.** The tea tray is constructed largely of ⅜-inch-thick material, not a standard thickness in anything other than plywood or particleboard. To get the required boards from 5/4 (five-quarter) stock, you need to resaw. While this is best done on a band saw, you can do it for this project on a table saw. Even given the kerf thickness of the latter, you should be able to get two ⅜-inch-thick boards from a single piece of 5/4.

To resaw on a table saw, clamp a featherboard to the saw table to keep the board against the rip fence; position it ahead of the blade, so the blade isn't pinched. To cut the slats, you have to saw through 3½ inches of material, so do it in two passes. Set the depth of cut to about 1⅞ inches and make a pass. Flip the board end for end (so the same face of the board rides against the fence), and make a second pass, parting the board. Plane the sawed surfaces to remove the saw marks.

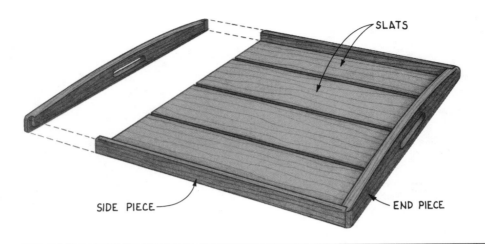

SLATS

SIDE PIECE

END PIECE

SHOPPING LIST—TEA TRAY

LUMBER
2 bd. ft. 5/4 white oak

HARDWARE AND SUPPLIES
Resorcinol glue

FINISH
Exterior-grade penetrating oil finish, such as CWF

CUTTING LIST—TEA TRAY

PIECE	NUMBER	THICKNESS	WIDTH	LENGTH	MATERIAL
End pieces	2	¾"	2"	15"	5/4 oak
Side pieces	2	⅜"	1"	19⅜"	5/4 oak
Slats	4	⅜"	3½"	19⅜"	5/4 oak

2. Make the end pieces. The trickiest part of making the tray is laying out the top curve in the end pieces. We established the curve using a strip of plastic laminate, which is thin and flexible. After establishing the high and low points of the curve on the stock, bend the laminate strip to form a pleasing arc connecting those points. While you hold the strip, have a helper trace the curve on the stock.

Cut the two end pieces to the size specified by the "Cutting List." Consult the *End View,* then lay out the curved top edges and the handles. Drill a ¾-inch-diameter hole at each end of each handle, establishing the rounded contours. Cut between the holes with a saber saw to complete the handle cutouts, then cut the curved tops.

Next, cut a ⅜-inch-wide, ½-inch-deep rabbet along the bottom edge and across each end.

Finally, radius the edges that will be exposed with a router and a ¼-inch rounding-over bit.

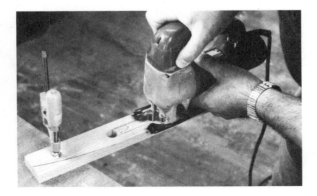

Drill ¾-inch holes for the ends of the handle, then cut between the holes with a saber saw. To get clearance for the saw blade, clamp the workpiece so it projects beyond the edge of the workbench.

TIP

The jointer, if you have one, is an excellent tool for cutting rabbets. The setup is fast and easy; the rabbet is super clean. Adjust the fence to the width of the rabbet, set the depth of cut to the depth of the rabbet, and make the cut. Yes, you can cut the rabbet in one pass; cutting the ½-inch-wide, ⅜-inch-deep rabbet in the tray end is equivalent to jointing ¹⁄₁₆ inch from a 3-inch-wide board. In all probability, you *will* have to remove the guard, but the fence covers all but a fraction of an inch of the blades, and even that fraction is housed by the workpiece as you cut.

3. **Cut and assemble the sides and slats.** Cut the sides to size and radius the edges. Glue them to the end pieces to form the tray's frame.

Cut the four slats to size and radius their edges. Turn the tray frame upside down, and glue the slats to the end frames, spacing the slats evenly. Sand, and apply a clear finish. If you are concerned about food coming in contact with the trays, use a nontoxic finish like Behlen's Salad Bowl Finish, which contains only ingredients approved by the federal Food and Drug Administration for use in contact with food when dry.

TEA TRAY PLAN VIEWS

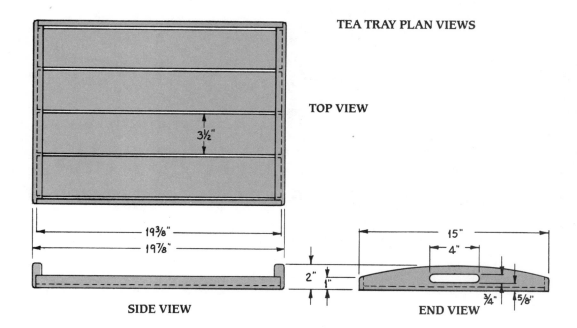

TOP VIEW

3½"

19⅜"

19⅞"

2" 1"

15"

4"

¾" ⅝"

SIDE VIEW

END VIEW

ACADIA BENCH AND CHAIR

Giving the Classic Garden Bench a Whorl

The genesis of this design is this: English garden benches are everywhere. College campuses. Public parks. Private yards. They're sold in mail-order catalogs. In deck and landscaping showrooms. Furniture stores. Even department stores. So we couldn't very well create the definitive outdoor furniture project book without an Americanized English-style garden bench.

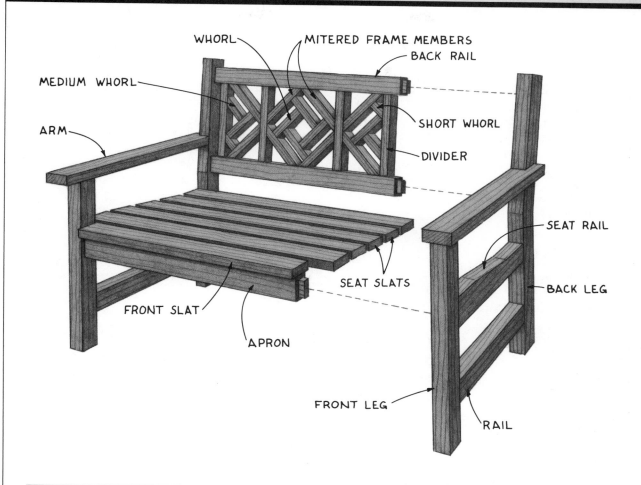

WHORL

MITERED FRAME MEMBERS

BACK RAIL

MEDIUM WHORL

ARM

SHORT WHORL

DIVIDER

SEAT RAIL

BACK LEG

FRONT SLAT

SEAT SLATS

APRON

FRONT LEG

RAIL

SHOPPING LIST—BENCH

LUMBER

2¾ bd. ft. 4/4 white oak
12¼ bd. ft. 5/4 white oak
13½ bd. ft. 8/4 white oak

HARDWARE AND SUPPLIES

1 box #6 × 1⅝" galvanized drywall-type screws
Resorcinol glue

FINISH

Exterior-grade penetrating oil, such as CWF

SHOPPING LIST—CHAIR

LUMBER

1⅓ bd. ft. 4/4 white oak
7⅛ bd. ft. 5/4 white oak
12¼ bd. ft. 8/4 white oak

HARDWARE AND SUPPLIES

25 pcs. #6 × 1⅝" galvanized drywall-type screws
Resorcinol glue

FINISH

Exterior-grade penetrating oil, such as CWF

CUTTING LIST—BENCH

PIECE	NUMBER	THICKNESS	WIDTH	LENGTH	MATERIAL
Whorls	14	¾"	1"	6"	4/4 oak
Medium whorls	2	¾"	1"	5"	4/4 oak
Short whorls	2	¾"	1"	3½"	4/4 oak
Mitered frame members	16	¾"	1"	8½"	4/4 oak
Dividers	6	¾"	1"	12"	4/4 oak
Back rails	2	1⅛"	2½"	54½"	5/4 oak
Back legs	2	1¾"	4½"	34"	8/4 oak
Front legs	2	1¾"	2½"	22¾"	8/4 oak
Rails	2	1¾"	2¼"	17½"	8/4 oak
Seat rails	2	1¾"	3"	17½"	8/4 oak
Arms	2	1¾"	3"	23½"	8/4 oak
Apron	1	1¾"	3"	54½"	8/4 oak
Seat slats	5	1⅛"	2⅞"	56½"	5/4 oak
Front slat	1	1⅛"	2⅞"	53"	5/4 oak

CUTTING LIST—CHAIR

PIECE	NUMBER	THICKNESS	WIDTH	LENGTH	MATERIAL
Whorls	6	¾"	1"	6"	4/4 oak
Medium whorls	2	¾"	1"	5"	4/4 oak
Short whorls	2	¾"	1"	3½"	4/4 oak
Mitered frame members	8	¾"	1"	8½"	4/4 oak
Dividers	4	¾"	1"	12"	4/4 oak
Back rails	2	1⅛"	2½"	30"	5/4 oak
Back legs	2	1¾"	4½"	34"	8/4 oak
Front legs	2	1¾"	2½"	22¾"	8/4 oak
Rails	2	1¾"	2¼"	17½"	8/4 oak
Seat rails	2	1¾"	3"	17½"	8/4 oak
Arms	2	1¾"	3"	23½"	8/4 oak
Apron	1	1¾"	3"	30"	8/4 oak
Seat slats	5	1⅛"	2⅞"	32"	5/4 oak
Front slat	1	1⅛"	2⅞"	28½"	5/4 oak

But what should it look like?

Some are very plain, with heavy legs, slatted backs, bulky arms. Others are ornate, with broadly rounded contours and scrollwork backs. Embellished with carving, perhaps. One design purports to reflect the intricacies of herbal knot gardens. Phil Gehret had built a handsome garden bench a few years back, but it was pretty plain, so we opted for something a bit more stylish this time. The stylishness we settled on was inspired by, of all things, a fence. It's the fence you see in the photo, which is the fence Phil built around his patio a few years ago.

The finished chair and bench are large, heavy, solid, and spacious. Just what garden seating should be.

The setting I've always envisioned for these pieces is not a brick patio, but the grass under a huge oak tree. The long view is to a huge pond, edged by wooded hills and, at its far end, two granite domes. The pond is Jordan Pond, the granite domes are The Bubbles. The setting is in Maine's Acadia National Park. The picture is vivid enough and persistent enough that the chair and bench are labeled "Acadia."

And the best part, if you like irony, is that Acadia is the name the French gave their sixteenth-century colony that encompassed what is now Maine, New Brunswick, and Nova Scotia. A French-American name for an English garden bench. Perfect.

Builder's Notes

The single dominating characteristic of this project is the mortise-and-tenon joint. If my quick count is correct, the chair alone has 48 of them. I mention this not to scare you away from this project, but to focus on equipment. With the right tools, you can knock these joints out almost as easily as rabbet-and-dado joints.

Materials. The stock used in building the chair and bench is white oak. White oak is a strong, heavy American native. Teak is the traditional material of garden benches, but it seems an endangered material. And we're building an American garden bench here.

A plus for oak in this project is that it is hard and stands up well in mortise-and-tenon joints. In addition, white oak is a good choice for an outdoor project, since it is rot resistant.

Alternatives include the outdoor standbys, redwood and cedar. Both of these are rot resistant, but both are soft and will be less satisfactory given the number of mortise-and-tenon joints involved in the project. These woods will yield more lightweight pieces, which can be a plus.

Other materials aren't called for. Well, some resorcinol to glue the parts together, a couple of screws to attach the parts to the back legs, a quart of finish. But that's it.

Tools and techniques. A hollow-chisel mortising attachment for the drill press is what you need to build

TOOL LIST

Backsaw	Planer
Band saw	Rubber mallet
Bar or pipe clamps	Ruler
Drill	Sander(s)
Pilot hole bit	Sandpaper
Drill press	Saw for crosscutting
⅜" mortising chisel	Screwdriver
and bit	Table saw
⅜" plug cutter	Dado cutter
Countersink bit	Miter gauge
Hollow-chisel	Tack cloth
mortising attachment	Tape measure
Jointer	Try square
Paintbrush	

this chair and bench. If you don't have one, get one. Break it in on this project.

Especially if you tend to be a power-tool woodworker, the mortise is an obstacle. The traditional technique for mortising involves a fair amount of handwork, paring the walls of mortises that have been roughed out with a drill. A drill press enables you to bore the holes quickly and uniformly, but you still have to cut away the ridges left between the holes; it is still handwork.

The glory of the mortising attachment is that it bores a square hole. Setup is no more time-consuming than setting up to rough the mortises, and the drill press

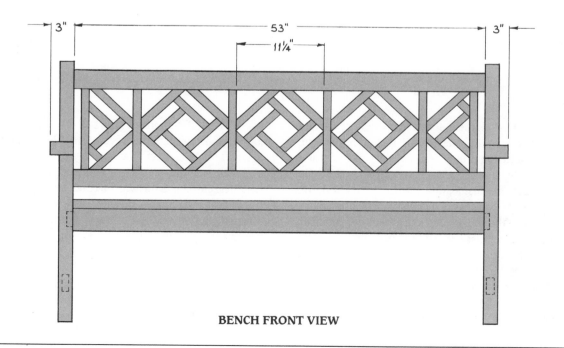

BENCH FRONT VIEW

CHAIR PLAN VIEWS

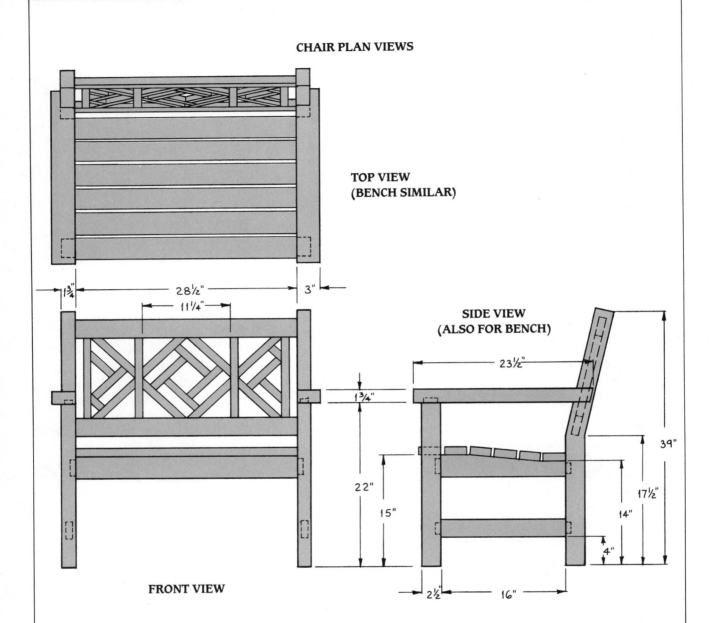

**TOP VIEW
(BENCH SIMILAR)**

**SIDE VIEW
(ALSO FOR BENCH)**

FRONT VIEW

work is all the work there is. When you retract the quill and switch off the drill press motor, the mortise is done.

The mortising attachment consists of a cast-iron yoke that holds a hollow chisel, the chisel and a special auger bit that fits inside, and a fence and hold-downs that secure the workpiece. The yoke, which is split to accommodate the chuck, attaches to the quill and holds the hollow chisel just below the chuck. The chisel fits into a socket in the yoke, and the auger is inserted into the bottom of the chisel and slid up into the chuck. The fence/hold-down is bolted to the drill press table and adjusted to hold the workpiece tightly to the table in just the right fore-and-aft alignment.

To "drill" a mortise, you pull on the quill feed, lowering the chisel to the wood. It's hard to tell, but the auger actually contacts the wood first, boring a round hole and augering the waste chips up and out of the hole. The chisel hits the wood second, just a hair behind the auger, and squares the hole. The waste it cuts is augered out with the rest of the waste. The hold-down comes into play as you retract the quill; it holds the workpiece tightly so you can pull the tightly wedged chisel out of it.

Several sizes of chisels are available. The ⅜-inch chisel, which probably gets the most use in our shop, makes a ⅜-inch-square hole. Cutting a full mortise invariably involves boring a row of holes, sometimes two or three rows of holes. As you skim through the directions for this project, I think you'll find that the ⅜-inch chisel was used exclusively.

Other than the mortiser, the essential tool is a table saw with a 1½- to 2-horsepower motor and a sharp blade. Ripping 8/4 (eight-quarter) oak can bog a lesser machine. A dado cutter to fit the table saw will expedite the cutting of tenons.

1. Prepare the stock.
To prepare your hardwood for use, you need to joint and plane it to reduce it to working thicknesses and to smooth the faces and edges. Following the "Cutting List," crosscut the boards to rough working lengths first, and mark each piece so you know what its intended use is. (Of course, you'll have to remark them before long, since dressing the boards will remove your labels.)

To dress each board, smooth one face on the jointer, then joint one edge. Run the board through the planer as many times as is required to reduce it to the desired thickness. (When planing a lot of parts of a common thickness, the usual practice is to set the cutters, run all of them through, reset the cutters and run them all through again, and so forth. That way, all the boards will end up at the same thickness.) Finally, rip the boards to within 1⁄16 inch of the final width, then trim away that last 1⁄16 inch and at the same time smooth away the saw marks on the jointer.

The result is a board whose surfaces are flat and at right angles to their neighbors, and whose faces are parallel to each other.

There are some alternatives, although the results won't always be ideal. The best alternative, if you lack a jointer and planer, is to buy from a lumberyard or dealer that can surface the boards to your specifications.

2. Make the back inserts.
The diamond-whorl back inserts are composed of many small pieces, all of which are mortised and tenoned. Making the inserts is not difficult so much as tedious. Given the number of mortises that must be cut—the chair back alone has 32 mortises—a hollow-chisel mortising attachment is a virtual necessity.

The only difference between the chair and the bench, as far as the back inserts go, is the number of full diamond whorls. The chair has a single full whorl and two halves, the bench has three full whorls and the two halves.

Begin by trimming the various whorls, mitered frame members, and dividers to the lengths specified by the "Cutting List." Check the *Back Insert Parts Layout* and, as you trim the pieces to length, miter the ends of the appropriate parts.

Cut the tenons on these pieces next. No particular layout on the pieces is necessary; it's all in the tool setups. Set the table saw's rip fence to govern the length of the tenons first. Adjust the depth of cut, and with the workpieces cradled one by one in the miter gauge, trim away the waste. Make three or four passes to cut one face of each tenon. To cut the angled tenons, simply adjust the angle of the miter gauge; the position of the rip fence remains unchanged. The corners of the latter tenons are trimmed away on the band saw.

The whorls have a square-cut tenon on each end. The mitered frame members have mitered tenons on

Cut the tenons on the mitered frame members on the table saw. Adjust the rip fence to govern the length of the tenon, and set the miter gauge to the miter angle. Two or three passes over the saw blade should complete each face.

Lay out the mortises on all the whorls at the same time. Line them up side by side, align them with a square, as shown, then scribe lines across all of them. Marking the ends of the mortises is sufficient, since your drill press setup will orient the mortises uniformly across the width of the piece.

BACK INSERT PARTS LAYOUT

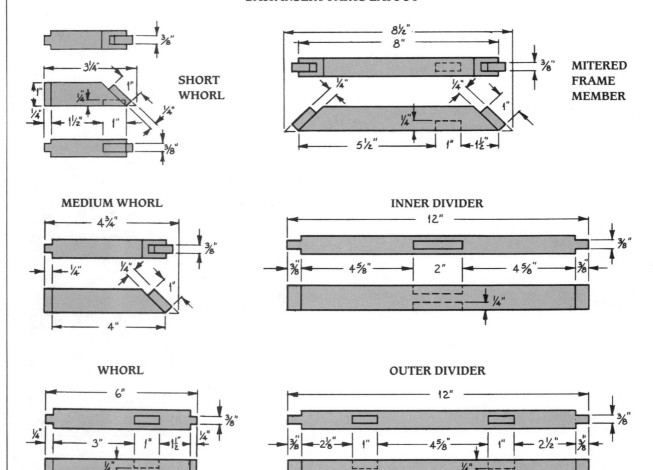

SHORT WHORL

3/8"
3¼"
1"
¼"
¼"
1½"
1"
3/8"

MITERED FRAME MEMBER

8½"
8"
3/8"
¼"
¼"
1"
5½"
¼"
1"
1½"

MEDIUM WHORL

4¾"
3/8"
¼"
¼"
1"
4"

INNER DIVIDER

12"
3/8"
3/8"
4⅝"
2"
4⅝"
3/8"
¼"

WHORL

6"
3/8"
¼"
3"
1"
1½"
¼"
¼"

OUTER DIVIDER

12"
3/8"
3/8"
2½"
1"
4⅝"
1"
2½"
3/8"
¼"

both ends. The short and medium whorls have one square-cut tenon and one mitered tenon.

Cut the mortises next. The mortises are all the same width—⅜ inch—and are all centered across the width of the parts. The tool setup thus is the same for all the parts. What changes is the length of the mortises,

and this is what you need to mark on the various parts. Scribe lines across the parts to indicate the position and length of the mortises. On one piece, lay out the sides of the mortise, and use this piece to set up the mortiser.

Next, install the mortising attachment and ⅜-inch mortising chisel on your drill press. Mount the fence on the drill press table and adjust it to properly position the mortise. Drill a test or two to refine the setup. When the setup is satisfactory, drill the mortises in all the parts. (When you cut the mortises in the short whorls, you'll discover that they cut into the mitered tenons, creating a small hollow and perhaps even causing a section of the tenon to break off. The assembly will still go together, so don't worry about it.)

3. Cut the back rails and assemble the back.
The two back rails are virtually identical, with tenons to join them to the side frames, and mortises for the various tenons of the back inserts. The inserts are flush with the front faces of the rails, so the mortises must be offset toward the front (the rails are thicker than the insert parts).

Following the *Back Rail Layout,* mark the location and lengths of the mortises on one edge of each rail. As with the back insert parts, you need only mark the ends

of each mortise, not the sides. After marking the mortises, mark the front face of each rail. The most direct approach: Set the two rails beside each other, marked edge to marked edge, and write "front" on the face of each.

Use the same setup to drill these mortises that you used to mortise the back insert parts. You will have to adjust the hold-down, of course, to accommodate the rails, which are wider than the back insert parts were. Be sure you set the rail's front against the fence when you do the mortising.

BACK RAIL LAYOUT

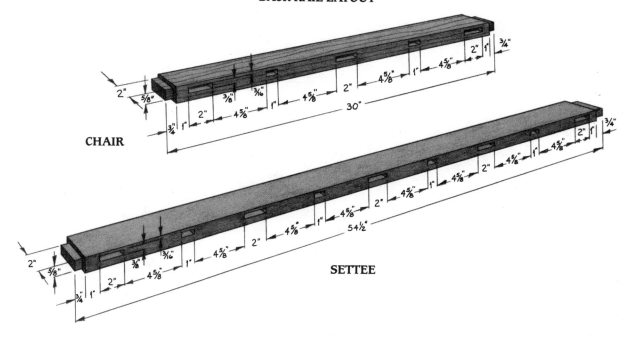

CHAIR

SETTEE

After cutting the mortises, tenon the ends of the rails. This operation can be performed on the table saw. Adjust the fence to govern the length of the tenons (¾ inch from the outside of the blade), set the depth of cut (to ³⁄₁₆ inch), and guide the rail with the miter gauge. The tenons are shouldered on both faces and edges. You can switch from your regular blade to a dado cutter to expedite the tenoning operation.

Assemble the back rails and the whorls. Carefully sand the sawed edges, and finish sand all the parts.

Before mixing the glue, however, do a dry run. This will give you a chance to ensure that everything fits as you want it to. Assuming all the joints do fit properly, pull the assembly apart and mix a batch of resorcinol glue. Resorcinol has a long "open time," meaning that it doesn't dry quickly. In practical terms, this means you can work deliberately, taking the time to be neat, to get all the little whorl parts assembled. You don't have to rush. Use a rubber mallet, if necessary, to drive joints closed; the rubber won't mar the wood.

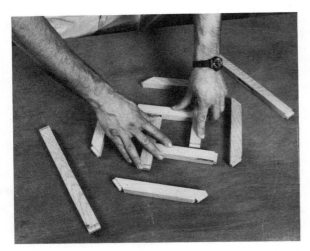

The diamond-whorl inserts have to be assembled in sequence, as demonstrated in this dry run. *Top left:* The central cluster is created by joining one whorl to the second, then joining a third to a fourth. The resulting two elements can be pressed together, forming the central cluster. *Top right:* Next, you add the mitered frame members, as shown. *Bottom:* Finally, you add the dividers. Assemble additional inserts in the same sequence and add them to the first. When all are joined, add the top and bottom rails to tie the whole works together.

The joints between the inserts and the rails are more likely than the others in this project to hold moisture. Resorcinol glue will fill any gaps in fit, and will seal the joint against moisture. Resorcinol also is runny and stains, so the real trick is to apply enough glue to really seal the joint while avoiding overflow that will mar the wood.

4. Cut the parts for the side frames. Cut the legs, rails, and seat rails to the sizes specified by the "Cutting List."

Normally, it is easier to make joinery cuts in a board before you cut it to an irregular shape. The back legs of this project are an exception to the general rule; the shape must be cut before the mortises. Lay out each back leg, as shown, on a 34-inch-long board. Note the grain direction. The layout shown minimizes the width of board needed. The trick is to locate the bend in the leg first, then methodically to extend the layout from that point. Cut out each leg on the band saw.

BACK LEG LAYOUT

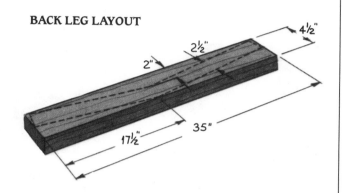

5. Cut the mortises. Whether you are building the chair or the bench, the general procedure is the same. Lay out the side assembly parts on a flat work surface. Lay out the mortises, as shown in the *Side Frame Joinery* drawing. You do need to completely lay out at least one mortise on each face of one leg to help set up the mortiser. Otherwise, you need only mark the ends of each mortise, since the setup will control the sides.

Use the mortising attachment to cut these mortises. Since all are ¾ inch wide, you can use the same ⅜-inch hollow chisel you used in previous steps. The mortises for the seat rails and stretchers can be cut in the front and back legs with a single setup, so do these first. To set up, set a front leg against the fence, then loosen the fence bolts. Lower the chisel to the workpiece and jockey the workpiece forward and back until you have the chisel properly positioned across the width of the stock. Tighten the fence bolts.

To cut the mortise, bore a series of square holes that open up the mortise from one layout line to the next. Pull the workpiece away from the fence, turn it, and butt the other side to the fence. Bore a second set of holes, doubling the width of the mortise.

To cut the mortises for the back rails, adjust the fence setting. This setting will also serve for cutting the apron mortises in the front legs.

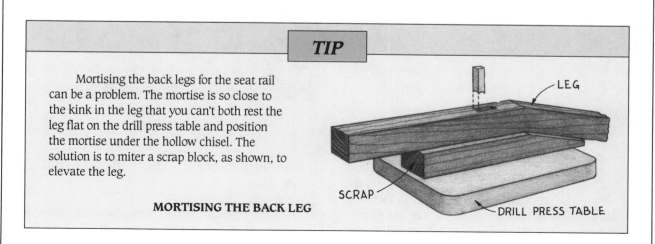

TIP

Mortising the back legs for the seat rail can be a problem. The mortise is so close to the kink in the leg that you can't both rest the leg flat on the drill press table and position the mortise under the hollow chisel. The solution is to miter a scrap block, as shown, to elevate the leg.

MORTISING THE BACK LEG

LEG

SCRAP

DRILL PRESS TABLE

SIDE FRAME JOINERY

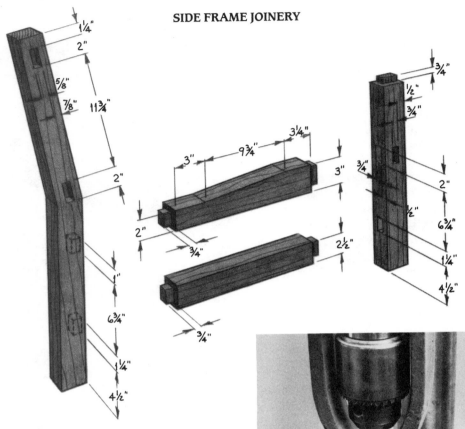

A drill press equipped with a mortising attachment can, in fact, bore a square hole. The key is the hollow chisel held by the yoke surrounding the chuck. The auger within the chisel cuts and excavates most of the waste, while the chisel simultaneously squares the sides of the hole. The hold-down attached to the fence enables you to back the chisel out of the workpiece.

6. Tenon the rails and front legs. The front legs are tenoned for the arm, and the rails and seat rails, of course, are tenoned for the legs. All are similarly sized. Cut them on the table saw using the same procedure used to tenon the back rails. Note here that the seat rails will have to be cut to shape after the tenons are cut, and that that operation will bring their rear tenons to the desired size.

Set the rip fence and the depth of cut, and guide the workpiece with the miter gauge. Since the mortises for these tenons are already cut, you can test your setup on a scrap and fit the tenon you cut on this scrap to one of the mortises. If the setup is dead on, cut the tenons.

Before moving to the assembly step, the seat rails need to be cut to shape on the band saw. As you can see from the *Side View,* the profile of the rails dips slightly (but gracefully) to the rear, the better to accommodate the sitter. The critical dimensions are shown, and the profile suggested. The easiest approach for you to take is to sketch your own profile using the critical dimensions as starting points. Cut the first rail, then use it as a template to lay out the second. Then carefully sand the sawed edges, and finish sand all the parts of the side assemblies.

7. Assemble the side frames. Dry assemble and clamp each side assembly to check for fit (and to practice the clamping routine). If the fit is satisfactory, assemble both units with glue.

After the clamps are set, stand the two assemblies side by side to be sure that one of them does not lean farther back than the other. This simple precaution can save you from building a twisted seat. Adjust the clamps to make the two frames line up before the glue dries.

8. Cut and fit the arms to the side frames. Trim the arms to the dimensions specified by the "Cutting List."

Fitting the arms to the side frame isn't too difficult if you work methodically. First, with the appropriate side frame laying on the workbench, set the arm in position, resting on the shoulder of the front leg tenon, and establish the alignment you want. Mark on the arm where it contacts the back leg. Scribe along the edge of the leg to transfer the leg's angle onto the edge of the arm. Mark along the bottom of the arm onto the back leg, too.

Using the marks as a starting point, lay out the notch on the arm. Cut it with a backsaw.

Measure from the mark on the back leg to the tenon, and transfer this measurement to the arm, marking across its bottom surface. Now set the arm in place, aligning this mark with the tenon. Trace around the tenon, then cut the second-to-last mortise in the project. Refit the arm to the side frame and refine the fit, if necessary.

Repeat the process to fit the other arm to its side frame. In the process, cut the *last* mortise of the project.

9. Cut and tenon the apron. The last part to be cut before the chair or bench can be glued up is the apron. This is a heftier, unmortised version of the back rails. Trim it to the length specified by the "Cutting List," then cut tenons on each end. Size the tenons to fit the mortises already cut for them in the front legs.

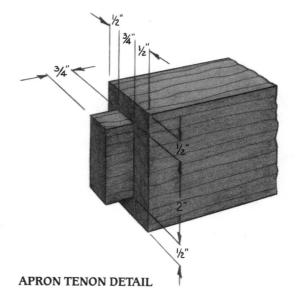

APRON TENON DETAIL

10. **Join the back assembly and the apron to the side frames.** Be sure you have a perfectly flat surface on which to set the legs as you clamp the unit together. Make a final dry run, both to make a final check of joint fits and to practice the assembly and clamping routine. If everything is satisfactory, repeat the process using glue.

Lay both side assemblies on the floor and apply glue to the mortises. Apply glue to the tenons on one end of the back assembly. Fit the tenons into their mortises. Install the apron. Spread glue on the remaining exposed tenons. With a helper, lift the assembly and insert the tenons into the mortises in the second side frame. Now set the unit on its feet and apply clamps, using cauls to prevent the steel jaws from marring the wood.

11. **Install the slats and arms.** While the glue sets, trim the seat slats to the lengths specified by the "Cutting List." Sand them. Using a ⅜-inch plug cutter, make a heap of plugs from scraps of the working stock. Try to match the color and figure of the slats.

Once the glue has dried in the frame joints, remove the clamps and install the slats. Drill countersunk and counterbored pilot holes and screw the seat slats in place. Cover the screw heads with the wooden plugs, gluing them in place. Set each plug carefully, aligning the grain in the plug with the grain of the slat. After the glue sets, pare the plugs flush and give them a touch-up pass with the finish sander.

Glue and screw the arms in place. The mortise is glued onto the tenon, of course, and a single screw is driven through the edge of the arm into the back leg. Conceal this screw beneath a wooden plug, too.

12. **Finish the bench or chair.** Sand the unit thoroughly and apply your favorite outdoor finish. Phil applied two coats of CWF, his favorite exterior-grade penetrating oil. The first coat is applied liberally and allowed to penetrate for about 20 to 30 minutes. Then, while the first coat is still wet, the second coat is brushed on. The oil needs to dry for 48 to 72 hours.

THE
DESIGNER
COLLECTION

MAHOGANY ENSEMBLE

Exotica Made from Commonplace Flooring

Challenged to come up with a different sort of chaise lounge, our woodworkers turned to 5/4 mahogany and the saber saw.

MAHOGANY ENSEMBLE CHAISE LOUNGE

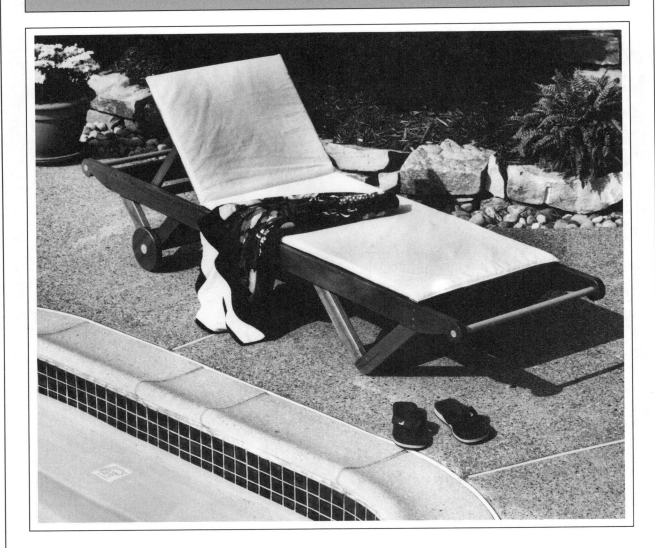

The genesis of this entire ensemble is this chaise lounge. An attractive, lean—but strong—wooden chaise lounge isn't easy to find. You certainly can't buy one for less than a king's ransom. And plans usually involve a load of 2 × 4s spiked together into a crate-like affair.

Thus challenged to come up with something a little different, Rodale woodworkers Fred Matlack and Phil Gehret turned to 5/4 (five-quarter) mahogany for their basic material and to the saber saw to execute a few embellishments.

The result is a chaise lounge that is interesting and relatively inexpensive to build, yet has great weatherability, good strength, and a lean, graceful appearance.

Too, the result was so inspiring that Fred 'n' Phil were sent back into the shop to create a folding serving cart, plans for which follow. That led to a plant cart project, and then to the chair and settee that round out the line.

All share the somewhat exotic material, the dowel-handle-in-scrolled-frame-end motif, the half-lap joinery.

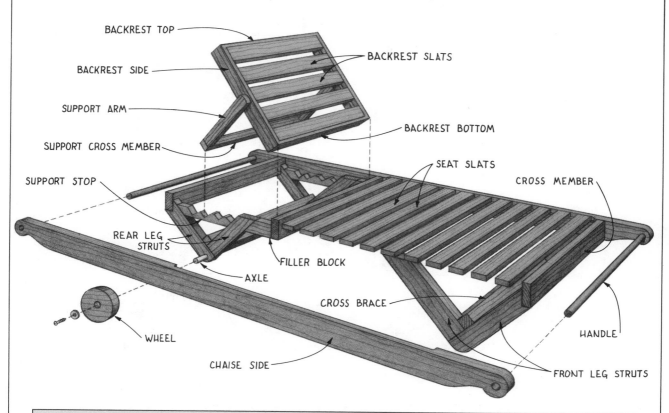

CUTTING LIST

PIECE	NUMBER	THICKNESS	WIDTH	LENGTH	MATERIAL
Chaise sides	2	1⅟₁₆"	3½"	89"	5/4 mahogany
Cross members	3	1⅟₁₆"	3½"	22¾"	5/4 mahogany
Handles	2	1" dia.		24⅛"	Hardwood dowel
Rear leg struts	2	1⅟₁₆"	2½"	14⅛"	5/4 mahogany
Rear leg struts	2	1⅟₁₆"	2½"	17"	5/4 mahogany
Front leg struts	2	1⅟₁₆"	2½"	17¾"	5/4 mahogany
Front leg struts	2	1⅟₁₆"	2½"	20¼"	5/4 mahogany
Cross braces	2	1⅟₁₆"	3⁹⁄₁₆"	22"	5/4 mahogany
Cross braces	2	1⅟₁₆"	2½"	19⅞"	5/4 mahogany
Seat slats	11	¾"	2½"	22¾"	1 × 4 mahogany
Backrest sides	2	1⅟₁₆"	2½"	19¾"	5/4 mahogany
Backrest top/bottom	2	1⅟₁₆"	2½"	20"	5/4 mahogany
Backrest slats	5	¾"	2½"	18½"	1 × 4 mahogany
Support arms	2	¾"	1½"	13"	1 × 4 mahogany
Support cross member	1	¾"	1½"	21½"	1 × 4 mahogany
Support stops	2	1⅟₁₆"	1½"	13½"	5/4 mahogany
Filler blocks	2	1⅟₁₆"	2¾"	5⅝"	5/4 mahogany
Axle	1	1" dia.		26½"	Hardwood dowel
Wheels	2	1⅟₁₆"	7" dia.		5/4 mahogany

SHOPPING LIST

LUMBER

1 pc. 5/4 × 12 × 8' mahogany (stair tread)
1 pc. 5/4 × 12 × 10' mahogany (stair tread)
3 pcs. 1" dia. × 36" hardwood dowel
4 pcs. 1 × 4 × 8' mahogany

HARDWARE AND SUPPLIES

2 pcs. 5⁄16" I.D. fender washers (minimum O.D. 1⅝")
2 pcs. 2" × 3" tight-pin hinges
2 pcs. ¼" × 1" roto hinges
1 box #6 × 2" galvanized drywall-type screws
Resorcinol glue

FINISH

Spar varnish

FABRIC AND NOTIONS

2¼ yd. 45" wide upholstery fabric
1 spool matching thread
1 pc. 1" × 21" × 22" foam rubber
1 pc. 1" × 21" × 48" foam rubber

CUTTING DIAGRAM

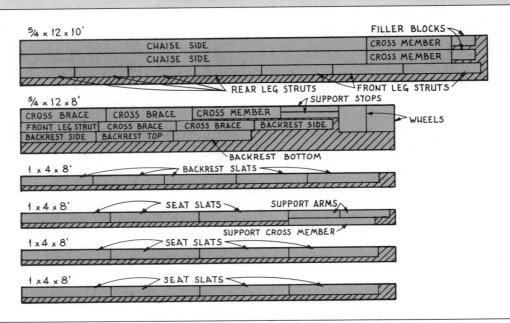

Builder's Notes

The chaise lounge is a good project for the wood-worker with intermediate skills who is looking for a challenge. It doesn't require a shopful of tools to build—a table saw, a router, a saber saw, and a good drill are the major requirements. But the material takes you a step away from standard dimensional lumber without burdening you with the need to surface—or to pay someone else to surface—rough-sawn boards.

Materials. Mahogany is a relatively stable hardwood that, in our locale, anyway, is readily available in dimensional lumber form. That is, several lumberyards

normally stock mahogany in nominal 1-inch thickness and nominal 4-, 6-, 8-, 10-, and 12-inch widths, as well as nominal 5/4-inch thick stair tread. Stair tread is nominally 12 inches wide (an actual 11¼ inches); one edge is rounded over (or "nosed"), thus diminishing the stock's useful width.

The qualifier "normally" applies because we didn't always find the particular material we wanted in stock at the time we wanted it. When we built the ensemble's planter cart and chair and settee, the situation was normal. But months earlier, when we built this chaise lounge and the folding serving cart, our local yards had 1-by mahogany only in the form of tongue-and-groove 1 × 4.

Mahogany, at any rate, is an unusual wood, but it's one that fits into the everyday lumberyard vernacular with which every woodworker is familiar. For the woodworker hesitant to tackle hardwoods because they are stocked unsurfaced and in unpredictable dimensions, this is good to know. Of course, some woodworkers may have qualms about using a tropical wood like mahogany. For this project, there are the usual outdoor-wood alternatives—redwood, cedar, cypress. Or you could try using oak, maple, or some other hardwood available in your area.

In this project, both 1-by and 5/4 stock are used. We felt the basic chaise frame needed extra girth, but we didn't want the bulk of 2-by stock. So we turned to the 5/4 thickness—it usually dresses out to an actual thickness of 1 1/16 inch.

An unusual bit of hardware—the roto hinge—is critical to two of the projects in this ensemble, including the chaise lounge. A roto hinge consists of two hardwood discs that sandwich a metal washer slightly larger in diameter than the discs. The assembly is riveted together, with the rivet acting as a spindle. The wood allows the hinge to be glued in place, completely concealed from view.

If you can't locate roto hinges in your locale, you will find them available through many mail-order woodworking suppliers. It is a good idea to have the hinge in hand before drilling holes for it.

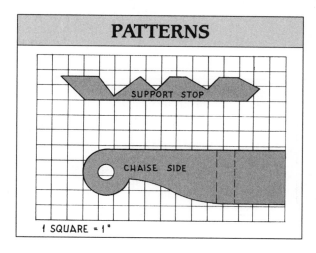

PATTERNS

SUPPORT STOP

CHAISE SIDE

1 SQUARE = 1"

Tools and techniques. This project is proof that you *can* do some out-of-the-ordinary projects without having a professional-level shop. A modest table saw, a basic-model router, a saber saw, and an electric drill are the principle tools required to build the lounger.

The saber saw comes into play to cut the scroll-like profiles on the ends of the sides. It also is used to cut odd-shaped notches in the leg struts and the support stops.

The router can be put to good use on this project: cutting the key dadoes, cutting the half-laps, rabbeting, rounding-over the edges of the piece. If equipped with a trammel attachment, the router can even be used to cut out the wheels. The step-by-step directions that follow include tips on jigs you can make to facilitate these router operations.

Finish. The finish we chose for all the projects in this ensemble is marine (or exterior) spar varnish. Made from tung and linseed oils or tung oil and phenolic resins, marine spar varnishes are *the* traditional clear outdoor finishes. In fact, for many years, they were the *only* clear outdoor finish.

What you need most of when applying marine spar varnish is patience. You want the oils to penetrate as deep as possible into the wood; to allow this, the varnish manufacturers add solvents to the mix that slow drying. So you must allow 6 to 24 hours between coats. Moreover, the manufacturers generally insist that many thin coats are better than a couple of thick coats. Three coats is just a minimum, six coats is preferable. Oh, and sand lightly between coats.

To prolong the finish, sand the piece and apply a fresh coat of varnish every year. Avoid leaving the furniture in the weather year-round, and minimize its exposure to direct sunlight.

Sewing. This project is a bit unusual in that we've included a cushion-making step, which involves not

TOOL LIST

Bar clamps	Ruler
Clamps	Saber saw
Drill	Sander(s)
1" dia. bit	Sandpaper
1" Forstner bit	Saw for crosscutting
Countersink bit	Screwdriver
Pilot hole bit	Sewing machine
Plug cutter	Table saw
Hand screw	Tack cloth
Paintbrush	Tape measure
Router	Trammel
3/8" rabbeting bit, piloted	Try square
1/4" rounding-over bit	Yardstick
3/4" straight bit	

PLAN VIEWS

1¹⁄₁₆"

22"

1¹⁄₁₆"

7" DIA.

1¹⁄₁₆"

TOP VIEW

RABBET FOR SLATS
³⁄₈" WIDE x ¾" DEEP

SIDE VIEW

10"

1" DIA.

1½" TYP.

2½" TYP.

45°

45°

45°

45°

3½"

14"

7" DIA.

8½"

24"

48"

8½"

89"

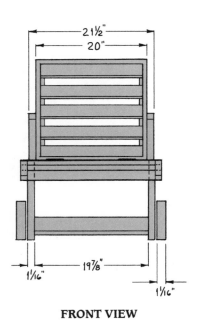

21½"

20"

19⅞"

1¹⁄₁₆"

1¹⁄₁₆"

FRONT VIEW

woodworking but sewing. If you are like me, you see sewing as an endeavor that *looks* pretty easy but is intimidating nonetheless. Without having actually done this sewing, I feel confident I could, especially with a little coaching.

The basic tool needed is a sewing machine, a standard, nothing-fancy sewing machine. You also need good scissors, some straight pins, maybe a few other oddments that anyone who sews will have. Depend on your coach.

The fabric we used is a natural-colored, 100 percent cotton sailcloth. It looks good in the photos, but it will get dirty quickly. Go to a fabric store and examine the goods. Sailcloth, you'll find, is a weight of cotton fabric that's between duck and canvas. You can use awning canvas, upholstery fabric, or any other sturdy fabric. While you are there, get thread to match the fabric you choose, and a slab or two of foam rubber.

Then follow the instructions. Still put off? Solicit help from someone who sews. Or hire the job out. Or just *buy* cushions.

1. Cut the chaise sides. Cut the sides to length from the 5/4 stock. Enlarge the chaise side pattern for the scrolled profile and the handle hole, and sketch it on both ends of each side. Cut the profile with a saber saw. Drill the 1-inch-diameter handle hole. To prevent the wood from splintering when the bit emerges, clamp a scrap back-up block to the workpiece.

With a router and a straight bit, cut three 1 1/16-inch wide, 3/8-inch deep dadoes to accept the cross members. Note the positions of the dadoes on the *Chaise Side Layout*. Because the largest commonly available straight bit is 3/4 inch, the trick here is to cut the dadoes to just the right width. A shop-made jig makes it easy to do.

Complete the joinery cuts on the sides by routing a

CHAISE SIDE LAYOUT

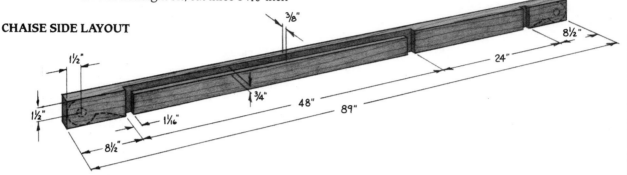

TIP

Since each chaise side has three wide dadoes, it is worth the trouble to make a modest router jig to help you cut them. To make the jig, you need two scraps of 1 × 4 stock about a foot long and two about 2 feet long. Fasten one guide strip (a long piece) to the two crossbars (the short pieces), making sure that the guide is exactly perpendicular to the crossbars.

Now calculate how far the second guide must be from the first to yield a dado that is 1 1/16 inches wide when using a 3/4-inch straight bit. Subtract the bit diameter from the base diameter, then add the width of the dado. Attach the second guide to the jig's crossbars, and cut a test dado on a scrap. If the dado is the correct width, your jig is ready to use on the side pieces. If the dado is too wide or too narrow, reposition the second guide.

To cut the dadoes, lay the jig on the side piece, as shown. Clamp the jig to both the workpiece and the workbench—we used a bar clamp for the former, a large hand screw for the latter. If you make your jig as large as we did, use an extra length of the working stock to support the overhang. In use, the two guide bars prevent the dado from inadvertently being cut too wide.

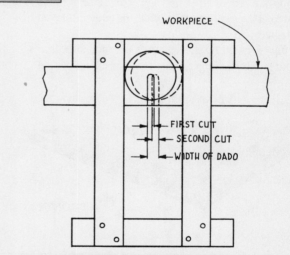

⅜-inch-wide, ¾-inch-deep rabbet along the top edge for the slats. The rabbet should extend from the front dado to the middle dado. Use a piloted rabbeting bit.

The final operation is to radius the inside edges of the handle cutouts, using a router and a ¼-inch rounding-over bit. The rest of the frame will be done after it is assembled, but the area around the handles will be difficult to reach with the router then.

2. Cut the cross members and handles, and assemble the frame. The cross members are cut from the 5/4 stock, the handles from 1-inch-diameter dowel.

After dry assembling the chaise frame to check the fits of the joints, apply glue and assemble the frame. Drive two or three 2-inch screws through the side and into the cross member at each joint. If a fully finished appearance is desired, countersink the screw heads and cover them with wood plugs.

After the glue has cured, rout a ¼-inch radius on the frame's edges. Doing this after assembly helps produce neat corners. Don't radius the rabbeted edges, of course.

3. Build the legs. The front and rear leg assemblies are constructed in the same way, but are slightly different sizes. To make each V-shaped assembly, two leg struts are joined in a half-lap joint. One strut is notched to fit the cross member, while the other is mitered at 45 degrees.

After crosscutting the leg struts to rough size, that is, about an inch longer than that specified by the "Cutting List," cut a half-lap on one end of each.

Glue up the assemblies. After the glue cures, lay out the miters and notches on the strut ends, scribe the 2½-inch-radius curve at the joints, and make these cuts with a saber saw.

Lay out and drill the 1-inch-diameter axle holes through the rear legs (the smaller pair).

Finally, radius the edges of the assemblies with a router and a ¼-inch rounding-over bit.

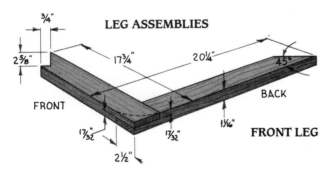

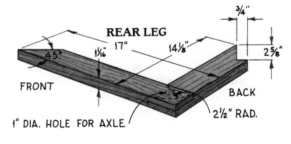

4. Cut and assemble the cross braces. Each brace is constructed from two pieces of 5/4 stock. The longer of the two pieces is notched on each end, and the shorter is glued to it, forming a V-shaped brace that fits into the crooks of the leg assemblies and holds them apart.

Cut the pieces to length, then lay out and notch the longer pieces. You can cut one, then use it as a template to lay out the other. Glue the second part of each brace in place. Finally, radius the edges of the assemblies with a router and a ¼-inch rounding-over bit.

CROSS BRACE ASSEMBLY

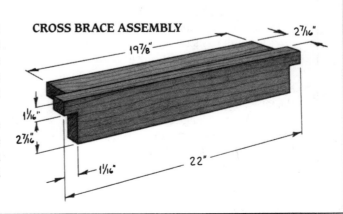

TIP

You can cut half-laps on several struts at the same time using a router and a straight bit, so long as you cut them as cross-laps. Since with a router you trim only ¼ inch or so at a pass, you need to leave stock at the butt ends of the struts to support the tool. After the laps are cut, you trim the struts to their finished length, removing this excess stock.

Set up the work first. Line up several struts edge to edge, with scrap pieces on the outside. Align the butt ends and clamp them tightly together. Clamp a straightedge to the scrap pieces to guide the router and position the shoulder cut. To establish the length of the laps, cut a scrap to use as a spacer between the clamped-on straightedge and the router.

Chuck the appropriate bit in the router, set the depth of cut to about ¼ inch, and cut the shoulder of the laps (top photo). Fit the spacer in place and make the end cut, which should leave a bar of stock at the butt ends of the struts (center photo). Remove the spacer and rout the waste material from between the first two cuts (bottom photo). Reset the depth of cut and repeat the three steps until the laps are cut to the required depth.

Finally, unclamp the struts and trim them to length.

5. **Install the legs and cross braces.** Glue and screw the legs in place on the frame.

Fit the braces in place. Install them with glue and screws, countersinking the screw heads and covering them with wood plugs for a finished appearance.

6. **Cut and install the seat slats.** The slats are cut from 1-by stock. Radius the slat edges, then install the slats, spacing them evenly apart.

7. **Build the backrest.** The backrest consists of a 5/4 frame with slats that match the seat slats. It is hinged to the lounge and supported by a U-shaped support assembly that is attached to the back with roto hinges.

Cut the backrest parts from the 5/4 stock. Using a router and a rabbeting bit, machine a ⅜-inch-wide, ¾-inch-deep rabbet along one edge of each frame member, as shown in the *Backrest Assembly* drawing. Cut a 1 1⁄16-inch-wide, ⅜-inch-deep rabbet across the ends of the top and bottom frame members. Since the width of the rabbet exceeds the capacity of rabbeting bits, machine these rabbets the way you cut the half-laps.

Drill a stopped hole in each side member for a roto hinge. These must be positioned accurately so the support will pivot easily. For the chaise lounge, we used a roto hinge that penetrates ¼ inch into the wood and requires a 1-inch-diameter hole. Be sure you have the hinge in hand before drilling the hole, and make the diameter and depth to suit that hinge. A Forstner bit is best for this job, but a brad-point bit will work. The important thing is to make a clean, accurate hole that is deep enough to receive the hinge without having a center point go clear through the wood.

Assemble the back with glue and screws. Countersink the screw heads and cover them with wood plugs.

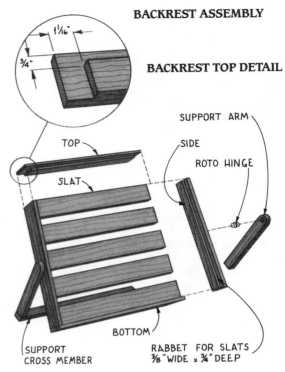

BACKREST ASSEMBLY

BACKREST TOP DETAIL

Round-over the edges of the back. Don't round-over the rabbeted edge. Cut the slats and round-over their edges. Install the slats.

---

8. **Build the support assembly.** Cut the support arms and cross member. In the arms, drill 1-inch-diameter stopped holes for the roto hinges.

To properly radius the edges of the support assembly, you should assemble it with screws but no glue, rout the edges, then disassemble it.

Then mount the arms on the backrest with the roto hinges. Glue the hinge into the holes in the backrest, then apply glue and fit the arm over the hinge. Fasten the cross member in place with glue and screws.

---

9. **Install the support stops.** Enlarge the pattern for the support stops and sketch it on 5/4 stock. Cut two stops using a saber saw. They should fit snugly between the ends of the leg struts. Screw them to the sides of the chaise.

Next, cut and install two filler blocks. The filler blocks fit between the middle cross member and the leg strut. They keep the back support from falling between the leg and the cross member if the back is pulled all the way forward. Screw the blocks to the chaise sides.

Finally, using two tight-pin hinges, install the backrest and the backrest support.

---

10. **Make the wheels.** The wheels are cut from 5/4 stock. They are 7 inches in diameter, with a 1-inch-diameter axle hole in the center. The wheels can be cut using a saber saw or a router; if you use a trammel accessory, you can do a better job of avoiding flat spots on your wheels.

11. Finish the chaise. Be sure all exposed edges are radiused. Sand all the surfaces, and wipe the resulting dust from the wood with a tack cloth.

Apply at least three coats of the spar varnish with a high-quality, fine-bristle varnish brush. Coat all the surfaces, including the underside of the chaise. Take particular care to coat any exposed end grain. Remember that with spar varnish, many thin coats add up to a better, more enduring finish than a couple of thick coats.

After the last coat of the finish is dry, install the axle and wheels. Slip the axle through the holes in the rear leg assembly. Fit a wheel over each end of the axle. Although you don't want to pinch the wheels, you don't need play in the assembly. Mark where the axle can be trimmed so it will be flush with the wheel on either side. Remove the wheels and the axle, and trim the axle. Before reinstalling the axle, locate the center of each end and drill a pilot hole for the screws that will secure the wheels.

With the holes drilled, reinstall the axle and wheels. Insert a screw through a fender washer and drive it into the pilot hole in the end of the axle.

12. Make the cushions. Cut a 76-inch piece of 45-inch-wide fabric for the cushion cover. The fabric's grain should parallel the larger dimension. Fold the piece once across the short dimension, with the back of the fabric exposed. Stitch a seam along the 76-inch dimension, ½-inch from the edge. Turn the resulting tube right-side out, so the fabric's face is now on the outside, and center the seam on the bottom.

Flatten the tube and sew two seams across it, as shown in *Sewing the Cushion,* 24 inches and 25½ inches from one end. These seams create two separate seat-cushion compartments. Turn in the fabric edges at both ends of the cover and hem them.

Cut the cushions from 1-inch-thick foam rubber. The seat is 21 inches by 48 inches; the back is 21 inches by 22 inches.

Stuff the foam cushions into the covers. Pin the ends of the covers shut with a row of straight pins at least 1 inch from the hemmed edge of the covers—you may have to temporarily bunch up the foam to get the pins in. This allows enough room to guide the layers of fabric under the foot of the sewing machine. Fold in the corners of the top and bottom layers of fabric approximately 1¼ inches. Sew a line of stitches through the hemmed edges of both layers of fabric, closing the ends of the covers. Remove the pins, allowing the cushion to unbunch. Place the cushions on the chaise.

SEWING THE CUSHION

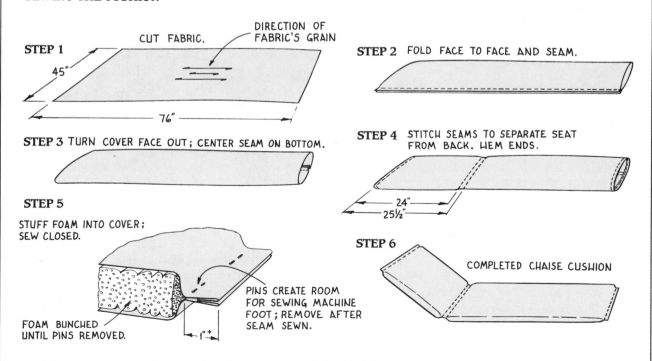

MAHOGANY ENSEMBLE FOLDING SERVING CART

Outdoor living isn't complete without a little something to nibble on. Burgers. Hot dogs. Barbecue chicken. Potato or macaroni salad. Chips. Iced tea or lemonade. Uummmm. That's real livin'.

This folding cart makes serving the picnic just a little more pleasant. The top surface is just a bit over 16 inches by 24 inches, expansive enough for a substantial cargo of food and drink. Load it with picnicstuffs in the kitchen, then wheel it out to the deck or patio and park it next to the grill. If you tile the top or use a big ceramic trivet to protect the wood, you can even use the cart as a base for a small gas grill or hibachi.

The top is hinged to the legs at the end you'll use to wheel the cart, so it won't collapse when you lift the handle opposite the wheels to move it. Moreover, because the legs are joined to each other and to the top with concealed hinges, the cart won't fall into a heap of parts when you attempt to fold it for storage.

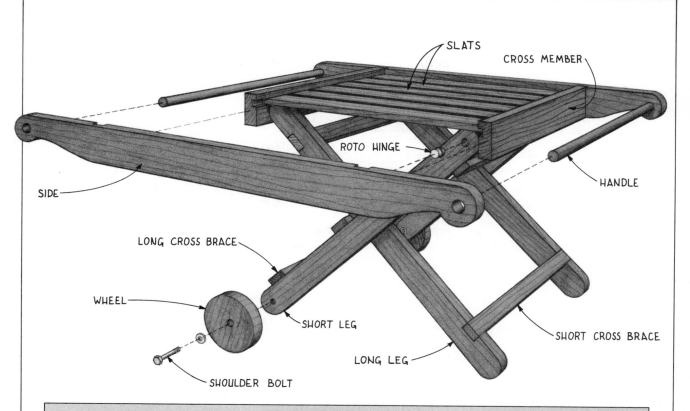

SLATS

CROSS MEMBER

SIDE

ROTO HINGE

HANDLE

LONG CROSS BRACE

WHEEL

SHORT LEG

SHORT CROSS BRACE

LONG LEG

SHOULDER BOLT

SHOPPING LIST

LUMBER
1 pc. 5/4 × 12 × 5' mahogany (stair tread)
1 pc. 1" dia. × 48" hardwood dowel
3 pcs. 1 × 4 × 8' mahogany

HARDWARE AND SUPPLIES
2 pcs. ½" × 1⅞" shoulder bolts
2 pcs. ⅜" flat washers
2 pcs. ⅜" T-nuts

HARDWARE AND SUPPLIES—CONTINUED
20 pcs. #6 × 1⅝" brass flathead screws
4 pcs. ¼" × 1" roto hinges
Resorcinol glue

FINISH
Spar varnish

CUTTING LIST

PIECE	NUMBER	THICKNESS	WIDTH	LENGTH	MATERIAL
Sides	2	1¹⁄₁₆"	3½"	44"	5/4 mahogany
Cross members	2	1¹⁄₁₆"	3½"	17⅛"	5/4 mahogany
Handles	2	1"		18½"	Hardwood dowel
Slats	6	¾"	2½"	25⅝"	1 × 4 mahogany
Long legs	2	¾"	1½"	38"	1 × 4 mahogany
Short legs	2	¾"	1½"	36"	1 × 4 mahogany
Long cross braces	3	¾"	1½"	16¼"	1 × 4 mahogany
Short cross braces	2	¾"	1½"	14¾"	1 × 4 mahogany
Wheels	2	1¹⁄₁₆"	7" dia.		5/4 mahogany

CUTTING DIAGRAM

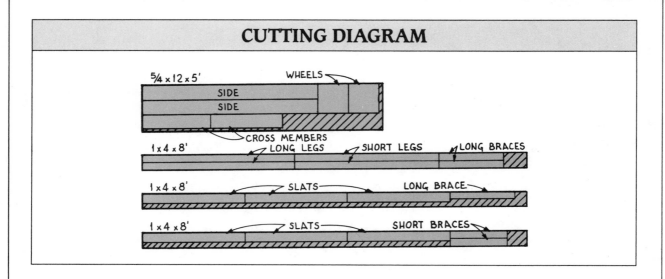

5/4 x 12 x 5'
WHEELS
SIDE
SIDE
CROSS MEMBERS

1 x 4 x 8'
LONG LEGS
SHORT LEGS
LONG BRACES

1 x 4 x 8'
SLATS
LONG BRACE

1 x 4 x 8'
SLATS
SHORT BRACES

PLAN VIEWS

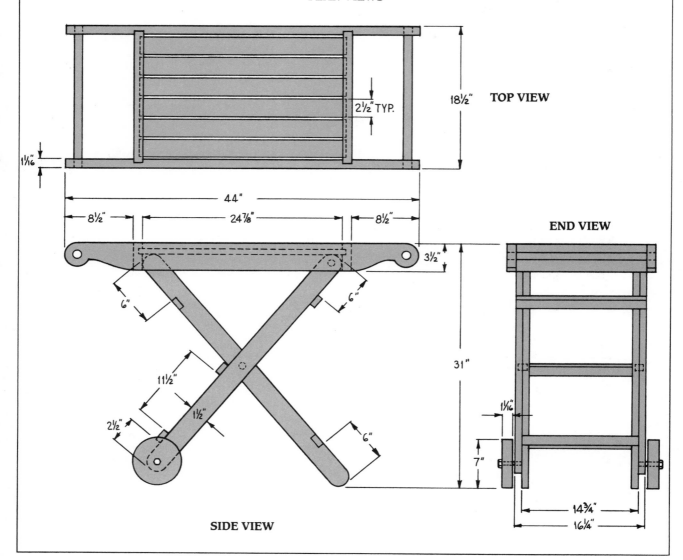

2½" TYP.

18½"   **TOP VIEW**

1 1/16"

44"

8½"   24 7/8"   8½"

END VIEW

3½"

6"   6"

11½"

1½"

2½"   6"

31"

1 1/16"

7"

14¾"

16¼"

SIDE VIEW

PATTERN

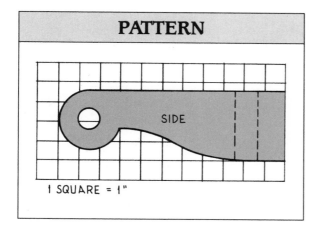

SIDE

1 SQUARE = 1"

TOOL LIST

Bar clamps	Ruler
Clamps	Saber saw
Compass	Sander(s)
Drill	Sandpaper
½" dia. bit	Saw for crosscutting
1" dia. bit	Screwdriver
1" dia. Forstner bit	Table saw
Pilot hole bit	Tack cloth
Paintbrush	Tape measure
Router	Trammel
¼" rounding-over bit	Try square
¾" straight bit	Wrench
Edge guide	

Builder's Notes

A companion project to this chapter's chaise lounge, plant cart, and settee and chair, the folding serving cart is constructed with the same materials and uses the same tools and techniques as those projects. If you are building only this project from the ensemble, then by all means read the "Builder's Notes" accompanying the chaise lounge project on page 158.

One hardware item, the shoulder bolt, is unique to the folding serving cart, but you should be able to get it at a well-stocked hardware store or home center. Sold as a replacement for a lawn-mower axle, a shoulder bolt usually has a ½-inch shank with ⅜-inch threads on the end. Because these bolts come in different lengths, you must match them to the wheels you make.

1. Cut the sides. Cut the sides to length from the 5/4 stock. Enlarge the side pattern for the scrolled profile and the handle hole, and sketch it on both ends of each side. Cut the profile with a saber saw. Drill the 1-inch-diameter hole. To prevent the wood from splintering when the bit emerges, clamp a scrap backup block to the workpiece.

With a router and a straight bit, cut two 1¹⁄₁₆-inch-wide, ⅜-inch-deep dadoes to accept the cross members. Note the positions of the dadoes in the *Top Joinery* drawing. Because the largest commonly available straight bit is ¾ inch, the trick here is to cut the dadoes to just the right width.

Since you have four dadoes to cut, it is worth the trouble to make a modest router jig to help you with this operation. To make the jig (which is shown in the previous project), you need four scraps of 1 × 4, each about a foot long. Fasten one guide strip to the two crossbars, making sure that the guide is exactly perpendicular to the crossbars. The crossbars should snugly embrace the workpiece, so there is no play when the jig is fitted in place.

TOP JOINERY

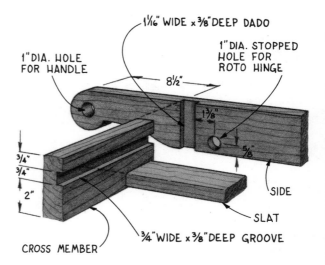

Now calculate how far the second guide must be from the first to yield a dado 1¹⁄₁₆ inches wide when using a ¾-inch straight bit. From the diameter of the router base subtract the bit diameter and add the width of the dado. That's how far apart the two guides should be. *Clamp* the second guide to the jig's crossbars, and cut a test dado on a scrap. If the dado is the correct width, fasten the second guide in place, then cut the dadoes in the sides.

Next lay out and bore the stopped holes for the roto hinges that join the top assembly to the leg assembly. A Forstner bit is the best tool for the job, but a brad-point bit will work. The important thing is to make a clean, accurate hole that is deep enough to receive the hinge without having a center point go clear through the wood.

Note: Roto hinges are glued in place. Available in a variety of both depths and diameters, it's a good idea to get the hinges first, then drill the holes to fit. For this project, we'd recommend a fairly large size. The hinge should be inserted ½ inch into the wood and should require a hole ¾ to 1 inch in diameter.

The final operation is to machine a ¼-inch radius on the inside edges of the handle cutouts. The rest of the frame will be done after it is assembled, but the area around the handles will be impossible to reach with the router then.

2. Cut the cross members, handles, and slats.

The cross members are cut from 5/4 stock, the handles from 1-inch-diameter dowel, and the slats from 1-by stock.

A ¾-inch-wide, ⅜-inch-deep groove must be plowed in each cross member to accept the slats, as shown in the *Top Joinery* drawing. This can be done using a table-saw–mounted dado cutter or a router equipped with an edge guide and fitted with a ¾-inch straight bit. If you rout the groove, be sure to make several passes, cutting deeper with each pass until the desired depth is achieved.

Using a router and a ¼-inch rounding-over bit, radius all the exposed edges of the slats.

3. Assemble the cart top. Dry assemble the

top to check the fits of the joints. Check also to ensure that there's sufficient clearance between the top edges and the slats for your piloted rounding-over bit. You need to radius the edges of the top, and doing it after assembly helps produce neat corners. If it appears that the pilot will mar the slats, remove them, reclamp the top frame (without glue, of course), and machine the interior edges.

Proceed with the glue-up. Apply a spot of resorcinol glue to each slat, but don't spread any in the groove for the slats. The spot of glue should anchor the slat in

position, yet still allow the wood to move with changes in humidity. One by one, insert the slats into the groove in one of the cross members. Use scraps of ¼-inch-thick stock as spacers to help you position the slats. After applying a dab of glue to the other end of each slat, work the second cross member onto them.

Now apply glue to the ends of the cross members and the dadoes in the sides. Fit the sides in place. Apply clamps across the assembly, one at each cross member.

After the glue has cured, use a router and a ¼-inch rounding-over bit to radius the frame's edges.

4. Cut the parts for the leg assemblies. Be-

cause one pair of legs has wheels, it is shorter than the other pair. And because the leg assembly without wheels fits inside the assembly with wheels, there are two different lengths of cross braces. As you cut the parts, label them lightly in pencil so you don't get them mixed up.

Lay out a 1¼-inch radius on both ends of each leg. Cut the radius with a saber saw or on a band saw. Sand the cut edges smooth, then, using a router and a rounding-over bit, radius all the edges of the legs only.

Don't radius the sections of the short legs where the cross braces will attach; mark these areas on the legs before you rout.

Notch the two long legs to accept cross braces, as shown in the *Leg Assembly* drawing. The short legs do not have the cross brace let in.

Lay out and drill the stopped holes in the legs for the roto hinges. As noted before, the holes should have a flat bottom, and you should have the hinges in hand to ensure the holes are properly sized for them. Locate the holes carefully so that the geometry of the leg assembly will be correct. Moreover, be sure you drill the holes for the leg hinges in one face of the short legs, and the holes for the top hinges in the opposite face.

Finally, lay out and drill the holes in the short legs for the T-nuts that secure the shoulder bolt axles. The ³⁄₈-inch T-nuts require ½-inch-diameter holes.

LEG ASSEMBLY

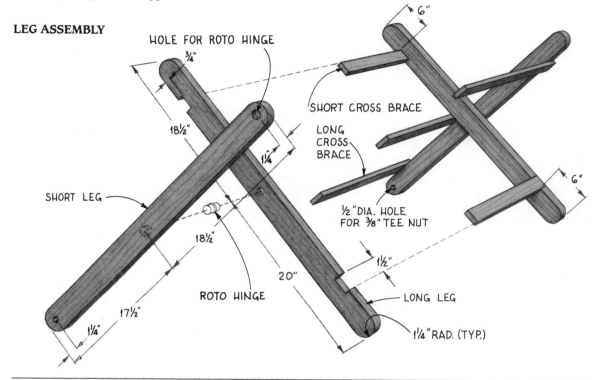

HOLE FOR ROTO HINGE
¾"
18½"
1¼"
SHORT LEG
18½"
ROTO HINGE
17½"
1¼"
20"
6"
SHORT CROSS BRACE
LONG CROSS BRACE
½" DIA. HOLE FOR ⅜" TEE NUT
1½"
6"
LONG LEG
1¼" RAD. (TYP.)

5. Assemble the legs.

Dry assemble the two leg units separately. With a router and a rounding-over bit, radius the cross braces so their corners blend into the legs. It is easier to do this before the legs and top are finally assembled.

Join the long legs and the short cross braces first. Use glue and two screws per joint. We used brass screws and left them exposed. Be sure the roto hinge holes face out. Glue the hinges in place. Glue the hinges in place on the top assembly as well.

One at a time, glue the short legs to the hinges, both those in the leg assembly and in the top. This goes best if you have help to manipulate the leg assembly while you coax the second short leg into place. Glue and screw the remaining three cross braces in place, as shown in the *Leg Assembly* drawing.

Test the fit of the roto hinge before gluing it in place. The metal washer between the wooden elements ensures the legs will be far enough apart to work smoothly. Note the area on the upper leg where the edges aren't rounded-over; this is where the cross brace attaches.

6. **Make the wheels.** The wheels are cut from 5/4 stock. They are 7 inches in diameter, with a ½-inch-diameter axle hole in the center. The wheels can be cut using a saber saw or router; if you use a trammel accessory, you can do a better job of avoiding flat spots on your wheels. Radius the edges of the wheels with a ¼-inch rounding-over bit in a table-mounted router.

7. **Finish the cart.** Be sure all exposed edges are radiused. Sand all the surfaces, and wipe the resulting dust from the wood with a tack cloth.

Apply at least three coats of the spar varnish with a high-quality, fine-bristle varnish brush. Coat all the surfaces, including the underside of the cart. Take particular care to coat any exposed end grain. Remember that with spar varnish, many thin coats add up to a better, more enduring finish than a couple of thick coats.

When the finish is dry, install the wheels. Insert the T-nuts from the inside of the leg. Use a ⅜-inch flat washer on the shoulder bolt to "capture" the wheel, and tighten the shoulder bolt into the T-nut.

A shoulder bolt has a segment of smooth shank that's larger in diameter than its threaded segment. It's probably used to hold the wheels on your lawn mower. Hold a washer at the hole in the wheel, fit the bolt through, and turn it into the T-nut in the leg.

TIP

With a shop-made trammel for your router, you can cut perfectly round wheels quickly and easily. The trammel is cut from ¼-inch plywood. Remove the plastic base plate from your router and attach the trammel in its place.

To cut the wheels for the cart, roughly lay both out on the wood. Drill their center holes.

Now chuck a small-diameter straight bit in the router and set the depth of cut to about ¼ inch. Slip a machine screw through the appropriate pivot hole in the trammel and into the center hole of the first wheel. Holding the bit just above the wood, turn on the router. Plunge the bit into the wood and swing the tool around the pivot, cutting a circular groove. Shift to the second wheel and repeat the process. Turn the stock over and start cutting the wheels from the second side, cutting two circular grooves around the center holes.

Now increase the depth of cut to ½ inch. Make a second cut on both sides for each wheel. If necessary, increase the depth of cut yet again, and rout the disks free.

MAHOGANY ENSEMBLE PLANTER CART

Flowers, shrubs, and trees are some of the nicest things about the outdoors. When we settle into our outdoor furniture, we're enjoying the sun, the breeze, the fresh air, *and* the flowers, shrubs, and trees—all the foliage and greenery we don't usually have indoors.

But you don't always have wonderful plants *right there* where you relax. Maybe the deck is elevated, or the patio tied into a driveway. Planters are nice in such situations, so we built this planter cart.

Designed around two huge clay pots, this cart allows you to keep colorful plants close by, regardless of where you are—on the deck or porch, terrace or patio. The cart enables you to move the plants to their favored conditions—always in the sun, always in the shade, whatever they prefer. The cart is attractive enough to have indoors; when cold weather arrives, protect your plants by wheeling the planter cart inside.

The cart borrows many of the ensemble's design and construction motifs: the scrolled handle brackets, the half-laps, the wooden wheels. As with the other projects in the ensemble, many of the elements are simply screwed together.

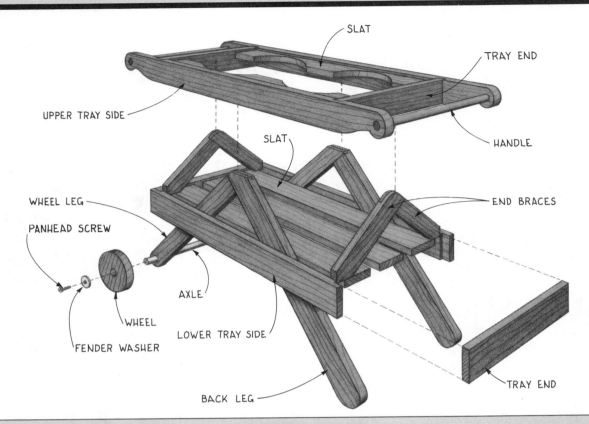

SLAT

TRAY END

UPPER TRAY SIDE

SLAT

HANDLE

WHEEL LEG

END BRACES

PANHEAD SCREW

AXLE

WHEEL

LOWER TRAY SIDE

FENDER WASHER

TRAY END

BACK LEG

SHOPPING LIST

LUMBER
2 pcs. 5/4 × 12 × 10' mahogany (stair tread)
3 pcs. 1" dia. × 36" hardwood dowel

HARDWARE AND SUPPLIES
1 box #6 × 2½" galvanized drywall-type screws
1 box #6 × 1¾" galvanized drywall-type screws

HARDWARE AND SUPPLIES—CONTINUED
2 pcs. #12 × 2" pan-head screws
2 pcs. ⁵⁄₁₆" I.D. fender washers (minimum O.D. 1⅝")
Resorcinol glue

FINISH
Spar varnish

CUTTING LIST

PIECE	NUMBER	THICKNESS	WIDTH	LENGTH	MATERIAL
Upper tray sides	2	1"	3½"	52"	5/4 mahogany
Tray ends	4	1"	3½"	17¼"	5/4 mahogany
Lower tray sides	2	1"	3½"	38"	5/4 mahogany
Slats	5	1"	3½"	36"	5/4 mahogany
Wheel legs	2	1"	2½"	30½"	5/4 mahogany
Back legs	2	1"	2½"	31¾"	5/4 mahogany
End braces	4	1"	2½"	13"	5/4 mahogany
Wheels	2	1"	6"	6"	5/4 mahogany
Handles	2	1" dia.		18¾"	Hardwood dowel
Axle	1	1" dia.		19"	Hardwood dowel

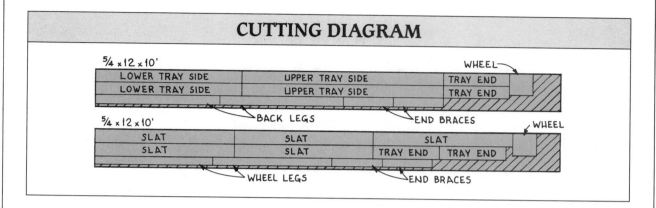

CUTTING DIAGRAM

Builder's Notes

A companion project to this chapter's chaise lounge, folding serving cart, and chair and settee, the planter cart is constructed with the same materials and uses the same tools and techniques as those projects. If you are building only this project from the ensemble, then by all means read the "Builder's Notes" accompanying the chaise lounge project on page 158.

The point worth noting is that wood doesn't always measure up to common standards. In this instance, the 5/4 (five-quarter) stock we purchased was a bit light of the common standard that 5/4 stock dresses out to—1 1/16 inches. It was only 1 inch thick. The dimensions recorded here are based on what we used.

If your stock lives up to the standard, you shouldn't have to fret. Cut the dadoes and rabbets a tad wider, the

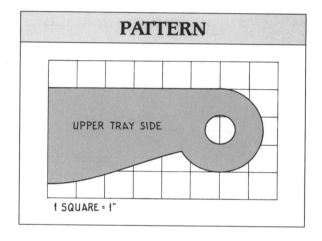

PATTERN

UPPER TRAY SIDE

1 SQUARE = 1"

laps a hint deeper. The extra thickness should have no other impact on your work.

---

1. Cut the parts for the upper tray. The cart is composed of two tray-like structures connected by the legs and two end braces. Start the project by making the upper tray, which has the scrolled ends and the handles.

Cut the sides, ends, and slats from the 5/4 stock and the handles from the dowel stock. Dado the sides for the ends, as shown in the *Upper Tray Joinery* drawing. Check the thickness of the stock, and cut the dadoes to the appropriate width. Use a router and a straight bit, and control the cut with the router jig described in the previous two projects in this chapter. The dadoes need only be ¼ inch deep.

To measure the pot, lay two scrap sticks against it. Shim them up so they clear the pot's rim. Measure between the sticks, adjusting their positions until they are both touching the pot and parallel. The distance between the sticks is the pot diameter.

PLAN VIEWS

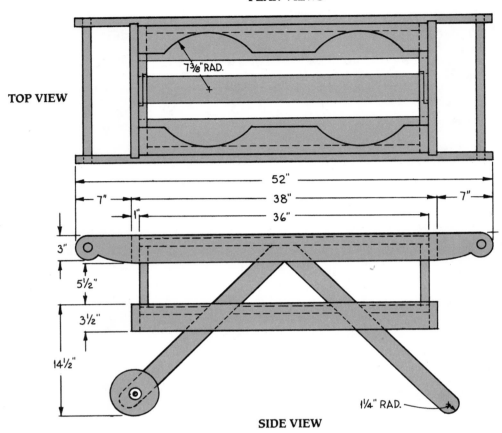

TOP VIEW

7⅜" RAD.

52"

7"   38"   7"

1"

36"

3"

5½"

3½"

14½"

1¼" RAD.

SIDE VIEW

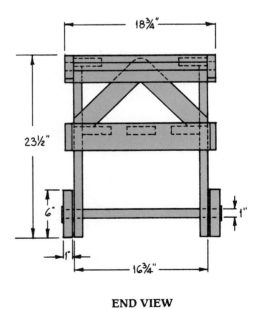

18¾"

23½"

6"

1"

1"

16¾"

END VIEW

TOOL LIST

Clamps	Saber saw
Combination square	Sander(s)
Drill	Sandpaper
⅜" plug cutter	Saw for crosscutting
1" dia. bit	Screwdriver
Countersink bit	Table saw
Pilot hole bit	Dado cutter
Paintbrush	Tack cloth
Router	Tape measure
¼" rounding-over bit	Trammel
¾" straight bit	Try square
Router, table-mounted	Yardstick
Ruler	

Now enlarge the pattern for the scrolled ends, transfer it to the sides, and cut the shape with a saber saw or on the band saw. Sand the sawed edges to remove saw marks. Then bore a 1-inch-diameter hole through the center of the scroll.

Finally, cut two arcs in each slat, as shown in the

Top View. These arcs should be laid out to accommodate the specific pots you will use in the cart. The pots we used were a bit over 14 inches in diameter just beneath their rims. Measure your pots and adjust the radius of the arcs, if necessary. After cutting the arcs, sand the sawed edges to smooth them.

UPPER TRAY JOINERY

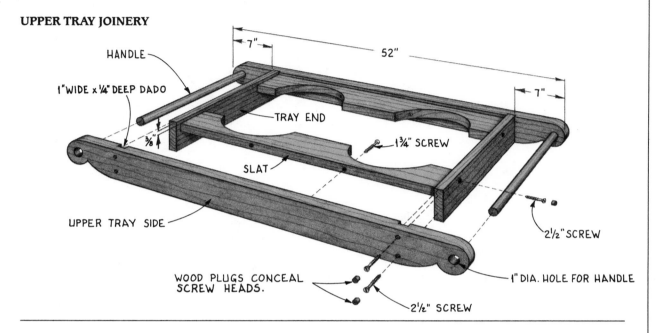

2. Assemble the upper tray. The initial step is to sand the parts and radius their edges. Use a router and a ¼-inch rounding-over bit to radius the edges that will be exposed. The interior corners of the framework should be left to be rounded during assembly so they can be blended for best appearance.

Assemble the sides and ends first. Be sure to incorporate the handles in the assembly at this time; it may be tough to drive them all the way through the holes after the frame is screwed together. Use resorcinol glue

and 2½-inch galvanized drywall-type screws. Countersink and counterbore the pilot holes for the screws so wood plugs can be used to conceal the screw heads. After the frame is assembled (but before the slats are attached), radius the inner perimeters—top and underside. That done, add the slats. Drive screws through the ends and sides into the slat edges, as well as through the edges of the slats (where the arcs reduce their width sufficiently) into the sides.

3. Make the lower tray. Cut the sides, ends, and slats for the lower tray. The ends fit into rabbets cut in the sides. Cut the rabbets as wide as the stock is thick and ¼ inch deep. Use a router and a straight bit guided by a straightedge clamped to the work.

Assemble the sides and ends temporarily with screws only, and radius the interior perimeter of the frame with the router and the rounding-over bit. This

done, back out the screws, disassembling the parts. Radius the remaining exposed edges of the sides, ends, and slats. Sand the parts.

Now glue and screw the slats between the ends. See the *Lower Tray Joinery* drawing. Be sure to counterbore all the pilot holes so the screw heads can be concealed beneath wood plugs. Don't attach the sides; they are attached after the tray is attached to the legs.

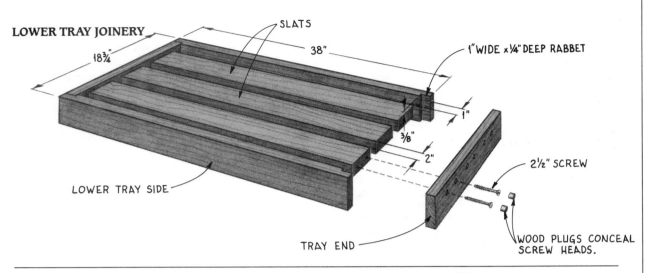

LOWER TRAY JOINERY

SLATS

18¾"

38"

1" WIDE × ¼" DEEP RABBET

1"

⅜"

2"

2½" SCREW

LOWER TRAY SIDE

TRAY END

WOOD PLUGS CONCEAL SCREW HEADS.

4. Make the leg and end brace assemblies.

Both the leg and end brace assemblies consist of two members joined in end laps, forming (when installed) inverted Vs.

Cut the parts to the sizes specified by the "Cutting List." Each piece has a lap cut on one end; do this next. Laps can be cut with several different tools: radial arm saw, table saw, or router. Since all members are the same thickness and width, one setup will serve for all. After cutting the laps, round off the foot ends of the legs; scribe a 1¼-inch radius on the leg, then cut it with a saber saw or on the band saw. Drill a 1-inch-diameter hole for the axle through the two wheel legs (the shorter legs); see the *Leg Assembly* drawing for the hole's location. Finally, trim the ends of the end braces, as shown in the *End Brace Assembly* drawing.

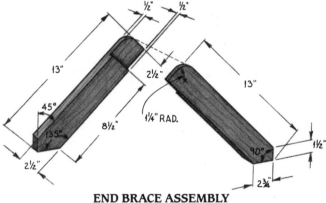

½" ½"

13"

2½"

13"

45°

135°

8½"

¼" RAD.

1½"

2½"

90°

2¾"

END BRACE ASSEMBLY

Glue up the assemblies with resorcinol glue. Be sure you mate a back leg and a wheel leg in each leg assembly. After the glue sets, trim the lap joints. The end braces are rounded slightly. The leg assemblies are trimmed on a 45 degree angle. Finally, radius the edges of these parts with a router and a ¼-inch rounding-over bit, and sand them carefully.

LEG ASSEMBLY

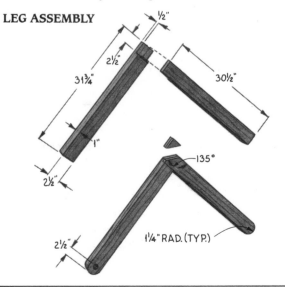

½"

2½"

31¾"

30½"

1"

135°

2½"

1¼" RAD. (TYP.)

2½"

TIP

Use a piece of the working stock as a measuring tool when setting the table saw fence for cutting laps. When you are joining two pieces of equal width in the lap joint, the length of the laps equals the width of the stock. Butt the stock against the fence, and adjust the fence to align the other edge of the stock with the *outside* of the blade.

5. Assemble the cart.

Assembly of the cart is contrary; it progresses from the top down. The upper tray is already assembled. Turn it upside down on your workbench. On the bottom of the slats, mark the midpoint (one mark on each slat). Similarly, mark the centerline (the line that splits the angle between the legs) on each leg assembly. Set a leg assembly in place and line up the centerline of the assembly with the centerline of the upper tray. Align the legs and drive 1¾-inch screws through the legs into the back of the upper tray sides. While you should drill pilot holes for these screws, the holes don't need to be counterbored, since the screws aren't obviously visible.

Attach the lower tray next. Cut four spacer blocks of equal length—5½ inches. Stand the blocks on the edges of the upper tray and prop the lower tray—turned upside down, of course, and still without its sides—on them. To stabilize the legs while you drill pilot holes and drive screws, clamp them to the lower tray slats. Run a couple of 2½-inch screws through each leg into the slats; these screws will be concealed by the sides. Now attach the sides, driving 2½-inch screws into the previously drilled (and counterbored) pilot holes. Complete this assembly phase by driving a 1¾-inch screw through each leg into the back of the side; counterboring the pilot holes for these screws is optional.

It is important to align the leg assemblies correctly when attaching them to the top tray assembly. Use a speed square, a combination square, or—as here—a drafting triangle. With one screw driven, you can rock the assembly slightly until you have the proper 45 degree angle. Note the pencil mark indicating the centerline of the leg assembly; it is aligned with a similar mark indicating the center of the tray assembly.

Cut four 5½-inch-long scraps to rest the lower tray on during its installation. These silent helpers keep the trays parallel, and they eliminate the need for clamping and adjusting and reclamping. Be sure the tray is upside down. The leg assemblies are still unstable, so clamp them to the tray while you drill pilot holes and drive screws.

The lower sides go on after the legs are secured to the lower tray. They need to be attached first to the ends, then to the legs.

6. **Make the wheels.** The wheels are cut from 5/4 stock. They are 6 inches in diameter, with a 1-inch-diameter axle hole in the center. The wheels can be cut using a saber saw; if you use a trammel accessory for the saw, you can do a better job of avoiding flat spots on your wheels. Radius the edges of the wheels with a ¼-inch rounding-over bit in a table-mounted router.

Prepare the axle by drilling a pilot hole in the center of each end.

7. **Finish the cart.** All the exposed screws, primarily those driven through the faces of the sides and ends, should be covered with wood plugs. Make your own plugs from the mahogany scraps, using a plug cutter chucked in a drill. A ⅜-inch-diameter plug will probably be the correct size. Apply resorcinol glue to the counterbore with a cotton swab and press the plug into the hole. After the glue dries, pare the plug flush with the surface with a chisel.

Sand the plugs, and touch up any rough spots on the cart and its wheels. Be sure all exposed edges are radiused. Wipe any dust from the wood with a tack cloth.

Apply at least three coats of the spar varnish with a high-quality, fine-bristle varnish brush. Coat all the surfaces, including the underside of the cart. Take particular care to coat any exposed end grain. Remember that with spar varnish, many thin coats add up to a better, more enduring finish than a couple of thick coats.

After the last coat has dried, fit the axle in place and install the wheels. Fit a wheel over the axle stub protruding from the leg and secure it with a pan-head screw and fender washer.

Like the ideal donut, a fender washer is all washer and very little hole. But it's the perfect retainer for the wheel. Just make sure the washer is larger in diameter than the axle. Install the wheels after the finish has dried.

MAHOGANY ENSEMBLE CHAIR AND SETTEE

To round out the Mahogany Ensemble, we needed some seats. Here they are: a chair and a settee.

Made with the ensemble's signature motifs, the pieces have the scrolled post tops, the half-lap joinery, the 5/4 (five-quarter) mahogany construction. Like the chaise lounge, the chair and settee are cushioned with foam rubber mats covered with natural sailcloth. Although

somewhat too erect to allow for total relaxation, they are a big improvement over picnic benches for outdoor socializing.

One of the nicest things about the assembly concept is that you can adjust the height and rake of the seat during construction. I'm pretty tall and unnecessarily large; Phil Gehret, who built a lot of this furniture, is less

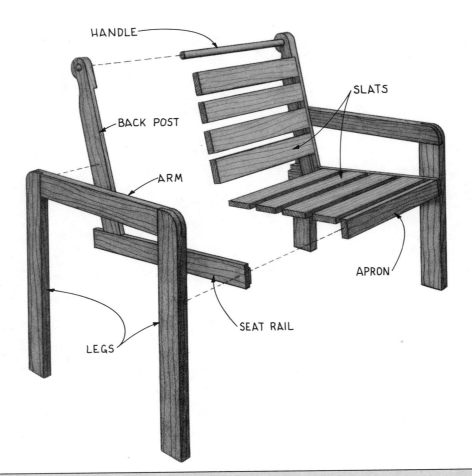

HANDLE

BACK POST

ARM

SLATS

APRON

SEAT RAIL

LEGS

SHOPPING LIST—CHAIR

LUMBER

2 pcs. 1 × 4 × 8′ mahogany
1 pc. 5/4 × 12 × 6′ mahogany (stair tread)
1 pc. 1″ dia. × 36″ hardwood dowel

HARDWARE AND SUPPLIES

1 box #6 × 1⅝″ galvanized drywall-type screws
Resorcinol glue

FINISH

Spar varnish

FABRIC AND NOTIONS

1⅛ yd. 45″ wide upholstery fabric
1 spool matching thread
1 pc. 1″ × 16″ × 21″ foam rubber
1 pc. 1″ × 18″ × 21″ foam rubber

SHOPPING LIST—SETTEE

LUMBER

4 pcs. 1 × 4 × 8′ mahogany
1 pc. 5/4 × 12 × 8′ mahogany (stair tread)
2 pcs. 1″ dia. × 36″ hardwood dowel

HARDWARE AND SUPPLIES

1 box #6 × 1⅝″ galvanized drywall-type screws
Resorcinol glue

FINISH

Spar varnish

FABRIC AND NOTIONS

2¼ yd. 45″ wide upholstery fabric
1 spool matching thread
1 pc. 1″ × 16″ × 41″ foam rubber
1 pc. 1″ × 18″ × 41″ foam rubber

CUTTING LIST—CHAIR

PIECE	NUMBER	THICKNESS	WIDTH	LENGTH	MATERIAL
Back posts	2	1″	2½″	24″	5/4 mahogany
Seat rails	2	1″	2½″	22″	5/4 mahogany
Apron	1	1″	2½″	20″	5/4 mahogany
Slats	8	¾″	3½″	20″	1 × 4 mahogany
Arms	2	1″	2½″	22″	5/4 mahogany
Legs	4	1″	2½″	24″	5/4 mahogany
Handle	1	1″ dia.		21″	Hardwood dowel

CUTTING LIST—SETTEE

PIECE	NUMBER	THICKNESS	WIDTH	LENGTH	MATERIAL
Back posts	3	1″	2½″	24″	5/4 mahogany
Seat rails	2	1″	2½″	22″	5/4 mahogany
Center support rail	1	1″	1¾″	21¼″	5/4 mahogany
Apron	1	1″	2½″	40″	5/4 mahogany
Slats	8	¾″	3½″	40″	1 × 4 mahogany
Arms	2	1″	2½″	22″	5/4 mahogany
Legs	4	1″	2½″	24″	5/4 mahogany
Handle	1	1″ dia.		41″*	Hardwood dowel

*Use 2 dowels, joined at the center support.

tall and more svelte. Chairs he built to accommodate himself don't comfortably accommodate me. But this design has the solution: As you'll see, you can clamp the parts together, give 'em a sit, and make some adjustments before final assembly. So I can raise the seat and tip it back just to accommodate *me*. It's nice.

Another plus is the cushion design. As covered, the seat and back cushions are a single unit. The cover is a simple fabric tube with a foam rubber slab stuffed into each end. A double seam stitched across the middle separates the seat from the back, but leaves them linked. The covers are simple enough to sew that even a woodworker can do it.

Builder's Notes

A companion project to this chapter's chaise lounge, folding serving cart, and planter cart, the chair and settee are constructed with the same materials and use

PATTERN

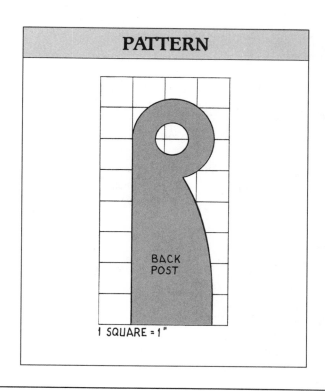

BACK POST

1 SQUARE = 1″

CUTTING DIAGRAM—CHAIR

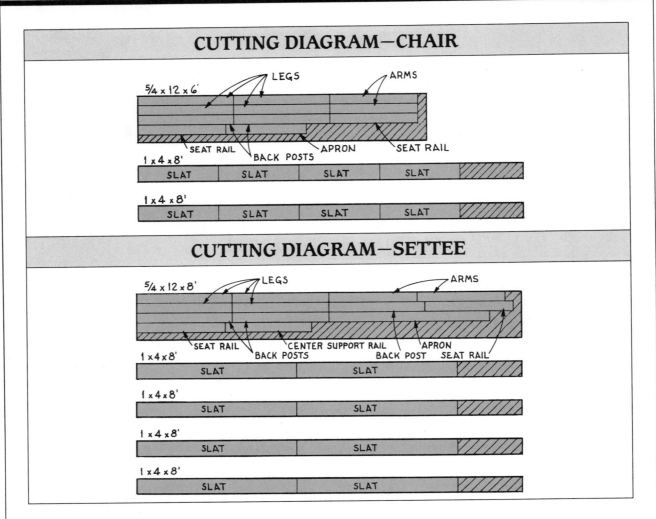

CUTTING DIAGRAM—SETTEE

the same tools and techniques as those earlier projects. If you are building only this project from the ensemble, then by all means read the "Builder's Notes" accompanying the chaise lounge project on page 158.

The point worth noting with this project is that wood doesn't always measure up to common standards. In this instance, the 5/4 stock we purchased was a bit light of the 1 1/16-inch standard that 5/4 stock usually dresses out to. It was only 1 inch thick. The dimensions recorded here are based on what we used.

If your stock lives up to the standard, you shouldn't have to fret. Cut the laps a hint deeper. The extra thickness should have no other impact on your work.

As is the case with many of the outdoor seats in this book, the chair and settee differ only in the length of the members that connect the side frames—in this case, the handle, slats, and apron. To bolster the structure, a center support rail is added midway between the side frames of the settee.

1. Cut and lap the arms and legs. Both the chair and the settee consist of two side frames, each made up of an arm and a pair of legs, and a seat assembly. Make the side frames first. To that end, cut the arms and legs to the sizes specified by the "Cutting List."

Cut the laps that join the legs and arm into a side frame. The legs are lapped on one end, the arms on both ends. These are easily cut on a radial arm or table saw using a dado cutter. On the table saw, guide the workpiece with the miter gauge and set the rip fence to govern the length of the lap. On the radial arm saw, clamp a stop to the backstop to govern the lap's length. Either way, you'll have to make three or four passes to complete each lap.

To set the depth of cut for a half-lap, make trial cuts on scraps of the working stock. This approach works whether you use a radial arm saw or table saw, and a standard blade or a dado cutter.

Set the depth of cut roughly, using a rule. Then set the miter gauge (or the arm) to a slight angle. Nip a corner of a piece of scrap. Roll the piece over and nip the opposite corner, so the two cuts intersect. By looking at the end of the piece where the cuts intersect, you'll be able to tell how you need to adjust the depth of cut. Adjust the setting, then try it on the new scrap.

In the photo, the scraps show settings that are (from left to right): just right, too deep, and too shallow.

2. **Assemble the side frames.** With resorcinol glue, assemble the side frames. Clamping each joint with a hand screw eliminates struggling with cauls needed to protect the woodwork from the metal pads or jaws of other sorts of clamps. But if C-clamps or speed clamps are what you have, they are more than adequate.

After the glue has set, scribe a 2½-inch radius on each lap joint, as shown in the *Side Frame Joinery* drawing, and round off the corners with a saber saw or on the band saw. Then radius the edges of these assemblies with a router and a ¼-inch rounding-over bit.

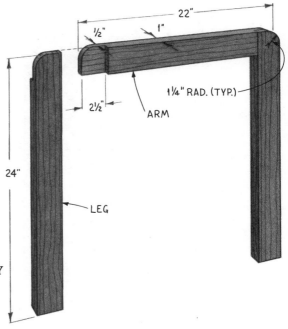

SIDE FRAME JOINERY

3. **Cut the parts for the seat assembly.** The seat assembly for the chair is composed of seat rails, back posts, slats, and an apron. The rails and posts are joined into two L-shaped frames by half-laps. In turn, the two frames are connected by the apron and slats, which nestle into rabbets cut in the rails and posts. The settee, besides having longer slats and apron, has a center support rail that's a trimmed-down seat frame.

Cut the necessary parts to the sizes specified by the "Cutting List."

Enlarge the pattern for the scrolled post top and transfer it to the posts. Cut the scroll with a saber saw or on the band saw. Bore the 1-inch-diameter hole for the handle.

CHAIR PLAN VIEWS

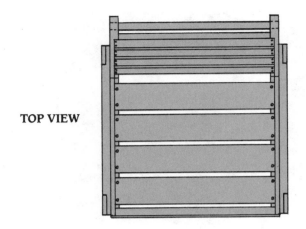

TOP VIEW

TOOL LIST

Clamps	Sandpaper
Compass	Saw for crosscutting
Drill	Sawhorses
1″ dia. bit	Screwdriver
Pilot hole bit	Sewing machine
Paintbrush	Table saw
Router	Dado cutter
¼″ rounding-over bit	Miter gauge
½″ rabbeting bit	Tack cloth
Ruler	Tape measure
Saber saw	Try square
Sander(s)	

FRONT VIEW

20″

1″

35½″

24″

±16½″

21″   1¹⁵⁄₁₆″

SIDE VIEW (ALSO FOR SETTEE)

3½″

¾″ TYP.

24″

3½″   ½″ TYP.

100°

22″

±14½″

2½″

22″

4. Cut the joinery in the rails and posts.
Study the *Rail-to-Post Joinery* drawing next, so you understand what needs to be accomplished.

Rabbet the rails and posts first. As shown, the rabbets are ½ inch wide and ¾ inch deep. On the rails, the rabbet for the slats extends from one end to the other. A rabbet is also cut across one end for the apron. On the posts, the rabbet for the slats is stopped, extending 20½ inches from the bottom. Note the orientation of the rabbet to the scrolled post top. *All the rabbets are on the inside face of each piece;* when assembled, the seat frames are mirror images of each other.

The rabbets can be cut with a router or on the table saw with a dado cutter. However you cut the rabbets, square the stopped end of the rabbet in the post with a chisel.

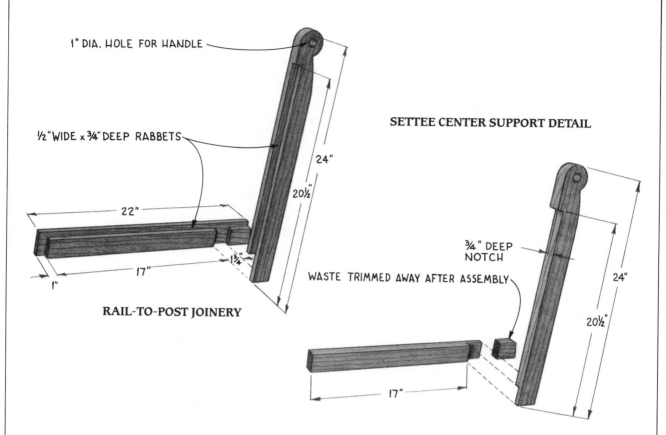

1" DIA. HOLE FOR HANDLE

½" WIDE x ¾" DEEP RABBETS

22"

17"

1"

1¾"

20½"

24"

RAIL-TO-POST JOINERY

SETTEE CENTER SUPPORT DETAIL

¾" DEEP NOTCH

WASTE TRIMMED AWAY AFTER ASSEMBLY

24"

20½"

17"

Cut the half-laps that join the rails and posts next. The laps on the posts are fairly straightforward, but those on the rails really make the case for the radial arm saw as the best tool for cutting laps. On this tool, you merely position the stop, set the arm's angle, and make the cuts.

The task is more complicated on the table saw. Begin the posts by mitering the lower ends; the miter, measured from the rabbeted edge to the butt end, must be 80 degrees. To actually cut the laps, set up the table saw with the dado cutter and position the rip fence as you did to cut the leg and arm laps. To cut the first lap, set the miter gauge to form a 100 degree angle with the fence. Pick the post that will lay in the miter gauge with its mitered end against the fence *and* the rabbet up. Cut the lap in it. Now readjust the miter gauge to form a 70 degree angle with the fence. Lap the other post.

The laps in the rails are harder to cut; you can't use the fence because the ends must be square rather than mitered, and the workpiece conceals the cut. So lay out the laps and extend the lines for the shoulder cuts onto the edges of the workpiece. Guiding the piece with the miter gauge, align the lines with the cutter and make the cuts. The laps in the rails are cut into the rabbeted face.

Note: The center support rail for the settee is

essentially a duplicate of a seat frame with the rabbet trimmed off. See the *Settee Center Support Detail*. The rail is specified by the "Cutting List" to be ¾ inch shorter and ¾ inch narrower than the seat rails. It is not rabbeted at all. The post is the same size as the other posts. Instead of rabbeting it, however, notch this post to the depth and length of the rabbets in the other posts. Cut laps in the center support parts just as in the seat frame parts.

TIP

If you choose to rout the rabbets in the posts and rails, you can use a ½-inch rabbeting bit and address the workpiece from its edge. To provide more surface area for the router to bear on, gang the two rails and two posts together and clamp them. Rout one rabbet. Shift the parts around to expose a new one, then rout the rabbet in it. And so forth. If you work this way, cut each rabbet in multiple passes, routing about ⅛ inch deeper with each pass.

SETTEE PLAN VIEWS

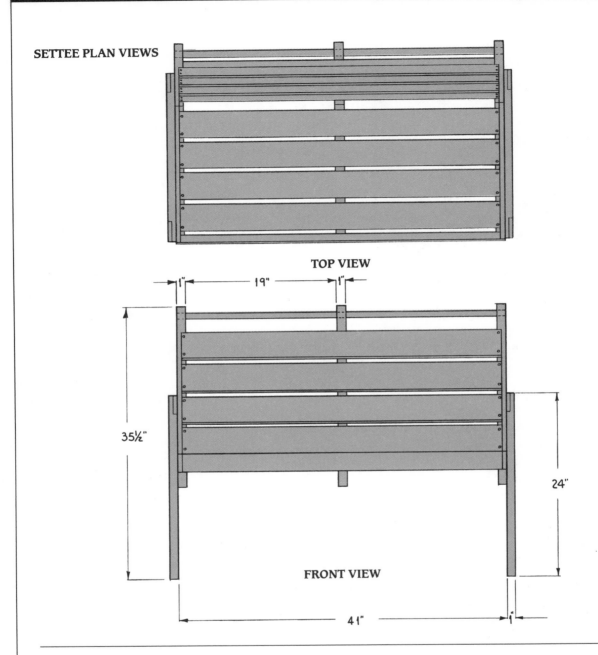

TOP VIEW

1" 19" 1"

35½"

24"

FRONT VIEW

41"

1"

5. Assemble the seat. Glue up the seat frames (and center support, if applicable) first, using resorcinol glue. After the glue has set, you can trim off the rear projection on the center support, since it serves no purpose. (On the seat frames, the projection is an attachment point for the side frames.) After the glue has dried and the clamps are off, radius all the exposed edges with a router and a ¼-inch rounding-over bit. Radius the edges of the slats and apron as well.

Attach the handle and the apron next, joining the two seat frames. Glue the handle into one seat frame, then add the other frame. (When making the settee, slide the center support onto the handle before adding the second seat frame.) With the frames linked by the handle, it's relatively easy to glue and clamp the apron in place.

After the glue has dried, install the slats. After drilling pilot holes, drive 1⅝-inch screws through the slats into the frames. Use two screws in each end of every slat. (Drive screws into the center support, too.)

6. Join the side frames to the seat assembly.

The seat is joined to the side frames by 1⅝-inch screws driven through the rails and posts into the legs. The construction of the chair allows you to fine-tune the seat's height and rake before you drive any screws, however. The *Side View* provides some positioning measurements to use as a starting point.

Set the seat assembly on its side on a couple of sawhorses. Set a side frame on it, aligning it as indicated in the *Side View*. Clamp the two assemblies together with C-clamps, speed clamps, or the like. Turn the unit over and position and clamp the second side frame.

Set the clamped-together chair on its feet and try it out. Make adjustments. Raise or lower the seat. Tilt it back a bit more. Make it more erect. When you are happy with the way the chair "sits," drill the pilot holes and drive the screws. Drive two screws each through the front of the rail into the front leg, through the rail's tail into the back leg, and through the posts into the arm-leg lap joint.

Setting the height and rake of the seat in the chair is a seat-of-the-pants process. After the seat assembly and the leg assemblies are glued and set, you can clamp these parts together. Use a clamp at each of four attachment points. Then sit in the chair and see if it is comfortable. Raise or lower the seat; rake the seat forward and back. With each adjustment, sit in the chair and see how it feels.

7. Apply a finish.

Do any touch-up sanding necessary, and wipe the resulting dust from the wood with a tack cloth. Be sure all exposed edges are radiused.

Apply at least three coats of the spar varnish with a high-quality, fine-bristle varnish brush. Coat all the surfaces, including the underside of the chair or settee. Take particular care to coat any exposed end grain. Remember that with spar varnish, many thin coats add up to a better, more enduring finish than a couple of thick coats.

8. Make the cushions.

Cut a 38-inch piece of 45-inch-wide fabric for the chair cushion cover. The pattern, if any, should parallel the larger dimension. Fold the piece once across the long dimension, with the back of the fabric exposed. Stitch a seam along the 38-inch dimension, ½ inch from the edge. Turn the resulting tube right-side out, so the fabric's face is now on the outside, and center the seam on the bottom.

Flatten the tube and sew two seams across it, as shown, 19 inches and 20½ inches from one end. These seams create two separate seat-cushion compartments.

Turn under the fabric edges at both ends of the cover and hem them.

Cut the cushions from 1-inch-thick foam rubber. The seat is 21 inches by 16 inches; the back is 21 inches by 18 inches.

Stuff the foam cushions into the covers. Pin the ends of the covers shut with a row of straight pins about 1 inch from the hemmed edge of the covers—you may have to temporarily bunch up the foam to get the pins in. This allows enough room to guide the layers of fabric under the foot of the sewing machine. Fold in the corners

SEWING CHAIR CUSHION

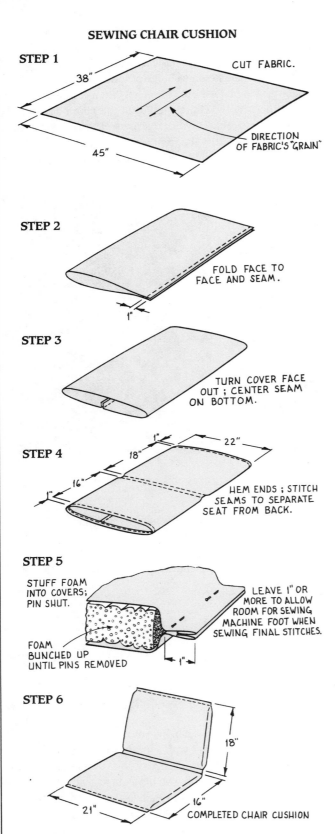

STEP 1

38"

45"

CUT FABRIC.

DIRECTION OF FABRIC'S "GRAIN"

STEP 2

FOLD FACE TO FACE AND SEAM.

1"

STEP 3

TURN COVER FACE OUT ; CENTER SEAM ON BOTTOM.

STEP 4

1" 22"
18"
16"
1"

HEM ENDS ; STITCH SEAMS TO SEPARATE SEAT FROM BACK.

STEP 5

STUFF FOAM INTO COVERS; PIN SHUT.

FOAM BUNCHED UP UNTIL PINS REMOVED

LEAVE 1" OR MORE TO ALLOW ROOM FOR SEWING MACHINE FOOT WHEN SEWING FINAL STITCHES.

1"

STEP 6

18"

16"

21"

COMPLETED CHAIR CUSHION

---

of the top and bottom layers of fabric about 1¼ inches. Sew a line of stitches through the hemmed edges of both layers of fabric, closing the ends of the covers. Remove the pins, allowing the foam to unbunch. Place the cushion on the chair.

The sequence is much the same in making the settee cushion, except that you must begin with two pieces of fabric 43 inches by 38 inches. Lay one on top of the other, face to face, and sew seams along both 38-inch dimensions, ½ inch in from the edges. This will form a 42-inch-wide by 38-inch-long tube. Turn the tube right-side out, with the seams on either side, and continue as in making the chair cushion. Stitch the two seams that form the cushion compartments, cut and insert the cushions, and sew the cover closed.

SEWING SETTEE CUSHION

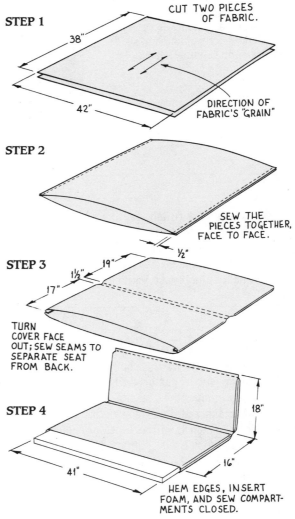

STEP 1

CUT TWO PIECES OF FABRIC.

38"

42"

DIRECTION OF FABRIC'S "GRAIN"

STEP 2

SEW THE PIECES TOGETHER, FACE TO FACE.

½"

STEP 3

19"
1½"
17"

TURN COVER FACE OUT; SEW SEAMS TO SEPARATE SEAT FROM BACK.

STEP 4

18"

41"

16"

HEM EDGES, INSERT FOAM, AND SEW COMPARTMENTS CLOSED.

SUN LOUNGER

The Old-Fashioned Hammock, Revisited

Traditionally, hammocks are strung between two more-or-less vertical objects that happen to be handy and heavy.

This is a hammock for people who don't have trees placed conveniently for support. Our portable model has a few advantages over the old standard. You don't need those stationary objects, for one. You can move the lounger to wherever the sun (or shade, if that's your pleasure) happens to be at a particular time of day. And if it's rainy, the lounger can be parked on a porch.

The frame is good looking, resembling Dali-esque glue-lam beams. And glue-lam beams is what they are. To make them, you rip a 16-foot-long oak board into thin strips, then glue the strips back together. To develop the vaguely W-shaped profile, the strips are clamped in a

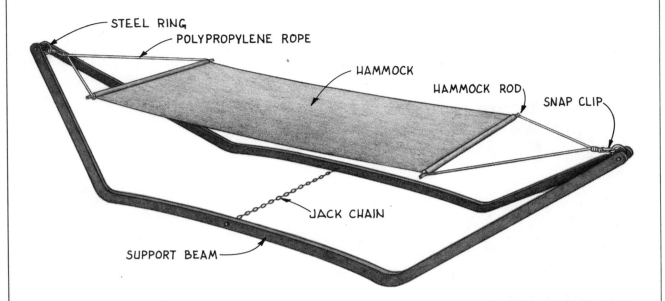

SHOPPING LIST

LUMBER

20 bd. ft. 5/4 white oak
1 sheet ¾" plywood
2 pcs. 1" dia. × 36" hardwood dowels

HARDWARE AND SUPPLIES

1 box #6 × 1¼" galvanized drywall-type screws
1 qt. resorcinol glue
Masking tape
2 pcs. ½" × 4" hex-head bolts, washers, and
    nylon-centered lock nuts
2 pcs. 3" dia. welded steel rings

HARDWARE AND SUPPLIES—CONTINUED

2 pcs. ⅛" galvanized eyebolts with 2 nuts each
2 ft. jack chain
30 ft. ⅜" dia. hollow-braided polypropylene rope
2 pcs. snap clips

FABRIC AND NOTIONS

3 yd. 34" wide canvas
1 spool matching thread

FINISH

Clear water repellent or clear exterior finish

CUTTING LIST

PIECE	NUMBER	THICKNESS	WIDTH	LENGTH	MATERIAL
Lamination form	1	¾"	20"	96"	Plywood
Support strips	4	¾"	4"	30"	Plywood
Stop blocks	4	¾"	4"	2¼"	Plywood
Lamination plies	32	³⁄₁₆"	1"	16'	White oak
Hammock rods	2	1" dia.		36"	Dowel

shop-made plywood form while the glue sets. The result-ing support beams are strong but springy, adding bounce to the hammock.

Connecting them are two bolts, run through holes drilled in the beam ends. The bolts are left loose and the holes are drilled oversize, so the members can swing away from one another. Captured on the bolts between the beams are steel rings, to which the hammock ropes are tied.

The hammock itself is but a minor sewing project. If you can laminate the support beams, you can deal with the hammock.

PATTERN

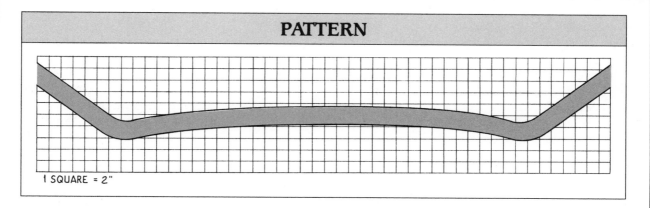

1 SQUARE = 2"

Builder's Notes

In an odd sort of way, this is truly a backyard project. Because those 16-foot-long laminations are a bit unwieldy in the shop, and also because the excess glue dripping from them can be messy, we put this one together outside the workshop. Out in the driveway.

This project was one of Fred Matlack's design and construction contributions.

Materials. We used oak for the frame. It is sturdy, has a good deal of spring, and looks good when laminated. Other good choices would be hickory and ash.

Regardless of the wood you use, the stock should be reasonably straight and clear, because knots and deviations in the grain direction will weaken the plies. The plies must be 16 feet long.

As noted in other hardwood projects in this book, you need to scout around for hardwoods; they aren't stocked at every building center. And this project's demand for 16-foot clear boards may keep you scouting longer than another project. To get the plies required to make the two support beams, Fred used two 16 footers that were about 6 inches wide; each board provided all the plies for one support beam.

Unless you have a jointer and a planer, you have to have the lumber dealer mill the wood to smooth it and reduce it to the required thickness. With this particular project, you need only have one face and one edge milled, since that's all you need to rip the lamination plies. During lamination, the individual plies will slip and slide, yielding beams with irregular faces. You'll have to sand them smooth.

The glue used is the outdoor builder's standby—resorcinol. If you've never used this glue, be prepared for a jolt when you buy the quart this project requires. Resorcinol is expensive, costing three to four times as much as yellow glue.

What makes resorcinol worth the expense for out-door projects is that it is completely waterproof. It has a lengthy assembly time, which means, in terms of this project, that it won't dry before you get the plies "painted" and assembled in the lamination form. But it also has a long clamping time, so you have to leave the clamps on for eight to ten hours while it sets.

Two ingredients, a powder and a liquid resin, must be mixed just before use. Use an expendable container to mix the glue—the bottom of a plastic milk or bleach jug, for example—and a likewise expendable paint brush to apply the glue. It's probably better to mix too little (and to have to mix two or three batches while you work) than to mix too much and to have to toss out the leftover. When mixed, the glue is somewhere between mulberry purple and brown in color, depending on the particular brand. It will stain wood and clothes, so be careful where it drips and what it smears on. Unlike

TOOL LIST

Bar or pipe clamps	Router
(at least 5)	¼" rounding-over bit
Belt sander, portable	Ruler
Circular saw	Saber saw
Clamps (at least 12)	Sandpaper
Drill	Sawhorses
⅛" dia. bit	Screwdriver
⅜" dia. bit	Sewing machine
¾" dia. bit	Table saw
Pilot hole bit	Tack cloth
Finishing sander	Tape measure
Hand screws	Try square
Pad sander	Wrench
Paintbrush	

other woodworking glues, it does not dry clear. You will be able to see thin, dark lines between the plies of the lamination. But resorcinol can handle the demanding job of rearranging your oak board in novel shapes—it is both flexible and waterproof.

The hammock sling is made from standard canvas. We used natural-colored canvas, but you might want to shop around for striped awning canvas.

Tools and techniques. There are two major machine operations in this project—ripping the plies and sanding the laminated support beams. Ripping the plies is a basic table saw operation. Given the length of the plies, you will need an outfeed table to support them as they come off the saw. It is very helpful to have an assistant to handle the outfeed operations—turning the plies as they leave the saw and keeping them properly organized.

The sanding operation is more tedious than difficult. When they come out of the clamps, the support beams will be uneven, with some plies having slid a bit high, others a bit low. You just have to sand the surfaces flat and smooth to get a good appearance. The beams are too big to move, so you need to use a portable belt sander to do the job.

The major technique is laminating the beams. If you've never glued up laminations before, don't be intimidated. The long, thin plies are merely awkward to handle. Get yourself some help—it doesn't have to be skilled help, just another pair of hands. The process is not complicated.

The oak plies are long and supple enough that you don't have to steam or soak them. The plywood form bends the plies into a series of curves and holds them in position until the glue hardens and preserves the shape. You'll need clamps to force those plies; the job requires five bar or pipe clamps and as many smaller clamps (of any sort) that you can muster.

A key "tool" in the process is the plywood lamination form, which you make. The plywood need not be the highest grade—neither side needs to be "good." But the form should be flat, so select a sheet that doesn't undulate, as cheaper grades sometimes do.

PLAN VIEWS

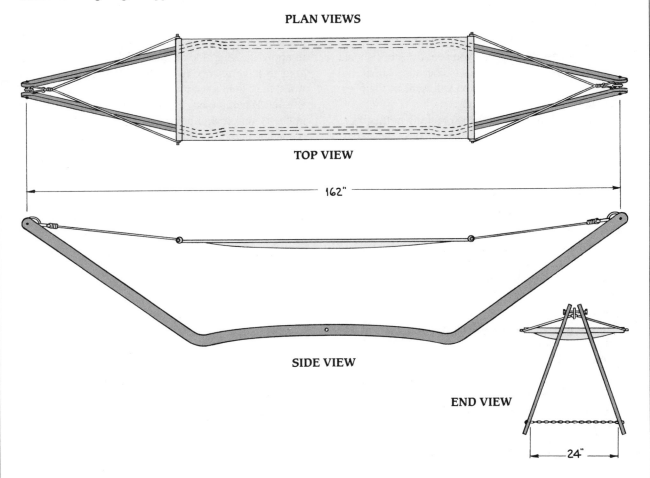

TOP VIEW

162"

SIDE VIEW

END VIEW

24"

1. **Make the plywood lamination form.** From a full sheet of ¾-inch plywood rip a 20-inch-wide piece for the lamination form. Rip two 4-inch-wide strips as well. A full sheet of plywood is pretty awkward to maneuver, so don't try. Rest the plywood on sawhorses and make the cuts with a circular saw. (Set the remaining piece aside for some future project.) Crosscut the two 4-inch-wide strips into the four support strips and the four stop blocks.

Enlarge the pattern and lay out both edges of the support beams' curves on the plywood, as shown in the *Plywood Lamination Form* drawing. Use a saber saw to cut along these lines, and discard the 3-inch-wide strip you cut away. It is important that the two edges *not* be the same; you can't simply lay out one line, cut the plywood in two, and expect to have a satisfactory form. The top edge of the beam has a modestly different profile than the bottom edge.

Having cut the form, attach the four support strips to the underside of the form's base element, positioning them roughly as shown in the *Plywood Lamination Form* drawing. Attach a stop block to each support.

During the gluing process, you rest the form's cap element on these strips back against the stops. This gives you a manageable starting point for applying the clamps. (If you build the form as specified here, you'll need two or three clamps that will open at least 28 inches. You can shorten the support strips a couple of inches to accommodate slightly shorter clamps, but not much more than that.) To help you center the strips in the form, measure and draw a centerline across the form, which is to say, a line 4 feet from either end. During the lamination operation, you align centerlines marked on the individual plies with the centerline on the form.

To complete the form, apply a heavy coat of paste wax to the curved edges and the support strips. This will help prevent glue drips and glue squeeze-out from bonding the lamination to the form.

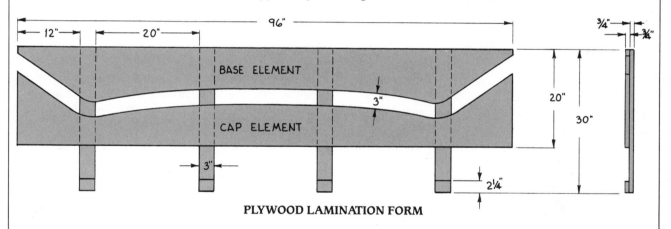

PLYWOOD LAMINATION FORM

2. **Cut the plies.** You need 32 plies in all, 16 for each support beam. It's a good idea to rip a few extras in case any of the plies are so knotty as to be unusable.

Before cutting the stock, mark a centerline across each face, that is, a line 8 feet from either end. During glue-up, you align the mark on each ply with the centerline drawn on the lamination form. Make all of these lines heavy enough to be easily visible while you work.

Here are our plies as they left the saw—same order and orientation. If these were to be glued up in this way, there would be a weak spot where the knots are. To avoid that, as mentioned in the text, you should flip every other strip end for end. That will compensate for the knots and yield a stronger lamination.

TIP

It's easy to get mixed up as you rip the plies. You need to flip every other ply end for end, as well as roll it over. To provide a quick visual check, mark the boards before you rip them. *On one face only,* draw a line on each side of the centerline. When you bundle up the plies, every other one should have three lines across it.

To enhance the strength of your lamination, you want to avoid reassembling the board you rip. So alter the grain structure (and disperse defects) by reorienting every other ply. As you rip the plies, keep them in order. But flip every other one end for end and roll it 180 degrees.

In doing this job, you'll be maneuvering a very long, heavy board. It's a good idea to have a helper manning the outfeed end of the operation, sliding the plies free of the saw and keeping them organized. You may find it easier to just bundle the plies as they come from the saw, then reorient alternating plies afterward.

3. Glue up the plies. Here comes the BIG step. Given the length of the plies and the nature of the glue, you may want to move out of the shop, as we did. To support each beam during its lamination, Fred set out several sawhorses. Use two horses to support the lamination form, and position two others to support the portion of the beam that extends beyond the form on either side.

Lay half of the plies—16 of them—edge to edge, face up, across the lamination form and the sawhorses. The ends should be flush. At intervals, apply masking tape across the undersides, linking all of them together. This will keep them in position while you apply the glue.

While conventional wisdom stipulates that you apply glue to both mating surfaces, in this particular project, it's probably better to flout convention. Don't worry about both sides; get a thorough, generous coat of glue spread on one face and be done with it. Work quickly but methodically. When the plies have been covered evenly, remove the tape strips and, one at a time, turn the plies on edge and stack them against each other in the form. You have to bend them slightly to fit them in the gap between the form's base element and its cap element. Align the centerline on each strip with the centerline on the form. Allow the plies to sit loosely in the form until all 16 are in place. Make sure that you haven't gotten glue on the outer surfaces of the top and bottom plies, or they may adhere to the form itself.

Apply strips of wide masking tape to the bottom of the strips before spreading the glue. Taping the pieces like this—a piece at each end, maybe a piece or two toward the middle—will keep the strips aligned. It also will keep them close together, so you don't have a lot of your expensive glue running between the strips and dripping on the floor. Pull off the tape after spreading the glue.

Use resorcinol glue, which is runny and stains like mulberries. Mix the contents of the two packages—one a powder, the other a syrup—according to the directions on the package. Fred used the bottom of a plastic milk jug for a container, an old paint brush as an applicator. Just paint it on, getting a heavy coat on one side of each strip.

Apply your two or three longest clamps to the form, positioning them to bear on the center and the deepest curves. Tighten these clamps alternately, a bit at a time, to gradually bend the plies. As soon as you can, add a couple more clamps. Keep tightening until you see glue expressed from between the plies.

The form spreads the clamping pressure, so that five clamps applied to the form should be enough.

After the form is taken care of, move on out to the ends, using at least a half-dozen clamps—C-clamps, hand screws, or quick clamps will do—on either end. Allow the glue to dry thoroughly before loosening the clamps. Remove the first beam from the form, and repeat the whole process to make the second one.

Here's the lamination in the form. The support beams are big and the glue is messy, so we did the job outdoors. The boards projecting from beneath the plywood are parts of the form, attached to the wider element only. You rest the loose element of the form on them, back against the stop blocks. Apply the glue to the plies, then turn them one by one and fit them into the gap between the form's elements. Apply the clamps, bending and compressing the strips together.

4. Complete the support beams. As the beams come out of the form, they are rough and probably streaked with rivulets of dried resorcinol. The ends are ragged. Round off the ends first. Scribe a 1½-inch-radius curve at each end of both frames. Using a saber saw, carefully cut along the line.

At the center of each curve, drill a ¾-inch-diameter hole for a bolt.

The next—and prolonged—operation is to sand the beams smooth. This is another good job for the outdoors.

Use a coarse belt on your belt sander and just sand and sand until the faces and edges of the beams are smooth and the resorcinol rivulets are eradicated. Remember that the dark glue lines between the plies will always be visible; you can't sand them out. Ease the edges, either by sanding or using a router and a ¼-inch rounding-over bit. Switch to finer belts as the work progresses, and finish up with fine-grit paper in a pad sander.

Finally, apply a couple of coats of an exterior-grade finish. Fred used CWF, a brand of penetrating oil. With

penetrating oils, you brush on a generous coat, allow it to penetrate for 20 to 30 minutes, then brush on a second application. Allow it to dry for two or three days.

After the gluing is completed and the clamps are off, you must round off the ends. Use a saber saw.

5. Bolt the frames together. The frames are joined together with hex-head bolts at either end. A deliberate mismatch of bolt to hole results in a lot of play, which allows you to spread the bottoms of the beams. Voilà! A hammock support.

With a helper at the far end steadying the two beams, drop a washer over the bolt and insert the bolt in the hole at your end of the first frame. As the bolt emerges, slide a 3-inch-diameter steel ring over the bolt, then push the bolt through the hole in the second frame. Add a second washer and a stop nut. The stop nut has a nylon insert that binds in the bolt's threads. You probably won't be able to turn it more than a couple of times with your fingers, which is the point. It will hold at whatever point you stop turning (with a wrench). Threaded only partway onto the bolt, it allows the frames to be spread apart.

Repeat at the other end of the frame.

Here's how the two beams are bolted together. The diameter of the bolt is smaller than the diameter of the holes, and the bolt is longer than the combined thickness of the beams. The result is play, which allows the base to be spread. The ring hung on the bolt between the beams is for the hammock ropes.

To prevent the beams from spreading too far, install a chain between them, as shown in the *End View.* Drill a ⅛-inch-diameter hole in the center of each frame for an eye bolt, as shown in the *Side View.* Install the bolts, with the eyes facing in. Run a 24-inch length of chain between them, attaching the links by opening the eyes of the bolts.

6. Make the hammock. The hammock is a piece of canvas stretched between two rods and suspended on ropes. Cut a piece of canvas, approximately 34 inches by 86 inches. Notch the corners, as shown in the *Hammock Layout,* and stitch a ½-inch hem along all the edges.

Next, sew pockets along four sides. Those across the ends will accommodate the 1-inch-diameter dowels. The longer side pockets accommodate suspension ropes. To sew the pockets across the ends, fold over 2 inches of the canvas with the hem on the inside and stitch along the existing hem stitches. The side pockets must be folded over the rope they'll accommodate; otherwise, you'll have a devil of a time threading the rope through them. Cut two 14-foot lengths of ⅜-inch-diameter hollow-braided rope. Fold the canvas over the first piece and use some straight pins to secure the fold while you stitch the seam. As with the end pockets, the hem should be on the inside, and the seam should follow the hem stitches. Remove the pins as you sew. Repeat the process to stitch the second side pocket.

Before slipping the dowels into their pockets, you must drill holes near the ends for the ropes to pass through. The ⅜-inch-diameter holes are 3 inches from either end of both dowels. The two holes in each dowel should be parallel. Drill the holes, slide the dowels in the pockets, and thread the ropes through the holes.

TIP

To hold each dowel and keep it from rolling while you drill the rope holes, lay it in a V-jig. You can quickly make one from a scrap of 2 × 4. Plow a V-groove (or a flat-bottomed groove, for that matter) the length of the scrap. So long as the groove is narrower than the dowel's diameter, the jig will work.

HAMMOCK LAYOUT

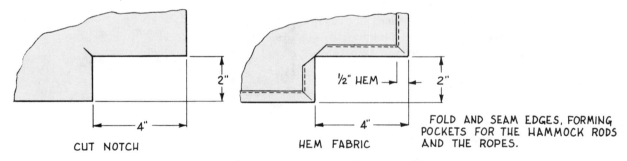

CORNER DETAIL BEFORE HEMMING   **CORNER DETAIL AFTER HEMMING**

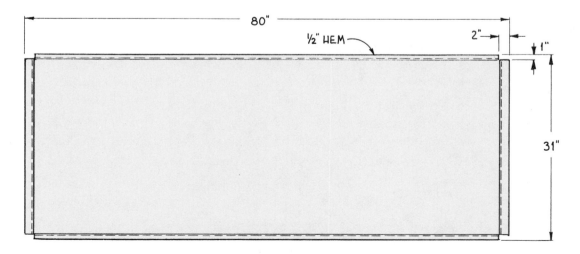

7. Suspend the hammock. The completed hammock is suspended between the two metal rings. To make it easy to remove the hammock and take it in out of the weather, Fred linked the ropes to snap clips, which connect to the metal rings in, well, a snap.

Take some time to equalize the amount of rope at each end of the hammock. Having done this, loop the rope around the dowel, as shown in the photo. At each end of the hammock, loop both ropes through a single snap clip, then backsplice them. The backsplice—you can only backsplice hollow-braided rope, not twisted rope—makes a tidy connection, not an outsized lump.

Backsplicing uses the same principle as Chinese handcuff toys. The braid of rope is opened up so the free end can be forced into the rope, surrounded by the braided strands. When the rope is pulled, the braid closes back up, tightening around the end. Like the handcuff toy, the more you pull, the tighter the braiding grips the cord it surrounds.

To make the splice, fashion a tool from a scrap of aluminum flashing (or other easily malleable sheet metal). Working several inches from the end of the rope, push the braided strands together so you can insert your tool, as shown in the *Backsplicing Detail.* Thread the free end of the rope through the snap clip and then into the tool. Pull both the tool and the rope on through. Give the rope and loop a yank and the splice is complete.

To secure the rope to the dowel, pass it through the hole, around the dowel, and back through the loop you've made.

BACKSPLICING DETAIL

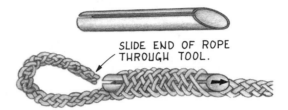

BEND A PIECE OF ALUMINUM FLASHING INTO A TUBULAR TOOL.

SLIDE END OF ROPE THROUGH TOOL.

PULL TOOL THROUGH, LEAVING ROPE END WITHIN BRAID.

8. Assemble the hammock. You're almost there. Spread the frame members until the chain between them is taut. Then attach the snap clips to the rings at either end. Settle back into the hammock, tuck your hands behind your head, let your eyelids fall closed. Then, according to Fred's handwritten shop notes, "Zzzzzzz."

VINEYARD ENSEMBLE

Classy, Comfortable, Cushioned Cedar Seating

After toiling in the vineyards all day, this is the sort of cushy seating you deserve. Deep, soft cushions and a footrest. You may never move again.

VINEYARD ENSEMBLE SETTEE AND CHAIR WITH OTTOMAN

After working hard in the yard and garden, or playing hard on the court, you deserve a break—and a comfortable place to sit while enjoying the fresh air. This smart ensemble fills the bill perfectly. The chair and matching ottoman offer the cushiness of a living-room–bound Barcalounger. The whole set reflects the refinement of indoor furniture, while retaining the clean lines and distinctive design of a custom-made patio ensemble. Imagine yourself . . . nested in the chair or settee . . . feet up . . . the Sunday paper and a tumbler of chilled orange juice on the table at your side. . . .

Get the picture? Build the set!

SHOPPING LIST—CHAIR AND OTTOMAN

LUMBER

2 pcs. 4 × 4 × 8' clear western red cedar
2 pcs. 4 × 4 × 10' clear western red cedar
1 pc. 1" dia. × 48" birch dowel

HARDWARE AND SUPPLIES

4 pcs. #6 × 3" galvanized drywall-type screws
Resorcinol glue

FABRIC AND NOTIONS

3⅓ yd. muslin, min. 31" wide (chair cushions)
1½ yd. muslin, min. 31" wide (ottoman cushion)
1 spool matching thread

FABRIC AND NOTIONS—CONTINUED

3⅓ yd. upholstery fabric, min. 31" wide (chair slipcovers)
1½ yd. upholstery fabric, min. 31" wide (ottoman slipcover)
1 spool matching upholstery thread
3 pcs. ¾" × 23" hook-and-loop tape
8 lb. shredded foam

FINISH

Leave natural, or apply clear exterior finish

SHOPPING LIST—SETTEE

LUMBER

2 pcs. 4 × 4 × 12' clear western red cedar
1 pc. 4 × 4 × 10' clear western red cedar

HARDWARE AND SUPPLIES

4 pcs. #6 × 3" galvanized drywall-type screws
Resorcinol glue

FABRIC AND NOTIONS

6⅔ yd. muslin, min. 31" wide (cushions)
1 spool matching thread

FABRIC AND NOTIONS—CONTINUED

6⅔ yd. upholstery fabric, min. 31" wide (slipcovers)
1 spool matching upholstery thread
2 pcs. ¾" × 23" hook-and-loop tape
5 lb. shredded foam

FINISH

Leave natural, or apply clear exterior finish

CUTTING LIST—CHAIR AND OTTOMAN

PIECE	NUMBER	THICKNESS	WIDTH	LENGTH	MATERIAL
Back legs	2	2½"	3"	36"	Cedar
Arms	2	1"	3½"	31"*	Cedar
Hand grips	2	¾"	1"	3½"	Cedar scraps
Front legs	2	3½"	3½"	18"*	Cedar
Side rails	2	1½"	3½"	24"	Cedar
Front rail	1	1½"	3½"	26½"	Cedar
Back slats	6	1"	3¼"	26½"	Cedar
Seat slats	4	1"	3¼"	28"	Cedar
Ottoman legs	4	3½"	3½"	12"*	Cedar
Ottoman front rails	2	1½"	3½"	26"	Cedar
Ottoman side rails	2	1½"	3½"	21½"	Cedar
Ottoman slats	4	1"	3¼"	27½"	Cedar
Ottoman handles	2	1" dia.	22"		Birch dowel

*Dimensions of piece before tapers or shapes are cut

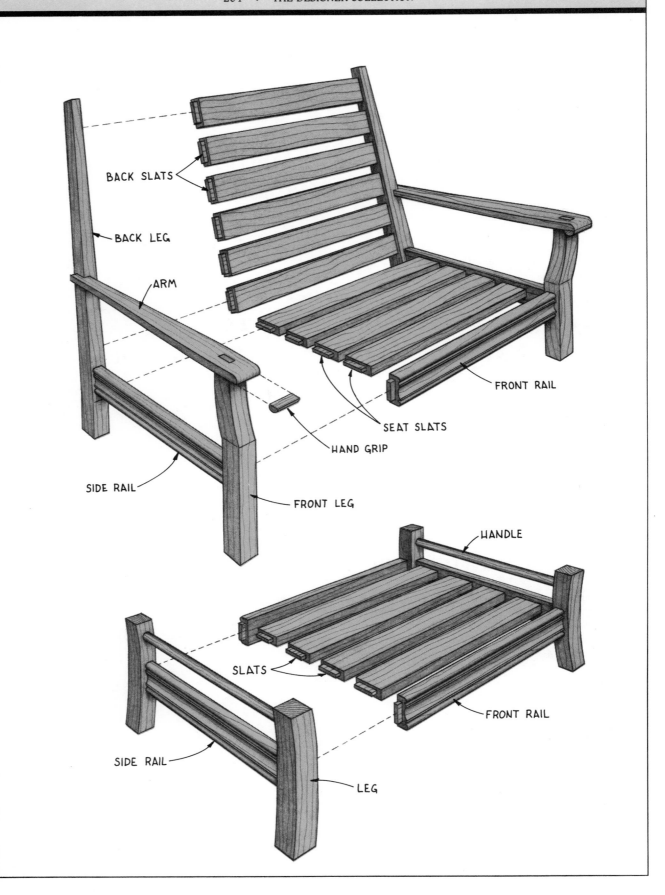

BACK SLATS

BACK LEG

ARM

SIDE RAIL

FRONT LEG

HAND GRIP

SEAT SLATS

FRONT RAIL

HANDLE

SLATS

FRONT RAIL

SIDE RAIL

LEG

CUTTING LIST—SETTEE

PIECE	NUMBER	THICKNESS	WIDTH	LENGTH	MATERIAL
Back legs	2	2½"	3"	36"	Cedar
Arms	2	1"	3½"	31"*	Cedar
Hand grips	2	¾"	1"	3½"	Cedar
Front legs	2	3½"	3½"	18"*	Cedar
Side rails	2	1½"	3½"	24"	Cedar
Front rail	1	1½"	3½"	51½"	Cedar
Back slats	6	1"	3¼"	51½"	Cedar
Seat slats	4	1"	3¼"	53"	Cedar

*Dimensions of piece before tapers or shapes are cut

CUTTING DIAGRAM—CHAIR AND OTTOMAN

4 x 4 x 10'
BACK LEG · BACK LEG · FRONT LEG · FRONT LEG

4 x 4 x 10'
BACK SLATS · BACK SLATS · SEAT SLATS · SEAT SLAT · OTTOMAN SLATS

4 x 4 x 8'
ARM · OTTOMAN SLATS · OTTOMAN LEGS · OTTOMAN FRONT RAILS

4 x 4 x 8'
SIDE RAILS · OTTOMAN SIDE RAILS · OTTOMAN LEG · FRONT RAIL · ARM

CUTTING DIAGRAM—SETTEE

4 x 4 x 10'
BACK LEG · BACK LEG · FRONT LEG · FRONT LEG

4 x 4 x 12'
BACK SLATS · BACK SLATS · ARMS

4 x 4 x 12'
FRONT RAIL · SEAT SLATS · SIDE RAILS · SEAT SLAT

Builder's Notes

The Vineyard Ensemble is one of the more challenging projects in this book. If you tackle it, you must deal with several different band saw operations, an unusual table saw setup, and the cutting of more than three dozen mortise-and-tenon joints. And if you make your own cushions, there's *sewing* involved, too.

Your reward is a set of outdoor furniture that, if you *could* buy it, would cost a couple of thousand dollars.

As with other projects in this book that include a chair *and* a settee, the settee is just a wider version of the chair. The side frame assemblies are identical; for the settee, you simply cut the slats and front rail longer (compare the cutting lists). Although the photos on the following pages show building procedures for the settee, the construction sequence and techniques are the same for both pieces.

Materials. We chose to make the project of western red cedar for its natural beauty and resistance to decay. We made the ensemble from 4 × 4s. From this we resawed the boards needed for the slats, rails, and arms.

PATTERNS

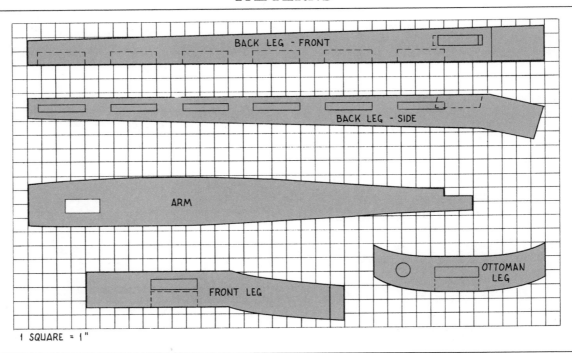

BACK LEG - FRONT

BACK LEG - SIDE

ARM

OTTOMAN LEG

FRONT LEG

1 SQUARE = 1"

If you want to avoid the resawing, you can buy 2-by stock for the rails, 5/4 (five-quarter) stock (usually stocked as decking) for the slats and arms.

Though the cedar *is* naturally decay resistant, this is not really the sort of furniture you'd thoughtlessly leave out in the rain. A protected patio or porch is a more appropriate setting. A finish of some sort is appropriate. You can use a clear penetrating oil finish. If more out-door protection is desired, apply either a clear water repellent or an exterior preservative stain.

An upholsterer can make the cushions for you, but they're easy enough to make yourself if you have basic sewing skills.

All the materials you need are to be had at a fabric or upholstery shop. You need fabric to make a cover for the cushions (muslin is durable, relatively inexpensive, and widely available), as well as a fabric (probably colored or patterned) for slipcovers. And you need mate-rial to fill the cushions. Ultimately, we used shredded foam. Slabs of foam rubber by themselves—we tried them—give the cushions an unappealingly angular look and an uninvitingly firm feel. We tried cutting the foam slabs slightly undersized, then wrapping them with polyester batting to soften the sharp edges. But eventually, we settled on the shredded stuffing because it produced cushions that were a balm for sore bodies.

Tools and techniques. This is a project for the well-equipped shop. It is very much a band saw project, though the table saw and the drill press are also key tools.

The band saw is used for the obvious operations, such as cutting the arms and legs. But it is also used to resaw the 4 × 4 stock into 1-inch-thick arms and slats and 1½-inch-thick rails. No other tool will perform these tasks as well.

You use the table saw to cut the wide coves in the rails of each piece. Setting up for the cove cuts on the table saw is a trial-and-error process; it may take as much time to set up the saw and fence to get the cove cut just right as it will to make the actual cuts.

Finally, you have to master the mortise-and-tenon joint. There are 28 mortise-and-tenon joints in the chair, another 16 in the ottoman. We cut the tenons on the table saw, the mortises using a mortising attachment on the drill press. The tenons can also be cut on the band saw or using a router. The mortise can be roughed out with a drill and finished with a mallet and chisel. But if you have a drill press, this ensemble might be just the excuse you need to justify the purchase of a mortising attachment.

A note on overall planning is in order. Because some of the setups are so difficult to duplicate, it's wise to make all possible use of them before breaking them down.

Take the cove-cutting setup, for example. The rails on all the furniture pieces have identical face profiles. Once you've set up the table saw to make cove cuts for one piece of furniture, it makes sense to cut coves for any of the other pieces you intend to make. But to do that, you have to have all the rails rough-cut on the table saw. So to avoid using the same machine to do two things at once, apply a production-line method. Decide ahead of time all the pieces you are going to make. Organize the parts and the routines, so you can perform all like operations at one time. Rough-cut the parts for all the furniture pieces at one time, cut all the mortises, cut all the coves, and so forth.

It will save you time in the long run.

---

1. **Rough the parts from the 4 × 4 stock.** Crosscut the parts following the *Cutting Diagram* and the "Cutting List," then resaw the appropriate blanks to produce the thinner pieces, such as the arms, rails, and slats. *Don't taper or shape any pieces yet.*

Few saws for crosscutting have the capacity to cut a 4 × 4 in a single pass. You'll probably have to mark each cut on opposing faces and make two passes to complete the cuts. A circular saw or radial arm saw is good for the job.

With the stock reduced to manageable lengths, resawing the stock for arms, slats, and rails is a band saw operation. After the parts are resawed, use a hand plane, a light cut on a jointer, or a sander to smooth the surfaces. The soft cedar will cut fast, so be especially careful if you are using a belt sander.

---

2. **Shape the face profile on the rails.** Make the first cuts with a router equipped with a ½-inch beading bit. See the *Rail Cross Section Detail* for the location of the bead cuts. Make trial cuts on scrap to perfect the setup, then cut beads on all the rails. (Save your "best" scrap piece for testing the cove setup.) Then rout a ¼-inch-radius roundover on the inner edges of the rail, as shown.

To complete the face profile, machine a cove on the rails using the table saw. To do this, you must feed the workpiece over the saw blade at an angle. Only a tiny amount of material can be removed at one time, so cut the cove in a series of passes.

The trickiest part is the setup.

Draw the desired cove profile on the butt end of a scrap. (Size the cove so that there is a ⅛-inch flat between the bead and the cove; the depth of the cove is not critical.) Move the saw's rip fence out of the way (or remove it completely). Set the depth of cut to equal the maximum depth of the cove. Align a straight board—to serve as an auxiliary fence—more or less diagonally across the saw table, just in front of the blade.

Adjust the shape of the cove by changing the angle of the auxiliary fence: Moving the fence more parallel to the blade will give a narrower cove at a given blade height, while moving the fence more perpendicular to the blade will give a wider cove at the same blade height.

With this in mind, set the scrap behind the blade and against the fence. Sight along the auxiliary fence at table height, adjusting the angle until the blade just obscures

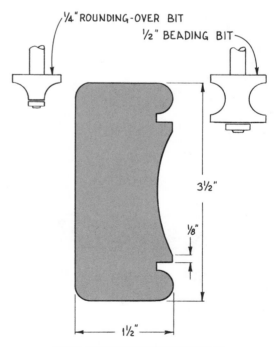

RAIL CROSS SECTION DETAIL

CHAIR PLAN VIEWS

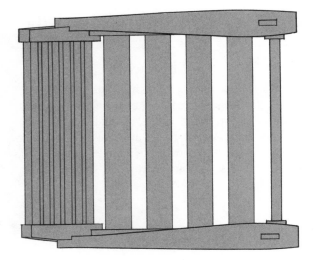

TOP VIEW

TOOL LIST

Band saw
Block plane
Circular saw
Clamps
Drill
  Pilot hole bit
Drill press
  Hollow-chisel mortising
    attachment
Hand plane
Mallet
Marking gauge
Paintbrush
Pipe clamps

Router
  ¼" rounding-over bit
  ½" beading bit
Sander(s)
Sandpaper
Sawhorses
Screwdriver
Sewing machine
Table saw
  Dado cutter
  Miter gauge
Tack cloth
Tape measure
Try square

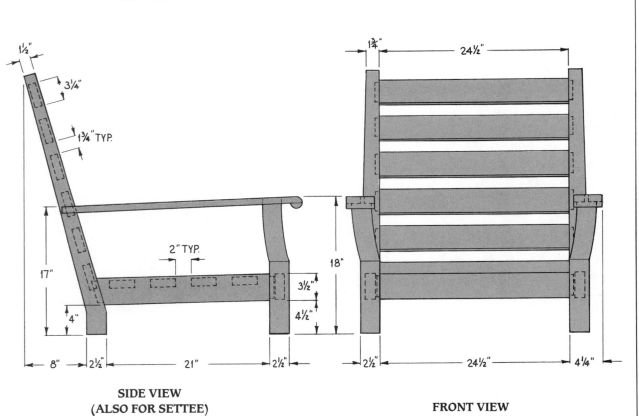

**SIDE VIEW
(ALSO FOR SETTEE)**

FRONT VIEW

the marks on the end of the scrap. Clamp the fence in position.

Now test your setup. Crank down the blade so that it cuts only about 1/16 inch deep and start cutting. After each pass, raise the blade about 1/16 inch. Your test isn't done until you achieve the maximum depth desired. This is because raising the blade on most table saws moves it backward or forward at the same time. There's no guarantee the center of the cut will remain in the same place, so you can't be sure whether the cove you want is the cove you'll get until you've carried the process through to completion.

If your test proves the setup to be right on, then start cutting coves in the rails. If not, then unclamp the auxiliary fence and make adjustments to the angle, based on whether the cove needs to be wider or narrower.

After drawing the cove profile on the end of the rail, position the rail and auxiliary fence as shown. "Eyeball" the blade's profile against the marked cove profile, adjusting the fence angle to make the cut wider or narrower. The space between the auxiliary fence and the blade dictates, of course, where the cove will be in relation to the edge of the workpiece.

OTTOMAN PLAN VIEWS

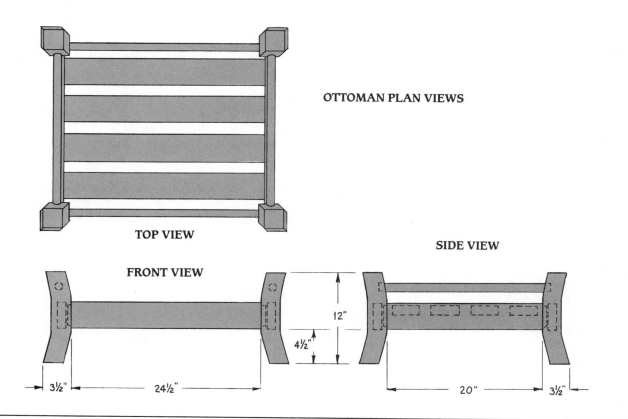

TOP VIEW

FRONT VIEW

SIDE VIEW

12"

4½"

3½"   24½"   20"   3½"

Feed the rail across the blade, beaded side down. It's best to make several light passes, raising the blade a bit each time, until full depth is reached, rather than trying to remove all the stock in a single pass. Attempting to cut the cove in one pass will probably stall the machine and could damage your saw motor.

3. **Lay out the legs.** The front, back, and ottoman legs have mortises that must be laid out and cut before you completely shape the legs. Especially if you are using a mortising attachment on a drill press to make the mortises, the stock must be square to properly perform the operation. Note that the chair legs are *mirror images,* not duplicates. As you lay out these legs on the 4 × 4 stock, be sure you lay out a right leg and a left leg. Note that while the chair legs are mirror images, all four ottoman legs are identical.

Lay out the mortises and curves at the same time. For the front legs, enlarge the pattern and make a template (including a hole for the mortise) of cardboard or thin plywood. Set the two leg blanks side by side in front of you. Trace the template on one blank. Flip the template over, and trace it on an adjoining face of the same blank. Repeat the process on the second blank, but be sure you lay out a *mirror image* of the first blank. Finally, lay out the tenon for the arm on each leg. As shown in the *Front Leg Detail,* the tenon is located ½ inch from the outside face of the legs.

The ottoman legs should be laid out from the pattern. Enlarge it and make a template, from which you can lay out the legs.

TIP

To help establish and maintain the proper left-leg/right-leg orientation when laying out the back legs, cut just their front profiles. Then position them as shown to lay out the slat mortises. At this point, either leg could be a right or a left. Marking the mortise locations makes one the left, the other the right; this approach ensures that you end up with a left leg and a right leg. It also helps you expedite uniform mortise layouts. Use a combination square to transfer the mortise locations from one leg to the other, and a marking gauge to scribe the mortise sides.

4. Lay out the mortises in the rails. Lay out the locations for the mortises on the (chair and ottoman) side rails, as shown in the *Rail Layouts* drawing. To ensure that the slats fit squarely between the rails and at a uniform setback from the edge, lay out each pair of rails at the same time. Use a square to mark mortise locations across both rails at the same time, then scribe the sides of the mortises with a marking gauge.

RAIL LAYOUTS

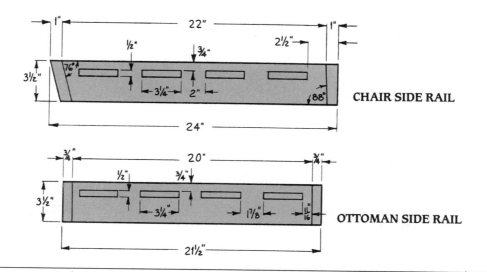

CHAIR SIDE RAIL

OTTOMAN SIDE RAIL

5. Cut the tenons on the slats and rails. On both ends of each slat, lay out and cut a tenon ½ inch thick by 3¼ inches wide by 1 inch long (the same width as the slat itself—there are no shoulders on the narrow ends of the tenons).

Lay out and cut the tenons on the ends of each rail to the dimensions shown in the *Rail Tenon Detail.* The shoulders of the chair side rail tenons are NOT square (see the *Rail Layouts*). The shoulders of the front tenons are cut at an 88 degree angle, the shoulders of the rear tenons at a 76 degree angle. The end of the rear tenon should be cut parallel to the shoulders, but the end of the front tenon can be left square.

We cut all the tenons using a dado cutter in a table saw. Set the depth of cut to match the width of the shoulder. Position the rip fence so the distance from the *outside* of the cutter to the fence face equals the length of the tenon. Butt the end of the workpiece against the fence

RAIL TENON DETAIL

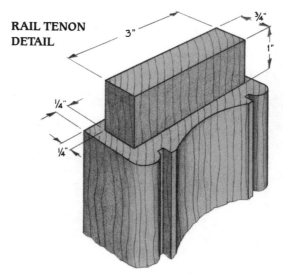

and guide it over the cutter with the miter gauge. Make as many passes as necessary to form the tenon.

6. Cut all the mortises. By waiting until now to cut the mortises, you can set up a more efficient production line to finish them all at once. Also, since the tenons have been cut, you can test fit them in their mortises.

The standard mortise-cutting technique is to rough out the mortises with a drill bit slightly smaller in diameter than the finished width of the mortise. Then you cut to the layout lines with a chisel. When working with a drill press, clamp a makeshift fence to the table, so you can position the mortises uniformly and accurately. And set the depth stop, so that all the mortises are roughed to a uniform depth—usually about 1/16 inch deeper than the tenons are long.

We chose another approach. We cut all the mortises using a mortising attachment on a drill press. This device, which combines a chisel with a drill bit, "bores" a square hole. This eliminates the handwork of squaring each mortise with a chisel.

Note: The mortises (in the legs) for the chair side rails are somewhat out-of-the-ordinary. See the *Side View* and the patterns. In the front leg blanks, these mortises must be cut deeper than the others, since the true depth must be measured not from the surface you are working with at this point, but from the final profile. In the back legs, the mortises must be cut at an angle. Tilt the drill press table to the correct degree (or cut a wedge to fit underneath the leg to achieve the same effect). Stand a try square on the lower section of the leg. When the blade is parallel to the bit, the angle is correct.

7. **Cut out the legs.** Use the band saw. Cutting the back legs is pretty straightforward. Rest the leg on its back and saw the side taper. Then turn the leg onto the inner face and cut the back profile.

The front legs are less straightforward. First, you must cut the tenon for the arm, then you must shape the leg with compound cuts. Cut two opposing sides first—sides 1 and 2 in the *Front Leg Detail.* Then, tape the waste pieces back to the blank—use masking tape. Cut the other sides—sides 3 and 4 in the illustration. Remove the waste and any remaining tape.

The ottoman legs also require compound cuts, and they should be cut in the same manner as the front legs.

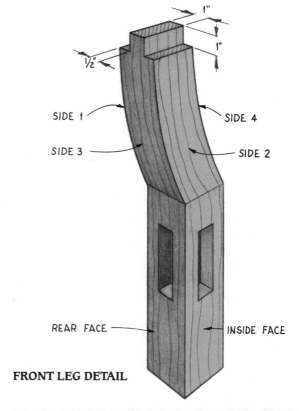

FRONT LEG DETAIL

Cutting the "double profile" front legs requires cutting along the layout lines on one face, then rolling the workpiece 90 degrees and cutting along the lines on the second face. *Above:* To provide a square, steady, and safe bearing surface for making the second series of cuts, you must tape the waste from the first series of cuts back in place, then cut. *Right:* When all the cuts are done, remove all the waste and peel away tape scraps.

SETTEE PLAN VIEWS

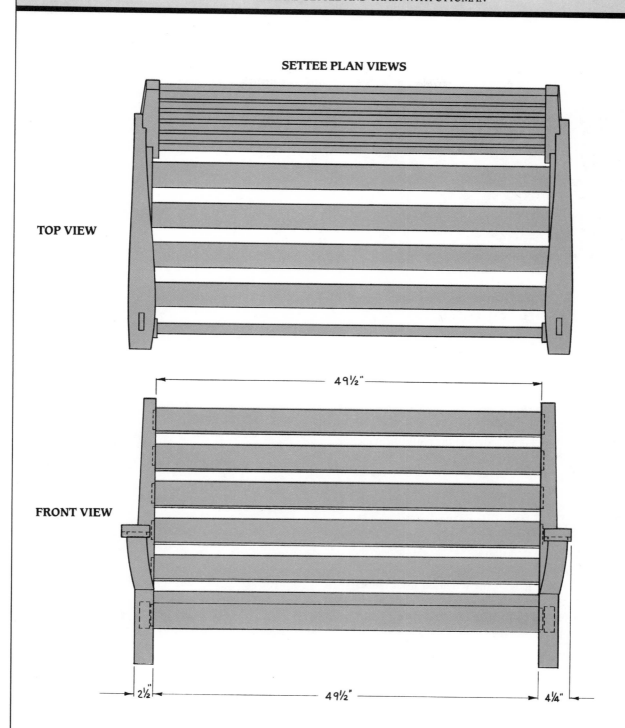

TOP VIEW

FRONT VIEW

49½"

2½"   49½"   4¼"

8. **Cut out the arms.** Enlarge the pattern for the arms and transfer it to the roughly sized board set aside for the arms. Cut out two ¾ inch by 1 inch by 3½ inch hand grips from scrap, and round the shapes on the band saw. Glue the grips to the underside of the front edge of the arms. After the glue sets, cut the arms on the band saw. Make the cuts with the grip facing up, and cut slightly outside the marked layout lines. Round-over the front edge of the arms and grips on the band saw or with a rasp. Sand the completed arms.

Cut out the shape of the hand grips on the band saw and glue them to the front of the arm piece, as shown. Spring clamps hold the grips in place while the glue dries.

9. **Assemble the chair side frames.** First, dry assemble the legs and rails to make two side frames. The joint between the side rail and the front leg has a slight misfit built into it—the top and bottom of the tenon slope up into a mortise that has no slope. The cedar is soft enough to make a force-fit possible. If you don't want to force the fit, give the top cheek of the tenon a lick or two with a block plane to taper it to fit.

Radius all the exposed edges of the parts (including the arms) with a router and a ¼-inch rounding-over bit.

Fit the arm in place next. Position the arm on the side frame and mark the arm location on the back leg. Then mark the mortise by tracing the tenon atop the front leg onto the bottom of the arm. Cut out the mortise, and check the fit of the joint. Adjust if necessary.

Now, disassemble the frames. Apply glue to both the frame mortises and the tenons, reassemble the frames and clamp them. Apply glue to the tenon on the front leg and to the mortise through the arm, then drive the arm down over the tenon. Drill a pilot hole and drive a 3-inch screw through the side of the arm into the leg tenon, and another through the side of the arm into the back leg. Leave the side frame clamped overnight.

If you don't have a large supply of clamps, glue one side frame at a time.

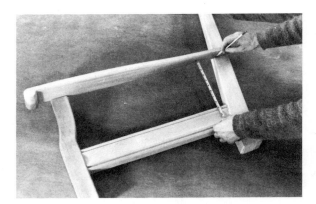

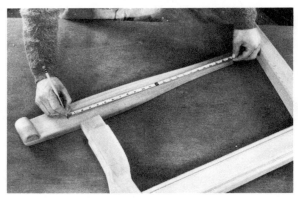

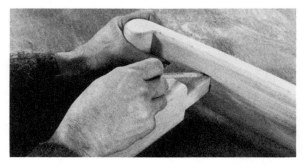

Fitting the arm to its side frame is a key part of the assembly process. *Top:* Position the arm parallel to the rail by measuring between the parts with a tape at front to back. Mark the arm position on the back leg. *Center:* Next, measure from the mark on the leg to the front-leg tenon, and transfer the measurement to the arm. *Bottom:* Finally, center the arm over the front leg, aligning the tenon to the mark on the arm. Trace the tenon onto the arm.

When gluing up the side assembly, a little masking tape can serve as extra hands, holding the cauls—scrap blocks that prevent the clamp jaws from marring the good wood—against the legs, making it easier to apply the clamp. Cut a wedge-shaped caul to fit behind the back leg and provide a square clamping surface.

10. **Complete the chair assembly.** It is usually a good idea, in an assembly process like this one, to conduct a dry run. You have the opportunity to check how all the joints fit and make any necessary adjustments. You also have the chance to coordinate your movements with your helper. Yes, you probably need one for this process.

For final assembly, start with a side assembly on your bench, with the mortises up. Apply glue to the mortises of one side frame first, then to the tenons. Insert the slats into the side frame. Apply glue to the mortises in the second side assembly. Upend the first assembly to insert the slat tenons into the mortises in the second side assembly.

(The reason you do it this way is to keep the glue from running out of the mortises and all over your project. Resorcinol glue, as you probably know, is runny and stains whatever it touches a dark maroon. You don't want to apply too much to the tenons, for if they are properly snug, assembly will "squeegee" the glue off the tenons' cheeks and onto their shoulders. Once there, it will squeeze out and make a mess. So you want to apply the glue in the mortise, but you don't want it to drip out on the project or on you during assembly. Keep the mortises oriented so the glue can't drip out.)

Once the project is assembled and all the tenons are set firmly into their mortises, use one pipe clamp or bar clamp to clamp the back. Carefully set the project on its feet and apply additional clamps to pull all the joints tight. Keep the clamps on overnight.

After the glue has set, trim the front-leg tenons flush with the top of the arms.

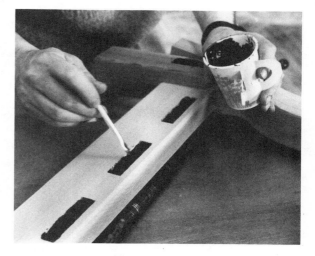

Assembly begins with the application of an even coat of glue on the sides of the mortises. A paper cup is a good mixing pot for the two-part resorcinol glue, and an inexpensive acid brush is a good reusable applicator.

TIP

During the dry run, as you fit each tenon to a particular mortise, lightly mark a number on both parts at the joint, so you won't accidentally mix up their locations when you disassemble the pieces for gluing. Cedar is very soft, so don't pencil too heavily.

How do you get all those slats fitted into all those mortises? It isn't as hard as you might think. *Top:* One by one, coat the tenons on the front rail and the slats with glue, then push them into the mortises in one side assembly. *Center left:* When that's done, steady the second side with scraps under the legs, and upend the assembly with the slats and rail. This will teach you the value of snug joints; it they aren't snug, the slats will drop out. *Center right:* Try to align as many of the tenons as you can over their mortises as you lower the project onto the second side assembly. *Bottom left:* A good approach is to cock the assembly slightly, working the front rail into position first, then the slat closest to it, then the next slat, and the next. Try not to smear glue on the legs and side rail as you line up the joints. Resorcinol has a long open time, so you needn't rush. *Bottom right:* After all the tenons have dropped into place, apply a single clamp to the back, primarily to hold the slats between the back legs while you lift the project and set it on its feet. Then apply more clamps and tighten them to close the joints.

11. **Assemble the ottoman.** If you choose to buy standard 1-inch birch dowel for the handles, it can be cut to length and stained to match the color of the red cedar. If you have a lathe, you can turn the handles from cedar scrap left over from cutting the slats.

Dry assemble the parts to check the fit of the joints, and make any adjustments before proceeding. When you're sure everything fits well, assemble the ottoman with resorcinol glue and clamp overnight to dry.

12. **Apply a finish.** Sand all surfaces smooth and apply the finish of your choice. We recommend a water repellent or a clear penetrating exterior finish.

Cushions

If you're handy with a sewing machine, making these cushions for the chair, matching ottoman, and settee will be a snap. If sewing is new to you, this is a good project to get you started. All the seams are straight and simple. Get a friend to show you how to thread the sewing machine's bobbin and needle, and how to stitch a straight line—that's all there is to it.

The cushions are designed to be protected with slipcovers. For the cushions themselves, use muslin, as we did. For the slipcovers, buy upholstery fabric that will be heavy enough to wear well and that is pleasing to your eye. Depending upon the weight of the slipcover fabric, you may need to buy a heavy gauge needle for the sewing machine, and heavy upholstery thread, too—check with the clerk at the fabric store for guidance.

The seat and back cushions for the settee are the same size as those for the chair—just make two of each.

1. **Stitch the cushions.** For each chair/settee cushion, cut two pieces of muslin that are 31 inches by 58¾ inches. For the ottoman cushion, cut the muslin to 31 inches by 52¾ inches.

Do one cushion at a time. Hem the ends of the muslin. To do this, fold over about ½ inch of cloth, bringing the good, outside surface of the fabric—known as the "right" side in sewing parlance—over the less attractive, less colorful side that will end up inside the finished cushion—known as the "wrong" side. Make another ½-inch fold over the first fold. Sew along the center of the fold.

After hemming both ends, fold the cloth in half, wrong sides together, bringing the hemmed edges together.

CUSHION SEWING SEQUENCE

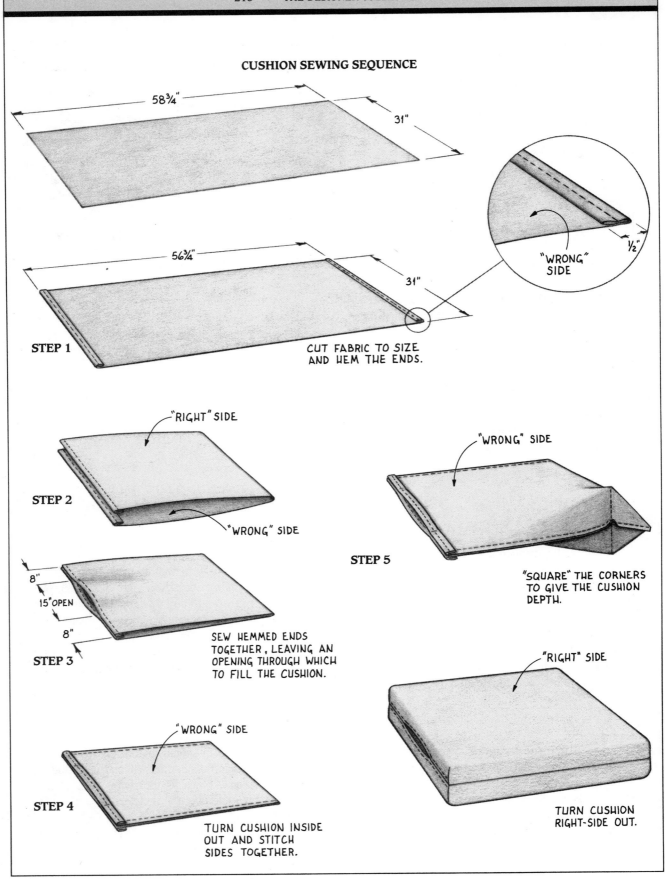

58¾"

31"

56¾"

31"

½"

"WRONG" SIDE

STEP 1

CUT FABRIC TO SIZE
AND HEM THE ENDS.

"RIGHT" SIDE

STEP 2

"WRONG" SIDE

STEP 5

"WRONG" SIDE

"SQUARE" THE CORNERS
TO GIVE THE CUSHION
DEPTH.

8"

15" OPEN

8"

STEP 3

SEW HEMMED ENDS
TOGETHER, LEAVING AN
OPENING THROUGH WHICH
TO FILL THE CUSHION.

"WRONG" SIDE

"RIGHT" SIDE

STEP 4

TURN CUSHION INSIDE
OUT AND STITCH
SIDES TOGETHER.

TURN CUSHION
RIGHT-SIDE OUT.

Stitch the hemmed edges together at the ends, leaving the center open; this is the opening through which you will stuff the cushion.

Now turn the cover inside out, so the right sides are together. Using a ½-inch seam allowance (which means aligning the seam ½ inch from the edge of the cloth), sew the unhemmed edges together to close the open side. The result is a flat pouch.

To give the cushion depth, sew a short seam at each corner, perpendicular to those already sewn. To do this, pick up the "pouch" and separate the two layers of fabric near a corner, pulling them away from one another. Fold the fabric flat and neat in a new plane; the previously sewn seam should bisect the corner, as shown. Stitch a seam across the corner, forming a triangle; the length of this seam will determine the thickness of the cushion. It should be about 5 inches long. Repeat for each corner of each cushion.

Turn the cover right-side out, and it is ready to be stuffed.

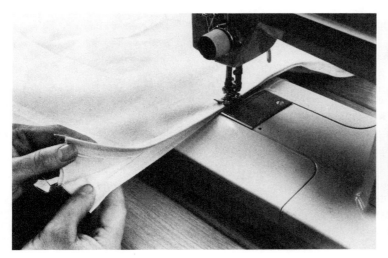
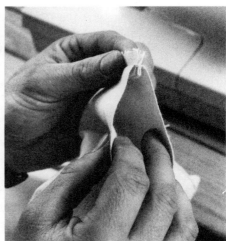

Left: The sewing required to make the cushions is as simple as stitching a straight seam on the sewing machine. *Right:* After hemming the ends of the fabric, fold the cloth so the hems overlap. Sew through both hems, along the hem stitches, forming a seam that turns the strip of cloth into a loop. This seam is on the surface, and you'll want this to be on the back of the cushion.

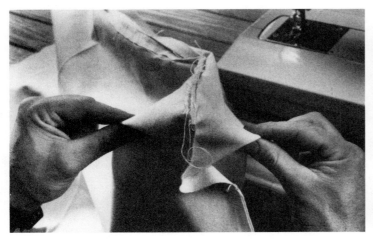

Squaring the corners of the cushions is easier to do than to describe. *Left:* As shown, you pull the layers of the cushion apart to create a plane perpendicular to the seams sewn so far. *Right:* After smoothing out the wrinkles, you stitch diagonally across the corner, thereby establishing cushion depth. The farther from the corner you position the seam, the longer it will be, and the fatter the cushion will be.

2. Stuff the cushions. The shredded foam we used was packaged in 1-pound bags, and we used about 2½ bags per cushion.

Open the package, fit the opening inside the cushion, then shake the stuffing out of the package and into the cushion. Fill each cushion to the girth you desire, but remember that you must be able to pinch the opening closed and stitch it on the sewing machine.

When you have stuffed the cushions and sewn them closed, the basic cushion is completed. Although you can use them like this, the covers will get dirty pretty quickly, and they'll be hard to clean. Better you should make slipcovers for them.

3. Stitch the slipcovers. The slipcovers are made in the same way as the cushions, except that you use hook-and-loop strips (Velcro) to close the openings rather than sewing them closed. Moreover, you'll probably want to use colored or patterned upholstery fabric.

Cut the slipcover fabric for each cushion. The cut sizes for the slipcovers match the sizes for the muslin given in step 1. Hem the edges as you did in making the covers.

Cut a 23-inch length of hook-and-loop tape (each length has a hook strip and a loop strip) for each cushion. Separate the hook strips from the loop strips. Sew a hook strip on the wrong side of the fabric, centered along the hemmed edge. Sew a loop strip on the right side of the fabric, centered on the opposite hemmed edge, as shown.

The side seams of the cushion are sewn with the fabric inside out—that is, with the wrong side exposed. Turn the fabric right-sides-together and mate the hook-and-loop strips. Using a ½-inch hem allowance, sew along the (unhemmed) sides.

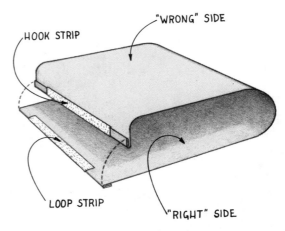

HOOK-AND-LOOP POSITION

Square the corners next. At each corner, pinch the cloth between the thumb and fingers and pull, separating the layers. Flatten the corner, align the seams atop one another, and sew the diagonal seam.

Open the hook-and-loop strip and turn the fabric right-side out.

4. Put the slipcovers on the cushions. Stuff the cushion into the slipcover, and close the hook-and-loop strips.

Now, fluff up the cushions, put them on the chair and ottoman, and try them out—aaahhhh!

VINEYARD ENSEMBLE TABLE

This small table is just the right size to keep an ice-cold drink, a plate of snacks, and a few of your favorite books or magazines within arm's reach while kicking back in the chair or settee.

Essentially a (larger) sibling to the ottoman, the table has basically the same appearance. Though more elongated, the table legs, like the ottoman legs, are made with compound cuts on the band saw. The decorative profile for the rails is identical. Again echoing the ottoman's construction, slats form a shelf beneath the top. A relatively square, fairly smooth cut flagstone (also known as a stepping or gauged stone) serves as the top.

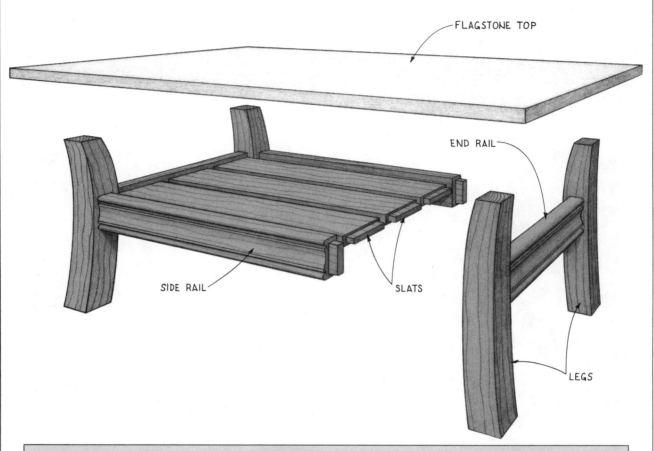

FLAGSTONE TOP

END RAIL

SIDE RAIL

SLATS

LEGS

SHOPPING LIST

LUMBER

1 pc. 4 × 4 × 12' clear western red cedar

HARDWARE AND SUPPLIES

1 flagstone, approx. 1" × 24" × 36"
Rescorcinol glue

FINISH

Leave natural, or apply clear exterior finish

CUTTING LIST

PIECE	NUMBER	THICKNESS	WIDTH	LENGTH	MATERIAL
Legs	4	3½"	3½"	17"	Cedar
Side rails	2	1½"	3½"	25½"	Cedar
End rails	2	1½"	3½"	13½"	Cedar
Slats	3	1"	3½"	26¼"	Cedar

CUTTING DIAGRAM

4 x 4 x 12'

SIDE RAILS   END RAILS   SLATS

| LEG | LEG | LEG | LEG | | | | |

PATTERN

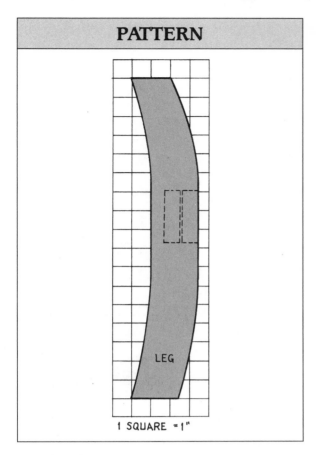

LEG

1 SQUARE = 1"

TOOL LIST

Band clamp
Band saw
Chisel
Circular saw
Drill
   Various-size wood-boring bits
Drill press
   Hollow-chisel moritising
     attachment
Hand plane
Paintbrush
Pipe clamps
Router
   ¼" rounding-over bit
   ½" beading bit
Sander(s)
Sandpaper
Sawhorses
Short bar clamps
Table saw
Tack cloth
Tape measure
Try square

Builder's Notes

A companion project to the settee and chair with ottoman that opened this chapter, the table is constructed with the same materials and uses the same tools and techniques as those earlier projects. By all means read the "Builder's Notes" accompanying the settee and chair with ottoman project on page 205.

The one item that is unique to the table is the top. Before building the table, we shopped at a landscaping center and found the flagstone you see as the tabletop. With the stone in the shop, we established the length and width of the table and went to work on the wood.

It might be most economical for you to do likewise. Buy a suitable stone for the top, and once you have it, adjust the table dimensions to suit. To alter length, simply increase or reduce the length of the side rails and slats. To change the width, you'll have to alter the width of the slats, or the space between the slats, or the number of slats, as well as the length of the end rails.

Shop for the stone at rock quarries, landscaping and gardening centers, and building supply centers.

1. **Rough the parts from the 4 × 4 stock.** Crosscut the parts following the *Cutting Diagram* and the "Cutting List," then resaw the appropriate blanks to produce the rails and slats. *Don't shape any pieces yet.*

Because few saws for crosscutting have the capacity to cut a 4 × 4 in a single pass, you'll probably have to mark opposing faces and complete each cut in two passes. Cut the stock with either a circular saw or a radial arm saw as on the chair.

With the stock reduced to manageable lengths, resawing the stock for slats and rails is a band saw operation. After the parts are resawed, use a hand plane, a light cut on a jointer, or a sander to smooth the surfaces. The soft cedar will cut fast, so be especially careful.

PLAN VIEWS

TOP VIEW

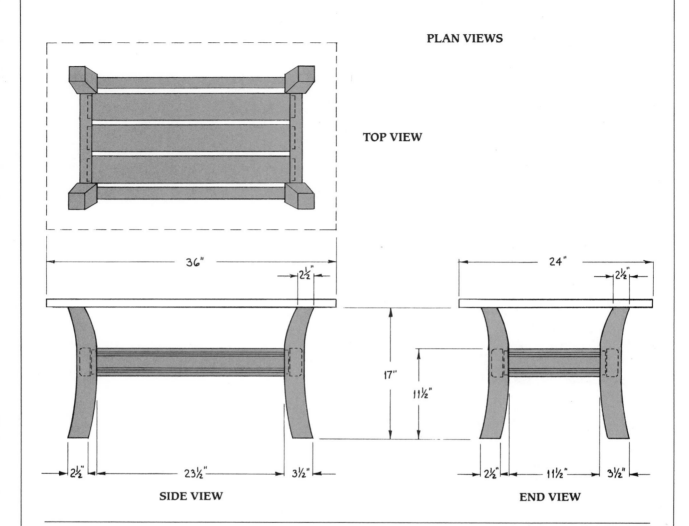

36"

2½"

24"

2½"

17"

11½"

2½" 23½" 3½"

2½" 11½" 3½"

SIDE VIEW

END VIEW

2. Make the rails and slats. Shape two edges of the rails with a ½-inch beading bit in a router, then machine a ¼-inch radius on the other two edges. Machine a cove on the rails with a table saw, as you did the chair and ottoman rails (see step 2 of the Vineyard Settee and Chair with Ottoman project on page 207).

Lay out and cut the tenons on both ends of each rail, as shown in the *Tenon Detail*. Then lay out the mortises in each end rail for the slats, as shown in the *End Rail Layout* drawing.

On both ends of each slat, lay out and cut a tenon ¾ inch thick by ¾ inch long by 3¼ inches wide, with a ⅛-inch shoulder on all four sides.

Cut the mortises next. We cut all the mortises using a mortising attachment on a drill press, which eliminates the handwork of squaring each mortise with a chisel. When working with a drill press, clamp a make-

TENON DETAIL

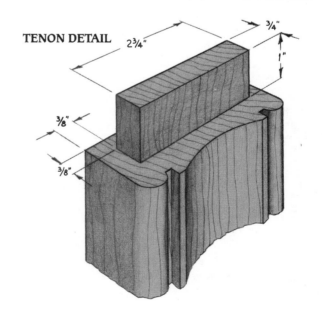

2¾"

¾"

1"

⅜"

⅜"

shift fence to the table, so you can position the mortises uniformly and accurately. And set the depth stop, so that all the mortises are roughed to a uniform depth—usually about 1/16 inch deeper than the tenons are long.

You can, of course, rough out the mortises with a drill bit slightly smaller in diameter than the mortise width. Then cut to the layout lines with a chisel.

END RAIL LAYOUT

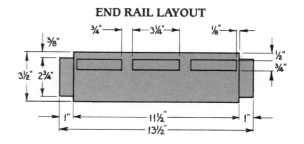

3. Make the legs. Since the legs' front and side profiles are identical, you can use the same pattern for both. Enlarge the pattern (including the size and location of the mortise), make a durable—cardboard or plywood—template, and use it to lay out the leg blanks.

Cut the mortises *before* cutting the leg profiles. Use the same techniques to mortise the legs as you did to mortise the rails in step 2.

Next, cut the profile of each leg on the band saw. Use the same technique as for the front legs of the chair and the ottoman legs—cut two opposing sides first, reattach the waste pieces with tape, then cut the other two sides.

4. Assemble the table. Dry assemble all the parts to make sure the joints fit properly. Make any needed adjustments.

Glue the side rails between the legs to make two leg assemblies. Then, glue and clamp the three slats to the end rails. Finally, join the two leg assemblies to the end rails, and clamp the whole thing by tightening a band clamp around the four legs, even with the rails. Keep clamped overnight, or until glue has cured completely.

Lightly sand the surfaces of the table and apply the same finish used on the chair, ottoman, and/or settee.

The flagstone top doesn't need to be attached. Because of its weight, it won't blow off, and it is unlikely to be jarred off center. Simply set the stone on the tops of the legs. If necessary, trim the tops of the legs so the stone sits squarely and firmly on the leg assembly.

Assembling the table involves making up three subassemblies—joining a pair of legs to each side rail and joining the slats to the end rails—then joining the subassemblies. The top is a gravity fit; it's heavy enough to stay put without adhesives or fasteners.

WHEELWRIGHT SERVING CART

Serving You a Woodworking Challenge

If you can buy spoked wheels like the ones on this serving cart, why on earth would you *make* them?

Because you never have. Because you want to. *Because you can.*

This is the kind of project that separates the woodworkers from the do-it-yourselfers. Woodworkers are always looking for the next challenge. With a shop full of expensive tools, you don't want to build one sawbuck picnic table after another. You want *challenge.* And here it is: a practical, sturdy, unique, attractive outdoor project.

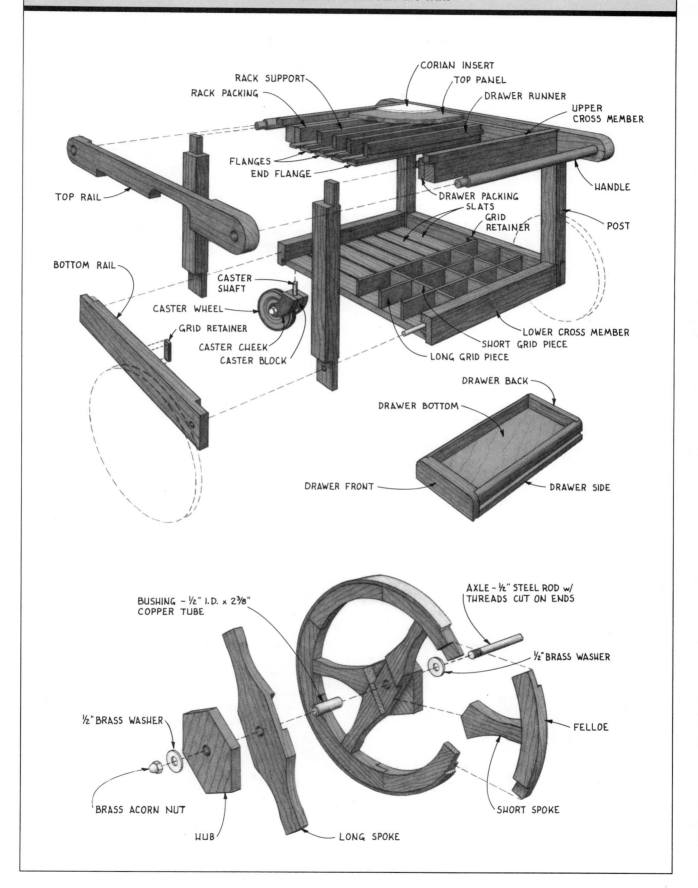

RACK SUPPORT
RACK PACKING
CORIAN INSERT
TOP PANEL
DRAWER RUNNER
UPPER CROSS MEMBER
HANDLE
FLANGES
END FLANGE
DRAWER PACKING
SLATS
GRID RETAINER
POST
TOP RAIL
BOTTOM RAIL
CASTER SHAFT
CASTER WHEEL
GRID RETAINER
CASTER CHEEK
CASTER BLOCK
LONG GRID PIECE
SHORT GRID PIECE
LOWER CROSS MEMBER
DRAWER BACK
DRAWER BOTTOM
DRAWER FRONT
DRAWER SIDE

BUSHING – ½" I.D. x 2⅜" COPPER TUBE
AXLE – ½" STEEL ROD w/ THREADS CUT ON ENDS
½" BRASS WASHER
½" BRASS WASHER
FELLOE
BRASS ACORN NUT
HUB
LONG SPOKE
SHORT SPOKE

SHOPPING LIST

LUMBER

7 bd. ft. 4/4 white oak
10⅓ bd. ft. 5/4 white oak
15 bd. ft. 8/4 white oak
2 pcs. 1¼" dia. × 36" oak dowel
1 pc. ¾" BC plywood, 2 × 4'
1 pc. ¼" AC birch plywood, 2 × 2'

HARDWARE AND SUPPLIES

1 box #6 × 1⅝" galvanized drywall-type screws
1 box #6 × 2½" galvanized drywall-type screws
2 pcs. #6 × 1¼" galvanized drywall-type screws
4 pcs. #6 × ¾" roundhead screws
4 pcs. #6 × 2" galvanized drywall-type screws
1 box galvanized 6d finishing nails
1 box 1" brads

HARDWARE AND SUPPLIES—CONTINUED

1 pc. ½" dia. × 28" round steel rod
2 pcs. ⅜" dia. × 3½" all-thread rod
2 pcs. ½" brass acorn nuts
4 pcs. ⅜" brass acorn nuts
4 pcs. ½" brass washers
2 pcs. ¾" brass washers
2 pcs. ½" × 2⅜" copper tubing
6 pcs. ¼" × ¾" × 36" rubber hold-down straps
1 pc. 20" × 27⅞" Corian
34 pcs. #4 × 1" brass flathead screws
Resorcinol glue
Contact cement

FINISH

Exterior-grade penetrating oil, such as CWF

TOOL LIST

Band saw
Bar or pipe clamps
Block plane
Clamps
Drill
  ⅛" bit
  ½" bit
  13/16" bit
  1" bit
  Pilot hole bit
Hammer
Jointer
Paintbrush
Planer
Radial arm saw
  Dado set
Router
  ¼" rounding-over bit
  ¼" straight bit
  ⅜" rabbeting bit, piloted
  ⅜" core box bit
  ¾" straight bit

Router—continued
  Edge guide
  Trammel jig
Router, table-mounted
Ruler
Saber saw
  Trammel attachment
Sander(s)
Sandpaper
Saw for crosscutting
Sawhorses
Screwdriver
Table saw
  Dado cutter
  Miter gauge
Tack cloth
Tape measure
Try square
Wrench
Yardsticks

The spoked wheels may be the biggest challenge in building this cart, but they are far from the only challenge. There are casters to make, too. You have to cut and surface 8/4 (eight-quarter) oak, which will tax the horsepower of your saws and test the edges of all your cutting tools. You have to do some resawing; you have to craft some unique joints. It is a challenge, but clearly it can be done.

The nexus of two needs and two minds begat this project. Both of the needs and one of the minds were Phil Gehret's. First, he needed a serving table or cart to round out a garden furniture set he had made. Second, he needed to find a use for a fairly large piece of Corian, the range cutout left when he installed his kitchen countertops. Corian is expensive, so you don't cavalierly toss out leftovers. You build things around them.

So Phil put his mind to work and created a design. Though it works with his garden furniture, it works with other pieces as well, such as the Acadia Bench and Chair or the Terrace Ensemble (if you like this cart better than that ensemble's tea trolley). There aren't fancy embellishments, just rounded edges and ends. The design is smooth and contemporary, without being trendy or transitory.

The second mind belonged to Fred Matlack. Fred hatched the design and engineering of the wheels. Why buy it, he'll say, if you can make it? So Fred sketched out his wheel plan, and Phil picked at it to satisfy himself that it would work. Then he built the cart.

Builder's Notes

This is one of those projects that's fun to tackle. Phil Gehret, who always welcomes the opportunity to try a new twist or flourish, gave himself latitude. And

CUTTING LIST

PIECE	NUMBER	THICKNESS	WIDTH	LENGTH	MATERIAL
Top rails	2	1¾"	3½"	42½"	8/4 oak
Bottom rails	2	1¾"	3½"	30"	8/4 oak
Posts	4	1¾"	2½"	22½"	8/4 oak
Upper cross members	2	1¾"	3½"	20"	8/4 oak
Lower cross members	2	1¾"	3½"	18¾"	8/4 oak
Handles	2	1¼" dia.		22"	oak dowel
Top panel	1	¾"	20"	27⅞"	¾" plywood
Rack packing	1	¾"	2"	18½"	4/4 oak
Rack supports	4	¾"	2"	20¼"	4/4 oak
End flanges	2	⅜"	1¾"	20⅝"	5/4 oak
Flanges	3	⅜"	2¾"	20⅝"	5/4 oak
Drawer front	1	1¾"	2¼"	9¾"	8/4 oak*
Drawer back	1	¾"	1¾"	9"	4/4 oak
Drawer sides	2	¾"	2¼"	18⅞"	4/4 oak
Drawer bottom	1	¼"	9"	18⅞"	¼" plywood
Drawer runners	2	5/16"	¾"	18½"	4/4 oak
Drawer packing	1	¾"	2⅜"	18½"	4/4 oak
Slats	6	1"	2½"	28"	5/4 oak
Center slat	1	1"	1¾"	28"	5/4 oak
Caster wheels	2	¾"	6"	6"	4/4 oak
Caster shafts	2	¾" dia.		4½"	oak dowel
Caster blocks	2	⅞"	2½"	3"	5/4 oak
Caster cheeks	4	¾"	4"	6½"	4/4 oak
Felloes	12	1"	3"	12"	5/4 oak
Long spokes[†]	4	¾"	2"	16½"	4/4 oak
Short spokes[†]	4	¾"	2"	7¼"	4/4 oak
Hubs	4	¾"	3½"	4"	4/4 oak
Long grid pieces	3	⅜"	2"	18½"	5/4 oak
Short grid pieces	3	⅜"	2"	14"	5/4 oak
Grid retainers	2	¼"	½"	2"	scrap

*Cut from top rail; see step 2.
[†]Trim to final length at assembly; see step 13.

used it. So the construction is sturdy, but not *completely* straightforward.

Materials. The principal material used in the cart's construction is white oak, which bears up under outdoor use better than its cousin, red oak. The reason Phil used oak, of course, was that he was matching existing oak furniture. You can make the cart of some other wood if you prefer.

Note that you need to buy three different thicknesses: 4/4 (four-quarter), 5/4 (five-quarter), and 8/4 (eight-quarter). With hardwoods, you probably will have to do some shopping to find what you need, and you will have to do some calculating to get the particular boards that will yield the parts you need. Since hardwoods generally are stocked in random widths and random lengths, you have to keep the "Cutting List" handy as you examine the boards. You have to imagine what pieces you can cut from each board. If you are like me, you'll be thinking about the board-foot cost of the material and trying to squeeze the maximum usable stuff from each board.

Be generous with yourself and buy some extra. (I always tell myself that.) Select boards that are wider and longer than you think you'll need. Get an extra piece or two. It's easy to miscalculate there at the lumberyard. Moreover, it's not uncommon to uncover defects as you joint and plane lumber. An extra board or two can save the day should you uncover a serious defect. Or if you

PATTERNS

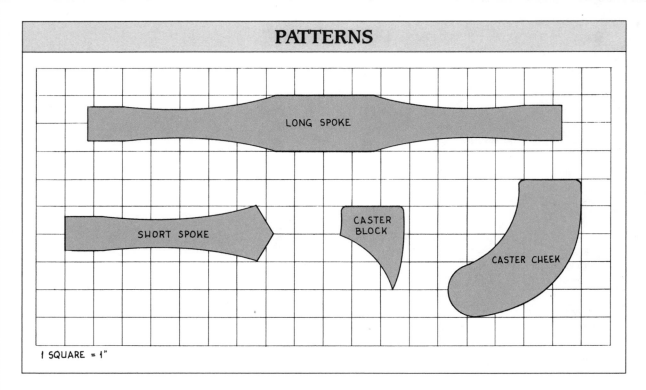

LONG SPOKE

SHORT SPOKE

CASTER BLOCK

CASTER CHEEK

1 SQUARE = 1"

simply miscalculate. (The extra board that becomes surplus is the beginning of the next project.)

If you select a standardized material like redwood, cedar, or pine, keep the actual thicknesses of both the stock and the parts you need in mind. The posts and rails, for example, will have to be resawed from 4-by stock unless you have 3-by available in your locale.

The adhesive of choice for most of this project is resorcinol glue. It is expensive, it stains, and it leaves a visible maroon-brown glue line. But it's very strong and completely waterproof.

To glue the rubber "tires" to the wooden wheels and casters, use contact cement. When he first built the cart, Phil used a silicone adhesive caulk, but it gave up the bond after about a year on the patio. When he reapplied the tires to the wheels, he used contact cement, and that has held the rubber to the wood ever since.

Contact cement's most common use is to bond plastic laminates to whatever they need to be bonded to—countertops, shelves, walls, cabinets. To use it, you apply a coating to *both* mating parts and allow the coatings to dry. Only then do you put the two parts together. The instant the coatings touch, they bond. No second chances if you didn't have the parts quite lined up. No clamping necessary, though.

In this project, you probably should use a brush as an applicator. Clean up with a proprietary solvent, lacquer thinner, or acetone.

One of Phil's little twists is the use of rubber hold-down straps for tires. These are strips of heavy rubber with a metal hook at each end. I noticed that our local hardware store has a couple of varieties of hold-downs. Any one will do, I think, though Phil used hold-downs manufactured by The Radiator Company.

As previously noted, the cart has a Corian top. Corian is a synthetic material made by DuPont. Hard and durable, stain- and grease-resistant, easy to clean, Corian makes wonderful, rich-looking countertops. Although it can be scratched and scorched, minor mars can be sanded out. Good for a countertop, in sum, and thus good for a serving cart top.

Corian is relatively easy to work with carbide-tipped cutters. The color permeates the material, so you don't have to struggle with edge-banding. You can glue pieces of it together using a special glue, creating virtually invisible seams.

Despite its desirability, the Corian insert has to be an option in this project. Its cost is just stupifying. A 30-inch by 49-inch piece of ½-inch Corian—the minimum size in that thickness—retails locally for $205. That's for a piece roughly one-third the size of a sheet of plywood. (Imagine paying more than $600 for a single sheet of ½-inch plywood.) Note also that the minimum size is more than twice what you need.

Two alternatives seem to present themselves. The first is to telephone counter fabricators and see what

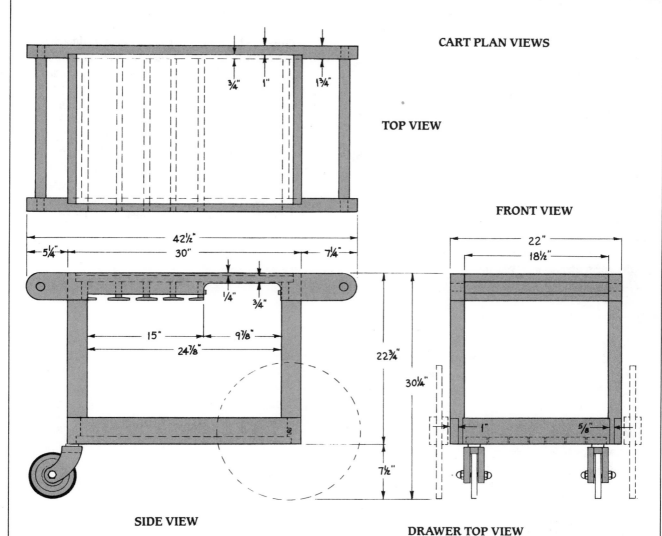

CART PLAN VIEWS

TOP VIEW

FRONT VIEW

SIDE VIEW

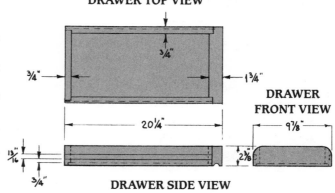

DRAWER TOP VIEW

DRAWER FRONT VIEW

DRAWER SIDE VIEW

they'll charge for the piece. The second is to substitute a less costly material. Buy or make a butcherblock insert, make an insert covered with plastic laminate, or cement ceramic tile to the top panel.

Tools and techniques. The tool requirements of this project aren't unusual—a table saw and a band saw, a drill, a saber saw, and a router, all common power tools. But the demands you'll place on some of them may be more than they (and you) are used to. Eight-quarter oak, for example, isn't your everyday stock. Ripping it takes a sharp blade and horsepower.

Cutting interior curves on the band saw is an unexceptional operation, but cutting short-radius curves where neither part is waste (and where the stock is almost 2 inches thick) probably isn't. It takes a sharp, narrow blade and operator confidence. Practice on scrap to create that confidence.

The joinery isn't all that complicated—laps and dadoes and rabbets. But there *are* those little twists. The "relieved lap joint," for example. Used to join the members of the cart's frame, it's a joint like no other, but it is only a slightly modified lap joint. In doing the posts, the twist is that the setup for cutting one face isn't right for cutting the opposing face. On one side, the cut is 1 inch deep, on the other, it's ⅛ inch deep. The cutting itself is straightforward, it's the layout that's a little tricky. You just have to be very methodical and you have to lay out each post so that, when the saw's howling, you can quickly determine the appropriate face for each cut.

The wheels, which may seem daunting to make, result from a series of twists on routine woodworking techniques. The long spokes are lapped, just not at the usual right angle. The felloes that form the rim look botched when first assembled, but you only need a narrow portion sawed from the center of the rough rim. Hollowing out the caster-wheel centers with the router seems right. But cutting them from their square blanks with the router seems, well, *different*. These are all just little *twists* on what you may be used to.

Finish. The "Shopping List" and the directions stipulate an exterior-grade penetrating oil as a finish. You don't have to use this finish any more than you have to make the cart from white oak.

Many of us have favorite finishes that we tend to use for almost everything we make in the shop. Phil has used penetrating oil, and specifically a product called CWF, on many projects he made for this book. It's *his* favorite. You brush on two coats, the second within a half-hour of the first. Obviously, it's easy to apply, and you clean the brush once, not twice. The finish is about as durable as other clear outdoor finishes. So that's what he uses.

But if *you* have a favorite other than penetrating oil, by all means use it.

1. Prepare the stock and rough-cut the parts. To prepare your hardwood for use, you need to joint and plane it to reduce it to working thicknesses and to smooth the faces and edges. Following the "Cutting List," crosscut the boards to rough working lengths first, and mark each piece so you know what its intended use is. (Of course, you'll have to re-mark them before long, since dressing the boards will remove your labels.)

To dress each board, smooth one face on the jointer, then joint one edge. Run the board through the planer as many times as is required to reduce it to the desired thickness. (When planing a lot of parts of a common thickness, the usual practice is to set the cutters, run all of them through, reset the cutters and run them all through again, and so forth. That way, all the boards will end up at the same thickness.) Finally, rip the boards to within 1/16 inch of the final width, then trim away that last 1/16 inch and, at the same time, smooth away the saw marks on the jointer.

The result is a board whose surfaces are flat and at right angles to their neighbors, and whose faces are parallel to each other.

There are some alternatives, although the results won't always be ideal. The best alternative, if you lack a jointer and a planer, is to buy from a lumberyard or dealer that can surface the boards to your specifications.

2. Lay out and cut the top rails. Study the *Top Rail Layouts*. Note that there is a right rail and a left one, and that the differences between them go beyond mirror imaging. The left rail is cut out for a drawer and for the glass rack. The right is not.

Lay out the two rails. Cut the dadoes for the posts first, using a router and a straight bit. Rest the rails side by side on the workbench to dado both at the same time. Clamp two straightedges across them to guide the router in cutting the first dado, positioning them so you can't cut the dado too wide. Cut the dado progressively, trimming about ¼ inch deeper with each pass, until the required depth is achieved. After the first dadoes are cut, move the straightedges to guide the cutting of the second.

Cut the stopped rabbet for the top panel next. This is a two-pass operation on the table saw. To cut the bottom of the rabbet, set the depth of cut to the width of the rabbet, and position the rip fence to establish the depth. What you must do is turn on the saw, then carefully lower the workpiece onto the blade, slide it forward to complete the cut, then lift the end up off the blade. You must only cut between the dadoes.

After cutting the bottoms of both rabbets, change the setup slightly. Now the depth of cut must match the rabbet's depth. Position the fence to keep the waste to the outside of the blade (and thus avoid having the blade kick it back at you). Again, you must lower the workpiece onto the blade, make the cut, then lift the workpiece off the

TOP RAIL LAYOUTS

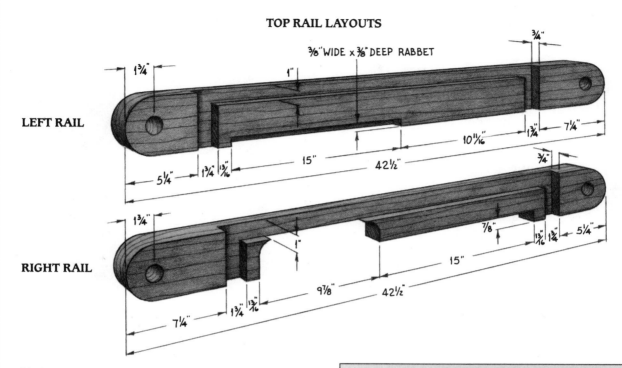

blade, cutting only between the dadoes.

With a router and a ⅜-inch rabbeting bit, cut the stopped rabbet for the glass rack flanges in the bottom inner edge of the non-drawer side.

Drill the 1-inch-diameter holes for the handles.

Finally, step up to the band saw. Round off the ends of both rails first. Then cut out the edge of the drawer-side rail for the drawer—be sure to save the cutout to use as the drawer front—and for the glass rack.

> **TIP**
>
> Because you are going to use the "waste" from the drawer cutout as the drawer front, you have to complete the cut with a single, continuous pass. The more narrow the blade you have in your band saw, the tighter you can round the corners of the cutout.

Making a stopped cut on the table saw requires you to plunge the workpiece onto the blade. In the case of the stopped rabbets in the cart's top rails, the blade is hidden from view; you must put guide marks where you *can* see them. On the saw table, use strips of tape to mark the nearest and farthest exposed points of the blade. On the workpiece, mark the beginning and the end of the stopped cut. Use the front edge of the saw table as a fulcrum; rest the workpiece's edge against it. Jockey the workpiece forward and back to align your marks, then pivot the work down onto the saw blade.

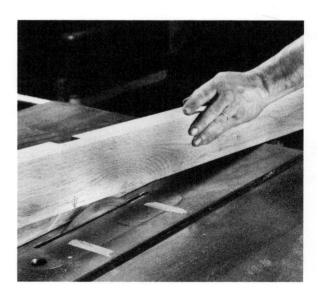

3. **Cut the joinery on the posts.** The posts join the rails and cross members in what might be called "a relieved lap joint." It is just a little unlike anything else I've encountered. This, of course, doesn't mean the post joinery is difficult to cut. It is not. In essence, you cut tenons on the posts (they just don't fit into mortises).

Lay out the posts carefully, since each one is unique. Follow the *Post Layouts.* The basic cuts are made on the table saw or radial arm saw with a dado cutter. Make the 1-inch-deep cuts on all the posts, then reset the depth of cut and make the ⅛-inch-deep cuts.

Finally, working at the band saw, cut away the designated area of the top tenons.

POST LAYOUTS

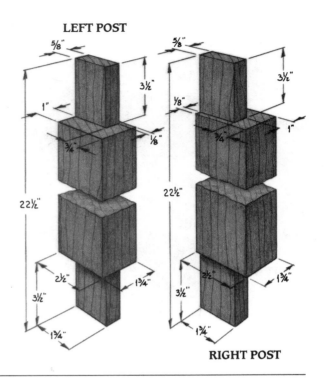

LEFT POST

RIGHT POST

4. **Cut the bottom rails and assemble the side frames.** Take up the bottom two rails next. These are lapped on their ends. Cut the laps using the same basic setup you used for the posts, which is to say, on the radial arm saw or table saw with a dado cutter.

Dry assemble the side frames to ensure that all the joinery fits properly. Sand the individual parts, then glue them together with resorcinol glue. Use care in mixing and applying the glue, since it stains. Drips and squeeze-out can mar your cart. Because resorcinol is a gap-filling glue, high-pressure clamping isn't necessary. Just make sure the assemblies are square and flat, and that the joints are snug.

After the glue has set, use a router and a ¼-inch rounding-over bit to radius all the exposed edges of the side frames. Clamp the frame to your workbench to keep it from shifting away from you as you push the router.

5. **Make the handles and cross members.** The two side frames are joined together by the cross members and the handles. Before you can assemble the cart frame, you need to prepare both the cross members and the handles.

Cut the handle tenons on the table saw. Set the

miter gauge roughly parallel to the saw arbor and clamp the bar to the saw table so it can't move. Set the fence-to-blade distance to equal the length of the tenon (measure from the outside of the blade). Set the depth of cut to remove only the amount of waste you want removed—in this case, ⅛ inch. Stand behind the saw, and cradle the handle dowel in the miter gauge. With the saw running, carefully feed the workpiece into the blade and rotate it. The fence keeps the tenon from getting too long; the miter gauge holds the work perpendicular to the blade. This is not something you can do with the saw guard in place.

The lower cross members are slightly shorter than the upper cross members. To join the side frames, the ends of the cross members fit into the shallow recess created by the ⅛-inch-deep lap cut made on the inside of the posts. Before assembly, the rear lower cross member must be grooved for the axle. Do it on the table saw with a dado cutter, positioning the ⅝-inch-wide, ⅝-inch-deep groove 1¼ inches from the cross member's top edge. The front lower cross member must be drilled for the caster shafts. The center points for the 13/16-inch-diameter, 3¼-inch-deep holes should be about 2 inches

TIP

Don't invite kickback! When cutting rabbets on the table saw, be sure you set up the second cut so the waste is to the outside of the blade. Never trap it between the blade and the fence. Oh, you may get away with it more often than not. But you'll remember ever after that one time when the blade *fires* that blunt projectile at your groin.

from either end, and 1 inch from the front edge of the crosspiece.

The upper cross members must be rabbeted for the top panel and notched so they join the side frames by both abutting and overlapping the "tenons" on the posts. Cut the rabbets with two passes on the table saw. Cut the notches on the band saw, sizing them as shown in the *Upper Cross Member Detail*.

Finish up your work on these parts by sanding them.

UPPER CROSS MEMBER DETAIL

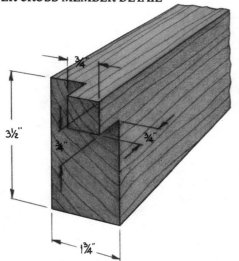

AXLE GROOVE DETAIL

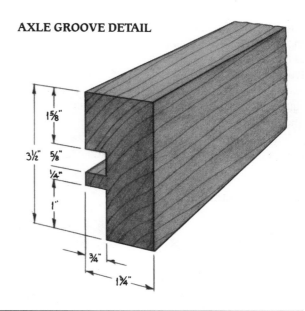

6. Assemble the cart frame. The cart frame parts are assembled using resorcinol glue and galvanized drywall-type screws. Before actually assembling the frame, do a trial run to check how well the parts fit together and to practice the routine. There are any number of approaches that can work. You may want

some help in holding the assembly together and applying clamps.

The idea, of course, is to position the handles and cross members between the side frames. If you do clamp the frame, position the clamps so you have access to the joints, so you can drill pilot holes and drive screws through the side frames into the ends of the cross members. The handles are captured between the side frames and don't need further fastening. And once the screws are driven, the clamps can be removed.

After the clamps *are* removed, use the router and the rounding-over bit to radius the exposed edges of the cross members, blending the corners where appropriate.

With a ½-inch bit, drill holes for the rear axle. Gauge the positions of these holes for the position of the groove for the axle in the lower rear cross member.

Finally, cut the top panel to size and set it in place. A handful of 6d finishing nails can be driven to hold the panel in place. Pilot holes will enable you to drive the nails in the oak.

---

7. Cut and install the glass rack components. The glass rack consists of supports (plus one piece of packing) and flanges. As shown in the *Glass Rack Detail,* the supports are attached to the underside of the top panel, and the flanges are then attached to the supports.

Trim the rack packing to fit between the front posts, and attach it to the front cross member with two or three 1⅝-inch galvanized screws.

Notch the supports to fit the cart next. With the cart frame upside down on the workbench, mark each support for cutting. First, set the support on the cut-out rail and butt the end against the far rail; mark along the inner edge of the cut-out rail on the support. Then set the support on the top panel and mark along the cut-out rail on the support's end (obviously, the support will be too long to fit between the rails, so you'll have to cock it; just be sure it is flat against the panel). With a try square, extend the lines until they meet, then cut to the lines on the band saw.

Install the supports by driving 1⅝-inch galvanized screws through the top panel into the top edge of each support. One support must be flush with the edge of the drawer cutout, since it will also support the drawer runner. The other three supports are spaced evenly between that support and the packing.

Finally, resaw and chamfer the flanges, then install them. The flanges are ⅜ inch thick and are most economically produced by resawing 4/4 or 5/4 stock (to get

---

TIP

Make sure the flanges are adequately backed when you cut the chamfers on them. To the rip fence, attach a facing strip—a piece of ¾-inch plywood, for example—that's at least as high as the flanges are wide. To keep your fingers well clear of the blade as you cut the chamfers, press the flange stock against the fence with one push stick, and propel the stock with another.

GLASS RACK DETAIL

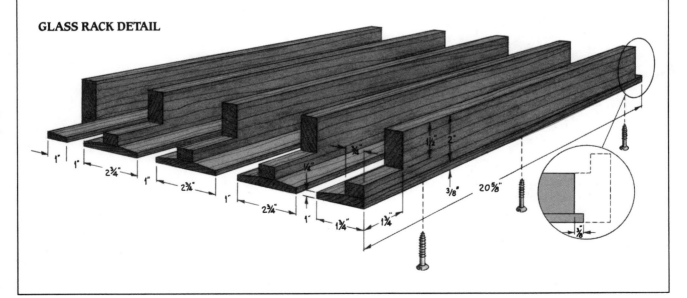

two flanges from each piece). If you resaw on the table saw, as Phil did, use 5/4 stock. If you use a band saw, you can probably use 4/4 stock.

Chamfer the end flanges along one edge only, the three inner flanges along both edges. Do this on the table saw. On some saws, you'll have to retract the blade completely, move the rip fence to the left of it, then raise and tilt it.

Finally, set the flanges in position and screw them to the bottom edges of the supports.

---

8. Build and install the drawer. Assemble the rough-cut parts for the drawer, including the runners.

The drawer joinery can be cut on the table saw or using a router and various bits. The front must be rabbeted (¾ inch wide by ⅜ inch deep) across both ends for the sides, and grooved (¼ inch wide by ⅜ inch deep) parallel to the bottom edge for the drawer bottom. The sides, similarly, must be rabbeted for the back and grooved for the bottom. But they must also be grooved for the drawer runners (¾ inch wide by 5/16 inch deep). See the *Drawer Detail.*

Chuck a ¾-inch straight bit into your router and fit it with an edge guide. Cut the rabbets first, doing both the sides and the front. Change the guide setting and depth of cut, then machine the runner grooves in the sides. Switch bits and reset the depth of cut and the guide position once more, then groove both sides and the front for the bottom. Finally, switch to a ⅜-inch core box bit and rout a finger groove along the bottom edge of the

drawer front, centered about ½ inch from the front edge.

Assemble the drawer with resorcinol glue and galvanized 6d finishing nails. Unless you are remarkably deft with a hammer, you ought to drill pilot holes for the nails. Join the front and one side, then fit the bottom into its grooves and add the second side, then the back. Drive a couple of nails through the bottom into the back. With a block plane, round-over the outer edges of the drawer sides to match the rounded corners of the drawer front.

To install the drawer in the cart, you must first fit the runners to their grooves in the drawer sides. The runners must be sufficiently smaller than the grooves to allow free movement, but not so much smaller that the drawer will rattle up and down. If the runners stick in the grooves, use a block plane to remove a shaving or two.

If necessary, trim the drawer packing to fit the cart, then install it with two or three galvanized screws. Attach the runners, one to the packing, the other to the glass rack support, using 1-inch brads.

DRAWER DETAIL

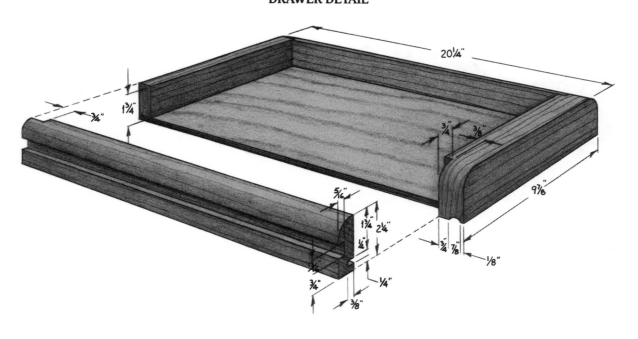

9. **Cut and install the slats.** The slats fit into a rabbet cut around the inner perimeter of the cart frame bottom. With the cart upside down, cut the ⅜-inch-wide, ¾-inch-deep rabbet with a router and piloted rabbeting bit. The rabbet is too deep to be cut in a single pass; rather, you should nibble away about ¼ inch of waste at a time. When the rabbet is cut, square the corners with a chisel and mallet.

Round-over the long edges of each slat before installing the slats. Use 1⅝-inch galvanized screws, driven through the slats into the cross members, to attach the slats. Put the narrow slat in the middle.

---

10. **Make the caster wheels.** Each caster consists of a housing with a shaft, and a wheel with an axle. Make the wheels first, then assemble the housings. Finally, assemble the two parts and mount the resulting units on the cart.

While it might seem natural to turn the wheels, Phil actually made them using a router and a trammel jig. Drill the center hole for each of the two caster wheels in their respective blanks. Fit the trammel jig to the router, then chuck a small-diameter straight bit in place and set the depth of cut to about ¼ inch. The radius of the wheels is 3 inches, so slip the pivot through the appropriate hole in the trammel and into the blank's center hole. With the router held just above the workpiece, turn it on and plunge the bit into the wood. Swing the router around the pivot, routing a circular groove. Adjust it to cut a bit deeper and increase the depth of the groove. Keep cutting deeper and deeper until you break through.

After both wheels are cut out, rout the decorative recesses shown in the *Caster Detail*, using the same technique, but with different bits. Sand the wheels to smooth them and to soften the various edges.

Phil cut the "tires" used on the wheels from 36-inch-long rubber hold-down straps. Cut the end off such a strap. Wrap the rubber around the first wheel and cut off enough to fit the wheel. Apply contact cement to both the rubber strap and the wheel rim. When the cement has dried, apply the tire to the rim. Since the adhesive bonds upon contact, you have to have the tire aligned properly on your first try; you won't be able to pull it off easily and reapply it. At intervals around the wheel, drill pilot holes through the tire and into the wheel, then drive 1-inch brass screws. Use six or seven screws per wheel.

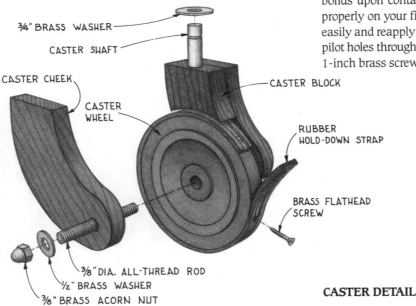

¾" BRASS WASHER

CASTER SHAFT

CASTER CHEEK

CASTER WHEEL

CASTER BLOCK

RUBBER HOLD-DOWN STRAP

BRASS FLATHEAD SCREW

⅜" DIA. ALL-THREAD ROD

½" BRASS WASHER

⅜" BRASS ACORN NUT

CASTER DETAIL

---

11. **Make the caster housings.** Enlarge the patterns for the caster cheeks and blocks, make plywood or cardboard templates, then lay out four cheeks and two blocks. Cut them on the band saw. Using a wheel as a guide, lay out the axle hole on one cheek piece. Line it up atop the other three and drill all at the same time.

Before gluing up the housings, dry assemble each one. With a clamp securing the assembly—a block sandwiched between two cheeks—fit a wheel in place with its axle (the axle is a short piece of threaded rod). You want the wheel to turn very freely and not bind between the cheeks or against the block. Both the wheel and the housing will shrink and swell with changes in the weather, and you want the parts to be assembled with enough clearance to ensure that they'll work regardless of the weather. If necessary, cut a thicker block or trim away the concave arc. When you are satisfied, glue up the housings.

After the glue has cured, radius the exposed edges with the router and the rounding-over bit. Drill the hole in the housing for the caster shaft, then glue the shaft in place.

The caster shafts fit into holes you drilled in the lower front cross member earlier. As with the wheel, the shaft must swivel without binding; check it, and, if necessary, bore the hole a bit larger. Use a large brass washer as a bushing between the caster and the cart; fit the washer over the shaft before inserting the shaft in the hole in the cross member.

To keep the casters in the holes, Phil drilled a screw pilot hole that intersects the shaft hole on a tangent. Then he filed a groove around the shaft. When the shaft is inserted and a screw driven, the screw passes through the groove, allowing the shaft to turn but not to drop out.

Make the groove around the top end of the caster shaft using a round file. Achieving the kind of action you want is a trial-and-error process. You have to insert the caster, drive the retaining screw, and see how it swivels. If it binds, withdraw the screw, pull the caster, and file.

12. Make the wheel rims.

The felloes are the rim segments. Cut half-laps on the ends of the felloes, glue them into a hexagonal frame, then cut the rim from the frame.

A great tool for cutting these half-laps is the radial arm saw equipped with a dado cutter. It's easy to set the angles required, and as you cut you can see the lap being created. Nevertheless, it is not the only tool that can be used to make the laps. If you do the job on the table saw, miter the ends of the felloes, then lap them. Use the dado cutter. Set the rip fence to limit the length of the lap to 1½ inches, and guide the workpiece with the miter gauge set to a 60 degree angle.

When you glue up the felloes—use resorcinol glue—you'll see that the laps don't lap at the edges; around the outside of the frame, there will be triangular protrusions, and around the inside, there will be triangular gaps. Don't worry about these. You'll be cutting the rim from the center of the frame, where the laps *do* lap.

To cut the rim, use a saber saw with a trammel attachment. To provide a pivot point, you must make a wheel center from scrap. Cross-lap two scraps of wood.

Set the rim frame on top of this unit and scribe along the inner edges of the frame on the temporary spokes. Trim off the spokes on the lines, and the center will fit snugly inside the rim frame. With a tape measure, roughly

SPOKED WHEEL PLAN VIEWS

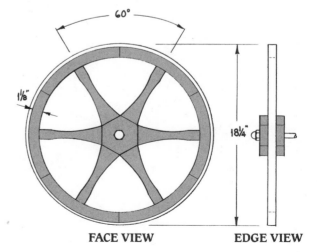

FACE VIEW   **EDGE VIEW**

estimate how you will take the rim from the frame, and locate the center point on the temporary wheel center. The inner diameter of the rim is 16 inches, the outer diameter 18¼ inches. The center point will be the pivot for the saber saw's trammel attachment. You shouldn't have to scribe the rim layout, but you can if you want to.

Clamp the work to the workbench, overhanging the edge. Cut the outer edge first, then the inner edge. Sand the completed rims, and radius the inner edges with the router and the rounding-over bit.

To cut the rim, clamp the rim frame overhanging the workbench edge. Obviously, you'll have to shift the work several times. As you progress, stick little scraps into the kerf to prevent it from shifting or pinching the blade.

13. **Make the spoke assemblies.** Each spoke assembly consists of two double spokes, which are cross-lapped together, and two single spokes, which are sandwiched with the double spokes between two hubs.

Note: If you are comparing the dimensions on the various drawings with the size specified by the "Cutting List," you've noted a disparity. The spokes are slightly long at this point. You don't trim them to their final length until they are assembled and you are ready to join them to the wheel rims.

Cut the cross-laps first, using a table saw or radial arm saw equipped with a dado cutter.

Next enlarge the patterns for the spokes, make cardboard or plywood templates, and trace the templates on the appropriate spoke blanks. Cut the spokes on the band saw, then radius their edges with a router and a rounding-over bit. At the same time, lay out the four hubs and cut them on the band saw, then round-over their exposed edges (this is best done using a table-mounted router).

Glue up the spoke assemblies next. Glue the double spokes together first. Then lay the double spoke assemblies on a piece of waxed paper, apply glue to the ends of the single spokes and butt them into place, and glue one hub atop the intersection of the spokes. High clamping pressure doesn't improve the bond of resorcinol glue, so it is enough to simply set a weight atop the hub until the glue sets. Laying the spokes out on the workbench like this keeps them flat while the glue cures, and the waxed paper keeps the glue from bonding them to the workbench. After the glue cures, turn the spoke assembly over and glue the second hub in place, just as you did the first.

Finally, drill the axle holes through the spoke assemblies.

Each spoke assembly consists of two long spokes, two short spokes, and two hubs. The long spokes are cross-lapped together, and the short spokes butt into the wide crotches formed when the long spokes are joined. A hub is glued to either side, reinforcing the joinery.

14. Join the spoke assemblies and rims.
The spokes are joined to the rims by screws driven through the rims into the ends of the spokes.

The first task is to trim the spokes. With the assembly resting on the workbench, set the rim on top and line it up. Make sure it is centered. Then mark along the rim on each spoke, and when you are done, trim the spokes on the band saw.

The spoke assembly should now fit precisely inside the rim. Line up the spokes so they join the rim midway between lap joints. If needed, a couple of spring clamps can hold the two assemblies in alignment while you drill the pilot holes and drive the screws that hold the set elements together.

Now mount the tires, just as you did on the caster wheels. The biggest difference here is that you'll need two hold-down straps for each wheel. Cut the first piece of strap, test fit it to the wheel, and mark where it begins and ends on the rim. Apply contact cement to both the wheel rim and the rubber strap. After the cement has dried, apply the strap to the wheel. Of course, the two parts bond upon contact, so be sure the strap is lined up with your mark and the rim before you press it in place. Drill pilot holes and drive small brass screws to help secure the tire. Trim the second strap to fit the remaining arc of the wheel, then mount it the same way you did the first segment. Repeat the process to complete the second wheel.

15. Cut and assemble the bottle rack.
The pieces composing the bottle rack are cross-lapped together. Cut the notches using a dado cutter in the table saw. Cut all the long grid pieces at one time, then all the short pieces. Lay out the notches on one piece of each length. Set the dado cutter to the desired width and adjust the saw's depth of cut to the desired setting. Test the setup on scrap. Stack all the pieces of one length, the marked piece on top, then stand them on edge in the miter gauge with a piece of scrap behind them to prevent tear-out. Line up the marks and make the cuts. Repeat the process with the pieces of the other length.

The bottle rack is an egg-crate sort of affair. The pieces composing it are cross-lapped together, forming a grid of 4¼-inch-square compartments, just the right size for the typical wine bottle. The grid pieces are not glued together, nor are they glued to the cart. The assembly can be removed and disassembled for cleaning.

Assemble the rack in place, then position and screw the retainers to the inside of the lower rails. Use two brass screws in each retainer.

16. Apply a finish to the cart.
Remove the wheels, casters, and bottle rack from the cart. Touch-up sand the cart, wheels, casters, and bottle rack if needed. Apply a finish.

Phil used CWF, an exterior-grade penetrating oil. Following the manufacturer's instructions, we brushed on a liberal application, let it soak into the wood for about 20 minutes, then brushed on another coat. The project should be coated everywhere—underneath as well as the top. Apply the finish to the drawer, too. DON'T, however, apply the finish to the caster shafts or the holes for them. We let the finish dry for two or three days before putting the cart together and pressing it into patio service.

17. Complete the cart. After the finish has thoroughly dried, install the wheels and casters and make a decorative top.

The caster axles are short pieces of threaded rod. Fit the caster wheel in place, slip the axle in place, then tighten a brass acorn nut on either end of the axle. Insert the caster shafts in their holes and drive the retaining screws.

The axle for the spoked wheels needs to be threaded on both ends so you can use nuts to secure the wheels. Phil used a die to cut threads on the ends of a steel rod; if you don't have this metalworking tool, use a threaded rod for the axle. To act as bushings between wheels and axle, Phil cut 2⅜-inch lengths of ½-inch (inside diameter) copper tubing. Slide the axle in place, fit a brass washer over each end, add the wheels and bushings, another washer on each end, then turn on the brass acorn nuts and tighten them.

Set the cart on its wheels, and slide the drawer in place.

Complete the cart by cutting a piece of ½-inch-thick Corian to cover the top panel. After cutting it to size, radius the edges with a router and a *carbide-tipped* rounding-over bit. The Corian is merely set in place, not glued.

TIP

A couple of 1-inch-diameter holes drilled through the top panel can make it a lot easier to remove your Corian insert for cleanup. Position them in the area of the drawer. To remove the Corian, pull out the drawer. Stick a finger in the hole and push up on the Corian. The lift should be enough to allow you to hook your fingers beneath the Corian and remove it from the cart.

SOUTHWESTERN ENSEMBLE

Unassuming, with Just a Touch of Flair

Inspired by the sturdy yet stylish furniture often found gracing adobe patios and plazas in the Old Southwest, this set will fit into almost any outdoor sitting spot in the country. By no means primitive, its construction requires some pretty fancy joinery.

SOUTHWESTERN ENSEMBLE CHAIR AND BENCH

From a design standpoint, this is a chambray work shirt, jeans, and *turquoise* bracelet kind of thing—low key, unassuming, with just a touch of flair. The chair and bench are deceptive. Their design is low key, but their details are exquisite. And the construction is done *right,* even though it means hard work.

This is just the sort of bench (or chair) you'd spend $800 or more on from a custom landscaper. Expensive. You'll never find it at Wal-Mart.

From a construction standpoint, this is a great project for the experienced woodworker who is looking for a challenge. It's got a lot of mortise-and-tenon joints, including a three-part one where the knee, leg, and seat rail come together. For the woodworker into setups and

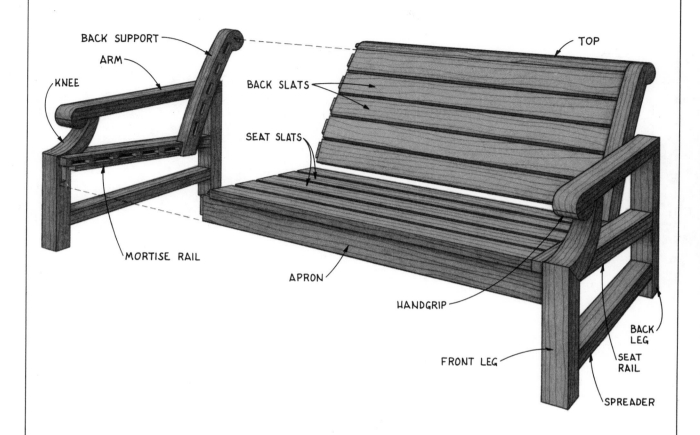

BACK SUPPORT

ARM

KNEE

BACK SLATS

SEAT SLATS

TOP

MORTISE RAIL

APRON

HANDGRIP

FRONT LEG

BACK LEG

SEAT RAIL

SPREADER

SHOPPING LIST—CHAIR

LUMBER

3 pcs. $4 \times 4 \times 8'$ clear all-heart cedar
1 pc. $4 \times 4 \times 4'$ clear all-heart cedar

HARDWARE AND SUPPLIES

8 pcs. #6 $\times$ 2″ galvanized drywall-type screws
6 pcs. #6 $\times$ 3½″ galvanized drywall-type screws
Resorcinol glue

FINISH

Exterior-grade penetrating oil, such as CWF

SHOPPING LIST—BENCH

LUMBER

5 pcs. $4 \times 4 \times 8'$ clear all-heart cedar

HARDWARE AND SUPPLIES

8 pcs. #6 $\times$ 2″ galvanized drywall-type screws
6 pcs. #6 $\times$ 3½″ galvanized drywall-type screws
Resorcinol glue

FINISH

Exterior-grade penetrating oil, such as CWF

CUTTING LIST—CHAIR

PIECE	NUMBER	THICKNESS	WIDTH	LENGTH	MATERIAL
Arms	2	2"	3"	23"	Cedar
Front legs	2	2"	3"	15"	Cedar
Back legs	2	2"	3"	22"	Cedar
Spreaders	2	2"	3"	22½"	Cedar
Seat rails	2	2"	3"	24"	Cedar
Knees	2	3"	3¼"	9¼"	Cedar
Hand grips	2	1½"	3"	3½"	Cedar
Mortise rails	2	1⅛"	2"	18"	Cedar
Back supports	2	2"	3½"	22¾"	Cedar
Back slats	5	1⅛"	3⅜"	20"	Cedar
Top	1	2"	3½"	20"	Cedar
Apron	1	1⅛"	3"	24"	Cedar
Seat slats	5	1⅛"	3⅜"	21¼"	Cedar

CUTTING LIST—BENCH

PIECE	NUMBER	THICKNESS	WIDTH	LENGTH	MATERIAL
Arms	2	2"	3"	23"	Cedar
Front legs	2	2"	3"	15"	Cedar
Back legs	2	2"	3"	22"	Cedar
Spreaders	2	2"	3"	22½"	Cedar
Seat rails	2	2"	3"	24"	Cedar
Knees	2	3"	3¼"	9¼"	Cedar
Hand grips	2	1½"	3"	3½"	Cedar
Mortise rails	2	1⅛"	2"	18"	Cedar
Back supports	2	2"	3½"	22¾"	Cedar
Back slats	5	1⅛"	3⅜"	44"	Cedar
Top	1	2"	3½"	44"	Cedar
Apron	1	1⅛"	3"	48"	Cedar
Seat slats	5	1⅛"	3⅜"	45¼"	Cedar

general techniques, there's probably a new setup or two he or she can try.

Phil Gehret, the Rodale woodworker who built this, remains enthusiastic about it. It was a pleasant change, he says, from the usual "glue-and-screw project" he's called upon to produce. He feels it looks good, and it definitely was a challenge to make.

Builder's Notes

The Southwestern Ensemble is good *woodworking*. Forget outdoor furniture. Don't think backyard. This is resawing and dressing lumber, it's mortise-and-tenon joinery, it's custom-making fine furniture.

If this book has done nothing else for you, at least it should have dispelled the usual notions of what "home-made" outdoor furniture looks like. This ensemble is the perfect antidote to those notions. Forget the sickly green of pressure-treated lumber, the galvanized nail heads. We're not building a deck here, we're making *furniture*. This is *real* woodworking.

Materials. We settled on cedar for the seats and tables. Cedar is a solid choice for outdoor projects, since it is attractive, naturally rot resistant, and readily available. Moreover, it's a western species, so it seems a particularly appropriate choice for a contemporary southwestern design motif. (Actually, there are species of cedar native to the eastern United States as well as to other

TOOL LIST

Backsaw	Jointer
Band saw	Paintbrush
Bar clamps or pipe clamps	Router
Block plane	¼" rounding-over bit
Chisels	Ruler
Clamps	Sander(s)
Drafting triangles	Sandpaper
Drill	Saw for crosscutting
Pilot hole bit	Sawhorses
Drill press	Screwdriver
1" dia. bit	Spring clamp
Hollow-chisel	Table saw
mortising	Dado cutter
attachment	Tack cloth
Hammer	Tape measure
Hand screws	Try square

wood and sapwood in your stock. And a penetrating oil finish such as we used tends to emphasize the contrast between heartwood and sapwood colors. The weight is fine here: Although the bench is massive, it doesn't weigh much (it's a lot easier to move around than, say, the Acadia Bench, which is made of oak). Moderate strength is satisfactory for the use here. The softness, however, *is* something of a drawback; the wood is easily dented as you work it on your shop's cast-iron tools. Cutting tools, especially chisels and planes, must be *sharp* to slice the cedar fibers. You'll know immediately when some honing is due, for the cedar fibers will tear, bunch up, and crush over your tool's cutting edge, rather than sever cleanly. Fred Matlack jokingly calls it "balsa cedar."

Tools and techniques. This is a project for the woodworker who is pretty well "tooled up" (although I suspect that no woodworker considers himself or herself to have any but the *essential* tools). The band saw and table saw are essentials here. The jointer is a near essential for dressing the resawed lumber. A drill press with a hollow-chisel mortising attachment is a genuine time-saver, but not an essential. Cedar is soft, and using a chisel to clean up fully housed mortises that have been roughed out at the drill press or with a portable electric drill would be relatively easy.

In building the prototype chair and bench, Phil Gehret started with 4 × 4 posts, which are stocked at

areas of the globe—we've all heard of the Cedars of Lebanon, haven't we? But western red cedar has been marketed for years, and a lot of us tend to think of cedar as western, period.)

Western red cedar is generally straight-grained, but it is lightweight, somewhat soft, and only moderately strong. The heartwood is reddish brown, in contrast to the light sapwood. Unless you pay the extreme premium to get heartwood only, you *will* have a mixture of heart-

PATTERNS

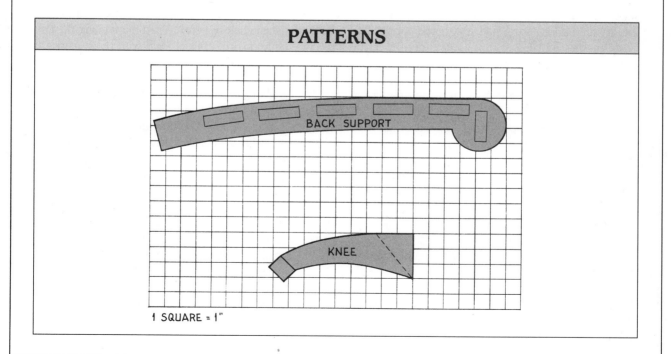

1 SQUARE = 1"

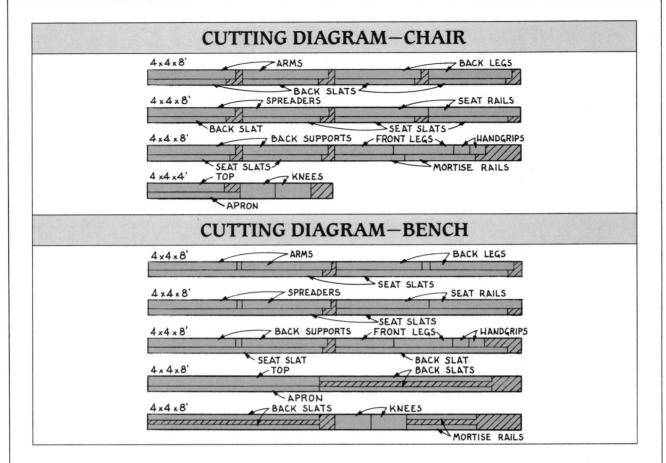

CUTTING DIAGRAM—CHAIR

CUTTING DIAGRAM—BENCH

lumberyards across the nation in a nicely dressed state. Of course, 4 × 4 means that the posts are an actual 3½ inches square. Each *Cutting Diagram* shows how you extract the various parts from the posts. Though the posts are dressed when you begin, you need to resaw them to reduce both the thickness and the width to obtain the required parts. This cutting dictates that you redress the lumber, and it is most easy to do on the jointer.

A key technique, one that arises most frequently when crafting one-of-a-kind pieces, is "laying out to fit." When you work from a plan (regardless of whether it is a published plan or a self-developed plan), you generally use a ruler or a tape measure to position joints. "The mortise is so many inches from the side, and yay many inches from the end; it's so wide and so long." Et cetera, et cetera. This approach works very well. So long as the plan is accurate and the parts are fabricated with precision.

But when you have no plan, or if you have no assurance that the parts are precisely like those in whatever plan you do have, then you "lay out to fit." In this project, you should use the side frame parts themselves to mark the joinery cuts. Put the legs on the workbench, then place the rails across them. Move the parts until they are arranged just the way you want them to be in the finished chair or bench. Then mark along the rails onto the legs with a pencil. And with those marks as jumping-off points, complete the layout work necessary before cutting mortises and tenons.

Similarly, you need to make curved braces to reinforce the joint between the side rails and the end frames. These braces are hard to duplicate. You need to make four, and you should not be surprised to discover each of the four you make is different from the other three. And given this, you can see how problematic it will be to lay out mortises for these braces from a dimensioned plan.

So what you do is lay out the mortises using the actual braces. Eventually, what you may find is that the approach saves you time here and elsewhere.

Finally, note that this bench and matching chair, like some of the others in this book, have identical side frames; the bench simply has a wider seat and back. If you want to make both, you'll save time by laying out, cutting, and joining the corresponding parts for each at the same time.

BENCH PLAN VIEWS

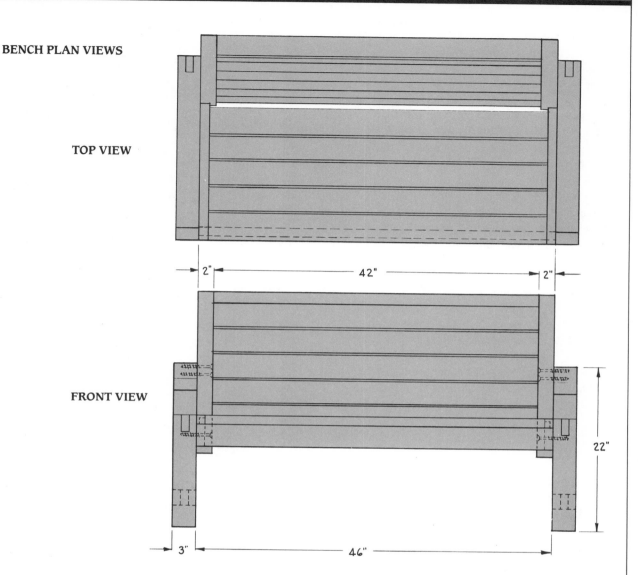

TOP VIEW

FRONT VIEW

2" 42" 2"

22"

3" 46"

Finish. Every outdoor project, regardless of whether it's made of a naturally rot-resistant wood like cedar, needs a finish. That's because rot isn't the only threat to the structural integrity of an outdoor project. The sun's heat bakes the natural oils and resins out of wood. Its ultraviolet rays turn the wood gray and cause its surface to disintegrate; the process is called photodegradation. Surface moisture soaks in when it rains, then migrates back out when the sun shines and the humidity declines. The resulting tension amongst the wood cells causes cupping and even opens up cracks.

Moreover, naturally rot-resistant woods aren't entirely so. The heartwood is, but the sapwood isn't. Unless you specify—and *pay* for—all heartwood, you'll get some sapwood, and the sapwood, exposed to moisture, will rot.

So put a finish on the wood.

SIDE VIEW (ALSO FOR CHAIR)

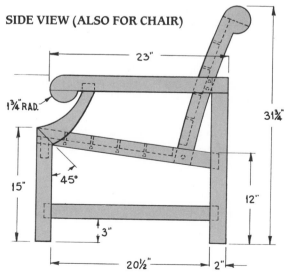

23"

1¾" RAD.

31¾"

45°

15"

12"

3"

20½" 2"

Having spent something of a premium for cedar, both for its weatherability and for its attractiveness, you won't want to paint it (although paint is probably the *best* finish for an outdoor project). Neither will you want to stain it. Use a varnish, picking one that's specially formulated for outdoor use. Or use an exterior-grade penetrating oil. We used such a product, called CWF, on the bench and chair, as well as many other projects in this book.

At the very least, apply—and reapply every year—a water repellent or a water-repellent preservative. A water repellent reduces water movement through the wood, primarily by sealing the surface with paraffin. You've seen the ads with the wet boards, the water all beaded up like on a freshly waxed car; applying a water repellent is a lot like waxing the wood. By reducing surface penetration of water, the water repellent reduces the shrinking and swelling, and thus reduces internal stresses that cause cupping and cracking.

A water-repellent preservative is the water repellent with fungicides added to prevent mildew and fungi that can discolor the wood surface.

CHAIR PLAN VIEWS

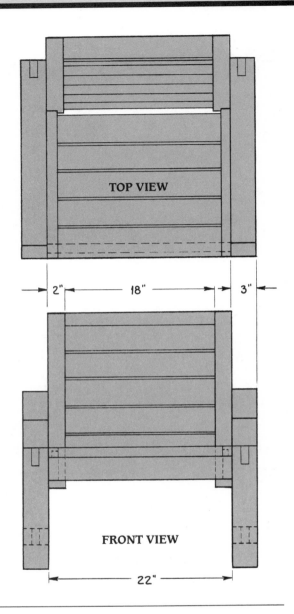

1. Cut the parts. All the parts for the chair and bench are cut from 8-foot lengths of cedar 4 × 4s. Most of the cedar has to be resawed to yield 2-inch-thick pieces for the framework and 1⅛-inch-thick pieces for the slats. It makes sense, given the nature of the job, to rough out all the parts for the project at the outset, rather than cutting parts as you go.

Study the appropriate *Cutting Diagram* first. Begin by crosscutting every 8 footer into two 4 footers. This gives you more manageable timbers for resawing.

You can resaw on the table saw or the band saw. On the table saw, the operation takes two passes, but the blade is rigid, and the tool is equipped with a rip fence,

so the cuts are likely to be true. You make one pass, cutting about halfway through the timber, then flip the piece end for end and make a second cut, severing the timber. On the band saw, the cut requires only a single pass, but the kerf, though narrow, tends to wander. In addition, you need to make a fence or pivot to clamp to the saw table.

In either case, you should joint the sawed face to smooth it. When you make your cuts, be sure to establish dimensions that allow for these jointer cuts. After resawing and jointing the boards to their final thickness, turn to the table saw to rip them to the widths listed for them in the "Cutting List."

Label each piece as you rough it out.

2. Lay out the side frame joinery. The side frame has an entertaining variety of mortise-and-tenon joints. Work methodically to avoid mistakes. Don't do anything with the knee just yet, and hold off on the mortise for it in the arm, too. Study the *Side Frame Joinery* drawing carefully before you begin.

The joints connecting the spreader and the legs are easy to lay out (and cut), as is the joint between the back leg and the arm.

The joints that connect the seat rail to the legs (and knee) are a bit more problematic. The most accurate way to lay out these joints is to lay out the parts and use them to mark key orientation lines on each other. Position the legs, then set the seat rail atop them, using the measurements indicated on the *Side View*. Scribe along both the top and bottom edges of the rail onto the legs. Likewise, mark the plane of the legs onto the rail. With a ruler and square, extend these lines onto the adjacent faces of the parts, as necessary, and complete the layout work.

The one tricky item here is the shoulder cut for the rail's front tenon. This cut must be made at 45 degrees from the line you scribed along the leg. It is NOT 45 degrees from either edge of the rail itself.

The mortise-and-tenon joint that connects the front leg, knee, and seat rail is tricky to lay out and cut. This is what the joint looks like before glue-up.

SIDE FRAME JOINERY

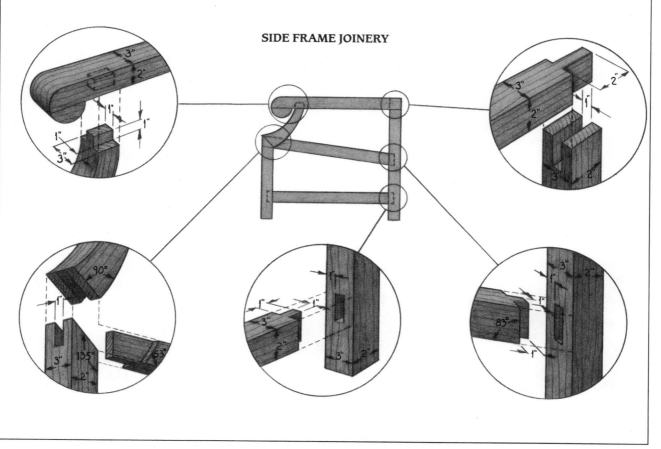

3. **Cut the side frame joinery.** A fair number of different tools come into play in making the side frame joinery, including a few hand tools. We don't seem to use them much any more.

Start by cutting the mortises. The spreader mortises in the legs can be done the traditional way, by boring out most of the waste at the drill press, then squaring the holes with a chisel. Cedar is soft and the chisel work should go quickly. You can also bore out the rail mortise in the back leg, but shim the upper end of the leg so the mortise is cut at an angle matching the orientation lines you scribed across the leg. The open (or slot) mortise atop the back leg (for the arm) can be cut on the band saw, but the somewhat similar mortise atop the front leg must be cut with a backsaw and chisel because its bottom is angled. Cut the sides of this latter mortise with the backsaw, down to the layout lines, then chisel out the waste.

Tenon the spreaders and arms next. These tenons are straightforward, and can be cut on the table saw using a dado cutter or at the band saw. At the band saw, cut the shoulders, then the cheeks, removing the waste. Following the old woodshop saying, save the (layout) line when cutting, then trim the individual tenons to fit their respective mortises.

The tenons on the rails are less straightforward because of their angled shoulders. Remember that the cedar is soft, so it isn't much work to cut these tenons with a backsaw.

TIP

Cedar is soft and easy to cut with a hand saw, but sharpen your chisels before putting them to use on it. The wood's fibers crush *very* easily, and a chisel that's less than razor sharp will crush and tear the fibers rather than sever them.

---

4. **Make the knees.** To make a knee, enlarge the pattern, make a template (Phil used lauan plywood), and trace the template onto the knee blank. On the band saw, cut (only) what will be the front surface (the concave curve).

To form the slot mortise, make repeated stopped cuts on the table saw. The dotted line on the pattern indicates the "bottom" of the slot. In the ideal, this would be a flat surface, but because the table saw blade is circular, the bottom will actually be concave. From the butt end of the knee blank, measure 2¼ inches and make a pencil mark. (Were you to scribe a line from this point to the opposite front corner of the blank, you'd have the pattern's dotted line.)

Set the blank beside the table saw blade with the curved surface up and crank the blade to a height that aligns with the top edge of the blank. Then lift the end of the blank until both the top edge of the blank and the pencil mark are on the arc of the blade. Measure the gap between the saw table and the bottom of the blank, then cut a scrap to fill it. Nail the scrap to the bottom of the blank.

With the workpiece set up, clamp a stop block to the rip fence so you can't feed the workpiece into the blade too far.

Set the fence and make one cheek cut. The process thereafter is one of making a cut, moving the fence slightly, making another cut, moving the fence slightly, making yet another cut. And so on, until you have just the width of slot that you need.

With the slot complete, you can remove the scrap and, on the band saw, cut the curved back surface.

After marking the height and depth of the mortise on the side of the knee, align the marks to the blade, as shown, then cut a shim block from scrap and tack it under the knee blank to hold the proper position.

All that's left is the tenon for the arm. Cut this to fit. Dry assemble the legs, spreader, seat rail, and knee. Rest the arm across the back leg and the knee, and scribe along the underside of the arm onto the knee. This is the tenon's shoulder. With this line as a starting point, lay out the rest of the tenon, then cut it with a backsaw.

Clamp a stop block to the rip fence to arrest the cuts at the desired depth. Make a series of cuts to hollow out the mortise. Guide the knee blank with the fence, nudging it farther away from the blade after each cut.

5. **Assemble the side frames.** Begin each side frame assembly operation with a dry run. This offers the opportunity to check how all the joints fit, but equally important, it allows you to complete the knee-arm joinery. What remains to be done is to lay out the mortise in the underside of the arm. With all the other side frame members assembled, set the arm in position and trace around the knee's tenon onto it. Cut the mortise inside the lines, and pare it (or the tenon) as necessary to refine the fit.

When you are satisfied with the way the joints fit, knock the assembly apart. Sand the individual parts. Glue the hand grip to the arm; a spring clamp will hold the grip in place 'til the glue sets. Now reassemble the side frame using resorcinol glue. Coat both mating parts, but don't be too generous; anything more than a bead of squeeze-out along the glue line will stain the cedar. Clamp the assembly to hold the parts reasonably tight and perfectly square, but with resorcinol, high-pressure clamping isn't necessary.

Repeat to assemble the second side frame (and any additional ones).

After the clamps are off, radius the exposed edges of each assembly with a router and a ¼-inch rounding-over bit.

6. **Make the mortise rail.** The mortise rails house the seat slat tenons. They attach to the inner faces of the seat rails. There's a left rail and a right one, so don't make them duplicates.

If you haven't already done so, trim these rails to the size specified by the "Cutting List." Since this rail overlays the seat rail, the front end of it is not square; lay the rails in position, scribe along the leg to mark them, and trim the ends.

Lay out the mortises on the rails, as indicated in the *Mortise Rail Layout* drawing, then cut them.

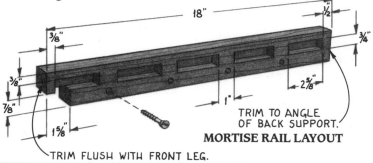

MORTISE RAIL LAYOUT

TRIM TO ANGLE OF BACK SUPPORT.

TRIM FLUSH WITH FRONT LEG.

7. Cut the apron mortises. The apron extends from one side frame to the other, helping to link the frames together and trimming out the front of the seat. It is recessed ½ inch from the front edges of the legs, and fits tight against the bottom of the front seat slat. To join it to the front legs, you must lay out and cut mortise-and-tenon joints.

The first operation is to notch the mortise rails so the apron can fit against the front slat. The notch should be 1 inch by 1⅜ inches; done properly, it will just intersect the front mortise.

APRON JOINERY DETAIL

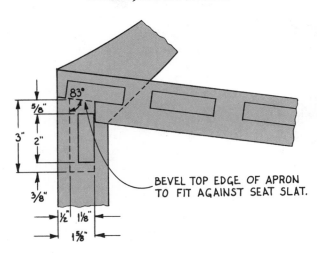

BEVEL TOP EDGE OF APRON TO FIT AGAINST SEAT SLAT.

Set the mortise rail in place and lay out the apron mortise on the front leg, as shown in the *Apron Joinery Detail.* Remove the mortise rail and cut the mortise. The mortise will bottom out against the seat rail tenon at the top.

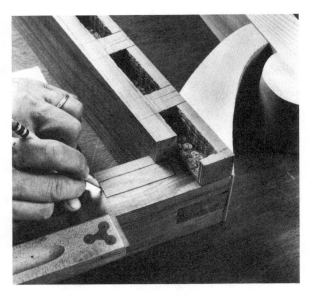

After the side assembly is glued up and the mortise rail made, you have to lay out and cut a mortise to house the apron tenon. As shown, you have to cut away a corner of the mortise rail so the apron can seat tightly against the leg.

8. Make the back supports. The back supports have a gently curved profile that's cut on the band saw. Then a half-dozen mortises are cut into it for the back slats and the top. To simplify things, lay out the profile and the mortises from a template.

Enlarge the pattern and transfer it to a piece of ¼-inch plywood or hardboard or a piece of heavy posterboard. Cut the profile and the mortises.

Now trace the layout onto the two back support blanks, running the pencil around the outside for the shape of the supports, and around the inside of the cutouts to delineate the mortises. Since there's a left support and a right one, you have to flop the template before tracing around it onto the second support. Cut the profile on the band saw, then cut the mortises.

Finally, with the router and the rounding-over bit, radius the edges of the supports that will be exposed.

9. Cut and tenon the apron, top, and slats. Trim the parts to the lengths specified by the "Cutting List."

The apron and the slats have the same tenon dimensions, so all can be cut using the same setup. No layout work is necessary. Do it on the table saw with a dado cutter. If you stack the cutters to make a ⅝-inch-wide cut, you can complete each tenon surface with two passes. Crank the depth of cut to ⅜ inch. Set the rip fence 1 inch from the *outside* of the cutter. Butt the end of the workpiece against the fence and guide it with the miter gauge. The first pass cuts the shoulder, the second pass—pull the workpiece away from the fence for it, of course—finishes the surface. Cut one face and both edges. The tenons are flush with the other face of the piece (and be sure you make both tenons on each piece flush with the same face).

With the router and the rounding-over bit, radius the four edges of all the slats and the bottom edge of the apron.

The top's two tenons can be laid out, then cut to the lines on the band saw.

10. Assemble the back. Before gluing the parts of the back together, dry assemble them to check how the joints fit. Make any necessary alterations. While the top and back supports are still assembled, scribe around the edges of the supports on the ends of the top. Disassemble these parts. The top eventually must be planed or sanded to a profile matching that of the supports. To minimize this post-assembly work, make a

series of bevel rips now to remove as much of the waste as possible.

Using resorcinol glue, assemble the back slats, top, and back supports. As in gluing up the side frames, be careful to evenly coat the mortises and tenons with glue, but don't overdo it, since squeeze-out will stain the cedar. And because the glue is runny, the best assembly approach is to lay out the supports—mortises up—and insert the slats into one of them. With a helper if necessary, upend this unit and drop the exposed tenons into the mortises in the other support. You avoid having glue dribble out of the mortises this way.

Finally, as you apply the clamps, take special care not to nick or dent the cedar with them. Use cauls between the wood and metal clamp jaws. After the glue has dried and the clamps are off, scrape off any beads of dried glue and touch-up sand this assembly.

After the joinery is cut, the back supports and the top are dry assembled, as shown. Trace around the back support's roll onto the shoulders of the top. Then rip bevels along the top to remove as much of the waste as possible.

11. Assemble the seat. Before the seat assembly—side frames, apron, and slats—can be put together, the mortise rails must be attached to the side frames. Use glue and 2-inch screws for this. Drill pilot holes so you don't split the wood.

The top edge of the apron must be beveled slightly to achieve a close fit against the front slat. You can do this with a block plane or on the table saw. Test the joinery by assembling the unit without glue. Make any adjustments necessary.

The assembly of the seat proceeds much as the

back did. Coat the mortises and the tenons evenly with resorcinol glue. Keep the mortises facing up so the glue doesn't run out and stain the wood, and push the tenons down into them. After the apron and the slats are fitted into one side frame, have an assistant help you upend it so you can lower the exposed tenons into the mortises in the other side frame. Apply the clamps with care, since this wood dents easily.

After the glue dries, clean up the glue lines and touch-up sand the unit.

12. **Join the back to the seat.** The end is near. The back and the seat must still be assembled, and the top shaped.

The back is joined to the seat with six 3½-inch screws. With your assistant, slide the back into position, as shown in the *Bench Side View,* and clamp it with hand screws. Drill pilot holes, two through each support into the arm, one through each support into the seat rail. Drive the screws. And remove the hand screws.

With the top now secured at a comfortable working height, plane or sand it to its final contour. With fine-grit sandpaper, touch up the entire chair or bench.

Protect your work with an exterior-grade finish. Phil applied two coats of CWF, an exterior penetrating oil. The first coat of this product is applied generously with a brush. After it has penetrated for 20 to 30 minutes, but before it has dried, the second coat is applied. As with most penetrating oil finishes, the drying is protracted, taking as much as 72 hours.

After the piece is assembled, you can use a block plane, as shown, or a belt sander to complete the shaping of the top. The block plane has to be very sharp, the belt sander used with considerable care.

SOUTHWESTERN ENSEMBLE COFFEE AND SIDE TABLES

To accompany the chair and bench, Phil Gehret crafted two tables with gridwork tops. To wed the tables to the seats in a design sense, he used the chair's knee as a brace. Too, the tables share the blocky cedar legs and rails. Visually, they belong together.

There's no grand rationale for the gridwork tabletops. They're just different. Neat. And you learn a new setup that can be used in other projects.

Like the bench, the construction sequence, in a nutshell, is to glue up the side frames, then cut a mortise-and-tenon joint for the rails that link the two side frames, then install the gridwork.

The materials are the same, with the exception that you need some construction adhesive in addition to the resorcinol glue. And you need to buy some 1-by cedar from which to cut the gridwork parts.

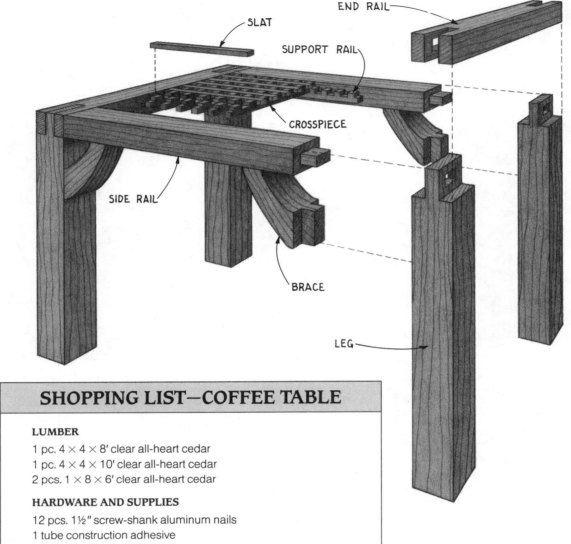

SLAT

END RAIL

SUPPORT RAIL

CROSSPIECE

SIDE RAIL

BRACE

LEG

SHOPPING LIST—COFFEE TABLE

LUMBER

1 pc. 4 × 4 × 8' clear all-heart cedar
1 pc. 4 × 4 × 10' clear all-heart cedar
2 pcs. 1 × 8 × 6' clear all-heart cedar

HARDWARE AND SUPPLIES

12 pcs. 1½" screw-shank aluminum nails
1 tube construction adhesive
Resorcinol glue

FINISH

Exterior-grade penetrating oil, such as CWF

SHOPPING LIST—SIDE TABLE

LUMBER

1 pc. 4 × 4 × 8' clear all-heart cedar
1 pc. 4 × 4 × 10' clear all-heart cedar
1 pc. 1 × 8 × 6' clear all-heart cedar

HARDWARE AND SUPPLIES

12 pcs. 1½" screw-shank aluminum nails
1 tube construction adhesive
Resorcinol glue

FINISH

Exterior-grade penetrating oil, such as CWF

CUTTING LIST—COFFEE TABLE

PIECE	NUMBER	THICKNESS	WIDTH	LENGTH	MATERIAL
Legs	4	3"	3"	15"	4 × 4 cedar
End rails	2	2"	3"	20"	4 × 4 cedar
Side rails	2	2"	3"	36½"	4 × 4 cedar
Braces	4	3"	3¼"	8¼"	4 × 4 cedar
Support rails	2	1¹⁄₁₆"	1¼"	30½"	1 × 8 cedar
Crosspieces	22	1¹⁄₁₆"	1¼"	14"	1 × 8 cedar
Slats	10	1¹⁄₁₆"	½"	30½"	1 × 8 cedar

CUTTING LIST—SIDE TABLE

PIECE	NUMBER	THICKNESS	WIDTH	LENGTH	MATERIAL
Legs	4	3"	3"	22"	4 × 4 cedar
End rails	2	2"	3"	20"	4 × 4 cedar
Side rails	2	2"	3"	24³⁄₁₆"	4 × 4 cedar
Braces	4	3"	3¼"	8¼"	4 × 4 cedar
Support rails	2	1¹⁄₁₆"	1¼"	18³⁄₁₆"	1 × 8 cedar
Crosspieces	13	1¹⁄₁₆"	1¼"	14"	1 × 8 cedar
Slats	10	1¹⁄₁₆"	½"	18³⁄₁₆"	1 × 8 cedar

CUTTING DIAGRAM—COFFEE TABLE

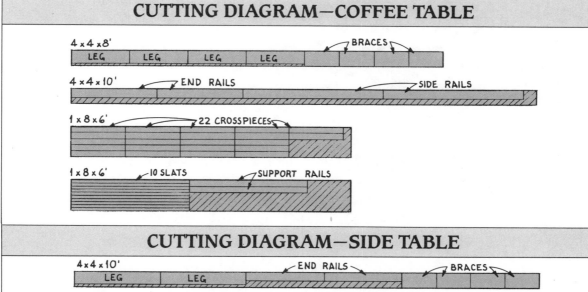

CUTTING DIAGRAM—SIDE TABLE

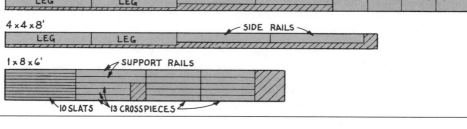

Builder's Notes

A companion project to this chapter's bench and chair, the gridded tables are constructed with the same materials and use the same tools and techniques as the earlier project. If you are building only this project from the ensemble, then by all means read the "Builder's Notes" accompanying the chair and bench project on page 246.

The only additional note here is a caveat about the 1-by cedar. According to Rodale's woodshop director Fred Matlack, 1-by cedar seems to run a bit light, which is to say it is $1\frac{1}{16}$ inches thick rather than the ¾-inch thickness we've become accustomed to expect of 1-by. In some cases, the cedar may be as thin as ⅝ inch.

TOOL LIST

Band saw
Bar clamps or pipe clamps
Caulking gun
C-clamps
Chisels
Circular saw
Drill press
   1" dia. bit
   Hollow-chisel
     mortising
     attachment
Hammer
Jointer
Paintbrush
Router
   ¼" rounding-over bit
Sander(s)
Sandpaper
Saw for crosscutting
Saw for ripping
Sawhorses
Screwdriver
Table saw
   Dado cutter
   Miter gauge
Tack cloth
Tape measure
Try square

SIDE TABLE PLAN VIEWS

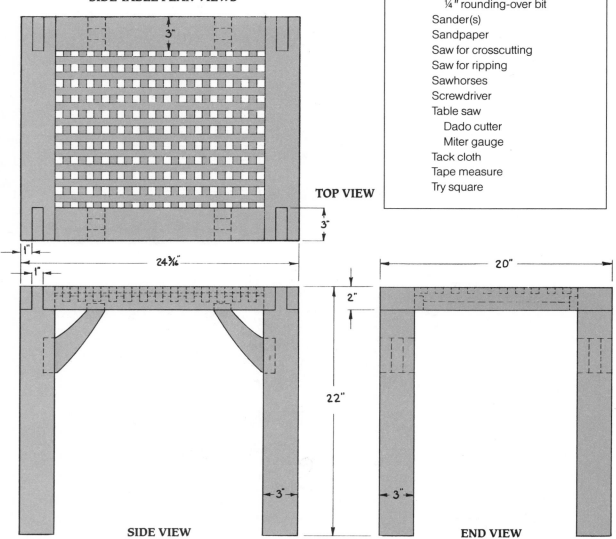

TOP VIEW

SIDE VIEW

END VIEW

COFFEE TABLE PLAN VIEWS

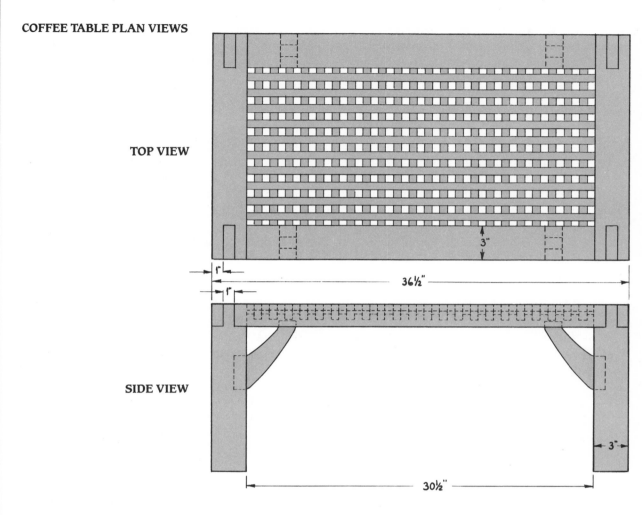

TOP VIEW

3"

1"

1"

36½"

SIDE VIEW

30½"

3"

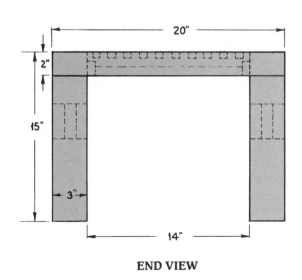

20"

2"

15"

3"

14"

END VIEW

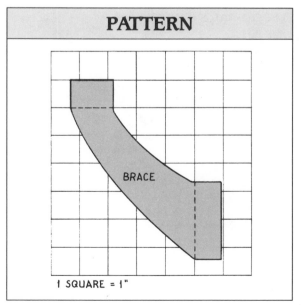

PATTERN

BRACE

1 SQUARE = 1"

What we experienced in building the tables is reflected in the "Cutting List." If the material you lay your hands on is a true ¾ inch, or is ⅝ inch, this shouldn't make a bit of difference. The ultimate dimensions of the gridwork stem from the stock you use, rather than a tape measure. In addition, you start at the middle and work to the ends when making the crosspieces, so any discrepancy between our directions and your material will be bumped to the ends of these pieces. It shouldn't make a difference.

1. Cut the legs, end and side rails, and braces. Start with the 4 × 4s and cut them into the pieces specified by the "Cutting List." Use a circular saw or radial arm saw for the crosscutting. The girth of the cedar may dictate that to sever each part from the stock you must cut into opposing faces (that is, make a cut, roll the stock 180 degrees, then make the second cut).

After the parts are cut to length, most of them need to be resawed to the correct thickness, then ripped to the proper width. These cuts can be made either on the table saw or the band saw.

On the table saw, resawing the 4 × 4s takes two passes, but the blade is rigid, and the tool is equipped with a rip fence, so the cuts are likely to be true. You make one pass, cutting about halfway through the 4 × 4, then flip the piece end for end and make a second pass, completing the cut. On the band saw, each cut requires only a single pass, but the kerf, though narrow, tends to wander. In addition, you need to make a fence or pivot to clamp to the saw table to guide the cuts.

In either case, you should joint the sawed face to smooth it. When you make your cuts, be sure you allow for these jointer cuts. After jointing the resawed boards to their final thickness, turn to the table saw to rip them to the widths listed for them in the "Cutting List." To smooth the cut and remove saw marks, joint each part after ripping it to width.

Label each piece as you rough it out.

2. Make the end frames. Regardless of which table you are making, the end frames consist of two legs and an end rail. These parts are joined in slot (or open) mortise-and-tenon joints. Despite being resawed and

LEG-TO-RAILS JOINERY

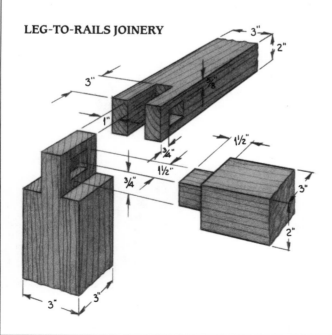

TIP

Instead of fussing with a ruler, use the parts themselves to dimension the joints. Lay a leg across the rail, its edge flush with the rail's end. Scribe along the opposite edge to mark the bottom of the mortise for the leg tenon. Similarly, rest a rail on the leg and scribe along it to mark the shoulder cuts for the leg tenon.

ripped, the parts are still bulky, so the band saw may be the best power tool for cutting these joints.

Do the mortises in the rails first. Lay them out, then cut them. Although you can remove the bulk of the waste on the band saw, you will have to finish the mortise bottom with a sharp chisel. (If the chisel isn't sharp, it will crush and tear the soft fibers of the cedar, rather than cleanly severing them.) Lay out and cut the tenons next.

When the joints are cut and fitted, glue the end frame members together with resorcinol glue.

3. Cut the side rail joinery. The side rails are connected to the end frames by mortise-and-tenon joints. The side rail's tenon is long enough to penetrate the tenon on the end rail, thus locking the end frame joinery.

Lay out the mortises, as shown in the *Legs-to-Rails Joinery* drawing. These can easily be cut in the usual manner by drilling out the majority of the waste, then squaring the corners and paring the mortise walls with a sharp chisel.

Next, tenon the rails on the table saw. Set up the saw with a dado cutter. Position the rip fence 1½ inches from the outside of the cutter to control the tenon length. Set the depth of cut to ⅝ inch. Test the setup on scrap to ensure the resulting tenons will fit the mortises (particularly that they not be too thin), and save the scrap for testing the next phase of the setup. When the setup is correct, guide the rails with the miter gauge and cut the top and bottom surfaces of the tenons. Reset the depth of cut to ¾ inch and test the setup on the scrap you set aside. Assuming the setup is correct, cut the sides of the tenons.

---

4. Make the braces. The table's brace corresponds to the knee in the bench/chair. And, in fact, in laying out the braces, Phil Gehret used the template for the knee. So the profile is very much the same. The procedure in this step is to tenon the blank from which the brace is to be cut, then to lay out and cut the brace.

Start with the blanks for the braces. Without shortening them, miter their ends. This will probably entail multiple passes unless you do the job on the band saw.

Next, cut 1-inch-thick, 1-inch-long tenons on the ends. This is a table saw task. Set the rip fence 1 inch from the outside of the blade, and set the depth of cut to 1 inch (test the setting to be sure it is correct). Working

Above: After the brace blank has been mitered, cutting the raw tenons is an easy table saw operation. Use the rip fence, as shown, to guide both the shoulder cuts and the cheek cuts. In this photo, the shoulder cuts are completed and the cheek cuts are being finished up.

Top right: With the raw tenons cut, lay out the shape of the brace using a template, in this instance the same template that was used to lay out the knees for the chair and bench. Since the brace is shorter than the knee, alignment marks have been penciled on the template. *Bottom right:* After marking the curves, the lines have to be squared onto the rough tenons, so they too can be cut to their final dimensions. Use a small square, as shown, to extend the line from the arc across the shoulder to the tenon cheek. Note on the already-marked tenon that the lines on the tenon cheek are perpendicular to the shoulder cut.

on one blank at a time, slide it along the fence to make the shoulder cuts, then turn it and, still guiding the work with the fence, make the cheek cuts.

Now enlarge the brace pattern and make a template from plywood or posterboard. Position the template on the first brace blank. Mark the template so you can position it in the same way on subsequent blanks, then scribe along its contours on the blank. Repeat on the other three braces. Finish the layout work by dropping lines down the tenon shoulders and across the tenon cheeks, so these can be cut properly. Use a small square to ensure the lines are perpendicular.

Finally, cut the braces on the band saw.

5. Cut the mortises for the braces. The mortises for the braces are laid out from the braces themselves. To do this, dry assemble the table and rest it upside down on the workbench. Assign a specific brace to each of the four corners and mark both the braces and the corners so you don't get them mixed up.

Lay out each pair of brace mortises in turn. Set the brace against the leg and side rail, as shown in the *Brace Mortise Layout* drawing, with the shoulder of the brace against the inner surface of the leg and the bottom surface of the rail, the tenon cheeks against the sides of the leg and rail. Be sure the braces are properly oriented, that is, with the fatter end against the leg, the narrow end against the rail. Tick the edges of the leg and rail to mark the extremities of the tenons. Remove the brace and square these tick marks across the leg and rail. These lines delineate the ends of the mortises. Since the mortise must be 1 inch wide and centered on the leg (or rail), laying out the sides is easy.

Cut the mortises and trim them (or the tenons) to refine the joint's fit. Dry assemble the table's framework by fitting the braces in the rails, then sliding the end frames into position on the rail and brace tenons. If the assembly goes together without a hitch, you are ready to make the gridwork.

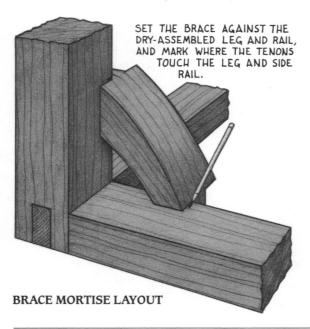

SET THE BRACE AGAINST THE DRY-ASSEMBLED LEG AND RAIL, AND MARK WHERE THE TENONS TOUCH THE LEG AND SIDE RAIL.

BRACE MORTISE LAYOUT

USING A SQUARE, EXTEND LINES ACROSS THE LEG AND RAIL FROM THE MARKS. THEN SCRIBE THE SIDES OF THE MORTISES.

6. Make the parts for the tabletop grid. The tabletop grids consist of two support rails that are attached to the side rails, a number of crosspieces that fit into notches in the supports, and a number of slats that fit into notches in the crosspieces. All the notches are the same size, and all are cut with a dado cutter on a table saw using a finger-joint jig. If you make both the tables, you need 35 of the denticulated crosspieces, and they all have to be the same, or you won't be able to fit the slats in place.

The first step in the sequence is to rip and crosscut the two supports, all the crosspieces, and all the slats to size. Cut extras of the crosspieces and the slats. You need at least one extra of each piece to make the finger-joint jig. You can also use a scrap or two of the slat material in setting the width of the dado cutter.

Next you must set up the saw.

Mount the dado cutter and adjust it until the width of the dado matches the width of the slat stock. Make cuts in scrap and see how your scrap slat fits. It should be snug.

To complete the initial setup, you must establish the rip fence position for making the first two cuts in each crosspiece. There is a dentil at the middle of each crosspiece, that is, a hump rather than a notch. The width of the dentils is exactly that of the notches. With two pencil marks, lay out the center dentil on one crosspiece. Cradle this piece in the miter gauge and align one mark with the outside of the dado cutter. Then slide the fence up against the butt end of the crosspiece and lock it.

With this setup, you can drop a workpiece into the miter gauge, butt the piece against the fence, and make a cut. Spin the piece around and make a second cut, forming that center dentil. Every cut will be in the same place in relation to the end of the piece. And every piece will be identical. With the setup thus established, make

two cuts in each crosspiece, including at least one extra crosspiece.

Now assemble the jig used to cut the rest of the notches. Lock the fence and slide it out of the way. Put the left notch of the extra crosspiece over the cutter and slide the miter gauge against it. Screw the crosspiece to the miter gauge. Then insert a short piece of the slat material—the key—into the free notch.

You are now ready to knock out those crosspieces. There are only 176 more notches to cut if you're making the coffee table, 104 more if you're making the side table (280 if you're making both tables). You fit a crosspiece in the jig, notch over the key. Cut a new notch, adjust the crosspiece to fit that new notch over the key, then cut another. Et cetera, et cetera, et cetera.

This is the tedious part of the project. But it is *very important* to cut all the notches carefully. You won't

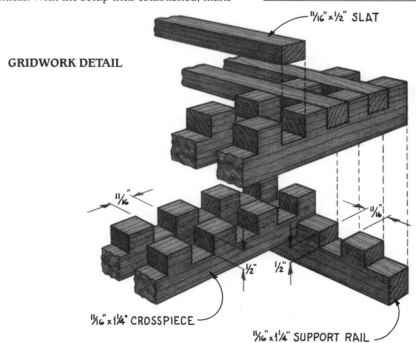

GRIDWORK DETAIL

¹¹/₁₆" × ¹/₂" SLAT

¹¹/₁₆" × 1¹/₄" CROSSPIECE

¹¹/₁₆" × 1¹/₄" SUPPORT RAIL

realize how important until you try to fit the slats in place. Remember that cedar is pretty soft, and each time you push a notch over the key, you are scraping the key, maybe denting it a tad if you rush and miss the alignment and use force. Your center two notches are going to be well positioned, because they were indexed off the rip fence. But the others will be indexed off the key, and a fractional error will be multiplied 'til you get to the outermost notch on a crosspiece.

So take it easy; replace the key a few times during the process.

The support rails are notched in the same way.

After establishing the width of the cut, you must locate the first cuts. *Top left:* With the pencil mark aligned with the dado cutter, slide the rip fence—gently—against the workpiece and lock it. *Top right:* The first two cuts on each crosspiece will center the first dentil. The backer between the workpiece and the miter gauge prevents tear-out as the cutter exits the back of the workpiece.

Center left: After all the crosspieces have the first two notches cut in them, replace the miter gauge's backer with the jig. With the jig's position established by fitting one of its notches over the cutter, slide the miter gauge into place and drive screws through it into the jig. *Center right:* Then fit a length of the slat stock into the other notch. *Bottom right:* You then cut notch after notch.

7. Assemble and finish the table. The parts are now completed, and you are ready to assemble the table. The first thing you need to do is sand all the parts. Then nail the supports for the gridwork to the side rails. Phil used 1½-inch screw-shank aluminum nails, which provide slightly better holding power than smooth-shank nails; you could use small galvanized screws or ring-shank nails.

Glue the table framework together next. Fit the braces to the side rails, then the side rails to the end frames. Use resorcinol glue.

When the clamps are off the table, install the gridwork. A complete dry assembly can be perilous, especially if the slats fit snugly. You may damage parts trying to disassemble the grid.

Use construction adhesive to secure the grid parts together. Resorcinol glue, which is used to glue all the mortise-and-tenon joints in this project, is both runny and staining. It almost certainly will beget a mess and a purple-stained table. But a dot of construction adhesive in each notch, squeezed from a caulking gun, will hold the slat, be contained within the confines of the joint, be moisture resistant, and be strong.

Fit the crosspieces in place first.

The slats are fitted next, starting with the middle slats. These should fit best, since the two middle notches in each crosspiece were indexed against the rip fence and should be uniformly spaced. If the notches in individual crosspieces seem a tick out of alignment with all the others, try turning them around—that is, lifting them out of the support rails, spinning them end for end, then slipping them back in place.

Remember, during this assembly process, that the cedar is soft and will give in to *some* force. You don't want to overdo it, but you can force-fit here and there.

When the gridwork is completely installed, touch-up sand any parts of the table that need attention, then apply two coats of an exterior-grade penetrating oil.

Here's how the braces are incorporated in the leg-rail assembly. To successfully assemble the table, you must insert the brace tenon into the side rail mortise, then fit the side frame onto the brace and side rail tenons simultaneously. The table won't go together any other way.

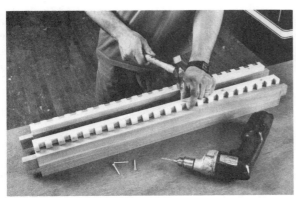

Install the gridwork supports with aluminum or galvanized nails. Because cedar splits very easily, drill pilot holes for the nails.

While a complete dry assembly of the gridwork isn't recommended, you probably ought to fit the crosspieces in place and visually check the alignment of their notches.

THE
TRADITIONAL
COLLECTION

ADIRONDACK ENSEMBLE

Inexpensive Lawn Classics

This chair with ottoman, matching settee, and side table is at home on the lawn, porch, or deck, be it at your Adirondack camp or just out in the backyard.

ADIRONDACK ENSEMBLE CHAIR WITH OTTOMAN

The Adirondack chair has become one of the classic pieces of outdoor furniture. Its flat-board, angular design is right at home in the backyard or on the deck or porch. Typically, it's parked on the lawn and left there all summer.

This popular chair apparently evolved from one called the Westport, which was designed and patented around the turn of the century. It was named for a small town in New York's Adirondack region. The Westport has the same simple, angular planes, but the back and seat are not slatted.

The chair is the mainstay of our ensemble, and you'll probably want to make several of them. The matching ottoman transforms the chair into a chaise lounge, which allows you to stick your feet up so you'll be sittin' easy.

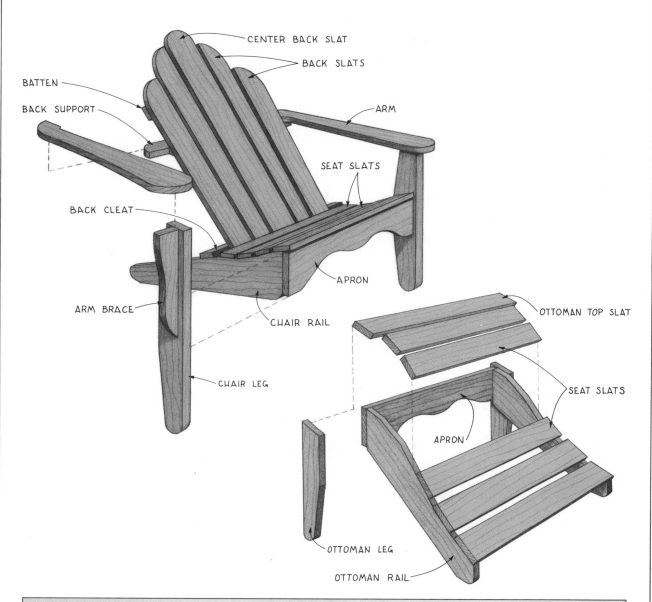

CENTER BACK SLAT

BACK SLATS

BATTEN

BACK SUPPORT

ARM

SEAT SLATS

BACK CLEAT

ARM BRACE

APRON

CHAIR RAIL

CHAIR LEG

OTTOMAN TOP SLAT

SEAT SLATS

APRON

OTTOMAN LEG

OTTOMAN RAIL

SHOPPING LIST

LUMBER

1 pc. 5/4 × 6 × 12' #2 white pine
1 pc. 5/4 × 4 × 10' #2 white pine
1 pc. 1 × 6 × 12' #2 white pine*
2 pcs. 1 × 4 × 10' #2 white pine
1 pc. 1 × 4 × 8' #2 white pine
1 pc. 1 × 3 × 4' #2 white pine

HARDWARE AND SUPPLIES

1 box #6 × 1¼" galvanized drywall-type screws
1 box #6 × 1⅝" galvanized drywall-type screws

HARDWARE AND SUPPLIES—CONTINUED

1 box #6 × 2" galvanized drywall-type screws
Wood putty
Resorcinol glue

FINISH

Exterior paint or clear finish of your choice

*Try to get one with two clear 30" lengths from which to cut the arms.

CUTTING LIST

PIECE	NUMBER	THICKNESS	WIDTH	LENGTH	MATERIAL
Chair rails	2	1 1/16"	5½"	31½"	5/4 × 6 pine
Chair legs	2	1 1/16"	3½"	21½"	5/4 × 4 pine
Ottoman rails	2	1 1/16"	5½"	24"	5/4 × 6 pine
Ottoman legs	2	1 1/16"	5½"	15½"	5/4 × 6 pine
Aprons	2	¾"	5½"	21½"	1 × 6 pine
Back cleat	1	1 1/16"	3½"	21½"	5/4 × 4 pine
Back support	1	1 1/16"	3½"	28½"	5/4 × 4 pine
Arms	2	¾"	5½"	29"	1 × 6 pine*
Center back slat	1	¾"	5½"	35½"	1 × 6 pine
Long back slats	2	¾"	3½"	33"	1 × 4 pine
Short back slats	2	¾"	3½"	29½"	1 × 4 pine
Arm braces	2	1 1/16"	3"	10"	5/4 × 4 pine
Batten	1	¾"	2½"	20"	1 × 3 pine
Seat slats	9	¾"	3½"	21½"	1 × 4 pine
Ottoman top slat	1	¾"	2½"	23⅝"	1 × 3 pine

*Cut from knot-clear piece of #2 pine.

CUTTING DIAGRAM

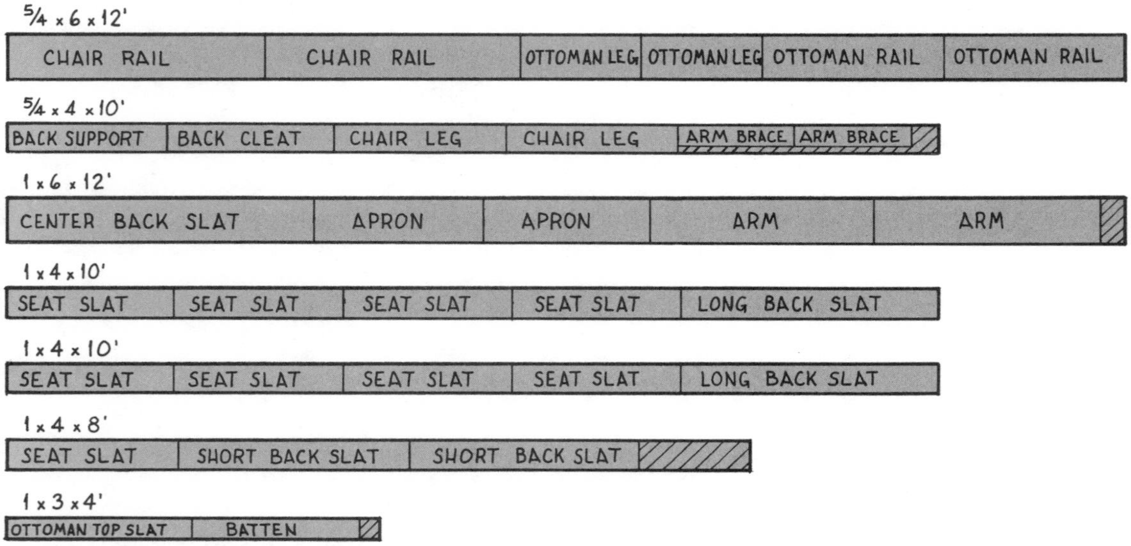

5/4 x 6 x 12'
CHAIR RAIL
CHAIR RAIL
OTTOMAN LEG
OTTOMAN LEG
OTTOMAN RAIL
OTTOMAN RAIL
5/4 x 4 x 10'
BACK SUPPORT
BACK CLEAT
CHAIR LEG
CHAIR LEG
ARM BRACE
ARM BRACE
1 x 6 x 12'
CENTER BACK SLAT
APRON
APRON
ARM
ARM
1 x 4 x 10'
SEAT SLAT
SEAT SLAT
SEAT SLAT
SEAT SLAT
LONG BACK SLAT
1 x 4 x 10'
SEAT SLAT
SEAT SLAT
SEAT SLAT
SEAT SLAT
LONG BACK SLAT
1 x 4 x 8'
SEAT SLAT
SHORT BACK SLAT
SHORT BACK SLAT
1 x 3 x 4'
OTTOMAN TOP SLAT
BATTEN

Comfortable chairs are usually considered difficult to construct. This one is not. The look of the chair belies its comfort. It *is* comfortable. And its construction *is* simple.

Because we planned to paint the set—white is common, but bright primary colors are great!—we used pine. Use waterproof glue, galvanized fasteners, and freshen the paint every couple of years, and your Adirondack ensemble will last for decades.

Builder's Notes

This set is easy to build. Many of the components are laid out from patterns, then cut out with a saber saw or band saw. The hardest job may well be that of enlarging all the patterns.

Materials. As with most outdoor furniture projects, you have several choices in woods, depending on what's readily available in your area. You can use a hard-

PATTERNS

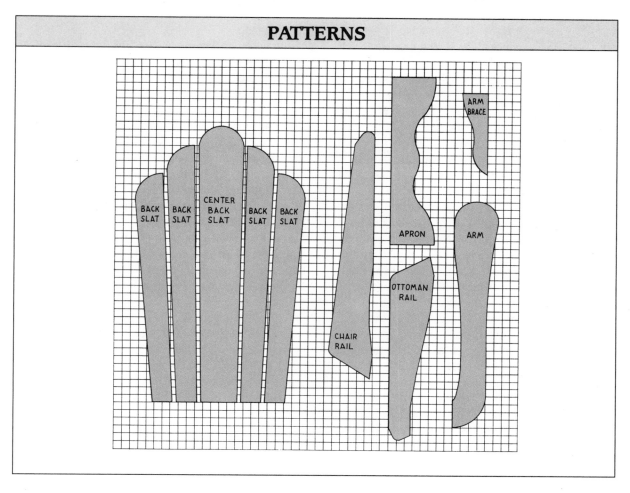

wood, such as oak or birch, covered with a clear exterior finish such as marine-grade spar varnish or exterior polyurethane. Redwood or red cedar are good choices when it comes to natural decay resistance and weatherability; pressure-treated wood is even more durable.

Because we planned to paint the set, we used #2 white pine. All of the pieces in the ensemble are cut from 1-by dimensional lumber (¾-inch dressed thickness) and 5/4 (five-quarter) stock (1 1/16-inch dressed thickness).

For assembly, use resorcinol glue, which is waterproof, and galvanized drywall-type screws, which are tailor-made for use with power screwdrivers.

Tools and techniques. This ensemble is very much a band saw project. We used one to round the ends of the legs and slats, taper the legs, and cut out the shaped parts shown in the patterns. If you don't have access to a band saw, a saber saw will do; the lumber thicknesses are within its capacity. Use a router and a ¼-inch rounding-over bit to radius the exposed edges of the various components.

Although most of the cuts are simple, making

clean, accurate taper cuts for the legs and back slats will require a bit of skill. After laying out the pattern on the stock, we used the band saw to cut the tapered sides just outside the marked line, then planed down to the line with a block plane.

With all the screws used to assemble the furniture

TOOL LIST

Band saw	Saber saw
Block plane	Sander(s)
Clamps	Sandpaper
Drill	Saw for crosscutting
Countersink bit	Saw for ripping
Pilot hole bit	Sawhorses
Framing square	Screwdriver
Paintbrush	Tack cloth
Router	Tape measure
¼ " rounding-over bit	Try square

in this ensemble, you need a good pilot hole bit, which consists of a tapered bit, a countersink, and a stop collar. The girth of the bit is matched to the screw gauge, and you adjust the bit to alter the depth of the pilot hole.

Patterns. Enlarge the patterns reproduced here to make full-size ones that you can transfer to the stock. Patterns for small parts can be enlarged on 4/4 graph paper (4 squares to the inch). For larger patterns, draw a grid of 1-inch squares on butcher paper, then sketch in the shape.

If you're making just one or two parts from the pattern, cut it out and affix it to the stock with a low-tack spray adhesive (available at art stores). For multiple parts of the same type, make a sturdy reusable pattern from stiff cardboard, ⅛-inch tempered hardboard (such as Masonite), or plastic laminate (such as Formica), from which you can trace the shape.

Finish. The finish we applied to the Adirondack Ensemble is actually the best outdoor finish: paint. The reason it is so good is that it covers and shields the wood from view. And thus from the sun.

Lovely, warm sunlight is remarkably destructive to bare wood. The heat bakes the moisture and resins out of the wood, and the ultraviolet (UV) rays discolor the wood and actually cause surface erosion. A clear coating like spar varnish deters the migration of moisture in and out of the wood, but it can't mitigate the harmful effects of ultraviolet radiation. In fact, the varnish itself is degraded by the ultraviolet radiation, which is the reason the varnish makers put ultraviolet absorbers (UVAs) in their products.

What really protects wood against UV degradation is shielding it from the sun. The pigment in paint does this.

According to researchers at the federal government's Forest Products Laboratory, the most durable outdoor finish is obtained by applying two coats of a high-quality acrylic latex paint over an oil-based primer. Oil-based paints are more impervious to moisture than latex paints, but they are less flexible. Regardless of how well it is sealed, wood swells and shrinks. The latex paint stretches and shrinks with the wood, while the oil-based coating eventually cracks. To prolong the life of the paint, the researchers recommend coating the wood with a water-repellent preservative before priming.

One last note on the finish. Knots in the wood you use will bleed through a painted finish. It may take a year or so, but it will happen. To prevent this, seal the knots with fresh shellac or prime the whole project with a pigmented shellac, such as Kilz or Bullseye.

All this takes a lot of time, but the time you invest now will come back to you with interest in years to come. A varnish or penetrating oil finish needs to be "refreshed" every couple of years. Your painted chair may not need recoating for ten years!

---

1. Cut and assemble the parts forming the lower frame assemblies. Start by cutting the legs and rails for both the chair and the ottoman from 5/4 stock. Take the dimensions for the legs from each *Side View* and lay out the pieces on the stock. Enlarge the rail patterns and sketch them on the stock. Use a band saw or saber saw to cut out the parts. Radius all the exposed edges using a router and a ¼-inch rounding-over bit.

Assemble the legs and rails with glue and 1⅝-inch screws, driving the screws through the rails into the legs. Be sure to make left and right assemblies (mirror images of each other). Line up the rails 1 inch back from the front edge of the legs. This setback provides for the thickness of the apron plus a ¼-inch reveal where it joins the legs.

Cut the front aprons from 1 × 6 boards. Enlarge the apron pattern, sketch it on the stock, and cut out the pieces. Attach the aprons to the front ends of the rails with glue and 2-inch screws. The edges of the leg should be ¼ inch proud of the faces of the aprons. Cut the back cleat and bevel it. Fasten it across the rails, 12 inches from the back end.

Finally, cut and attach the arm braces to the tops of the legs. Make sure the tops of the braces are perfectly flush with the tops of the legs.

Assemble the legs and rails with glue and two or three 2-inch galvanized screws at each joint. Make sure the assemblies are mirror images, not duplicates.

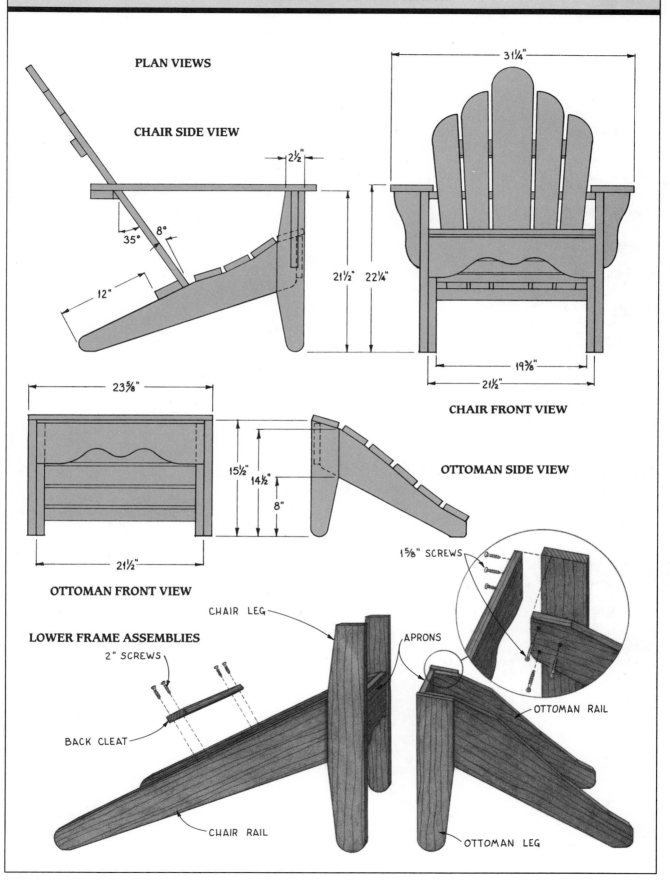

PLAN VIEWS

CHAIR SIDE VIEW

31¼"

2½"

35°   8°

12"

21½" 22¼"

19⅜"

21½"

CHAIR FRONT VIEW

23⅝"

15½" 14½" 8"

21½"

OTTOMAN SIDE VIEW

OTTOMAN FRONT VIEW

LOWER FRAME ASSEMBLIES

CHAIR LEG

1⅝" SCREWS

2" SCREWS

APRONS

BACK CLEAT

OTTOMAN RAIL

CHAIR RAIL

OTTOMAN LEG

2. **Cut and assemble the arms and the back support.** Cut the back support from 5/4 stock, and rip a 35-degree bevel along the front edge. Form 3½-inch-wide notches at each end by trimming away the bevel, as shown.

Cut the arms from 1 × 6 stock (use knot-free pieces, if possible), and rout ¼-inch radii all around the edges.

Glue and screw the arms to the back support, using 1¼-inch screws. Keep the curved ends of the arms flush with the ends of the back support and be sure the arms are 20½ inches apart at the front.

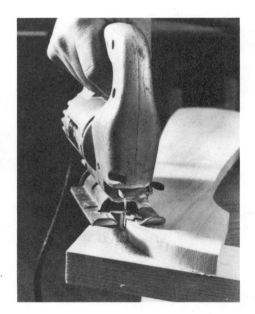

Shape the back support in stages. *Above:* Begin by notching the ends to remove the bevel. *Right:* After joining the back support to the arms, round off the ends of the support, using the arm's curve as a guide.

3. **Start the back assembly.** Enlarge the pattern for the center back slat, sketch it on the stock, then cut out the slat. Radius the edges with a router and a ¼-inch rounding-over bit. Then glue and screw the slat to the back cleat, using 1¼-inch screws. Be sure to center the slat on the cleat.

Now fasten the arm/back support assembly to the slat and the tops of the legs. You may want to temporarily clamp it in place and do a little measuring (or just plain eyeballing) to be sure it is where you want it before you actually fasten it. The slat should be centered on the back support, and the arms should be level.

ARM/BACK SUPPORT ASSEMBLY

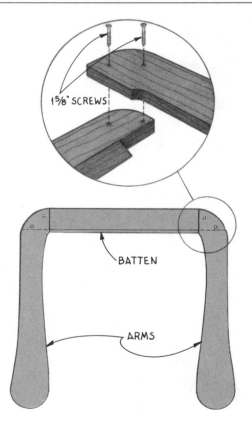

Aligning the arms and back support for assembly is easy, if a bit imprecise. Position the support on the arms and run a screw into each joint. Place a framing square next to an arm and the back support, and visually line up the pieces in relation to it. When you are satisfied that the arm and support are at right angles to each other, drive a second screw into the joint.

4. Cut and install the back, seat, and ottoman slats. The remaining back slats are cut from 1 × 4 stock. Radius the edges, then attach them to the back cleat and back support with glue and 1⅝-inch screws.

Enlarge the arm brace pattern and lay out two of the braces on 5/4 stock. Cut them out, radius the curved edges, and mount them against the arms and legs with glue and 2-inch screws.

Cut a batten and 10 seat slats. Radius all exposed edges, and attach these pieces to complete the chair and ottoman. Use 2-inch screws to attach the seat slats, 1¼-inch screws for the batten. Position the ottoman top slat so it caps the ends of the legs.

5. Apply a finish. Fill the screw holes with wood putty. Then sand, prime, and paint the chair and ottoman.

For the most durable finish, generously apply a water-repellent preservative to the sanded project. Allow this sealer to dry for as long as a week before shellacking the knots and priming the wood. Use an oil-based primer. After the primer dries, apply two coats of an exterior-grade latex paint. At each stage, pay special attention to the joints and to exposed end grain. Be sure these areas are thoroughly sealed.

TIP

Making screwheads "disappear" involves a combination of countersinking, puttying, and finish sanding. To start, countersink screws deeply enough to provide a foundation for the putty. We used a tapered pilot hole bit with an adjustable countersink to drill and countersink the screw holes before driving the screws. Immediately upon application, the putty should be just proud of the wood surface. The shrinkage of drying will reduce the bulge so you can quickly sand it flush with the wood surface. If you apply too little putty, you probably will have to add more, because it will shrink below the wood surface.

ADIRONDACK ENSEMBLE SIDE TABLE

A side table is a nearly essential component of the Adirondack Ensemble. The chair's arms *are* wide enough to accommodate a tall glass, but what will you do with that tray of snacks and ice-cold beverage pitcher? If you are making a brace of chairs and the settee, by all means, make a matching side table or two.

The table picks up the chair's slat lines for its tabletop slats. The table's aprons borrow the profile of the chair apron, and, of course, the leg profiles echo those of the chair. Made of the same materials, using the same joinery, the table is a natural companion to the chair and settee.

SHOPPING LIST

LUMBER

2 pcs. 1 × 4 × 8′ #2 white pine
1 pc. 1 × 3 × 10′ #2 white pine

HARDWARE AND SUPPLIES

1 box #6 × 1¼″ galvanized drywall-type screws
1 box #6 × 1⅝″ galvanized drywall-type screws
1 box #6 × 2″ galvanized drywall-type screws
Wood putty
Resorcinol glue

FINISH

Exterior paint or clear finish of your choice

CUTTING LIST

PIECE	NUMBER	THICKNESS	WIDTH	LENGTH	MATERIAL
Table legs	4	¾″	3½″	17¾″	1 × 4 pine
Side aprons	2	¾″	3½″	18″	1 × 4 pine
End aprons	2	¾″	3½″	11¾″	1 × 4 pine
Battens	3	¾″	1½″	10¼″	1 × 4 pine
Center top slat	1	¾″	3½″	33½″	1 × 4 pine
Long top slats	2	¾″	2½″	30″	1 × 3 pine
Short top slats	2	¾″	2½″	25″	1 × 3 pine

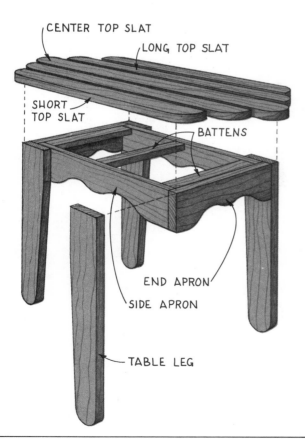

CENTER TOP SLAT

LONG TOP SLAT

SHORT TOP SLAT

BATTENS

END APRON

SIDE APRON

TABLE LEG

Builder's Notes

A companion project to this chapter's chair with ottoman and settee, the side table is constructed with the same materials and uses the same tools and techniques as its companion projects. If you are building only this project from the ensemble, then by all means read the "Builder's Notes" accompanying the Adirondack Chair with Ottoman project on page 274.

TOOL LIST

Drill
    Countersink bit
    Pilot hole bit
Paintbrush
Router
    ¼″ rounding-over bit
Saber saw
Sander(s)

Sandpaper
Saw for crosscutting
Saw for ripping
Sawhorses
Screwdriver
Tack cloth
Tape measure
Try square

CUTTING DIAGRAM

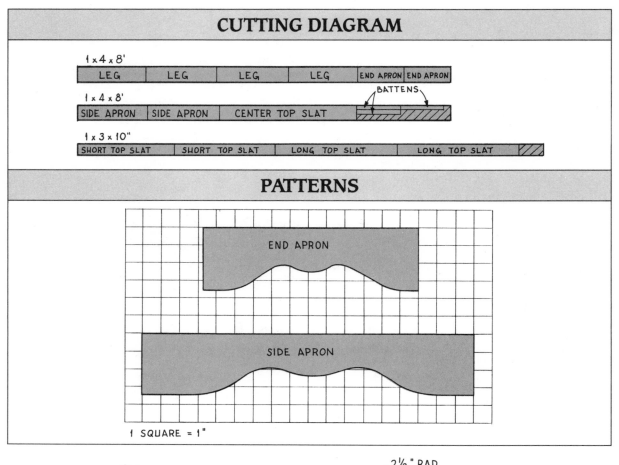

1 x 4 x 8'

| LEG | LEG | LEG | LEG | END APRON | END APRON |

1 x 4 x 8'

| SIDE APRON | SIDE APRON | CENTER TOP SLAT | BATTENS |

1 x 3 x 10"

| SHORT TOP SLAT | SHORT TOP SLAT | LONG TOP SLAT | LONG TOP SLAT |

PATTERNS

END APRON

SIDE APRON

1 SQUARE = 1"

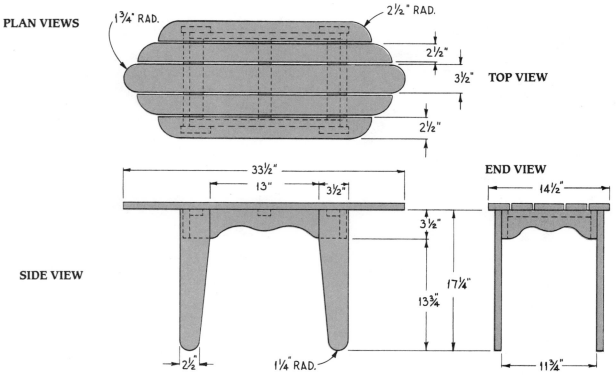

PLAN VIEWS

1¾" RAD.

2½" RAD.

2½"

3½"

TOP VIEW

2½"

END VIEW

14½"

SIDE VIEW

33½"

13"

3½"

3½"

17¼"

13¾"

2½"

1¼" RAD.

11¾"

1. Cut out and assemble the legs and side aprons for the table. Lay out the legs using the dimensions shown on the *Side View*. Note that they are tapered along one edge only, and their bottoms are rounded. Enlarge the side apron pattern and sketch it on the stock. Using a band saw or saber saw, cut out these parts. With a router and a ¼-inch rounding-over bit, radius all exposed edges.

Glue and screw the parts together, forming two U-shaped frames. Use 1¼-inch screws. The legs overlay the aprons. Keep the ends of the aprons 1 inch back from the outside edges of the legs.

TIP

It's a good idea to have two drill-drivers close at hand when assembling this project. Equip one with a pilot hole bit, which is a special combination bit that bores and countersinks a tapered pilot hole in one operation. Equip the other with a screwdriver bit. During assembly, line up the two (glued) pieces to be joined, holding them tightly in position with one hand. Pick up the drill with the other hand and bore the pilot hole. Still holding the workpieces, set down the drill, pick up the driver, and drive the screw.

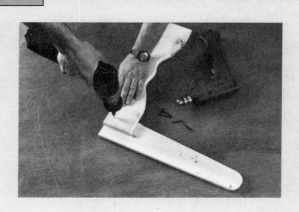

---

2. Complete the leg/apron assembly. Enlarge the end apron pattern and sketch it on the stock. Cut out the aprons, radius the edges, then glue and screw them to the ends of the side aprons with 2-inch screws, thus joining the two assemblies made in the previous step.

Cut three battens. Using 1⅝-inch screws, attach one to the inside of each end apron. The third batten is installed in the next step.

---

3. Make and install the top. Cut out the table-top slats, and round the ends as shown in the Top View. Arrange them facedown on a flat surface. Apply glue to the top surfaces of the leg/apron assembly, turn it upside down, and position it carefully on the slats. Drive 1¼-inch screws through the battens and into the slats. Glue and screw the third batten across the middle of the slats.

---

4. Apply a finish. Fill the screw holes with wood putty. Then sand, prime, and paint the table a color that will go well with your favorite set of tall glasses.

TIP

Before you paint your Adirondack furniture, be sure to prime knots with shellac or a pigmented shellac. If you don't, they will bleed through any paint you apply, blemishing your finished project.

ADIRONDACK ENSEMBLE SETTEE

This settee makes a congenial addition to the basic Adirondack chair/ottoman/table set. It seats two comfortably and generally encourages intimacy—that is, if both occupants can agree to share the center armrest.

If you're making the chair, it won't require much more work to build the settee because it's really just two chairs joined by a center leg/arm assembly and continu- ous seat slats and back support. Most of the remaining components are exactly the same as those used for the chair, so you can use the same patterns for both projects.

The ottoman for the chair also fits one side of the settee, so you might opt to make another pair of them— and two more side tables, if you're feeling especially ambitious.

SHOPPING LIST

LUMBER

1 pc. 5/4 × 6 × 12' #2 pine
1 pc. 5/4 × 4 × 16' #2 pine
1 pc. 1 × 6 × 12' #2 pine*
1 pc. 1 × 6 × 6' #2 pine
1 pc. 1 × 4 × 10' #2 pine
1 pc. 1 × 4 × 12' #2 pine
1 pc. 1 × 4 × 14' #2 pine
1 pc. 1 × 3 × 4' #2 pine

HARDWARE AND SUPPLIES

1 box #6 × 1¼" galvanized drywall-type screws
1 box #6 × 1⅝" galvanized drywall-type screws
1 box #6 × 2" galvanized drywall-type screws
Wood putty
Resorcinol glue

FINISH

Exterior paint or clear finish of your choice

*Try to get one with two clear 30" lengths from which to cut the arms.

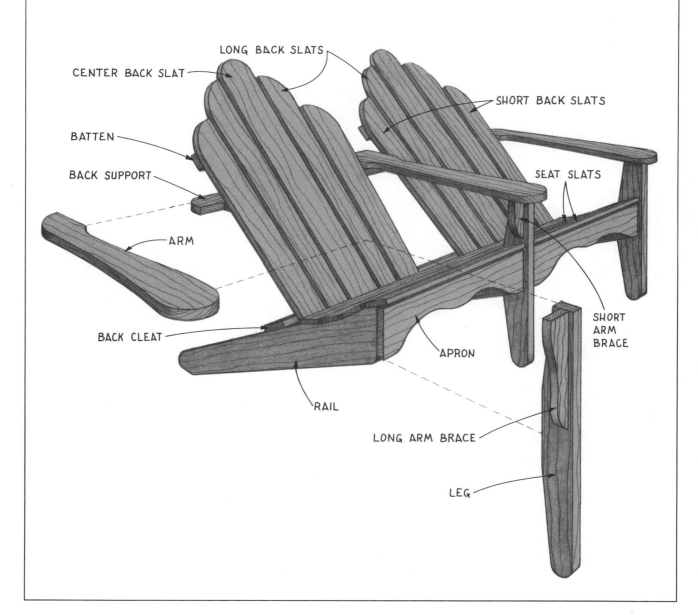

CUTTING LIST

PIECE	NUMBER	THICKNESS	WIDTH	LENGTH	MATERIAL
Rails*	4	1¹⁄₁₆″	5½″	31½″	5/4 × 6 pine
Legs*	3	1¹⁄₁₆″	3½″	21½″	5/4 × 4 pine
Aprons*	2	¾″	5½″	21½″	1 × 6 pine
Back cleat	1	1¹⁄₁₆″	3½″	44″	5/4 × 4 pine
Back support	1	1¹⁄₆″	5½″	51″	5/4 × 4 pine
Arms*	3	¾″	5½″	29″	1 × 6 pine†
Center back slats*	2	¾″	5½″	35½″	1 × 6 pine
Long back slats*	4	¾″	3½″	33″	1 × 4 pine
Short back slats*	4	¾″	3½″	29½″	1 × 4 pine
Long arm braces*	2	1¹⁄₁₆″	3″	10″	5/4 × 4 pine
Short arm braces	2	1¹⁄₁₆″	3″	5″	5/4 × 4 pine
Battens*	2	¾″	2½″	20″	1 × 3 pine
Seat slats	4	¾″	3½″	44″	1 × 4 pine

*Piece identical to that on Adirondack Chair
†Cut from knot-free section, if possible.

PATTERNS

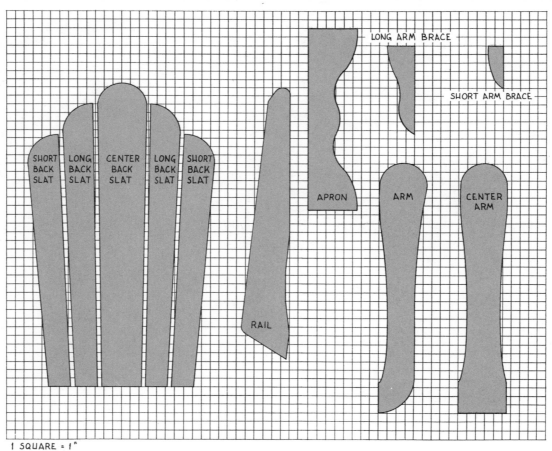

1 SQUARE = 1"

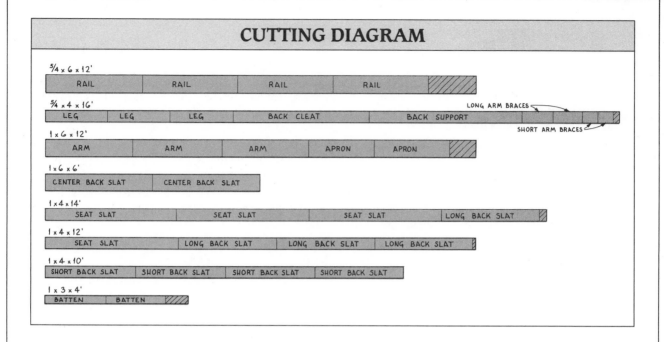

CUTTING DIAGRAM

5/4 x 6 x 12'
| RAIL | RAIL | RAIL | RAIL | |

5/4 x 4 x 16'
| LEG | LEG | LEG | BACK CLEAT | BACK SUPPORT | | | | | |

LONG ARM BRACES
SHORT ARM BRACES

1 x 6 x 12'
| ARM | ARM | ARM | APRON | APRON | |

1 x 6 x 6'
| CENTER BACK SLAT | CENTER BACK SLAT |

1 x 4 x 14'
| SEAT SLAT | SEAT SLAT | SEAT SLAT | LONG BACK SLAT | |

1 x 4 x 12'
| SEAT SLAT | LONG BACK SLAT | LONG BACK SLAT | LONG BACK SLAT | |

1 x 4 x 10'
| SHORT BACK SLAT | SHORT BACK SLAT | SHORT BACK SLAT | SHORT BACK SLAT |

1 x 3 x 4'
| BATTEN | BATTEN | |

Builder's Notes

A companion project to this chapter's chair with otto-man and side table, the settee is constructed with the same materials and uses the same tools and techniques as its companion projects. If you are building only this project from the ensemble, then by all means read the "Builder's Notes" accompanying the Adirondack Chair with Ottoman project on page 274.

1. Cut and assemble the parts for the leg/rail assemblies. Cut the three legs and the four rails for the leg/rail assemblies. To lay out the rails, enlarge the pattern. To lay out the legs, use the dimensions shown in the *Side View.* Use a band saw or saber saw to cut out the parts. Rout a ¼-inch radius on all the exposed edges using a router and a ¼-inch rounding-over bit.

To make the center leg/rail assembly, attach a rail to each side of one of the legs. During assembly, use a scrap of 5/4 stock as a temporary spacer to keep the rear ends of the rails apart (see photo). Glue and screw the rails onto the legs from both sides, using three or four 2-inch screws on each side. Make left- and right-hand leg assemblies next, attaching the legs to the rails with glue and 1⅝-inch screws. Drive the screws through the

rails into the legs. On all assemblies, position the front end of the rails 1 inch back from the front edge of the legs. This setback provides for the thickness of the aprons plus a ¼-inch reveal where they join the legs.

Next, enlarge the patterns for the aprons, transfer them to the stock, and cut out these pieces. Use glue and 2-inch screws to attach the aprons to the front ends of

The center leg/rail assembly is one of the design components used to join two "chairs" to make one settee. Attach a rail to each side of the center leg to form this component. Use a scrap of 5/4 stock as a temporary spacer to help align the rails during assembly.

the rails, thus joining the three leg assemblies at the front. Make sure the top edges of the aprons are flush with the top edges of the rails.

Now, cut the back cleat to length and rip an 8-degree bevel along the front edge. Attach the cleat across the top of the rails, 12 inches from the back end. Drive screws through the cleat into the outside rails first, then carefully align the middle rail assembly so it is properly centered before fastening the cleat to it. Use glue and 1⅝-inch screws.

To complete the assembly, enlarge the patterns for the arm braces, transfer them to the stock, and cut out these pieces. Fasten the arm braces to the legs with glue and 2-inch screws. Make sure the tops of the braces are flush with the tops of the legs.

LOWER FRAME ASSEMBLY

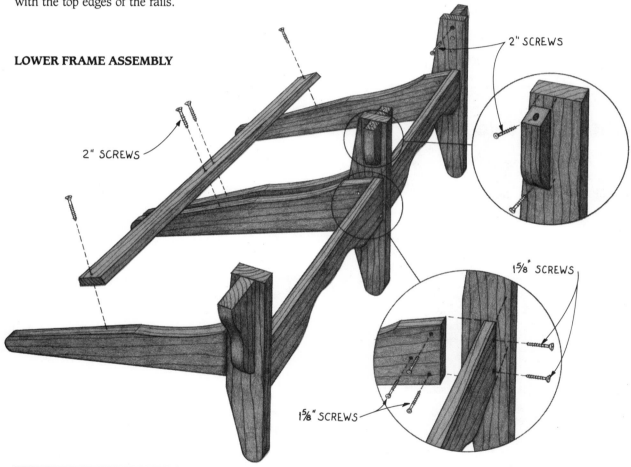

2" SCREWS

2" SCREWS

2" SCREWS

1⅝" SCREWS

1⅝" SCREWS

2. **Cut and assemble the arms and back support.** Cut the back support to length and rip a 35-degree bevel along the front edge. With a saber saw, trim away 3½ inches of the bevel at each end of the support, forming notches, as shown in the *Arm/Back Support Assembly* drawing.

Next, lay out and cut the left, right, and center arms (from clear, knot-free stock, if possible). Rout a ¼-inch radius around the exposed edges on both sides of each piece.

Join the arms to the back support with glue and 1⅝-inch screws. Lay out the pieces, as shown in the

PLAN VIEWS

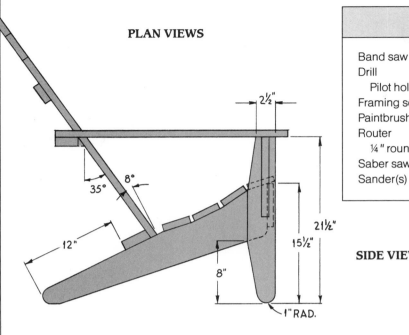

SIDE VIEW

TOOL LIST

Band saw	Sandpaper
Drill	Saw for crosscutting
Pilot hole bit	Saw for ripping
Framing square	Sawhorses
Paintbrush	Screwdriver
Router	Tack cloth
¼" rounding-over bit	Tape measures
Saber saw	Try square
Sander(s)	

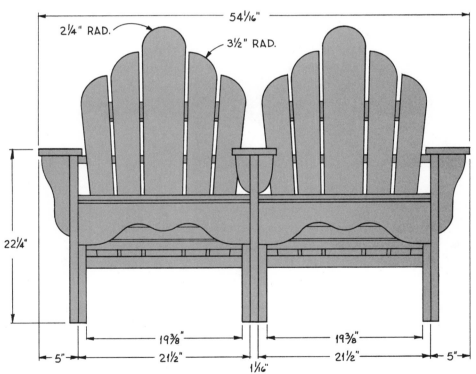

FRONT VIEW

Arm/Back Support Assembly drawing. Use a framing square to aid in visual alignment when joining the outer arms to the back support (see step 2 of the Adirondack Chair with Ottoman project on page 278). After the outer arms are attached, use two tape measures, as shown in the photo, to position the center arm equidistant between the outer arms.

Finally, use a saber saw to trim the edges of the back support to the same curve as that on the arms (see step 3 of the Adirondack Chair with Ottoman directions).

ARM/BACK SUPPORT ASSEMBLY

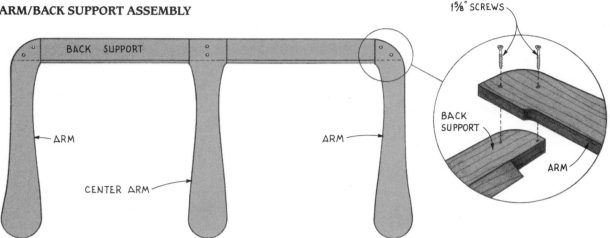

After the two outer arms are fastened in place, use two tape measures, as shown, to align the center arm between the outer ones. When the center arm is an equal distance from each of the outer arms—you'll have the same measurement on both tapes—drive a couple of screws through the support into the arm to secure it.

3. **Attach the center slats to the leg/rail assembly.** Enlarge the pattern for the center back slats, lay out two center back slats, then cut them out. Radius the edges with a router and a ¼-inch rounding-over bit.

Fasten each slat to the back cleat with a couple of 2-inch screws. Make sure each slat is centered between its rails and perpendicular to the cleat (use a framing square to aid in vertical alignment, if necessary).

Holding a center slat in position while you drill pilot holes and drive screws may seem more difficult than it is. Rest the meat of the slat on your shoulder and pinch the base against the cleat with one hand, while you operate a drill with the other. Aligning the butt edge of the slat flush with the edge of the cleat *should* ensure that the slat is perpendicular.

4. **Fasten the arm/back support assembly to the slats and the tops of the legs.** Set the arm/back support assembly in position. Make sure the arms are level (to establish this, simply set a level on an arm and watch the bubble while you move the back support up and down), then join the slats to the back support with glue and 1⅝-inch screws. Center the fronts of the arms on the tops of the legs and attach them to the legs and the arm support brackets with glue and 2-inch screws.

Use two spring clamps as an extra set of hands while leveling the arm/back support assembly. Roughly position the arms on the legs, then use a level to determine where the back support will attach to the center slats to ensure perfectly level arms. Clip a spring clamp on each slat and rest the assembly on them as you fine-tune the fit and complete the installation.

5. **Cut and install the back and seat slats.** Enlarge the patterns for the remaining back slats, laying out four slats from each pattern. Unlike the center slat, which has two tapered sides, only one side of these slats is tapered. Radius the edges, then attach them to the back cleat and back support with glue and 1⅝-inch screws.

Next, cut the seat slats and two battens. Use 2-inch screws to attach the slats to the leg/rail assembly and 1¼-inch screws to attach the battens to the slats.

6. **Apply a finish.** Fill the screw holes with wood putty. Then sand, prime, and apply the finish of your choice. After the finish dries, move the settee to a pleasant spot in the yard and invite a friend or relative to sit with you.

RUSH-SEATED PORCH ROCKER

Straight from America's Front Porch

Rocking on the porch. A traditional American pastime. In traditional *American* communities, the communities of *The Music Man* and *American Gothic* and Thomas Hart Benton. In scattered rural enclaves and on farms across the heartland: The hay's all stacked, the corn's growing noisily, and the porch rocker creaks contentedly. In bustling towns, wherever there are single houses with

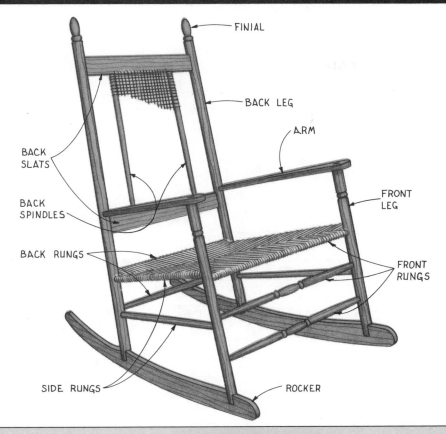

FINIAL

BACK LEG

ARM

BACK
SLATS

BACK
SPINDLES

FRONT
LEG

BACK RUNGS

FRONT
RUNGS

SIDE RUNGS

ROCKER

SHOPPING LIST

LUMBER
2 pcs. 1⅜" dia. × 40" oak dowel*
8¼ bd. ft. 8/4 oak

HARDWARE AND SUPPLIES
2 pcs. #6 × 3" galvanized drywall-type screws
4' mason's cord (or comparable string)
6 lb. ⁶/₃₂" fiber rush*

HARDWARE AND SUPPLIES—CONTINUED
Resorcinol glue
Transparent tape

FINISH
Penetrating oil finish for rush seat and backrest
Clear exterior finish for wood

*Available via mail-order from Constantine's,
2050 Eastchester Road, Bronx, NY 10461.

CUTTING LIST

PIECE	NUMBER	THICKNESS	WIDTH	LENGTH	MATERIAL
Back legs	2	1⅜" dia.		39"	Oak dowel
Front legs	2	1½"	1½"	20¼"	Oak
Front rungs	3	1"	1"	23"	Oak
Back/side rungs	6	1"	1"	18"	Oak
Finials	2	1⅜"	1⅜"	4"	Oak
Back slats	2	1½"	2½"	18"	Oak
Arms	2	¾"	3½"	20½"	Oak
Rockers	2	¾"	6"	35"	Oak
Back spindles	2	¾"	¾"	19"	Oak

PATTERNS

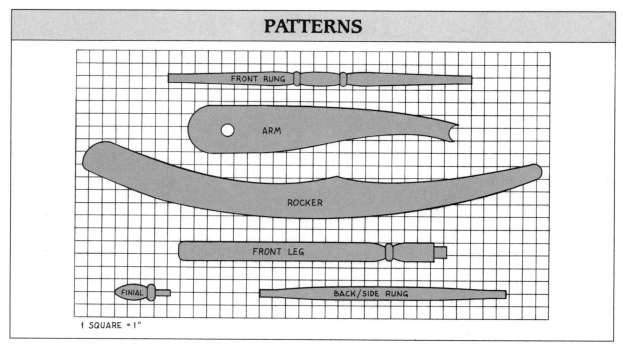

FRONT RUNG

ARM

ROCKER

FRONT LEG

FINIAL

BACK/SIDE RUNG

1 SQUARE = 1"

porches, sheltering trees, and a little street activity—kids running to the playground, folks walking to the corner store, families out for a Sunday stroll. There you sit and rock and quietly talk, pawing idly at the still air with a fan.

Okay, so here's a rocker you can build yourself. It's the traditional porch rocker, with turned legs, spindles, and rungs; a woven seat and back; and flat armrests. The square, angular design truly belies the rocker's comfort: The woven rush seat and back provide firm support, yet have more "give" than solid wood or wood slats. The low, wide armrests add to the rocker's comfort, enabling you to read, knit, or do other handwork without interference.

Builder's Notes

This rocker is one of the more advanced projects in this book. The instructions assume you have a well-equipped shop, with a table saw, drill press, band saw, and lathe, and the basic know-how to use them. The project will test your weaving skills, too.

Materials. You can use practically any hardwood for the rocker. A dense wood, such as oak, ash, or maple, is best for the rockers, because the bottom edges will need to withstand wear and abrasion.

In choosing materials, a pivotal part of the rocker is the back leg. Few home woodshop lathes—and that includes the one in our shop—have the capacity to turn

the 40-inch-long back legs. To circumvent this problem, we used manufactured 1⅜-inch by 40-inch dowels, purchased through the mail from Constantine's. (You'll note that the back legs are untapered and unembellished.) Because the dowels we bought were red oak, we used this wood for most of the rocker.

As with all hardwoods, oak isn't stocked at every lumberyard and it isn't available in predictable sizes. Thicknesses are standardized, but not widths and lengths. With a band saw—and you at least need access to one to make this project—you can rough-cut all the pieces you

TOOL LIST

Band clamps	Paintbrush
Band saw	Sander(s)
Bar clamps	Sandpaper
Bench vise	Sawhorses
Calipers	Scissors
Chisel	Screwdriver
Dividers	Spring clamps
Drill	Table saw
Pilot hole bit	Tack cloth
Drill press	Tape measure
Various-size drill bits	Trammel
Various-size Forstner bits	Try square
Framing square	Turning chisels
Lathe	

need for the rocker from an 8/4 (eight-quarter) plank. Dressed, the plank will be 1¾ inches thick, sufficient to yield the thickest parts (the legs and back slats). And using a band saw, you can easily resaw sections of the plank into thinner pieces to get the 1-inch square billets for the rungs, as well as the ¾-inch-thick rockers and arms.

The "Shopping List" specifies the purchase of 8¼ board feet of 8/4 oak. With hardwoods, you must keep the dimensions of the necessary parts in mind when you shop. A board might contain the requisite number of board feet without having the correct dimensions to give you the parts you need. For example, a 12-foot-long oak 8/4 × 4, should you find one, contains 8 board feet—almost enough for the rocker. But you wouldn't be able to cut the 6-inch-wide rockers from this board, and they represent almost 40 percent of your lumber need.

The seat and back of the rocker are woven of fiber rush. Fiber rush is made from a tough grade of paper twisted into a strand to simulate natural rush. It is usually sold in coils by the pound, rather than by length, in strand widths designated 3/32 inch, 4/32 inch, 5/32 inch, and 6/32 inch. You'll need approximately 6 pounds of 6/32-inch rush to do the back and seat of the rocker. We purchased the fiber rush for the seat and back from Constantine's.

Tools and techniques. To make the rocker just as shown, you need a lathe and lathe tools, along with basic spindle-turning skills. Great proficiency isn't required, since the ornamentation is pretty modest. In fact, this is a very good project for the beginning turner.

To cut the curved back slats, you must have (or have access to) a band saw. No other tool will do. You can, however, cut the arms with a saber saw.

To clamp the rocker, perhaps the easiest clamps to use are band clamps. Bar or pipe clamps work, but you need to use cauls with them to avoid marring the wood. If you do use pipe or bar clamps, cut V-shaped grooves into them to give them the best purchase on the curved surfaces of the legs and rungs.

Holes for the rungs are best bored on a drill press. Use Forstner bits to bore the required holes. You'll notice that the seat is wider at the front than at the back, which means that the rungs are not 90 degrees to each other where they join the legs. You'll want to make a "dogleg" fixture to aid in positioning the holes. The details for making the fixture are shown in step 6.

Weaving rush seats is a time-honored craft that takes a bit of practice to master. If this is your first shot at it, though, you can still expect reasonably good results for this project if you pay close attention to the instructions and take your time.

Weaving the rush seat and back requires no specialized tools or equipment; after weaving each course, you'll need to pack it tight against the previous one with a hammer and wood block. Weaving will take your full concentration: Read the directions carefully, making sure you fully understand the method before you start. The secret to a firm seat and back lies in keeping the strands taut as you weave and pack each course.

---

1. Cut all parts to size. Rip and crosscut all the parts for the rocker to the sizes specified by the "Cutting List." It helps if you label each part so you don't get them mixed up. Pieces for the arms and rockers should be milled to exact thickness.

---

2. Turn the rungs, front legs, and finials. Because turning on a lathe creates a lot of shavings, it's best to make all the turned parts at once and clean up just one mess afterward.

One by one, mount the billets for the front legs, rungs, and back spindles, as shown in the photos on page 296. Use the patterns as guides in turning the parts. When making the rungs and back spindles, turn the tenons first, then turn the body of the part to a pleasing curve that blends into the tenon.

The "Cutting List" specifies the exact lengths for the rungs, front legs, and back spindles. To minimize "whipping," it's best to keep the turnings as short as possible. You can do this by cutting the billets to the exact length. Where the turning attaches to the spur center on the headstock, leave a short portion of the tenon unturned. (A cone center on the tailstock enables you to turn all the way to the end). After removing the piece from the lathe, trim these ends with a chisel or pocketknife.

To mount billets for the various turned pieces, you must locate the center point on each end. *Left:* Scribe diagonals to do this. Kerf one end on the diagonal marks so you can attach the billet to the headstock.

Right: Then, as you adjust the lathe's tailstock to "capture" the billet, make sure its point penetrates the center point.

Left: To monitor your progress during turning operations, use calipers. Set the calipers to, for example, the diameter of the spindle's tenon. Begin the cut at the shoulder of the tenon. Periodically interrrupt your cutting to fit the calipers to the cut, as shown. When the calipers just drop over the cut, you have achieved the correct diameter. Turn the rest of the tenon in a series of similar cuts.

Right: After the tenons on each end are cut, begin to shape the rung or spindle profile. Work from the ends toward the middle, rounding the billet. Taper the piece from the middle to blend into the tenons.

3. Cut out the back slats. Rather than steam and bend the back slats to shape, we used a band saw to cut the curved slats.

Begin with stock about 1½ inches thick and about 2½ inches wide. Use a string compass or trammel to scribe the outer arc—it has a 50-inch radius—on the edge of the stock. Cut freehand along the line on the band saw. Next, set a pencil compass or dividers to ¾ inch and mark a parallel arc on the stock, using the newly cut edge as a guide. Then make the second cut.

Before leaving the band saw, use it to cut the tenons on the ends of the slats, as shown on the *Back Slat Layout.*

BACK SLAT LAYOUT

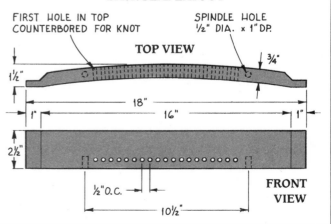

TIP

If you are skeptical about cutting the second face of the back slat freehand, use a pivot block to guide the cut. The block supports the narrow stock vertically, plus it ensures that the thickness of the piece will be uniform.

The pivot point of the block consists of two 45-degree cuts; the height of the block should equal the thickness of the board you'll be cutting. After drawing the cutting line on the stock, cut about 1 inch along the line. Then turn off the saw and clamp the block to the saw table, with its point against the stock directly opposite the blade. Restart the saw and complete the cut. Advance the workpiece with one hand, while guiding it against the pivot block with the other. Keep your hands clear of the blade, even when it's buried in the stock.

Note that the block can't be used for guiding the first arc, nor can it be used for cutting curved parts that vary in width, such as the rockers.

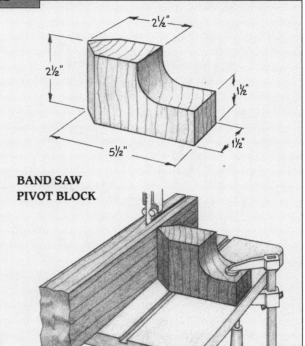

BAND SAW PIVOT BLOCK

4. Drill holes in the back slats for the back spindles and rush. Measure and mark the hole locations for the back spindles, as shown on the *Back Slat Layout*. Drill ½-inch-diameter holes 1 inch deep. Clamp the workpiece to your bench or drill press table to steady it while drilling.

The holes along the bottom edge of the top slat and the top edge of the bottom slat are used to thread the warp strands for the rush back. Decide which slat will be the top, and which the bottom, and drill the holes accordingly. As shown in the drawing, there are 19 holes in each slat, ¼ inch in diameter, spaced ½ inch apart. Counterbore the first hole on the left side of the top slat to ½ inch diameter and ¼ inch deep from the back side of the slat. This provides a recess to help conceal the knot you will tie in the rush warp at its starting point.

5. Notch the front and back legs for the rockers. As indicated in the *Side View,* the bottoms of the front and back legs are notched so they fit over the rockers. Since the rockers will be ¾ inch thick, make the notches ¾ inch wide. The bottoms of the notches are perpendicular to the length of the legs. Mark the notch locations and cut them on the band saw, making them 1½ inches deep.

6. Mortise the legs for the back slats and rungs. This is a key step in building the rocker. Each of the four legs has holes drilled in two planes, and all the holes must be aligned accurately if you are going to be able to assemble the legs, rungs, and slats. If you've never done this before, it can seem tricky, but the simple dogleg fixture we used makes the alignment operation easy.

PLAN VIEWS

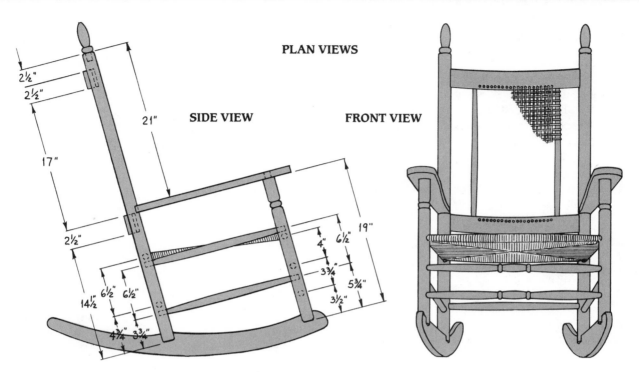

SIDE VIEW　　**FRONT VIEW**

TOP VIEW

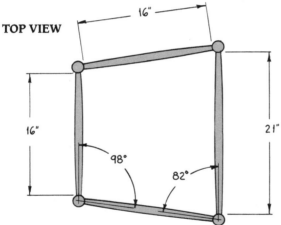

Lay out the mortises first. Use a square to mark the locations on the front and back legs for the rung mortises and the back slat mortises. Make sure you position the holes for mirror-image left and right legs.

To steady the turned legs for drilling, you'll need a V-block, such as you would use when drilling any cylindrical object. If you don't already have such a block, set your table saw or radial arm saw to make a bevel rip, then cut a V-groove about an inch wide in a scrap of 2 × 4 about 2 feet long. Clamp (or fasten temporarily with bolts) the V-block to the drill press table with the center of the groove directly beneath the bit.

To align the legs in the V-block so the axis of each hole will be correct, make the fixture shown in the *Dogleg*

Fixture Detail. Fit the fixture into the rocker notch in the leg and sight-align it with either the bit or the drill press table, depending upon which holes you are boring.

For example, to drill the round mortises for the front rungs in the front legs, fit the long leg of the fixture into the rocker notch. The mark for one of the mortises should be directly under the bit. Sight along the leg, aligning the fixture with the drill bit, rolling the leg slightly in the V-block as necessary to achieve the proper alignment. When the fixture is parallel with the bit, drill your hole. Each time you shift the leg to line up the next mark under the bit, recheck your alignment against the fixture.

This alignment setup is used for the front rung mortises (in the front legs), as well as the back rung and back slat mortises (in the back legs). To drill the side rung mortises in both the front and back legs, a different alignment setup is used.

DOGLEG FIXTURE DETAIL

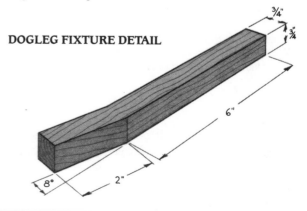

For these holes, fit the short leg of the fixture in the rocker notch, *then align the long leg parallel to the drill press table,* as shown in the photos. To make the alignment easier, cut a short 2 × 4 block and set it next to the V-block. Rotate the leg until the fixture is parallel to the block. (It will virtually rest on the block.) The kink in the fixture will position the leg to give you the correct axis for the side rungs in relation to the holes you drilled for the front or back rungs.

Drill the mortises with a Forstner bit, which yields a clean, flat-bottomed hole. The rung mortises, of course, are each a single hole. To make a slat mortise, drill a series of overlapping holes to rough it out, then use a chisel to square it up. Finally, drill a hole in the top of each back leg for the finials.

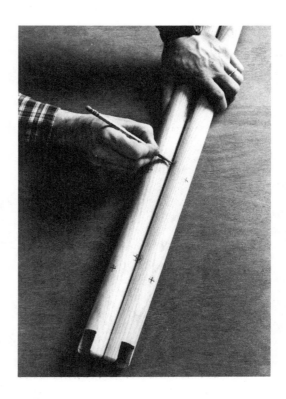

Right: Make sure you lay out the back slat mortises and rung holes to create left and right legs (mirror images) at front and back, rather than making identical parts. Perhaps the best way to do this is to mark one leg, then place the second beside it and transfer the position marks.

Cut four mortises for the back slats, two in each back leg. To do this, lay out each mortise, marking the length and width. *Far left:* Set the leg in the V-block, align it using the dogleg fixture, and drill a series of overlapping holes to excavate the bulk of the waste from the mortise. *Left:* Use a chisel to square the sides of the mortise.

Far left: To drill the mortises for the front and back rungs and the slats, fit the long leg of the dogleg fixture into the rocker notch, as shown. With the leg in the V-block, sight along the leg, aligning the dogleg fixture parallel to the drill bit, thereby rotating the leg into the proper alignment for drilling. *Left:* Align the leg for drilling the side rung mortises by switching the fixture so its short leg is in the rocker notch and its long leg is cocked to the side. Rotate the rocker leg so the fixture's long leg is parallel to the table; a scrap block set on the table makes the alignment easier to establish.

7. **Assemble the back spindles and the back slats.** Apply glue to the ends of the two back spindles and to the sockets in the back slats. Fit the parts together. When clamping them, lay the assembly facedown on a flat surface to avoid twisting it. After the glue dries,

sand and finish the assembly, because it's easier to do now than after you've woven the rush back. Be sure you don't apply finish to the tenons, however, since these get glued into the mortises in the legs.

---

8. **Weave the rush back.** It is a lot easier to weave the back before it is joined to the rocker itself. Clamp it in a vise and pull up a chair to it. It will take a lot of time, so you might as well be as comfortable as possible.

Start by setting up the back assembly for weaving after its finish dries. Secure it upright in a bench vise, sandwiching the bottom slat between two pads of styrene material to compensate for the curvature of the slat and to protect the finish. Make sure the holes for the rush are exposed.

Thread the warp; this is the set of vertical strands. Cut a 50-foot strand of rush, which should be long enough to both thread the warp and start the weave. Feed one end of the rush through the first hole (with the counterbore), tie a knot in it, then pull it back so the knot settles into the counterbore. Thread the free end of the rush through the remaining holes, as shown in *Threading the Warp*. Make sure each loop is taut. After you complete the warp, start right in on the weave.

Follow the *Weaving Sequence* to make the diamond

pattern we used for the back. This pattern requires you to alternate the over-under weave with each course.

After weaving each course, pack it tight. Without a strand above it, the course will tend to pop up the warp strands, pushing the weave away from the previous course. Use a scrap of hardwood, no more than a half-inch thick, to press down on the weave between each warp. To further tighten the weave, tap the stick with a hammer. (What you are really doing is packing the previous course, for the topmost weave will always pop up along the warp, no matter what you do.)

Initially, you will be able to thread the strand, also called the "weaver," over and under all the strands making up the warp. You pull the excess through easily, give the rush a sharp tug to pull it snug, then pack with the stick. But as you near completion, the warp will have so little "give" that you'll be reduced to threading the weaver over or under a single strand, then pulling through the excess, then threading it over another single warp strand, and so forth. At this point, you want to be working with a pretty short weaver. Not only is the

BACK WEAVING SEQUENCE

THREADING THE WARP

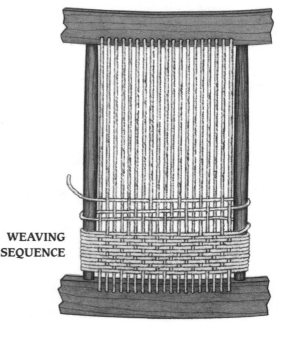

WEAVING SEQUENCE

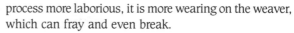

process more laborious, it is more wearing on the weaver, which can fray and even break.

Tie off the weave by wrapping the free end around the spindle for the last time and working it into the weave. You don't want to knot the rush and leave a lump to spoil the appearance of the weaving.

Left: Here's the basic setup for weaving the rush backrest. The back assembly is held firmly by the vise. The work area is free of clutter, the worker is comfortably seated.

Below left: Weaving one course for the back is a matter of looping the free end of the weaver around the spindle, then threading it over and under the warp strands in the required sequence, as shown. Then pull the excess through, yanking the weaver as taut as you can. Snug the weaver as tightly as possible against the previous course using your packing stick. *Below right:* Then pack the previous course, using the stick and a hammer. At each warp strand, fit the tip of the stick against the weaver and give the stick a rap.

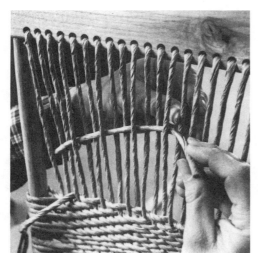

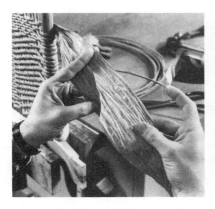

Above left: Fiber rush is made of a tough paper twisted into a strand to simulate natural rush. If you untwist and spread open the strand, you'll have a strip of paper 4 to 5 inches wide, as shown. *Above center:* To splice two strands together, untwist the ends of both the weaver and the new strand. With scissors, cut the ends at an angle, then tape them together with ordinary cellophane tape. Fold the splice with the tape inside, then fold again to ensure all the tape is concealed inside. *Above right:* Finally, carefully twist the splice, tightening it to blend into the strand.

9. Assemble the back assembly, the legs, and the rungs. Glue and clamp the woven back assembly between the back legs. Then, lay out the front rungs and front legs on a flat surface and glue and clamp them together. When making both assemblies, use a framing square to make sure they're clamped square. After the glue dries, connect the front leg assembly to the back leg assembly by installing the side rungs. Do not install the arms or rockers at this time.

TIP

When weaving the back and the seat, it's best to work with no more than 30 feet of rush at a time. If the strands are much longer, they'll be too unwieldy to work with; if much shorter, you'll end up making too many splices.

---

10. Weave the seat. Sand and finish the unfinished parts of the assembly you just made. When the finish dries, weave the rush seat.

The weaving sequence is a lot easier to show than it is to describe with words. The weaver winds over and under and around and over and under and . . . But you get the idea. Study both the photos and the *Seat Weaving Sequence* before you start. It is a lot easier than it sounds.

To start, you need to square up the seat opening—it's wider at the front than the back. You do this by filling the front corners. Tie two large loops of mason's twine to the back rung, then tie the end of the first strand of rush to one of them. Until you've squared off the opening, weave from one string loop across the front only (not across the back) to the other loop, then back again. To keep too many courses from bunching up in one loop,

Weaving the rocker seat is a matter of looping a continuous strand of rush in sequence around the rocker's rungs and itself. *Top:* Pass the coil of rush over and under and around the rungs, playing out the strand loosely. To keep the previous courses from loosening while leaving your hands free to thread the new course, use a spring clamp to pinch the taut weaver against a rung. *Center:* The photo shows how the strand is looped around the front and side rungs and itself, knitting an attractive seat surface. *Bottom:* After threading the rush fully around the seat, go back around, pulling it tight, while carefully aligning the strand next to previous courses. Reset the spring clamp and repeat the process. Note that here you can splice strands of rush with knots, so long as you position them where they will be hidden inside the weave. (Note also that, after finishing the seat weaving, we decided it would have been easier to do if the arms hadn't been in the way, and if the work didn't rock unpredictably. Weave yours before installing the arms and the rockers.)

SEAT WEAVING SEQUENCE

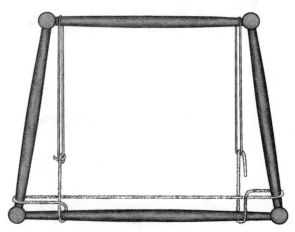 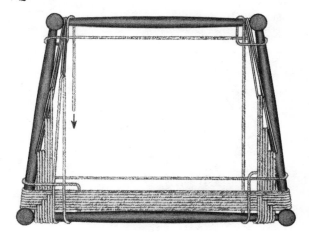

make additional loops, each slightly shorter than the previous one, to distribute the strands evenly. The *Seat Weaving Sequence* shows the path of the weaver through a typical course.

After you've squared off the opening, you weave around all four sides to fill in the seat. To make the seat *really* tight, you can use a stick and hammer, as you did when weaving the rocker back, to tighten each course against the previous one.

When you've finished weaving, "tuck" your loose end into the underside of the seat, making sure it's secure.

---

11. **Cut out and attach the arms.** Enlarge the arm pattern, and transfer it to the stock for the arms. Be sure to make mirror images, rather than two identical pieces. Cut out the basic shape of the arms on the band saw. Cut a radius in the back of the arms to fit around the back legs, as shown in the pattern, and test it for fit by positioning the arms against the leg. Make any minor adjustments for a tight fit, then center the front of the arm over the front leg and mark the front hole location. Drill the front hole, then glue the front of the arm to the front and back legs. Drive a #6 × 3-inch galvanized drywall-type screw through the back leg into the end of the arm for additional strength.

---

12. **Cut out and attach the rockers.** Enlarge the rocker pattern, and use it to lay out two rockers on the working stock. Cut them out. Radius the edges of these rockers, except where they will be covered by the notched legs, with a router and a ¼-inch rounding-over bit. Sand the rockers.

Glue the rockers into the notches in the legs. After the glue sets, drill a ¼-inch hole completely through the side of the leg at the notch (see the *Side View*) and drive a ¼-inch dowel into it to lock the rocker in place.

---

13. **Glue the finials on the back legs, sand all unfinished parts, and apply a finish.** After gluing on the finials, apply one coat of finish to all the unfinished parts of the rocker. Then, lightly sand the finished rocker with a fine-grit paper and apply a second coat of finish to the entire project. On the rush seat and back, use a penetrating oil finish or water sealer such as Thompson's Wood Protector or CWF. Clear surface finishes are too brittle and tend to crack.

OAK PORCH SWING

Turn-of-the-Century Graciousness for Your Porch

A porch is an architectural reminder to take time out. This porch swing is a further inducement. There is nothing practical whatsoever about a legless bench that hangs from the ceiling. You sit in it because you want to relax, without apologies.

This swing is just a generic, traditional-looking swing, not a replica of any specific swing. Nevertheless, it evokes the turn-of-the-century spirits of family, comfort,

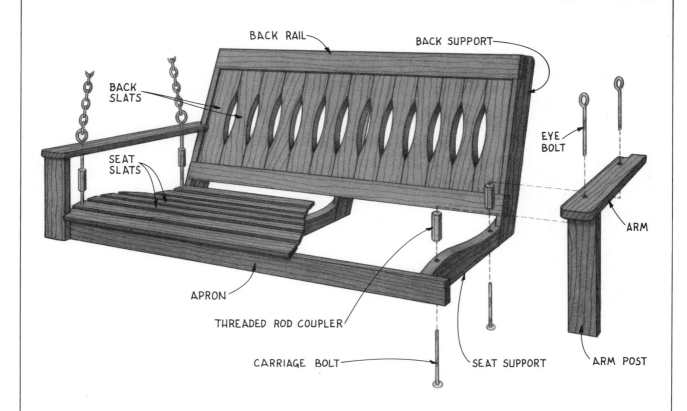

BACK RAIL

BACK SUPPORT

BACK SLATS

SEAT SLATS

EYE BOLT

ARM

APRON

THREADED ROD COUPLER

CARRIAGE BOLT

SEAT SUPPORT

ARM POST

SHOPPING LIST

LUMBER

15 bd. ft. 4/4 white oak
5 bd. ft. 5/4 white oak
4 bd. ft. 8/4 white oak

HARDWARE AND SUPPLIES

1 box #6 × 2" galvanized drywall-type screws
1 box #6 × 1¼" galvanized drywall-type screws
4 pcs. ⁵⁄₁₆" × 5" eyebolts
4 pcs. ⁵⁄₁₆" × 7" carriage bolts

HARDWARE AND SUPPLIES—CONTINUED

4 pcs. ⁵⁄₁₆" threaded rod couplers
4 pcs. ⁵⁄₁₆" nuts
2 pcs. ⅜" × 3" eyescrews
Chain as required
Resorcinol glue

FINISH

Clear water repellent or clear exterior finish

CUTTING LIST

PIECE	NUMBER	THICKNESS	WIDTH	LENGTH	MATERIAL
Back supports	3	¾"	3"	24½"	4/4 oak
Seat supports	3	1½"	3"	21½"	8/4 oak
Back slats	13	⅜"	3½"	15"	5/4 oak
Back rails	2	¾"	3"	47"	4/4 oak
Apron	1	¾"	2⅜"	51"	4/4 oak
Seat slats	7	¾"	2¼"	47"	4/4 oak
Arm posts	2	¾"	3½"	11"	4/4 oak
Arms	2	¾"	3½"	24½"	4/4 oak

TOOL LIST

Backsaw
Band saw
Bar or pipe clamps
Clamps
Drill
   5/16" dia. bit
   Countersink bit
   Pilot hole bit
Hammer
Jointer
Paintbrush
Planer
Pliers
Radial arm saw
   Dado set
Router
   1/4" rounding-over bit
   3/8" rabbeting bit
Saber saw
Sander(s)
Sandpaper
Sawhorses
Screwdriver
Table saw
   Dado cutter
   Miter gauge
Tack cloth
Tape measure
Wrenches

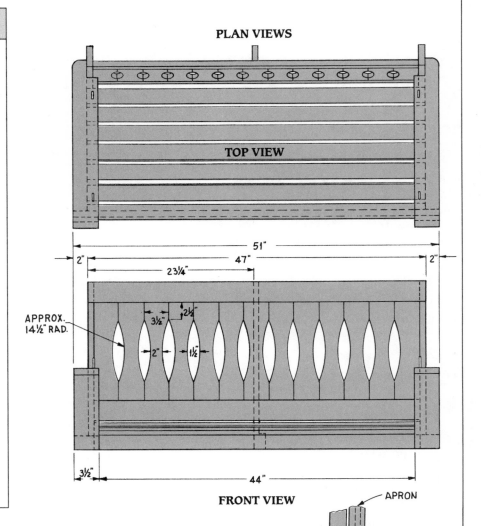

PLAN VIEWS

TOP VIEW

FRONT VIEW

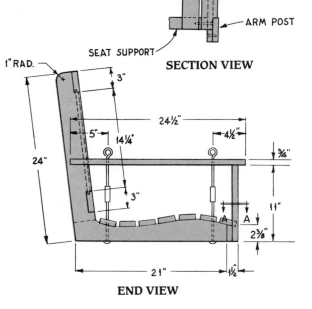

SECTION VIEW

END VIEW

and moderation in life's pace. The swing is quietly reminiscent of Victorian porch swings. Rather than elaborate gingerbread, though, it has a series of ellipses piercing the back. To me, this one belongs on a Victorian house's porch. Or on whatever porch you have.

Builder's Notes

This project offers few perils for most woodworkers. You do have to prepare hardwood stock in three thicknesses. And the joinery—mortise-and-tenon joints, lap joints—*sounds* a bit advanced, perhaps. But you *can* deal with these challenges.

Materials. Oak is a wood that was especially popular around the turn of the century. When you think of Victorian furnishings, you think of oak. As often as not, *dark* oak. So oak is a natural choice for this swing.

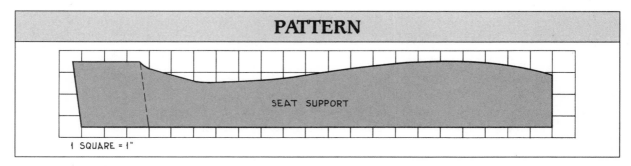

A note on *dark* is in order. Turn-of-the-century furnishings were dark because they were stained or fumed to make them that way. We liked the natural blonde of white oak, so we eschewed stains, using a clear finish. As long as the finish is maintained, the blondeness should survive. Unfinished and left in the weather (even if under roof), oak will darken.

Having selected oak, we picked white oak over red oak because it has more decay resistance than the red oak.

Hardwoods usually are stocked in a rough-sawn state. If you don't have a jointer and a planer, you must have the supplier dress the wood. The shopping and cutting lists assume you will resaw the 5/4 (five-quarter) stock to obtain the ⅜-inch stock for the slats.

The swing is assembled largely with screws. The only glued joints are the laps that join the two elements of the supports. The back slats are captured between the rails, which in turn are captured by the supports. And screws affix the rails to the supports. Screws also affix the seat slats, the arm posts, and the arms. In all cases, the screws used are the galvanized drywall type.

The hardware used to hang the swing shouldn't be hard to find at a respectable hardware store. If you shop at a place that displays its hardware in blister packs, there's one item you might not find: the threaded rod coupler. Looking like an overgrown hex nut, it links two threaded rods or bolts. You turn each rod about ½ inch into the coupler.

Tools and techniques. Though the swing looks pretty sophisticated, building it doesn't require sophisticated equipment operated with uncanny proficiency. If you have a shop with the basics—a table saw and assorted portable power tools—you should be okay. A band saw will expedite cutting the back slats and ease cutting the seat supports.

The joinery isn't tough, just a tad tedious. The mortise-and-tenon joints that link the back rails and back slats might easily be called tongue-and-groove joints. The mortise is really an open-ended groove, the tenons are offset, so that forming them is a matter of cutting a rabbet across each end of every slat. The tedium stems from the number of slats to be worked.

The one operation that's unusual among the projects in this book is resawing. The back slats are only ⅜ inch thick. Resawing thicker stock will save an enormous amount of time and wood. Working 4/4 (four-quarter) lumber down to ⅜ inch on a planer takes a long time, and it turns an awful lot of good wood into shavings, too. From a slightly heftier 5/4 board, you can resaw two ⅜-inch boards. Although the band saw generally is regarded as the best tool for resawing, swing-builder Phil Gehret resawed the slats on the table saw.

1. **Make the support frames.** Begin the construction process by building the three support frames. Cut the three back supports from ¾-inch-thick stock, and the three seat supports from 1½-inch-thick stock. Make them a bit long to provide a margin of error at the joints. Lay out the laps, as shown in the *Support Joinery* drawing; as you can see, only the seat supports are lapped. Note that the lap's shoulder is 7½ degrees off square, so the back will lean back. The lap is cut into the outside face of the two outer seat supports, but it can be in either face of the center seat support.

A radial arm saw equipped with a dado cutter may be the best tool for cutting the laps. It allows you to see the lap as you cut, and you can hog out the full ¾-inch depth of the lap in a single pass. (A router also allows you to see the cut as you work, but you should only trim about 3/16 inch from the lap with each pass, so the process will take longer.) Remember that the outer supports are mirror images of each other, not duplicates. And if you make the laps a tad longer than specified (because of your margin for error), be sure you leave yourself enough room for the seat.

SUPPORT JOINERY

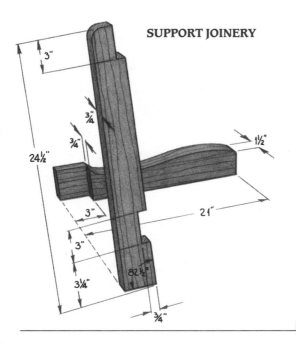

Cut the seat profile into the seat supports next. You can enlarge the pattern, or you can create your own profile, working off the high and low points indicated on the *End View.* In either case, transfer the profile to the three supports, then cut on the band saw.

Notch and trim the back supports next. Round off the top back corners of the three supports on the band saw or with a saber saw. All three must be notched to accommodate the back rails. The two outer supports get 3-inch-wide, ¾-inch-deep notches, as shown in the *End View.* The middle support has to be reduced in width from its top to the lower notch's bottom edge so the back assembly will nestle into it. Lay out these notches and cut them on the band saw.

Finally, glue up the pairs of supports, and secure the joints with clamps until the glue has dried. Trim both ends of each board at the joints, as shown in the *End View.*

2. Cut the back rails. Cut the two back rails to length. Round the top front edge of the upper rail, using a router and a ¼-inch rounding-over bit.

Plow a ¼-inch-wide, ⅜-inch-deep groove in one edge of each, using either a router or a dado blade on a table saw. The back slats' tenons will be held within these grooves. For the best appearance, you can make these stopped grooves, so they won't be exposed on the ends. Or you can glue a scrap of the working stock in the grooves at the ends. We left the grooves open.

Finish up the rails by sanding them smooth.

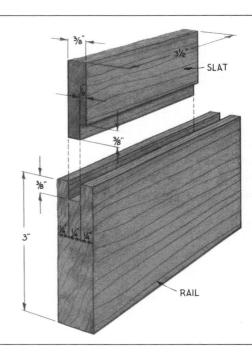

SLAT-TO-RAIL JOINERY

3. Resaw stock for the back slats. The back slats are cut from ⅜-inch-thick stock. Since this is not a standard thickness, you'll either have to pay extra to have the required amount of stock prepared for you, or you'll have to make it yourself. The best way to generate this stock is by resawing 5/4 stock.

The band saw is generally regarded as the best tool for resawing, but unless you have a thickness planer,

you may be better off doing the work on the table saw. The table saw blade makes a pretty wide kerf, but it is rigid and yields a sawed face that's parallel to the face that bore on the rip fence. You can, therefore, clean up the sawed face on the jointer or with a belt sander, and be reasonably assured both faces will be true. The band saw blade, on the other hand, while it does make a narrow kerf, tends to wander even when you use a fence

While it's possible to resaw stock free-hand on the band saw, you can be more accurate if you guide the board with a pivot. Clamped to the saw table as shown, the pivot braces the workpiece, keeping the cut from wandering, thus helping you to achieve a uniform thickness. The advantage of the pivot over a fence is that you can shift the feed angle without interrupting the cut. Using a marking gauge, or just a pencil and rule, mark a cutting line on the unjointed edge of each piece to be resawed. Cut with the jointed face of the stock held firmly against the pivot, turning the board as necessary—adjusting the feed angle, in other words—to hold to the line.

The pivot is made by cutting a piece of wood or plywood to approximately the shape shown, then cutting bevels on the edge, so the workpiece rides against a point rather than a surface.

(If the blade guide in the photo seems high, it is that way for a reason. The conventional wisdom is that the guide should

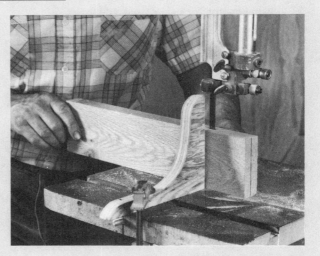

be set as close to the top of the workpiece as possible to minimize blade deflection. The problem is that the blade can deflect inside the cut. If the guide is close to the wood, you can't see the deflection. If it is well above the wood, as shown, you can see the deflection and react by adjusting the angle of feed.)

or pivot, yielding a somewhat uneven sawed face. And this can lead to unevenness and taper in the jointed or sanded piece.

Regardless of the approach you take, prepare the stock by squaring one face and one edge on a jointer; the board must rest squarely on the saw table and against the fence or pivot.

Use a featherboard to control the stock when resawing on the table saw. Position the featherboard just shy of the saw blade (so it doesn't pinch the blade) and tight enough against the stock to prevent kickback—its main purpose. Set the saw to cut just about halfway through the stock. Make one pass, then flip the board end for end and, keeping the same face against the fence as in the previous pass, make a second cut.

4. **Cut and tenon the back slats.** If necessary after resawing, cut the back slats to the size specified by the "Cutting List."

Turn one slat into a pattern for cutting arcs in the rest. First, find and mark reference points on the slat: the ends

of the arc and its high point. The arc begins (or ends) 2½ inches from either end; at its midpoint, its rise is ¾ inch. Connect these marks with a curved line. This line is roughly the arc of a 14½-inch-radius circle. Cut this slat, then use it as a template to lay out others, then

TIP

Laying out the back slats can be done any number of ways. You can use a template. Or mark high and low points, then connect the dots freehand.

We used a flexible strip of Formica scrap to form an arc we liked (and that connected the dots), then we traced the arc. To make this a one-man process, and to "capture" the arc so you can trace it again and again, make a short cut into each end of the scrap. Knot a string and catch it in the cut on one end. Flex the strip, then knot the string a second time, catching it in the kerf at the other end. Makes a little bow, like for archery. Mark the appropriate spots on the workpiece, line up the bow, and trace the arc.

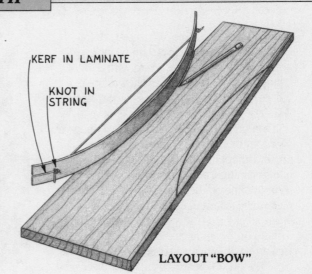

cut them as well. Note that the two end back slats have only one arc apiece, so hold two slats aside, cutting only a single arc in them. After cutting all the slats, sand them, particularly the sawed edges.

Tenon the slats next. The tenons are offset, so cutting them is a matter of rabbeting each end of every slat. You can do this on a table saw using a standard blade and a tenoning jig. Or you can use a ⅜-inch rabbeting bit in a router to form them. To save setup time, Phil used the table saw's standard blade and made multiple cuts to form the tenons. Set the rip fence ⅜ inch from the *outside* of the blade to control the length of the tenons. Using the miter gauge to guide the slat, make a pass with the slat end butted against the fence, cutting the shoulder. A couple more passes will complete the tenon. Before cutting the slats, test the setup on a scrap, and test the fit of the tenon in the grooves in the rails. Adjust the thickness of the tenons to get a snug fit.

Save layout and cutting time by stacking and cutting three or four slats at a time (obviously, with the pattern marked on the top slat). This is something to do on a band saw, not with a saber saw. Hold the stack together, all the slats in alignment, with tape. That way you can focus entirely on cutting accurately. Any tape will do—masking tape, duct tape, even packing tape.

5. Assemble the back. You usually begin an assembly this big with a dry run. Partly to test how the joints fit, but also to practice the routine so you don't dribble glue all over while you try to figure how to fit two parts together, and so the glue doesn't set up before you're ready. You can cut to the chase here, because you really don't *need* glue. The slats won't fall out, since they're captured by the rails and the outer supports. And the rails are attached to the supports with screws. No

glue is needed there, either.

Fitting the rail-and-slat subassembly into the notches in the three back supports will doubtlessly go best if you have help. If you have to go it alone, keep the rail-and-slat assembly together with two or three bar or pipe clamps. The assembly fits into the notches cut into the back supports. With the assembly in place, drill two pilot holes through it at each place a frame member rests against a back support. Drive 2-inch screws into the holes.

6. Cut and attach the apron and seat slats. Cut the apron to size, beveling the top edge at 75 degrees to meet the front seat slat. Sand the apron. Then, holding the apron in place, drill two pilot holes through it and into each seat frame. Drive 2-inch screws into the holes.

Cut the seat slats from ¾-inch stock, and round what will be the exposed edges with a router and a ¼-inch rounding-over bit. Lay out the slats on the seat supports, arranging them an equal distance apart. With a pilot hole bit, drill two countersunk pilot holes through each slat into each support. Drive a 2-inch galvanized screw into each hole.

Finally, drill holes for the suspension hardware. As you will note on the *End View,* the holes penetrate the second slat (from the front) and the last (or rearmost) slat. Back out two screws on each side: the front screw in the second slat, the rear screw in the last slat. Drill 5/16-inch-diameter holes at these four points, through both the seat slats and the supports below.

---

7. Cut and attach the posts and arms. Cut the arm posts and arms to size. Fit the posts to the swing assembly, marking the front seat slat for the notches that are necessary to accommodate the posts. (See the *Section View.*) Cut the notches with a backsaw. This *can* be done with the slat in place—the post will conceal any scuffing of the apron that results—but you can easily back out the screws and remove the slat to notch it. Before machining the post edges with a router and a ¼-inch rounding-over bit, stand each post in place, noting the edges that will be exposed and marking where the rounded edges should blend into the rounded edges of adjoining parts. Rout the posts.

To install the posts, drive two 1¼-inch screws through the apron and into the post back, and drive a

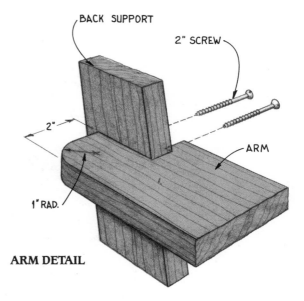

ARM DETAIL

single 2-inch screw through the post into the apron and support. Drill pilot holes for these screws first, of course.

Now turn to the arms. Round off the outer back corners and notch the back ends to fit around the back supports, as shown in the *Arm Detail.* As you did with the posts, set the arms in position, mark them, then round-over the appropriate edges. Attach the arms with 2-inch screws driven through the back support into the arm (as indicated in the *Arm Detail*) and through the arm into the posts. Again, drill pilot holes before driving these screws.

Finally, drill holes on the arms for the suspension hardware. These holes must align with those drilled earlier through the seat slats and seat supports.

The arm posts nestle against the apron and the front seat slat. Secure each one by running in two 1¼-inch screws from the back of the apron, as shown, and a 2-inch screw through the front of the post and the apron into the seat support.

The holes in the arms for the suspension hardware must be directly above the holes already bored in the slats and supports. *Left:* To "capture" the location of a hole in the seat, place a combination square on an arm, as shown, and align its rule with the hole below. Mark the edge of the arm. *Right:* Reposition the square to extend this mark across the top of the arm. Find a point along this line, ¾ inch in from the inside edge of the arm, and drill a 5/16-inch-diameter hole for the eyebolt.

8. Finish the swing. Sand any areas of the swing that need a touch-up. Apply whatever finish you've

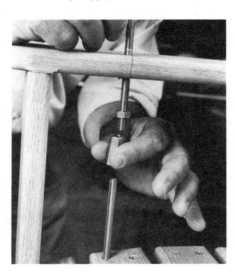

chosen. Because we wanted to show off the natural beauty of the oak used to make the swing, Phil applied two coats of Deft, a clear finish, to the swing shown.

Now install the suspension hardware. Insert the carriage bolts up through the holes in the supports and seat their heads with a tap or two of a hammer. Drop the eyebolts through the holes in the arms. Turn a nut onto one bolt in each pair, then link the pair with a threaded coupling. Hand-tighten the nut against the coupler, then use a pair of wrenches to further tighten the parts.

The eyebolts and carriage bolts come together like this. Turn a regular machine nut onto either the eyebolt (as here) or the carriage bolt. Follow it with a threaded coupler, turning the coupler until the bolt is about halfway through. Hand-tighten the nut against the coupler, then jam them together by tightening them with wrenches. Now thread the coupler onto the other bolt, turning the bolt-nut-coupler assembly until the other bolt is as far into the coupler as it will go.

9. Hang the swing. Suspend the swing from framework of substance, like the joists bearing the porch ceiling or the porch-roof rafters—it's got to support the dynamic weight of two or more "swingers," after all. Eyeball the likely trajectory of the swing, and try to minimize the chance that it will hit walls or railings. Pick a pair of joists or rafters that are at least as far apart as the width of the swing. Make sure the two points are on the same level. (Although you can hang it from points at two different heights, it won't swing evenly.) Drill pilot holes and turn eyescrews into them.

Attach the chain to the swing's eyebolts by opening the eyes enough to slip links over them. Close the eyes. Run chain from the eyebolts to the eyescrews, and open the eyes of the screws to hold the links that will put the swing at the right height. Close the eyes, and remove the excess links unless you anticipate adjusting the swing's height.

From time to time, check that the eyescrews are still securely anchored in the joists or rafters. And bring a couple of wrenches out to make sure that the lock nuts and threaded couplers are snug against each other.